Ecological Revolutions

CAROLYN MERCHANT

· ·

Ecological Revolutions

Nature, Gender, and Science in New England

The University of North Carolina Press

Chapel Hill and London

Library of Congress Cataloging-in-Publication Data
Merchant, Carolyn.
Ecological revolutions : nature, gender, and science in New
England / by Carolyn Merchant
p.   cm.
Bibliography: p.
Includes index.
ISBN 0-8078-1858-5 (alk. paper). — ISBN 0-8078-4254-0 (pbk. :
alk. paper)
1. Human ecology—New England—History. 2. New England—Economic
conditions. 3. Indians of North America—New England—Economic
conditions. 4. Human ecology—Philosophy—History. I. Title.
GF504.N45M47   1989   89-30945
304.2'0974—dc19   CIP

The paper in this book meets the guidelines for permanence and
durability of the Committee on Production Guidelines for Book
Longevity of the Council on Library Resources.

Printed in the United States of America
93   92   5   4   3

This book was published with the assistance of the H. Eugene and
Lillian Lehman Fund of the University of North Carolina Press.

Portions of this book have appeared in somewhat different form in
Carolyn Merchant, "Perspective: Restoration and Reunion with Nature,"
Restoration and Management Notes 4 (Winter 1986): 68–70, and in
Carolyn Merchant, "The Theoretical Structure of Ecological
Revolutions," *Environmental Review* 11, no. 4 (Winter 1987): 265–74.

Frontispiece: An Indian fur trader symbolically surveys the effects of three centuries of transformation of the New England landscape. Indian ecologies based on gathering, hunting, fishing, and horticulture were transformed by European colonists practicing settled agriculture and overseas trade. Colonial ecology was in turn transformed by the advent of internal transportation networks and an industrial economy.
Source: Horace T. Martin, *Castorologia* (Montreal: W. Drysdale, 1892), p. 60.

To the memory of my ancestress

Mary Barnes

convicted of witchcraft

Hartford, Connecticut, 1662

and to my mother

Elizabeth Barnes Holcomb

Contents

Preface   xiii

1
Ecology and History   1

PART ONE
The Colonial Ecological Revolution   27

2
Animals into Resources   29

3
From Corn Mothers to Puritan Fathers   69

4
The Animate Cosmos of the Colonial Farmer   112

PART TWO
The Capitalist Ecological Revolution   147

5
Farm Ecology: Subsistence versus Market   149

6
The Mechanization of Nature: Managing Farms and Forests   198

7
Nature, Mother, and Industry   232

Contents

8
Epilogue: The Global Ecologual Revolution   261

Appendixes   271

Appendix A
Foods of Southeastern New England
Indians, 1600–1675   271

Appendix B
Pelts Exported by John Pynchon, 1652–1663   273

Appendix C
Profile of Fifteen Inland Massachusetts Towns   275

Appendix D
Land Use in Concord, Massachusetts   282

Appendix E
Products of the New England Forest, 1840   286

Notes   287

Bibliography   327

Index   363

Figures, Tables, and Maps

Figures

Frontispiece   ii & iii

1.1 Conceptual Framework for Interpreting
Ecological Revolutions   6

2.1 Variations of the Beaver Hat, 1600–1800   43

2.2 Blaeu's Map of New Belgium and New England   53

3.1 Plymouth Colony Home Lot   88

4.1 Curiosities of Nature and Art in
Husbandry and Gardening   124

4.2 The Anatomy of Man's Body, 1712   136

4.3 The Anatomy of Man's Body, 1782   138

5.1 Agricultural Ecology of a New England Farm   154

5.2 A Primeval Forest of Central New England,
Petersham, Massachusetts, 1700   158

5.3 An Early Settler Clears a Homestead,
Petersham, Massachusetts, 1740   159

5.4 Height of Cultivation for Farm Crops,
Petersham, Massachusetts, 1830   195

5.5 Farm Abandonment, Petersham, Massachusetts, 1850   196

6.1 Estimated Percentage of Forest Area in Each
New England State, 1620–1865   225

7.1 Woman Drawing in Warp Ends   238

7.2 Steam Locomotive Arriving at Walden   243

Tables

1.1 Ecological Revolutions   24

2.1 Indian Population of New England, 1610   39

3.1 Approximate Food Intake per Capita of
Southeastern New England Indians, 1605–1675   75

4.1 Source and Chemical Content of Fertilizers   120

8.1 The Global Ecological Revolution   266

Maps

2.1 Major Soil Groups in New England   32

2.2 New England Topography   34

2.3 Forest Types at the Beginning of
New England Settlement   35

2.4 Indian Tribes of New England, 1610   45

3.1 Colonial New England, ca. 1675   71

5.1 Isochronic Map of Settlement in New England   151

5.2 Fifteen Inland Massachusetts Towns, 1771   152

5.3 Canals of Nineteenth-Century New England   194

Preface

The world in which most Americans live today is the legacy of four centuries of transformation of land and life. We dominate an increasingly fragile earth, "mastering" a nature from which we are largely alienated. As a "people of plenty" we produce a cornucopia of goods at the expense of our environment, the Third World, and laboring peoples. In the process we endanger the earth for future generations. The native American and colonial past we have lost in many ways enjoyed a more vital relationship with nature, using it for subsistence and sustaining it for succeeding generations. This book attempts to recover our ecological past, to understand the transformation process, and to suggest goals for restoring health to the planet.

Ecological Revolutions explores for the New World some of the themes of my earlier book, *The Death of Nature: Women, Ecology, and the Scientific Revolution*: the roots of the environmental crisis, the roles of women in history, the change from nature as mother to nature as machine, and the place of science in the creation of the modern world. But *Ecological Revolutions* also offers a new synthesis of ways that humans and the biosphere have interacted over time. I examine how different human cultures—native American and Euramerican—occupied the same geographic space in close succession with differing effects on the environment. I use feminist insights to analyze reproduction and show how it interacts with production to give magnitude and direction to ecological transformations. I also place science in the broader context of human consciousness and ask how different cultures knew nature and how these ways of knowing have changed over time.

But this book is also a personal odyssey. My ancestors migrated from England to New England in the seventeenth century and then to New York State in the nineteenth century. One of my mother's ancestors was convicted of witchcraft and probably executed in Hartford, Connecticut. My father descended from a nineteenth-century railroad general manager and coal company president who dealt with native Americans in the westward expansion of white America. These roots symbolize a major theme of this book—the encounter of science, technology, and capitalism with nature conceptualized as woman.

I wish gratefully to acknowledge the assistance and support of Charles Sellers in deepening my understanding of American history and particularly the role of subsistence farming in the creation of American democracy. I have absorbed much of my perspective from his forthcoming book, *The Market Revolution and the Creation of Capitalist Culture, 1815–1846*, and without his advice, suggestions, and queries I would not have attempted this project.

I am also grateful to William Cronon for his book *Changes in the Land: Indians, Colonists, and the Ecology of New England*. Although my manuscript was completed before his book was published, the appearance of *Changes in the Land* has pushed me to expand and differentiate my approach from his. He has also furnished me with many helpful references and suggestions for continuing my research.

I am particularly indebted to Sandra Marburg, Marian Stevens, Elizabeth Bird, and Yaakov Garb who assisted me with the research for and preparation of the manuscript, tables, graphs, and illustrations and who offered helpful critical comments and suggestions throughout its various stages. I also thank Nita Davidson, Susanne Easton, Jonathan Kusel, and Kathleen Delate for assistance with numerous references and Margaret Henderson, Marguerite Versher, and Celeste Newbrough for help in manuscript preparation, copying, and indexing.

The research for the project was supported by the National Endowment for the Humanities, Division of Research, under grant RO–20269–82, "An Ecological History of the Northeastern United States, 1600–1850" between 1981 and 1983. This grant allowed me to travel extensively throughout New England to examine topography, wildlife, and natural areas and to visit numerous archives. I thank the librarians and personnel of state and local libraries, museums, and historical sites for their assistance and answers to my many questions. I am also grateful to the Agricultural Experiment Station of the University of California, project CA–B–CRS–4110–H, "Subsistence Farming in Colonial America and California: A Reevaluation," for support between 1981 and 1986.

I am indebted to Virginia Nelke, Brookes Spencer, and Nancy Spencer for a year's opportunity to practice farming, including the care and raising of horses, steers, sheep, and goats; milking, dairying, and sheep shearing; and barn and fence construction and repair. I thank Patricia Gahagan and James Gahagan for numerous discussions concerning deer hunting and fishing and the use of chickens, geese, goats, and pigs for household subsistence. I am likewise grateful to Frank Siebert who discussed the history of the Penobscot Nation with me, to Frank Patoine who showed me techniques of fur trading, and to Jim O'Brien who helped me learn New England tree species and beaver history.

I have absorbed much of my perspective on environmental issues and agricultural ecology from my colleagues in the Department of Conservation and Resource Studies and the Division of Biological Control at the University of California at Berkeley. I am particularly grateful for discussions with and articles written by Miguel Altieri, Claudia Carr, Donald Dahlsten, Sally Fairfax, Richard Garcia, Kenneth Hagen, Alan Miller, and Arnold Schultz.

Numerous other individuals have provided helpful suggestions and references. For these I wish to thank Ronny Ambjörnsson, William Ashworth, Ernest Callenbach, Jane Cate, Weston Cate, Allen Debus, Brian Donahue, Barbara Duden, Lena Eskelsson, Tore Frängsmyr, Susannah French, Stanley French, Robert Gross, Barbara Haack, Peter Haack, Alice Ingerson, Hans Jenny, Carol Karlsen, Kjell Jonsson, Barbara Leibhardt, Jonas Liljeqvist, Ingegerd Lundström, Bettye Hobbs Pruitt, Arthur McEvoy, William Meyer, Pamela Muick, Roderick Nash, Abby Peterson, Winifred Rothenberg, Sverker Sörlin, Bill Turner II, Elsie Wenström, and Donald Worster. I also wish to acknowledge the superb assistance of my editor Paul Betz and the design and technical staff of the University of North Carolina Press who brought this book to its felicitious completion. My sons David and John Iltis took an active interest in the project and asked many pertinent and difficult questions throughout its history.

Spelling in quotations from primary sources has been modernized.

Berkeley, California
October, 1988

Ecological Revolutions

1

. . . .

Ecology and History

Wherever [man] plants his foot, the harmonies of nature are turned to dis-
cords.... Indigenous vegetable and animal species are extirpated and sup-
planted by others of foreign origin ... with new and reluctant growth of vegeta-
ble forms, and with alien tribes of animals. These intentional changes and
substitutions constitute indeed great revolutions.
—George Perkins Marsh, *Man and Nature*, 1864

W hen Vermont statesman and author George Perkins Marsh
took up his pen to write to botanist Asa Gray in 1849, he revealed the concerns that would spark his quest to understand the
destruction of New England in a historical context. "I spent my early
life almost literally in the woods. A large portion of the territory of
Vermont was, within my recollection, covered with the natural forest.... Having been personally engaged to a considerable extent," he
confessed, "in clearing lands, and manufacturing, and dealing in
lumber, I have had occasion both to observe and to feel the effects
resulting from an injudicious system of managing woodlands and the
products of the forest." The changes that Marsh observed and docu-
mented in *Man and Nature* were the culmination of a history of European interactions with the land. They were reflected only belatedly in
the New World.[1]

New England is a mirror on the world. Changes in its ecology and
society over its first 250 years were rapid and revolutionary. Only
through a historical approach can the magnitude and implications of
such changes for the human future be fully appreciated. What took
place in 2,500 years of European development through social evolution came to New England in a tenth of that time through revolution.
This book delineates the characteristics of two types of ecological
revolution—colonial and capitalist—through the study of the New England exemplar. Yet the implications extend far beyond the confines
of New England. As the American frontier moved west, similar eco-

logical revolutions followed each other in increasingly telescoped periods of time. Moreover, as Europeans settled other temperate countries throughout the world, colonial ecological revolutions took place. Today, capitalist ecological revolutions are occurring in many developing countries in a tenth of New England's transformation time. In the epilogue, it is suggested that human beings are now entering a third type of revolution—a global ecological revolution—that encompasses the entire earth.

Between 1600 and 1860 two major transformations in New England land and life took place. The first, a colonial ecological revolution, occurred during the seventeenth century and was externally generated. It resulted in the collapse of indigenous Indian ecologies and the incorporation of a European ecological complex of animals, plants, pathogens, and people. The colonial revolution extracted native species from their ecological contexts and shipped them overseas as commodities. It was legitimated by a set of symbols that placed cultured European humans above wild nature, other animals, and "beastlike savages." It substituted a visual for an oral consciousness and an image of nature as female and subservient to a transcendent male God for the Indians' animistic fabric of symbolic exchanges between people and nature.

The second transformation, a capitalist ecological revolution, took place roughly between the American Revolution and about 1860. It was initiated by internal tensions within New England and by a dynamic market economy. Local factories imported natural resources and exported finished products. Air pollution, water pollution, and resource depletions were created as externalities outside the calculation of profits. The capitalist revolution demanded an economy of increased human labor, land management, and a legitimating mechanistic science. It split human consciousness into a disembodied analytic mind and a romantic emotional sensibility.[2]

Each of these "ecological revolutions" altered the local ecology, human society, and human consciousness. New material structures and technologies—maps, plows, fences, clocks, and chemicals—were imposed on nature. The relations between men and women through which daily life was maintained and reproduced were radically changed. And in turn the forms of consciousness—perceiving, symbolizing, and analyzing—through which humans socially constructed and interpreted the natural environment were reorganized.

My thesis is that ecological revolutions are major transformations in human relations with nonhuman nature. They arise from changes, tensions, and contradictions that develop between a society's mode of production and its ecology, and between its modes of production and reproduction. These dynamics in turn support the acceptance of new forms of consciousness, ideas, images, and worldviews. The course of the colonial and capitalist ecological revolutions in New England may be understood through a description of each society's ecology, production, reproduction, and forms of consciousness; the processes by which they broke down; and an analysis of the new relations between the emergent colonial or capitalist society and nonhuman nature.

Two frameworks of analysis offer springboards for discussing the structure of such ecological revolutions. In *The Structure of Scientific Revolutions* (1962), Thomas Kuhn approached major transformations in scientific consciousness from a perspective internal to the workings of science and the community of scientists. Scientific paradigms are structures of thought shared by groups of scientists within which problems are solved. When a sufficient number of anomalies challenges a scientific theory, scientists construct new paradigms, initiating scientific revolutions. The Copernican revolution in the sixteenth century, the Newtonian revolution in the seventeenth, Lavoisier's chemical revolution in the eighteenth, Darwin's evolutionary theory in the nineteenth, and Einstein's relativity theory in the twentieth are examples of major transformations within various branches of science.[3]

One of the strengths of Kuhn's provocative account is its recognition of stable worldviews in science that exist over relatively long periods of time, but that are rapidly transformed during periods of crisis and stress. One of its limitations is its failure to incorporate an interpretation of social forces external to the daily activities of scientific practitioners in their laboratories and field stations. Internal developments in scientific theories are affected, at least indirectly, by social and economic circumstances. A viewpoint that incorporates social, economic, and ecological changes is required for a more complete understanding of scientific change.

A second approach to revolutionary transformations is that of Karl Marx and Friedrich Engels. Their base/superstructure theory of history viewed social revolutions as beginning in the economic base of a particular social formation and resulting in a fairly rapid transformation of the legal, political, and ideological superstructure. In the most succinct statement of his theory of history, in 1859, Marx wrote: "At a certain stage of their development, the material productive forces of society come in conflict with the existing relations of production.... Then begins an epoch of social revolution. With the change of the economic foundation the entire immense superstructure is more or less rapidly transformed."[4]

For Marx, society is an integrated whole. A fabric of economic, political, and intellectual forces exists and evolves as a stable system for periods of time. But at particular times in history, changes are initiated in economic production that bring about rapid transformations in politics and consciousness. One weakness of this approach is in the determinism assigned to the economic base and the sharp demarcation between base and superstructure. But its strength lies in its view of society and change. If a society at a given time can be understood as a mutually supportive structure of dynamically interacting parts, then the process of its breakdown and transformation to a new whole can be described. Both Kuhn's theory of scientific revolution and Marx's theory of social revolution are starting points for a theory of ecological revolutions.

Science and history are both social constructions. Science is an ongoing negotiation with nonhuman nature for what counts as reality. Scientists socially construct nature, representing it differently in different historical epochs. These social constructions change during scientific revolutions. Similarly, historians socially construct the past in accordance with concepts relevant to the historian's present. History is thus an ongoing negotiation between the historian and the sources for what counts as history. Ecology is a particular twentieth-century construction of nature relevant to the concerns of environmental historians.

A scientific worldview answers three key questions:

1. What is the world made of? (the ontological question)
2. How does change occur? (the historical question)
3. How do we know? (the epistemological question)

Worldviews such as animism, Aristotelianism, mechanism, and quantum field theory construct answers to these fundamental questions differently.

Environmental history poses similar questions:

1. What concepts describe the world?
2. What is the process by which change occurs?
3. How does a society know the natural world?

The concepts most useful for this approach to environmental history are ecology, production, reproduction, and consciousness. The relations among animals (including humans), plants, minerals, and climatic forces constitute the ecological core of a particular habitat at a particular historical time. Through production (or the extraction, processing, and exchange of resources for subsistence or profit), human actions have their most direct and immediate impact on nonhuman nature. Human reproduction, both biological and social, is one step removed from immediate impact on nature: the effects of the biological reproduction of human beings are mediated through a particular form of production (hunting-gathering, subsistence agriculture, industrial capitalism, and so on). Population does not press on the land and its resources directly, but on the mode of production. Two steps removed from immediate impact on the habitat are the modes through which a society knows and explains the natural world —science, religion, and myths. Ideas must be translated into social and economic actions in order to affect the nonhuman world.

Because of the differences in immediacy of impact of production, reproduction, and consciousness on nonhuman nature, a structured, multi-leveled conceptual framework is needed (Figure 1.1). This framework provides the basis for an understanding of stability as well as evolutionary change and transformation. Although changes may occur at any level, ecological revolutions are characterized by major changes at all three levels. They are initiated by widening tensions between the requirements of ecology and production in a given habitat and between production and reproduction. These dynamics in turn support transformations in consciousness and legitimating worldviews.

Ecology and Production

In the ancient civilizations of Europe, Nature was an actress on the stage of history. Personified in Mesopotamia as the goddess Inanna, in Egypt as Isis, in ancient Greece as Demeter and Gaia, in the Roman world as Ceres, and in medieval France as Natura, Nature was the

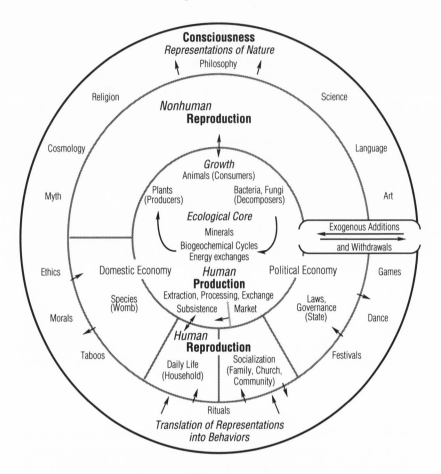

Figure 1.1

Conceptual Framework for Interpreting Ecological Revolutions. Ecology, production, reproduction, and consciousness interact over time to bring about
ecological transformations. The innermost sphere represents the ecological
core within the local habitat, the site of interactions between ecology and
human production. Plants (producers), animals (consumers), bacteria and
fungi (decomposers), and minerals exchange energy among themselves and
with human producers in accordance with the laws of thermodynamics and
the biogeochemical cycles. Introductions and withdrawals of organisms and
resources from outside the local habitat can alter its ecology. Human production (the extraction, processing, and exchange of resources and commodities)
is oriented toward immediate use as food, clothing, shelter, and energy for
subsistence or toward profit in mercantile trade and industrial capitalism.
With increasing industrialization, the subsistence-oriented sector declines
and the market-oriented sector expands (as indicated by the clockwise arrow).

bringer of life, fertility, famine, and death. The earth's interior was alive, active, and filled with small wombs, matrices, and caves within which the life on its surface germinated.

Since the scientific revolution of the seventeenth century, the West has seen nature primarily through the spectacles of mechanistic science. Matter is dead and inert, remaining at rest or moving with uniform velocity in a straight line unless acted on by external forces. Change comes from outside as in the operation of a machine. The world itself is a clock, adjustable by human clockmakers. Nature is passive and manipulable.

An ecological approach to history reasserts the idea of nature as historical actor. It challenges the mechanistic tradition by focusing on the interchange of energy, materials, and information among living and nonliving things in the natural environment. Through biogeochemical cycles, oxygen, nitrogen, carbon, phosphorus, sulfur, and other elements are circulated through living and nonliving things. Through the action of solar energy, chemicals are taken up by plants

---

The middle sphere represents human and nonhuman reproduction. The intergenerational reproduction of species and intragenerational survival rates influence ecological interactions directly in the case of nonhuman individuals or as mediated by production in the case of humans. In subsistence (or use-value) societies, production is oriented toward the reproduction of daily life in the household through the production of food, clothing, shelter, and energy (as indicated by the two-way arrow). For humans, the reproduction of society also includes socialization (in the family, church, and community) and the establishment of laws and governance that maintain order in the tribe, town, state, or nation.

Human consciousness, symbolized by the outermost sphere, includes representations of nature reflected (as indicated by the arrows) in myth, cosmology, religion, philosophy, science, language, and art, helping to maintain a given society over time and to influence change. Through ethics, morals, taboos, rituals, festivals, the dance, and games, they are translated into actions and behaviors that both affect and are affected by the environment, production, and reproduction (as indicated by the arrows).

The "semipermeable" membranes between the spheres symbolize possible interactions among them. Ecological revolutions are brought about through interactions between production and ecology and between production and reproduction. These changes in turn stimulate and can be simulated by new representations of nature and forms of human consciousness.

Source: Carolyn Merchant, "The Theoretical Structure of Ecological Revolutions," *Environmental Review* 11, no. 4 (Winter 1987): 268, reprinted by permission.

(producers), transferred to animals (consumers), and broken down into elements again by bacteria and fungi (decomposers). Plant production is the process of using the sun's energy to assimilate water, carbon dioxide, and minerals to provide energy for growth and reproduction. Primary production by plants supplies the energy that is ultimately consumed by animals and decomposers. In each transfer of materials and energy, some energy is lost to the environment in the form of heat in accordance with the second law of thermodynamics. Less energy is dissipated as heat in simple plant-animal or plant-human food webs than in more complex plant-animal-human webs.[5]

The activity of ecosystems is expressed through evolutionary and ecological succession. In evolutionary succession, new species evolve over long periods of time through natural selection, maintaining balanced ecological relationships among species. In ecological succession, changes in one community create ecological conditions that favor other communities as when lakes are gradually filled in by silt, followed by aquatic plants, grasses, shrubs, and trees to gradually become forests. When natural disruptions such as volcanoes, hurricanes, or fires alter an environment or when humans disturb ecosystems as by clearing and abandoning agricultural land, secondary succession occurs. Then weeds, grasses, pines, and hardwoods gradually replace each other over several decades.

Nonhuman nature, therefore, is not passive, but an active complex that participates in change over time and responds to human-induced change. Nature is a whole of which humans are only one part. We interact with plants, animals, and soils in ways that sustain or deplete local habitats. Through science and technology, we have great power to alter the whole in short periods of time. The relation between human beings and the nonhuman world is thus reciprocal. Humans adapt to nature's environmental conditions; but when humans alter their surroundings, nature responds through ecological changes.

Like the mechanistic paradigm, the ecological paradigm is a socially constructed theory. Although it differs from mechanism by taking relations, context, and networks into consideration, it has no greater or lesser claim to some ultimate truth status than do other scientific paradigms. Both mechanism and ecology construct their theories through a socially sanctioned process of problem identification, selection and deselection of particular "facts," inscription of the selected facts into texts, and the acceptance of a constructed order of nature by the scientific community. Laboratory ecology and field ecology merge through the replication of laboratory conditions in the field. The ecological approach of the twentieth century, like the mechanistic, has resulted from a socially constructed set of experiences sanctioned by scientific authority and a set of social practices and policies. The dominant paradigm in ecology draws heavily on economic metaphors such as producers, consumers, productivity, yields, and efficiency. Nature is cast as a computerized network of energy inputs and information bits that can be extracted from the environmental context and manipulated according to a set of thermodynamic equations.[6]

An ecological approach asserts the primacy of process in the natural world. It is rooted in ancient ideas about nature's inherent activity. Eastern philosophers expressed the inherent activity of nature as a dialectical movement between polar opposites. In ancient Greece, Heraclitus (d. ca. 470 B.C.) also spoke of change as an inherent tension between opposites: "Cool things become warm, the warm grows cool; the wet dries, the parched becomes wet." "Upward, downward, the way is one and the same." Their very opposition united them. The only constant, he believed, was the fact of change itself: "You could not step twice in the same rivers, for other and yet other waters are ever flowing on."[7]

The naturalists and alchemists of the Renaissance symbolized the activity within nature as a continual flux between male and female principles; the hermaphrodite was the androgynous unity of the opposites, the alchemic marriage of the masculine sun and feminine moon. Giordano Bruno (1548–1600) viewed change as a movement between contraries: everything comes "from contraries, through contraries, into contraries, to contraries." The coming together and dissolution of opposites was the cosmic process of change.

The mechanistic philosophy of the seventeenth century reconstructed the world as dead matter acted on by external forces. Nevertheless, its primary architects, Isaac Newton (1642–1727) and Gottfried Wilhelm Leibniz (1646–1716), sought the source of its evident internal activity. Newton, dissatisfied with his own cosmology of nature as mechanical laws and gravitational forces (described in his *Mathematical Principles of Natural Philosophy*, 1687), spent most of his life poring over alchemic and ancient texts looking for clues to the laws of vital life that would recruit new motion in a clocklike cosmos seemingly in danger of winding down. For Leibniz the source of energy lay in the unfolding vital lives of an infinity of self-active monads, like those basic to cabalistic and Eastern philosophies.[8]

Marx and Engels expressed the activity of nature as a dialectic within matter. The reciprocal interaction between human bodies and nature's matter was the key to ecological change. Both humans and nonhumans were real, active beings in constant interaction. Nature as impulse and tension was in continuous motion, transformation, and change. As an internally dynamic whole, the relations of nature, rather than the parts, were fundamental. From conflicts and tensions, a new totality was continually being produced.[9]

Although Marx and Engels ultimately opted for the domination of nature through technology and science, their insight into the interaction between human production and nonhuman nature is fundamental to the history of ecological thinking. As the whole within which humans live, nature was an extension of the human body. It provided the oxygen, nitrogen, phosphorus, and other elements necessary for food, clothing, shelter, and daily energy. In producing commodities for use and as well as for profit, humans appropriated its elements as resources. But like human ecologists today, Marx saw people as integral parts of nature. That "man lives on nature—means that nature is his body, with which he must remain in continuous interchange if he is not to die. That man's physical and spiritual life is linked to nature means simply that nature is linked to itself, for man is a part of nature."[10]

When humans use nonhuman nature, however, there are often unforeseen "ecological" consequences. "Because interaction is forgotten," complained Engels in his *Dialectics of Nature*, "our natural scientists are prevented from seeing the simplest things." "In nature nothing takes place in isolation." When people cut down the forests in ancient Asia Minor, they did not understand that they were also affecting the water reservoirs on which their life depended. Destroying forests in Italy dried out the springs needed for dairying. Goats grazing on the hillsides of Greece rendered them barren and susceptible to new species and diseases released when foreign ships landed in Greek ports. The unpredicted consequences nullified the original intention. "Each conquest," Engels chastised, "takes its revenge on us."[11]

Production in human systems is the counterpart of "nature's" activity. The need to produce subsistence to reproduce human energy on a daily basis connects human communities with their local environments. The production of food and fiber for human subsistence (or use) from the elements (or resources) of nature and the production of surpluses for market exchange are the primary ways in which humans interact directly with the local habitat. An ecological perspective unites human and nonhuman processes of production through exchanges of energy. The sun's energy, which is used by plants to produce energy for growth and reproduction, is transferred to animals, including humans, and returned to the environment through decomposition. All animals, plants, bacteria, and minerals are energy niches involved in the mutual exchange of energy, materials, and information.

Through human production systems, living and nonliving things become resources for humans. The word "resource" (to rise again) originally referred to Mother Earth's ability to restore herself. In 1650, Sir John Denham could write, "For whatsoever from our hand she [the earth] takes, Greater or Less, a vast return she makes. Nor am I only pleased with that resource." People could use the goods and gifts of the earth within a framework of reciprocity. By 1870, however, "resource" had donned its modern clothing. In his *Natural History of Commerce*, John Yeats wrote: "In speaking of the natural resources of any country, we refer to the ore in the mine, the stone unquarried, the timber unfelled, etc."[12]

Production is the extraction, processing, and exchange of natural resources. In traditional cultures exchanges are often gifts or symbolic alliances, while in market societies resources are exchanged as commodities. Over much of Western history, humans have produced and bartered food, clothing, and shelter primarily within the local community to reproduce daily life. When, instead, commodities are marketed for profit, as is the norm in capitalist societies, they are often removed from the local habitat to distant places and exchanged for money. Marx and Engels distinguished between use-value production (or production for subsistence) and production for profit. When people "exploit" nonhuman nature, they do so in one of two ways: they either make immediate or personal use of it for subsistence or they exchange its products as commodities for personal profit or gain. For New England's native Americans, plant and animal resources were gifts of nature to be used to take care of human needs. For colonial Americans engaging in mercantile trade, these same resources, exchanged as commodities, became sources of money and private property.

Like the word "resource," "production" has changed its meaning over time. To seventeenth-century writers, the living earth brought forth productions: "Metals are (as plants) hidden and buried in the bowels of the earth which have some conformitie in themselves, in the form and manner of their production." Eighteenth-century Americans who wrote natural histories of various places used the term "animal and vegetable productions" in discussing the power of nature to bring forth animals, trees, and herbaceous plants. By 1825, however, John McCulloch would define production not in nature's terms but in human terms: "By production, in the science of political economy, we are not to understand the production of matter, ... but the production of utility, and consequently of exchangeable value, by appropriating and modifying matter already in existence."[13]

Production has ecological implications. A society's patterns of production may modify and recycle matter and energy such that relative stability may be maintained within the habitat over long periods of time. On the other hand, the extraction of biotic elements (such as beaver or white pine trees) may be faster than their replacement through species reproduction or ecological succession. Or new species, such as agricultural crops, livestock, or pests, may be added. Human populations may increase or decrease through immigration and emigration, births and deaths, with implications for other species. The results alter habitat diversity and composition.[14]

New England is a significant historical exemplar because several types of production evolved within its present geographic area. Native Americans engaged primarily in gathering and hunting in the north and in horticulture in the south. Colonial Americans combined mercantile trade in natural resources with subsistence-oriented agriculture. The market and transportation revolutions in the nineteenth century initiated the transition to capitalist production.

Understanding the complex interactions between a society's ecology and production is enhanced through a systems perspective—an integrated view of the way in which the components function together. But while systems theories often describe integrated situations such as the way an indigenous culture has adapted to the local ecology, they may not successfully explain change over time. A dynamic rather than a static systems approach can better describe a continually evolving society and a changing environment. In contrast to closed mechanical systems whose parts are in equilibrium and are isolated from their surroundings, ecological and social systems are open—matter and energy are constantly being exchanged with the environment.

One approach to a dynamic theory of change over time is that of Ilya Prigogine and his follower Erich Jantsch who view open systems as dissipative structures, much like whirlpools in a rushing stream. Their structural dynamics hold them together for a time, but changes can cause them to dissolve and re-form. When a major disruption occurs, open systems may respond by reorganizing themselves from within. In equilibrium or near-equilibrium states, living systems are capable of absorbing and adapting to small disruptions. But when change is both rapid and radical, a major transformation can be initiated. The relationships become nonlinear and a new organization emerges. By analogy, human communities can develop ecologically sustainable relations with nature, can adapt to minor ecological disruptions, or can undergo major ecological and social transformations. Points at which major branchings in development occur are bifurcation points. Ecological revolutions are examples of major changes in ecology and society in particular periods and regions. In New England, historical bifurcation points within the evolutionary process can be identified as occurring *roughly* between 1600 and 1675 (the colonial ecological revolution) and between 1775 and 1860 (the capitalist ecological revolution).[15]

A second dynamic approach views systems as dialectical interactions. Tensions exist within a society and its ecology. Through mutual interaction, changes in one lead to changes in the other. Changes that affect production also affect ecology and vice versa. If the changes are of sufficient magnitude, the society as a whole and its ecology may both be radically altered. Because the ecological relationships between animals, plants, and minerals are intricate and societies are also structured in complex ways, it is helpful to focus on particular processes and interactions. Depletion, pollution, plant succession, and species reproduction are useful in understanding ecological changes. The interactions between these ecological processes and a society's patterns of production, reproduction, and consciousness help to explain the magnitude and direction of historical change.

Reproduction

To continue over time, life must be reproduced from generation to generation. The habitat is populated and repopulated with living organisms of all kinds. Biologically, all living things must reproduce themselves intergenerationally. All species—humans, other animals, plants, and microbes—increase, decrease, or maintain their populations depending on the balance between their reproductive potential and environmental resistance. Environmental conditions can alter the energy distribution between an organism's growth and its reproduction. Every species must produce enough offspring that survive to reproductive age without succumbing to adverse environmental conditions such as lack of water or food, unfavorable habitat or weather, parasites or disease, or competitors.[16]

For humans, reproduction is both biological and social. Biologically, each adult generation must maintain itself, its parents, and its offspring intergenerationally so that life itself may be passed on. Each individual must also reproduce its own energy and that of its offspring (intragenerationally) on a daily basis through gathering, growing, or preparing food and conserve it through clothing and shelter. Socially, humans must reproduce future laborers by passing on family and community norms. And they must reproduce and maintain the larger social order through the structures of governance and law (such as laws of property inheritance) and the ethical codes that reinforce behavior. Thus while production is twofold (oriented toward subsistence-use or market-exchange), reproduction is fourfold, having both biological and social articulations.[17]

Reproduction is the biological and social process through which humans are born, nurtured, socialized, and governed. Through reproduction sexual relations are legitimated, population sizes and family relationships are maintained, and property and inheritance practices are reinforced. In subsistence-oriented economies, production and reproduction are united in the maintenance of the local community. Under capitalism production and reproduction separate into two different spheres.

The biological reproduction of the human species is regulated by social and ethical practices that maintain, limit, or increase human population. These include mating patterns, fertility, nurturance, contraception, and abortion. Over human history, according to anthropologist Marvin Harris, cultures have used a wide variety of both malign and benign methods to regulate population. Malign techniques have included violence (warfare), deprivation (starvation), senilicide, infanticide, killing of female infants, assaults against pregnant women, clitoridectomies, neglect of preadolescent girls, and abortion. Benign methods encompass homosexuality, coitus interruptus, incest taboos, delayed marriage, postpartum sexual abstinence, masturbation, and prolonged lactation.[18]

Claude Meillassoux's *Maidens, Meal, and Money* (1981) best explains the necessary connections between biological and social reproduction in subsistence economies. Here production exists for the sake of reproduction; the production and the exchange of human energy are keys to the reproduction of human life. Food must be extracted or produced to maintain the daily energy of the producing adults, to maintain the energy of the children who will be the future producers, and to maintain that of the elders, the past producers. Reproducing life on a daily (intragenerational) basis through energy is thus directly linked to intergenerational reproduction of the human species.[19]

In the extraction economies of gathering, hunting, and fishing (such as those of the northern New England Indians), the return from the land is instant food that can be converted to human energy in order to reproduce daily life. The energy accumulated by the body during the past few hours is converted into energy during the next few hours. Some of that energy is spent in direct extraction during individual or collective food gathering. Additional energy is spent constructing the tools, weapons, traps, and cooking devices that mediate between humans and the land. More energy is used to maintain the social relations of the band. In gathering-hunting, there is no dead season and productive periods are separated from nonproductive periods by hours only. This mode of production cannot afford to use group energy to maintain the elderly—the past producers—or excessive or defective infants.[20]

Agriculture, in contrast to gathering and hunting, comprises a productive period of several months followed by a nonproductive period during which the stored food is consumed for energy. Such was the situation among the southern New England tribes and colonial farmers. Stored food allows for the support of the past producers—the tribal or family elders—whose energy contributes less to production than to the reproduction of the social relations within and between families and communities.[21]

Energy is not only used by people for maintaining daily life, it also circulates within society in the form of material products such as food and clothing. Enough surplus must be produced and stored over time to allow the children born in any one year to survive for fifteen to twenty years until they become adult producers. If harvests do not produce enough surplus or if some of the surplus is extracted by the state or a superior class, demographic growth will not occur. Additionally, enough surplus energy in the form of labor must be available to manufacture tools, cooking equipment, clothes, furniture, houses, barns, and outbuildings to produce and conserve the family's energy. Only after the community maintains and reproduces its own subsistence can demographic or commercial growth take place. Production for use takes precedence over the production of marketable surpluses. Production thus exists for the sake of reproduction.[22]

While the biological reproduction of life itself is possible only through the necessary connections between inter- and intragenerational reproduction, the community itself is maintained by social reproduction. In native American communities, male elders (sachems and shamans) usually bore the responsibility for decision making within the tribe and for negotiations with neighboring tribes. Under colonialism, men held the positions of responsibility within the town government. Through property and inheritance titles, they also reproduced the family farm as the unit of agricultural production from one generation to the next. Additionally, political, legal, and governmental structures helped to maintain the mode of production and reproduce the social whole.[23]

Women, according to Meillassoux, are exploited in agricultural communities to a greater degree than in the gathering-hunting bands because they are necessary both for the conversion of the agricultural product into edible food and for procreation. As biological reproducers, women circulate either by forcible abduction by a neighboring community, as in Indian warfare, or peacefully through "marriage," as for Indians and English immigrants. In either case, a woman is subordinate in juridical reproduction because she lives with her husband and gives her rights over her progeny and property to him. Her value begins at puberty when she becomes capable of bearing children, continues through motherhood as the reproducer of social norms in young children, and ends after menopause, unless as a widow she temporarily perpetuates the line of descent and property inheritance.[24]

Whereas Meillassoux was primarily interested in the concept of reproduction in subsistence societies, sociologist Abby Peterson formulated an analysis of reproduction in capitalist societies by looking at the gender-sex dimension in politics. Under capitalism, the division of labor between the sexes results in a situation in which men bear the responsibility for and dominate the production of exchange commodities, while women bear responsibility for reproducing the work force and social relations. "Women's responsibility for reproduction includes both the biological reproduction of the species (intergenerational reproduction) and the intragenerational reproduction of the work force through unpaid labor in the home. Here too is included the reproduction of social relations—socialization." With the change from subsistence to capitalist patriarchy, the relationship between production and reproduction is reversed. Under industrial capitalism, reproduction is subordinate to production.[25]

The work of Meillassoux and Peterson offers an approach through which the analysis of reproduction can be advanced beyond demography to include daily life and the community itself. The sphere of reproduction becomes fourfold, having two biological and two social manifestations: (1) the intergenerational reproduction of the species (both human and nonhuman), (2) the intragenerational reproduction of daily life, (3) the reproduction of social norms within the family and community, and (4) the reproduction of the legal-political structures that maintain social order within the community and the state. The fourfold sphere of reproduction exists in a dynamic relationship with the twofold (subsistence- or market-oriented) sphere of production (see Figure 1.1).

Production and Reproduction in Tension

How do reproduction and production interact? According to Engels in his *Origin of the Family, Private Property, and the State* (1884), "the determining factor in history is, in the last resort, the production and reproduction of immediate life . . . this itself is of a two fold character. On the one hand, the production of the means of subsistence . . . on the other, the production of human beings themselves." The reproduction of human beings is thus distinct from, but structurally related to, the production of the means of subsistence. A change in the mode of production from gathering-hunting to subsistence-oriented agriculture, or from subsistence agriculture to capitalist agriculture, will increase the capacity of the land to feed people. Intensification in agricultural production is made possible through advances in science and technology.[26]

Production and reproduction interact dialectically. When reproductive patterns are altered, as in population growth or changes in property inheritance, production is affected. Conversely, when production changes, as in the addition or depletion of resources or in technological innovation, social reproduction and biological reproduction are altered. A dramatic change at the level of either reproduction or production can alter the dynamic between them, resulting in a major transformation of the social whole. Whereas the colonial ecological revolution in New England resulted from external impacts wrought by Europeans on Indian production and reproduction, the capitalist ecological revolution was initiated by internal tensions between production and reproduction. Because of the colonists' low person-land ratio, each family had to reproduce its own labor force in order to produce subsistence for the family. On the other hand, a partible system of patriarchal inheritance meant that farm sizes decreased over three or four generations to the point that not all sons could inherit enough land to reproduce the subsistence system. The tensions between the requirements of subsistence-oriented production (a large family labor force) and social reproduction through partible inheritance (all sons must inherit farms) helped to create a wage labor supply of landless sons needed for the transition to capitalist agriculture.

Socialist-feminists have further elaborated the interaction between production and reproduction. In her 1976 article, "The Dialectics of Production and Reproduction in History," Renaté Bridenthal argues that changes in production give rise to changes in reproduction, creating tensions between them. For example, the change from a preindustrial agrarian to an industrial capitalist economy that characterized the capitalist ecological revolution can be described with respect to tensions, contradictions, and synthesis within the gender roles associated with production and reproduction. In the agrarian economy of colonial America, production and reproduction were symbiotic. Women participated in both spheres, since the production and reproduction of daily life were centered in the household and domestic communities. Likewise, children were socialized into production by men working in barns and fields and by women working in farmyards and farmhouses. But with industrialization, production of items such as textiles and shoes moved out of the home into the factory, while farms themselves became specialized and mechanized. Unmarried women were employed outside the home in textile production, or later in clerical work, while married women focused more of their efforts on the reproduction of daily life through housework. Production became more public, reproduction more private, leading to their social and structural separation. For working-class women, the split between production and reproduction imposed a double burden of wage labor and housework, while for middle-class women it led to an increase in domesticity and indoor housework.[27]

Ecological revolutions are generated through tensions and interactions between production and ecology and between production and reproduction. Changes may be externally stimulated as in the colonial ecological revolution or internally stimulated (and aided by external market incentives) as in the capitalist ecological revolution. As society responds to change, inherent tensions in its legitimating worldview and forms of consciousness begin to widen. Some assumptions about nature are elaborated and developed to support and lead the new directions; others are rejected as irrelevant and become the ideas of subordinate groups.

Consciousness

Consciousness is the totality of one's thoughts, feelings, and impressions, the awareness of one's acts and volitions. Group consciousness is a collective awareness by an aggregate of individuals. Individual consciousness and group consciousness are shaped by both environment and culture. In different historical epochs, a society's consciousness is dominated by particular characteristics. These forms of consciousness, through which the world is perceived, understood, and interpreted, are socially constructed and subject to change.

A society's symbols and images of nature express its collective consciousness. They appear in mythology, cosmology, science, religion, philosophy, language, and art. Scientific, philosophical, and literary texts are sources of the ideas and images used by controlling elites, while rituals, festivals, songs, and myths provide clues to the consciousness of ordinary people. How are the ideas, images, and metaphors that legitimate human behaviors toward nature translated into ethics, morals, and taboos? Anthropologist Clifford Geertz holds that religious beliefs establish powerful moods and motivations that translate into social behaviors. Also, ideological frameworks or worldviews "secrete" behavioral norms. According to Charles Taylor, particular frameworks give rise to a certain range of normative variations and not others because their related values are not accidental. When sufficiently powerful, worldviews and their associated values can override social changes, but if weak or weakened they can be undermined. A tribe of New England Indians or a community of colonial Americans may have a religious worldview that holds it together for many decades while its economy is gradually changing. Eventually, however, with the acceleration of commercial change, ideas that had formerly existed on the periphery or among selected elites may become dominant if they support and legitimate the new economic directions.[28]

For native American cultures, consciousness was an integration of all the senses with the body in sustaining life. In this mimetic consciousness, culture was transmitted intergenerationally through imitation in song, myth, dance, sport, gathering, hunting, and planting. Oral-aural transmission of tribal knowledge through myth and transactions between animals, Indians, and neighboring tribes produced sustainable relations between the human and the nonhuman worlds. The primal gaze of locking eyes between hunter and hunted initiated the moment of ordained killing when the animal gave itself up so that the Indian could survive. The very meaning of the gaze stems from the intent look of expectancy when a deer first sees a fire, smells a scent, or looks into the eyes of a pursuing hunter. For Indians engaged in an intimate survival relationship with nature, sight, smell, sound, taste, and touch were all of equal importance, integrated together in a total participatory consciousness.[29]

When Europeans took over native American habitats during the colonial ecological revolution, vision became dominant within the mimetic fabric. Although daily life for most colonial settlers, as for Indians, was still guided by imitative, oral, face-to-face transactions, Puritan eyes turned upward toward a transcendent God who sent down his Word in written form in the Bible. Individual Protestants learned to read so that they could interpret God's word for themselves. In turn, the biblical word legitimated the imposition of agriculture and artifact in the new land. The primal gaze of the Indian was submerged by the objectifying scrutiny of fur trader, lumber merchant, and banker who viewed nature as resource and commodity. Treaties and property relations that extracted land from Indians were codified in writing. Alphanumeric literacy became central to religious expression, social survival, and upward mobility.[30]

The imposition of a visually oriented consciousness by Puritans was shattering to the continuance of Indian animism and ways of life. The implications were similar to the loss of mimetic consciousness in Plato's Greece. According to philosopher Eric Havelock, Plato's critique of the oral mimetic heritage of Homer was devastating. The orator to Plato (as the shaman to the Puritan) was an imitator who indulged in extremes extending even to the howls and cries of animals. The oral tradition was not the creative, individualistic medium appropriate to the virtuous, but the distortive chicanery of the trickster who presented appearance as reality. Myth and poetry stood for the illusions of appearance, not the truths discernible to reason. The oral tradition was merely a catalog of repeated, remembered examples that predetermined human responses. The person who repeated by rote memory through song, poem, or myth was not an individual with a unique psyche, but a victim of hypnosis. No "I" stood apart from the collective consciousness to examine or criticize its spell. No "self" asserted its own independence and authority. For Plato, the emergence of the autonomous psyche signified the separation of the knower from the known, the subject from the object, and the analytical from the oral.[31]

Against poetry, Plato set his theory of pure forms, with mathematics as the exemplar par excellence of knowledge. The ideal forms of the triangle, the bed, and the good were exact, unchanging, and universal. The applied mathematician, the carpenter, and the philosopher attempted to copy these forms in matter, while the orator and the poet were content with word pictures. Mathematics, logic, and science, or *episteme*, were the true modes of knowing, and the self was the knowing subject. With the commercialization of the fur trade and the missionary efforts of Jesuits and Puritans, a society in which animals, plants, and rocks were equal subjects changed to one dominated by transcendent vision in which individual human subjects were separate from resource objects. This change in consciousness imposed by dominant elites characterized the colonial ecological revolution.

The rise of an analytic, quantitative consciousness was a feature of the capitalist ecological revolution. Capitalist ecological relations emphasized efficient management and control of nature. With the development of mechanistic science and its use of perspective diagrams, visualization was integrated with numbering. The printing press and perspective art linked the mental to the material through what sociologist of science Bruno Latour called "immutable mobiles." By reducing three-dimensional natural objects—oceans, rivers, beaver, birds, rocks, and ores—to two-dimensional inscriptions—maps, charts, drawings, diagrams, lists, graphs, curves, equations, papers, texts, files, and archives—quantitative features could be circulated unchanged. In a laboratory, observatory, or field station, they could be accumulated, arrayed, superimposed, compared, and reconstructed as a "natural" order. "The result," observed Latour, "is that we can work on paper with rulers and numbers, but still manipulate three-dimensional objects 'out there'. . . . Distant or foreign places and times [can] be gathered in one place in a form that allows all the places and times to be presented at once." The visual and material thus combined to produce power over nature through science. The capitalist ecological revolution was characterized by the superposition of scientific, quantitative approaches to nature and its resources. Through education analytic consciousness expanded beyond that of dominant elites to include most ordinary New Englanders.[32]

Forms of consciousness are power structures. When one worldview is challenged and replaced by another during a scientific or ecological revolution, power over society, nature, and space is at stake. Symbol systems, metaphors, and images express the implicit ethics of elites in positions of social power. Debates over scientific theories, argues historian of science Donna Haraway, are contests for power over the terms of discourse. According to French philosopher Michel Foucault, the history of power over nature is a history of spaces, spatial metaphors (habitat, soil, landscape, topography, terrain, region, and so on), strategies of control, and modes of mapping, tabulation, recordation, classification, demarcation, and ordering. Whereas space "used to belong to nature," when mapped by explorers and geographers, cataloged and inventoried by traders and naturalists, and coded by militarists and computer scientists, it can be controlled by an "eye of power" and subjected to unlimited surveillance. For Foucault, the vision obtained metaphorically through Jeremy Bentham's Panopticon, in which the radiating wings of an entire prison can be surveyed from a single central tower, is paradigmatic of the controlling scrutiny of the overseer. All things are made visible through the dominating, examining look of a cultural overseer located in a management center that controls not only social institutions, but also by extension nature, resources, national parks, wild rivers, endangered whales, herds of wild antelope, migrating warblers, and indeed the whole earth itself through satellite surveillance.[33]

Human consciousness socially constructs nature in different ways in different historical epochs and cultures. Humans negotiate "reality" with nonhuman nature. Indians constructed nature as a society of equal face-to-face subjects. Animals, plants, and rocks were alive and could be communicated with directly. For eighteenth-century New England farmers, nature was an animate mother carrying out God's dictates in the mundane world. Plants and even rocks grew on the earth's surface, but were created for human use and could be harvested as commodities. Nineteenth-century scientists, industrialists, and market farmers reconstructed them as scientific objects to be analyzed in the laboratory and as natural resources to be extracted for profit.

Ecological thinking constructs nature as an active partner. The "nature" that science claims to represent is active, unstable, and constantly changing. As parts of the whole, humans have the power to alter the networks in which they are embedded. Nature as active partner acquiesces to human interventions through resilience and adaptation or "resists" human actions through mutation and evolution. Nonhuman nature is an actor; human and nonhuman interactions constitute the drama. Viewed as a social construction, nature as it was conceptualized in each social epoch (Indian, colonial, and capitalist) is not some ultimate truth that was gradually discovered through the scientific processes of observation, experiment, and mathematics. Rather, it was a relative changing structure of human representations of "reality."[34]

Ecological revolutions, I argue, are processes through which different societies change their relationship to nature. They arise from tensions between production and ecology and between production and reproduction. The results are new constructions of nature, both materially and in human consciousness. The two parts of this book, on the colonial and capitalist ecological revolutions, reflect this structure and process of change. Chapters 2 and 3 show how the patterns of production and reproduction of the northern and southern New England Indians were integrated with their cosmologies and forms of consciousness on the eve of European colonization. Each of these two

Table 1.1
Ecological Revolutions

	Native American Society	Revolution 1 Colonial → Preindustrial Society	Revolution 2 Capitalist → Industrial Society
Nonhuman Nature	Nature as self-active: Corn Mother, active spirits Active subjects: animals, trees, rocks Named places	Nature as active vice-regent of God: virgin, mother Passive objects, commodities Mapping of space as private property	Nature as passive female: teacher of mechanical laws, moral model Scientific objects, natural resources Cartesian grid system to map land and planet
Human Production (economy)	Gathering-Hunting-Fishing Female farming: long-fallow/polycultures	"Extensive," subsistence agriculture, use-value economy in local communities; mercantile trade Male-Female production spaces	Intensive market agriculture, exchange value economy, market system permeates U.S. interior Male-dominated machine production

Human Reproduction			
—Biological	Steady state: equilibrium of populations	Growth of population: reproduction of labor force	Demographic transition, sublimation of sexuality into economic production ("spermatic economy")
—Social	Tribal villages: reproduction of daily subsistence	Family farm: farmer as midwife to nature; wife as midwife to humans	Nuclear households: home as sphere of female and mother; emotive, romantic
—Political	Tribal councils	Jeffersonian, agrarian politics	Hamiltonian, market politics
Forms of Consciousness	Mimetic consciousness: imitation, equality of all senses	Visual consciousness: domination of visual signs, signatures, written symbols	Analytic consciousness: domination of mental, disembodied intellect, numbering
Symbols of Nature	Animism, reciprocity between humans and nature	Organicism, religious retribution, fatalistic acceptance of nature	Mechanism, domination and mastery of nature
Knowledge	Monistic thinking: identification, face-to-face, subject-to-subject relationships	Analogical thinking: sympathy/antipathy, similarities/differences	Dualistic thinking: subject/object, mind/body, male/female

chapters discusses the process of ecological breakdown and introduction of new European patterns of production, reproduction, and consciousness as an externally caused transformation. Chapter 4 then describes how the European colonists' cosmology and consciousness were integrated with their own dual mercantile and subsistence economy. Yet this colonial system contained within itself economic and intellectual tensions that set the stage for the capitalist ecological revolution of Part II. In analyzing this second revolution, Chapter 5 first considers the strengthening of the subsistence sector of the economy as farmers moved inland beyond easy access to the mercantile sector and argues that internal tensions between the requirements of production and reproduction stimulated by European market opportunities led to the capitalist transformation. Described in Chapter 6 is the new mechanistic worldview that superseded the colonial cosmology and supported capitalist industrialization. Chapter 7 elaborates the new gender division of labor under capitalism as production and reproduction separate into two distinct spheres and the accommodation of women's roles and sensibilities to the new ecological order. Finally, the Epilogue sets New England in the context of the worldwide ecological crisis of today and argues that we may now be in the midst of a third, or global, ecological revolution (Table 1.1).

PART ONE

. . . .

The Colonial Ecological Revolution

2

· · · · · · · · · · · · · · · · · ·

Animals into Resources

To see nature as active is to recognize its formative role over geologic and historical time. Only by according ecology a place in the narrative of history can nature and culture be seen as truly interactive. Only by considering the ecological relationships within plant succession and animal-plant interdependences can the habitat be viewed as the scene of dynamic change and the locus of the reproduction of life. Indians exemplified the true meaning of ecology as *oikos* (house) by making the entire habitat, often a watershed, their home. With European colonization, however, home would constrict to the family farm and then to the houses of city dwellers, while nature would become increasingly distant from and controlled by culture.

Animals to New England's Indians were spiritual equals in their homeland. When hunted, fished, or gathered, they became resources, or gifts, that sustained human life. For Europeans engaging in mercantile trade, animals became resource commodities to be traded for private gain. As the homeland of native Americans constricted during the colonial ecological revolution, the status of animals as resources also changed.

The New England Habitat

Over eons in New England, hydrologic and geologic forces, plant succession, and the activities of animals operated together to form local habitats. Climatic forces created the annual rainfall of 40–45 inches, while the annual motion of the earth on its inclined axis set the frost-free growing season of 153–163 days in southern New England and the northern limit for corn and beans between the Saco and Kennebec rivers in Maine at about 44 degrees of latitude. Melting snows and surging rains cut through the underlying granite and metamorphic rock and carved out south-flowing rivers—to the disappointment of explorers and traders looking for navigable routes to the west.[1]

Igneous and glacial forces pushed up and carved the Green, White, and Berkshire mountain biomes and the fabled monadnocks that pimpled their level surroundings. Retreating glaciers deposited the stony drift of the uplands, frustrating generations of farmers trying to make the earth say corn and beans instead of rocks and stones. The easily leached soils rendered the forest floors acid beneath a thin surface of humus and leaf litter.[2]

Soil is a living thing. More living biomass is found below the ground than above. Although soil does not double its mass through reproduction as does a living organism, it teems with molds, bacteria, amoebas, ants, earthworms, millipedes, pill bugs, termites, and nematodes. To soil scientist Hans Jenny, soils have their own personalities and artistic beauty. "I have seen so many delicate shapes, forms, and colors in soil profiles that to me soils are beautiful. . . . As yet neither touch nor smell sensations have been accorded aesthetic recognition, but colors delight painters, photographers, and writers." Like many animals and plants, undisturbed soil species are rare and endangered and should have similar rights to preservation.[3]

The podzol soils (or spodosols) of the cool forested mountains of Vermont, New Hampshire, and Maine are light gray, ashlike layers lying just under the humus, taking their color from the silica remaining after the more soluble elements leach out. The rusty-colored clay subsoil, below, with its accumulations of iron and aluminum, mixes with the gray topsoil on plowing. The brown podzolic soils (recently redesignated alfisols and spodosols) of the less acidic, more favored farming lands of southern New England are yellowish-brown and contain more clay. In the sandy loams of the Connecticut Valley, sandstones and shales add a reddish tint (Map 2.1).[4]

By comparison with the fourteen-inch soils of the midwestern prairies, pristine topsoils in New England are a shallow two to four inches. They are more acid than prairie soils, contain less nitrogen, and are comparatively less fertile, but they are also less erosive and higher in phosphorus and potassium. They respond well when farmers add fertilizers such as lime (calcium oxide, CaO), which raises the pH and adds calcium, nitrogen from legumes, potassium from potash (potassium oxide, K_2O), and phosphorus from bones.

Four types of habitats held the natural resources that Indians and colonists would use for subsistence and fur traders, merchants, and

lumberers would exploit for profit. Coastal lowlands with their protected bays, river mouths, dunes, and sandy plains sustained fishing,
shellfish gathering, and coastal agriculture. River valley lowlands
contained the rich soils, meadows, rolling hills, woods, lakes, and
swamps that supported horticulture, gathering, and fishing. The eastern and western uplands on either side of the Connecticut Valley,
extending north to Vermont and New Hampshire, offered colder winters and stonier pastures than the adjacent lowlands. The mountain
forests with their cold lakes and fast-running streams provided farms
in their flat, meadowed intervales as well as resources for hunters,
fishers, and lumberers (Map 2.2).[5]

The "desolate wilderness" encountered by Pilgrims and Puritans
was in reality a parklike woodland that rippled westward in three
broad bands of modulated green from the Atlantic to the Hudson
River, extending northward from Long Island Sound to the Saint Lawrence. Three basic forest types, covering up to 95 percent of the area
on the eve of colonization, comprised the undulating bands. Pollen
profiles from New England bogs established the changing composition of the forest through time as the glacial ice sheets that covered
the land 13,500 years ago retreated. The species found in the three
zones today are essentially the same as in the precolonial era, although local compositions have been altered through ecological succession (Map 2.3).[6]

Farthest to the north is the coniferous forest of spruce, fir, and
northern hardwoods, extending from northeastern Maine through
the White and Green mountains of New Hampshire and Vermont to
the Berkshires in western Massachusetts. The northern forest is a
relict of glacial retreat, the hardy species requiring only a thin layer
of soil in which to establish their roots. Red spruce (*Picea rubens*)
dominates the high mountains accompanied by its constant companion, the balsam fir (*Abies balsamea*). Together they form dense, cool,
shady groves with little understory. Mingling among these softwoods
are the northern hardwoods. Along lake shores and cold rushing
streams are found the paper birch (*Betula papyrifera*) that helped to
sustain life for Indian and beaver, aspen (*Populus tremuloides*), the
beaver's favorite food, and red maple (*Acer rubrum*), its flowering red
stems glowing in early spring and its leaves a brilliant red in fall. In
the swamps grow black spruce and tamarack, while the lower mountain slopes support yellow birch, sugar maple, and beech.

The white pine zone somewhat to the south established itself as a

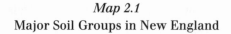

Map 2.1
Major Soil Groups in New England

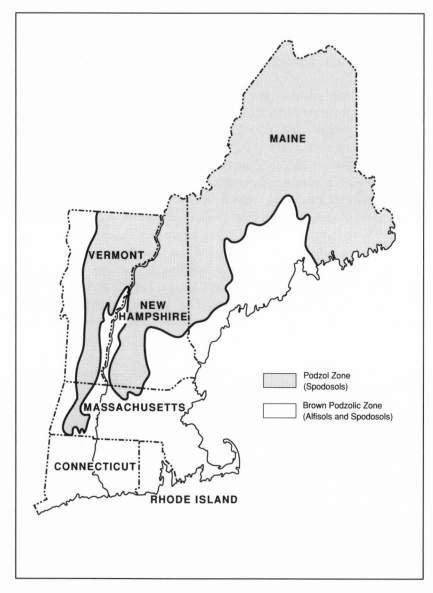

Podzols (now known as spodosols) are acid soils found in coniferous regions.
They yield pine timber, but base-needing agricultural crops do not do well in
them. Brown podzolic soils (now reclassified as alfisols and spodosols) are
less acid. Alfisols, found in deciduous forests, recycle calcium, thereby reduc-

second forest type as the glaciers retreated. The fast-seeding pioneer, white pine (*Pinus strobus*), 150 feet tall with 80 feet of clear trunk, was the famous mast tree of the colonial era. Hemlock (*Tsuga canadensis*), fabled companion to the "murmuring pines" of the "forest primeval," grew slowly only after dense shade and leaf mold had accumulated. Moving southward, the northern hardwoods begin to be replaced by oaks, hickories, and, in earlier times, the American chestnut.

In the third band, the oak forest of southern New England, the hardwoods come into their full glory. White oak (*Quercus alba*), which with its light, ash-gray bark, gigantic spreading canopy, and deep root system, contributed most to the majestic parklike feeling described by early explorers, was destined to supply shipbuilders and farmers with strong decking, planks, and rafters. Red oak (*Quercus borealis*), whose more porous, weaker, tawny wood was ideal for barrels and casks, grew on the higher slopes. The gnarled black oak (*Quercus velutina*), its pointed lobed leaves brilliant in autumn, was used for casks, fuel, and yellow dye. Chestnut oak (in Connecticut) and scarlet oak (around Massachusetts Bay and in Connecticut and Rhode Island) grew in the drier areas of the southern zone, while in wetter places basswood, ash, maple, and birch alerted Indians and settlers to the mull soils that would yield good crops. On the sandy coastal soils of Cape Cod, Rhode Island, and Connecticut, pitch pine contributed charcoal, turpentine, and tar.

Concord naturalist Henry David Thoreau (1817–62) first perceived the succession of plant forms in disturbed habitats. He saw in New England's trees and underlying vegetation an explosive regenerative power enabling them to "recover" their habitat when disturbed. Like Renaissance Neoplatonist and Stoic philosophers, he conceived of a formative power ordering the whole of nature. First, he speculated,

---

ing acidity and are agriculturally productive. Coastal sandy spodosols are poor in bases and need to be fertilized with calcium, magnesium, and potassium to be productive. River valley soils are entisols that retain fertility through periodic additions of organic matter from flooding. (Milo I. Harpstead and Francis D. Hole, *Soil Science Simplified* [Ames: Iowa State University Press, 1980], pp. 98–99, 92–95.)

Source: U.S. Department of Agriculture, *The Changing Fertility of New England Soils*, Agricultural Information Bulletin No. 133 (Washington, D.C.: U.S. Government Printing Office, 1954), p. 17, fig. 13.

Map 2.2
New England Topography

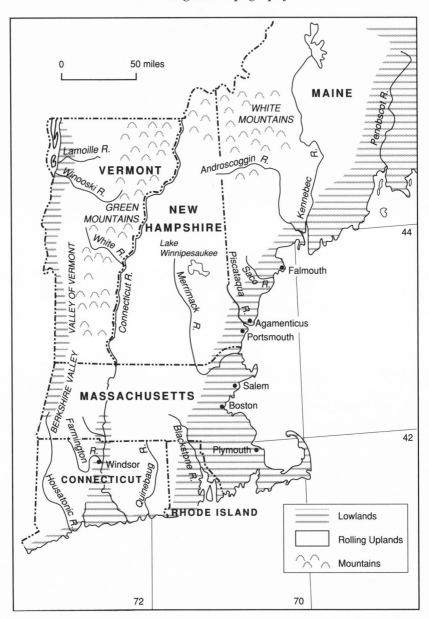

Source: William F. Robinson, *Abandoned New England: Its Hidden Ruins and Where to Find Them* (Boston: New York Graphic Society, 1976), p. 2.

Map 2.3
Forest Types at the Beginning of New England Settlement

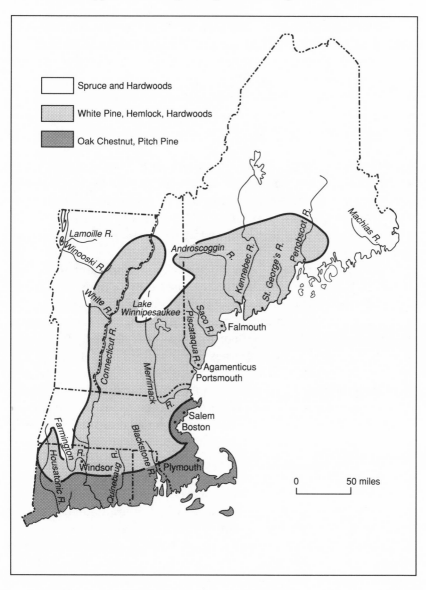

Source: Samuel F. Manning. *New England Masts and the King's Broad Arrow* (Kennebunk, Maine: Thomas Murphy, 1979), p. 20.

cherries, birch, poplar, and willow would regenerate themselves. Then would follow the other trees—evergreens such as pines, hemlock, spruce, and larch and hardwoods like oaks, chestnuts, beeches, and walnut. Nature would take back the forest from its human conquerors and ultimately obliterate any evidence of their presence.[7]

Modern ecologists describe in detail the plant succession that reforests the three different zones when old fields are abandoned. In the southern zone, red cedars sprout along pasture edges, followed by slender gray birches and black cherries. After these pioneers have established themselves, hardwoods like the oaks, hickories, white ash, and maples begin to return. In the pine zone, white pine seeds itself first, darkening the forest floor so that little else survives. But as the pines mature and decay, the shade-tolerant seedlings of red oak, black cherry, and maple grow up, to be succeeded eventually by the hardwoods. In the north, aspen, pin cherry, striped maple, and yellow birch take over first, followed by the northern hardwoods and conifers.[8]

To see nature as active, rather than as a mere constraint on human activities, is also to recognize the role played by animals in creating the landscape. In the forests, deer carved out winter browse yards as they grazed on tree leaves and grasses. Migrating passenger pigeons annually fertilized the forest floor with tons of droppings. Their dung, according to naturalist John James Audubon, "fell in spots not unlike melting flakes of snow" and once on the ground it "lay several inches deep, covering the whole roosting place." Extinguishing these birds deprived the forest soils forever of an important source of phosphorus. Especially significant for Indian and colonial farmers were the fertile beaver meadows that contrasted so sharply with the stony uplands.[9]

Over thousands of years, all over New England rich meadows with fertile soils had been created by beavers. Both Indians and whites recognized the beaver as an active agent in nature. Indians considered it to be more intelligent than humans. Naturalists made extravagant claims about the beaver's reasoning ability, powers of discrimination, and industry. Conservationists eulogized its engineering feats and labeled it the archetypal conserver of water resources. "The beaver," enthused Enos Mills, writing during the progressive conservation era of the early 1900s, has "prepared the way for forests and meadows, orchards and grainfields, homes and schoolhouses. . . . Elm avenues now arch where the low-growing willow drooped across the [beaver's] canal, and a populous village stands upon the seat of a primitive and forgotten colony."[10]

Engineering skills made beavers important molders of natural habitats. Their dams across upland streams transformed the topography. Capturing and holding water, soil, and sediment from nearby hillsides, beaver ponds raised the temperature of the cold rushing waters, producing plankton and aquatic insects favored by fish. Ranging from a few square feet to hundreds of acres in area, the ponds became diverse habitats for a variety of birds, fish, and plants. While the open water attracted waterbirds, the newly created rock islands, dead brush, cavity trees, and surrounding marshes lured woodpeckers, chickadees, phoebes, wrens, sparrows, thrashers, and bluejays.[11]

As the beavers expanded their colonies and raised the level of their dams, the small ponds grew to large lakes, trapping within their confines tree stumps that once lined their shores, falling leaves, rain-washed debris, and melting snows. Rather than being carried downstream, rich layers of sediment formed on the lake bottoms as the organic matter decomposed. As long as beavers maintained them, the dams stored floodwaters and slowed runoff during rainy periods, releasing the water slowly throughout the drier seasons like leaky sieves. Their channels, dams, and ponds operated like irrigation works and reservoirs to preserve watersheds and equalize stream flows.

But when a beaver colony exhausted its food supply and moved on, the abandoned dam released its waters, exposing flat tracts of muck in which meadow grasses took root. When fur traders removed the beavers or colonists broke down the dams, they accelerated the natural cycle. "These meadows," observed a nineteenth-century New Englander, "serve to feed great numbers of moose and deer, and are of still greater use to new settlers, who find a mowing field already cleared . . . and though the hay is not equally as good as English, yet it not only keeps their cattle alive, but in tolerable order; and without these natural meadows, many settlements could not possibly have been made."[12]

The European immigrants built much of their agriculture on the engineering of the ubiquitous beaver. At Hartford, Connecticut, a farmer eagerly planned to fence six acres "called beaver meadow." A Wethersfield widow inherited "five acres on the west side of Beaver Brook," and, at Haddam, a favored son received under his father's will "all my land at Beaver Meadow." Yankees peppered the land with the meadow builder's name: Beaver Brook, Beaver Creek, Beaver Lake, Beaver Dam Brook, Beaver Pond, Beaver Dam Pond, Beaver Meadow Village, and so on.[13]

The landscape created by waters, glaciers, forest succession, and animals was also altered by the first human inhabitants. Over 10,000 years ago Paleo-Indians ventured up New England's rivers for summer hunting with flint spears brought from farther south. Archaic Indians who followed them 7,000 to 5,000 years ago, as the tundra was being replaced by pine forests, hunted caribou with spears and fished with harpoons and hafted hooks. Their successors built circular bark houses and settled down in the warmer, drier hardwood forests, crafting cooking and eating bowls from soapstone. Around a thousand years ago, with the introduction of corn, a horticultural revolution further modified the southern New England forest. Algonkian horticulturists used fire to clear planting fields and create forest openings that attracted deer. Their frequent cool fires consumed the underbrush, but did not destroy mature trees or eliminate plant or animal species. The resulting fire-grass pastures and parklike groves, according to European colonizers, made "the country very beautiful and commodious," so that "scarce a bush or bramble or any cumbersome underwood" was to be seen.[14]

The vegetable, animal, and human inhabitants of precolonial New England constituted an integrated evolving ecosystem in 1600. The Indian population of New England on the eve of colonization in 1610 can be estimated by extrapolating from all known historical data on house, family, and village sizes and losses from epidemics and wars. Recent calculations give an estimate of 11,900 Abenaki in what is now Maine (about 0.2 persons per square kilometer) and upwards of 65,000 for southern New England or about 2.0 persons per square kilometer (Table 2.1). While horticulture predominated in the south (see Chapter 3), the northern tribes were primarily gatherer-hunter-fishers, growing some corn during favorable years. Women collected and processed maple syrup, ground nuts, berries, cattails, and medicinal and green plants; tended gardens; and crafted utensils and clothing. Men followed and trapped game and fowl for food and clothing, and engaged in net and canoe fishing on rivers and lakes. With European colonization, the New England habitat and its indigenous Indian tribes, animals, and plants began a period of disruption and adaptation to new conditions in what constituted New England's colonial ecological revolution.[15]

Table 2.1
Indian Population of New England, 1610

Abenaki	11,900
Pennacook	12,000
Massachuset	4,500
Wampanoag	5,000
Nauset and the island tribes	8,100
Narraganset	7,800
Pequot-Mohegan	3,500
Nipmuck-Connecticut Valley tribes	5,300
Wappinger Confederacy	13,200
Mahican	5,000
TOTAL	76,300

Sources: Data based on Sherburne F. Cook, *The Indian Population of New England in the Seventeenth Century*, University of California Publications in Anthropology, vol. 12 (Berkeley: University of California Press, 1976), p. 84; Dean R. Snow, *The Archeology of New England* (New York: Academic Press, 1980), pp. 31–42.

Europeans and Animals

The assumptions about animals, forests, and "savages" that fur traders, explorers, Puritan colonists, and Jesuit missionaries brought to the New England shores in the 1600s represented the vision of bourgeois elites and upper-class Europeans that human culture reigned supreme over wild nature. Emerging during the Renaissance and commercial expansion of the sixteenth century was a perception that bestial characteristics and animal-like passions in the human body and soul must be suppressed in all "civilized" humans. The polar opposites of "wildness" and "animality" were "civilization" and "humanity."

For Greeks and Romans the demarcations between people and animals had been less rigid than for Hebrews and Christians. The ancients populated their world with half-human gods and half-human animals, all manifestations of a universal matter. Fauns, satyrs, nymphs, and sileni were blatantly sexual beings that inhabited woodland pools and meadows, while centaurs, cyclops, and minotaurs lived darker lives in deserts, oceans, and untamed labyrinths. Completely human beings inhabited city states ruled by laws, while coun-

tryfolk, women, and slaves were destined to a lesser form of hu-
manness.

For Hebrews and Christians, humans and animals were rigidly
divided. While God in Genesis 1 gave humans dominion over fish,
fowl, and moving life, in the softer interpretation of Genesis 2 he
created the animals as helpmates for Adam. The mixing of humans
and animals through copulation was strictly forbidden. Moses was
commanded not to lie with any beast to defile himself, and women
were forbidden "to stand before a beast to lie down thereto." Lower
still than animality was wilderness—a moral state characterized by a
lack of blessedness in the soul and symbolized by exile in the desert,
the wastes, and the void. For Hebrews, God's righteousness could
restore blessedness and remove the curse of wilderness, while for
Christians God's mercy, dispensed through the Sacraments, provided
a restorative medicine.

To medieval theologians such as Aquinas, animal souls were characterized by sexual lust and ceaseless wandering. Humans could do-
mesticate them, use them for food and clothing, sacrifice them, or
destroy them without falling into sin. The danger for human souls
was that they might sink into a state of wildness beyond the possibility of redemption. For Dante, submission to lust meant eternal con-
finement to the second circle of hell.[16]

During the sixteenth century the lines drawn between animality
and humanity, wilderness and civilization, disorder and order sharp-
ened. Sexual lust was a mark of the failure of the higher mental
powers to control and subdue the bodily passions. Women's lapses
often resulted in the accusation of witchcraft. The wild, chaotic animal-like dances and sexual encounters of female witches with the
devil-goat at the witches' Sabbath revealed the weaknesses of females for the unbridled sexual lust of animal copulation. Errant
males were accused of sodomy or bestiality.

Explorers' tales of wild beasts and savage humans clothed in skins
fed fears of the animality to which humans could sink if the bonds of
civilized society were broken. While some early accounts of explorers
had reported Indians to be civil, merry, gentle, peaceful, and loving,
at a social level somewhere between beasts and humans on the Great
Chain of Being, other reports criticized their lack of clothing, crops,
culture, discipline, and government. Clothed in skins and eating wild
meat, they took on the characteristics of the beasts on which they fed.

As European elite culture set itself increasingly above nature as represented by its own medieval past and by New World savagery, a code of manners was adopted that self-consciously advocated the suppression of beastlike qualities in humans. Imitating animal characteristics, such as the slyness of a fox or the boldness of a lion, as advocated for a prince by Niccolò Machiavelli (1513), might be necessary to gain control in a social wilderness, but was not the mark of manners in an ordered civil state. Untamed human nature, as exemplified by Shakespeare's cannibal Caliban, could not be allowed to gain the upper hand in humans.[17]

The "civilizing" process, by which humans began to distance themselves from animal-like nature, altered many medieval customs and manners. In the Middle Ages, extravagant consumption of meat had been a mark of high rank. Although servants and grooms were allowed flesh or fish only once a day, the upper classes consumed enormous quantities of venison, fowl, and fish. Whole animals and birds with their feathers unplucked adorned the dinner table. Cattle, deer, and oxen were roasted on open fires in the dining hall; entire rabbits, lambs, and pigs were served and carved at the table.[18]

By the sixteenth century a code of table manners arose to distinguish human from animal behavior. Meat in the form of the whole animal was no longer brought to the table for carving with sharp knives. By the seventeenth century, meat carving ceased to be an essential accomplishment of the worldly courtier. Animals were slaughtered and prepared for consumption by butchers and cooks who cut them into small pieces and disguised them with sauces and spices. Food was to be eaten with the fork, not the fingers, and people were advised not to slurp or smack their lips like swine. Manuals dictated proper table manners. "Those who stand up and snort disgustingly over the dishes like swine belong with other farmyard beasts. To snort like a salmon, gobble like a badger, and complain while eating—these three things are quite improper," admonished Bonicino da Riva. "Do not slurp with your mouth when eating from a spoon. This is a bestial habit."[19]

The suppression of animal-like characteristics in the self meant changes in clothing codes as well. In the Middle Ages, fancy furs such as ermine and sable cloaks, fur-lined dresses, tiger skin jackets, and fox skin trimmings worn by English royalty had dazzled the courts. The nobility decorated their garments with choice miniver and sable, ermine being reserved for royalty. Nobles of lesser wealth could wear all furs but ermine and miniver. Yeomen and artisans of the lower classes were only allowed lamb, rabbit, cat, and fox for the linings of their winter garments, while the poor at the bottom of the social ladder were confined to sheepskin for warmth.[20]

Between 1600 and 1800 the ostentatious wearing of fancy furs by elites declined, to be replaced by the use of fur in a disguised, less obvious form—the beaver felt hat (Figure 2.1). Although kings, queens, and nobles retained their fur cloaks and trimmings, the great demand among gentlemen was for staple rather than fancy fur. The beaver hat was actually a fur-napped felt hat made by removing the soft inner barbed hairs of a beaver's fur from its pelt so that the barbs could stick to a felt base made of rabbit hair. It was the beaver's peculiar fate to have a pelt from which the best staple fur could be produced.[21]

By the 1580s Philip Stubbes, in his *Anatomie of Abuses*, reported that lords were sporting hats made from a curious sort of hair, "fetched from beyond the seas," and Ben Jonson wrote of a "new four pound beaver hat, set with enamel studs" as a prize for a bet. In the 1620s ladies began to wear large "beavers" that mimicked those of their spouses, and by 1638 the first flat-brimmed, flat-crowned beaver hats appeared. "The wearing of beaver hats," said Charles I in a royal proclamation of that year, "has of late times become much in use, especially by those of sort and quality."[22]

From then until the late nineteenth century, when silk hats replaced them, beaver hats were in great demand as hats of fashion, symbolizing entrepreneurial success among men and women of the expanding commercial sector. The high-crowned Spanish beaver, in favor at the time Charles I lost his head, was followed by the conical beaver of the Puritans, the broad-brimmed slouch hat of the Restoration, the plumed "shovel" hat of the Glorious Revolution, and the flat-crowned clerical and three-cornered cocked hats that prevailed throughout the eighteenth century.[23]

These attitudes about nature, animals, and the wild influenced the exploitation of the American shores by European merchant capitalists who financed expeditions and trade in the sixteenth and seventeenth centuries. The distancing of humans from nature that had evolved over several centuries from Graeco-Roman times to early modern Europe would have a revolutionary impact in the New World.

Figure 2.1

Variations of the Beaver Hat, 1600–1800. The beaver hat went through numerous modifications from the seventeenth to nineteenth centuries. In England "beavers" were popular among men and women of the commercial classes during the seventeenth century. Beavers were trapped in the New World, shipped to England where their pelts were made into hats, and then often shipped back to the colonies for sale. In America cocked hats were worn by troops during the American Revolution and flat-topped hats by the eighteenth-century clergy.

Sources: The images of seventeenth-century "beavers" are from Iris Brooke and James Laver, *English Costume from the Fourteenth through the Nineteenth Century* (New York: Macmillan Company, 1937), p. 208; reproduced courtesy of A. and C. Black Ltd., London. The other images are from Horace T. Martin, *Castorologia* (Montreal: W. Drysdale, 1892), p. 125.

Animal Ancestors

For the northern New England gathering-hunting tribes, no na-ture-culture demarcation separated the animal from the human world. A fuzzy rather than a sharp boundary existed between humans and their animal ancestors. Assumptions of human descent from ani-mals and their common generation from the earth mother indicate a fusion rather than a contradiction between the two worlds. An episte-mology of participatory consciousness based on the equality of all the senses led to knowledge and power. No separation between mind and body, thinking subject and passive object, animal and resource as yet existed.

The Eastern Abenaki (Dawn Land People) of present-day Maine comprised the tribes whose hunting territories lay in the river water-sheds from the Saco River in southern Maine northward to the Saint Lawrence. They included the Passamaquoddy who occupied the north-eastern coast of Maine surrounding Passamaquoddy Bay, the "place of the undertow people"; the Penobscot or Rock People to their west who lived "at the widening of the river"; the Norridgewock, or "peo-ple of the swift water," slightly farther west; and, adjacent to them, the "river abounding in shell-fish people," or Aroosaguntacook. In present-day New Hampshire and Vermont were the Pennacook and Western Abenaki (Map 2.4).

Similar to the coastal Algonkian Delaware and Iroquois tribes, who believed that they had emerged from the earth mother and were related to the groundhog which out of greater wisdom had remained behind, the Eastern Abenaki believed that the woodchuck was their maternal ancestor. Grandmother Woodchuck had raised their human ancestor, the shaman Gluskabe, and taught him the tricks of sur-vival—how to fish; how to hunt for rabbit, deer, and bear; and how to build canoes to hunt ducks.

Indian families, according to tribal beliefs, were directly descended from animal ancestors. An origin myth explains Gluskabe's creation of the Penobscot River homeland. To ease a terrible drought, Glu-skabe had felled a large tree on top of a thirst-causing monster, kill-ing him and creating the Penobscot River. When all the thirsty people began drinking the water, many were transformed into fish, frogs, and turtles. Future Indians took their names from these transformed relatives and retained an intimate connection with these blood rela-tions. For example, the Indian Eel family traced its origins to the

Map 2.4
Indian Tribes of New England, 1610

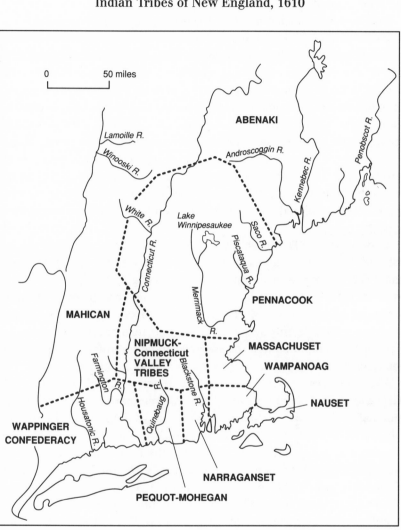

Source: Sherburne F. Cook. *The Indian Population of New England in the Seventeenth Century,* University of California Publications in Anthropology, vol. 12 (Berkeley: University of California Press, 1976).

water famine, subsisted on eels from a nearby saltwater marsh, and derived shamanistic powers from eel helpers.[24]

This totemic world was one of symbiotic participatory consciousness. Both thinking and perceiving differed from the causal consciousness that would soon emerge with European conquest. The interconnections among phenomena were governed not by the law of logical contradiction, but by that of participation. Indians were not subjects detached from objects of observation, but active communicants in a web of consciousness. The life principle flowed through their world, stopping in each animate and inanimate thing. Myths were collective representations of a reality common to the social group and aurally transmitted from one generation to the next, changing only slightly in communication. As such, myths became integral parts of the collective consciousness and thus of the recognized world.[25]

Common to the Penobscot, Passamaquoddy, Saint John's River Malecite, and Micmac Indians of lower Canada was a core of mythical tales concerning their animal ancestors. Originally, when the world was inhabited by half-human, half-animal creatures, Gluskabe changed their forms and characteristics to create the present-day animals, allowing only a few to retain their former shamanistic powers. Human shamans had the capacity to communicate with animal shamans, both having descended from common ancestors.

Many of these myths had ecological survival value. Gluskabe's Grandmother Woodchuck had taught him concern for future generations of Indians by insisting he leave some of the animals he hunted alive. When he made bags to capture all of the game animals, she chastised him: "Our descendants will in the future die of starvation. I have great hopes in you for our descendants. Do not do what you have done. You must only do what will benefit them, our descendants." Thereupon Gluskabe opened the bags and released the animals. Similarly, Gluskabe had once tricked all the fish in the ocean with a story that the world was coming to an end, convincing them that only his own river would remain. When all the fish swam up his river into his fish traps, Gluskabe took them to his grandmother so that she would no longer have a difficult time obtaining food. But again she was displeased: "Grandson you have not done well. All the fish will be annihilated. So what will our descendants in the future do to live?" Whereupon Gluskabe opened the basket and released the surplus fish.[26]

Many of Gluskabe's transformations directly aided his descendants' daily subsistence. To make the waters calm enough for fishing, Gluskabe tricked his grandfather, a large bird who continually flapped his wings making the winds on lakes too strong for canoes. To make rivers passable for canoes, he lowered the waterfalls.

Indians participated in these collective representations of the world through behavioral patterns. The symbiosis between humans and other animals inherent in tribal mythology was translated into daily life through rituals and taboos governing hunting practices. Myth and ritual together constituted an environmental ethic that operated to hinder overexploitation of animals. Prior to colonization, such ideas and practices were probably not consciously formulated as a conservation ethic, but were integral parts of the total fabric of tribal life and had a latent survival function. The life principle and material things circulated among humans and other humans, humans and animals, humans and plants, kinship groups and habitats, tribes and neighboring tribes.

Game animals were owned by a Great Being, Ketci-Ni-wes-kwe, and like the Indians lived in tribes of their own kind in social villages. Just as animals preyed on each other for food, so Indians preyed on animals. The Penobscot observed numerous regulations regarding the hunt in order to ensure plentiful supplies of game. Rituals governed the killing and disposal of the remains of game animals who had given up their lives for human sustenance, a process known as ordained killing.[27]

Through dreams, divinations, behavioral taboos, and spiritual preparations, human hunters prepared themselves to be, think, and behave like the animals they hunted. Dreaming of an animal indicated that the time to set out was at hand. During the hunt, humans and animals confronted each other as autonomous subjects, not as subject and object. Both hunter and hunted were intertwined in a process of outsmarting, confrontation, and negotiation. As face-to-face equals, the active gazes of interlocking eyes riveted animal power to human power. Wariness was matched by surprise. The individual hunter moved as one with his prey. When bands of human hunters joined together to outwit herds, tricks became group tactics. If the animal's time had come, it gave itself up to be killed.[28]

Hunting depended on mimicry. In participatory consciousness, all the senses are fused with body motions in mimesis. In contrast to the transcendent world of Judeo-Christian religion dominated by the visual sense (illumination, light, seeing) and the mathematical, analytic world of modern science dominated by the disembodied intellect (mind's eye), participation precludes separation. The hunt fuses touch, hearing, and the active eye. In hunting for survival, the gaze is active and participatory. It has not yet been tamed by seeing the prey as resource object. In the meeting of like with like, distance as space between is collapsed. Communication is direct and immediate. The objectivity that is dependent on distancing has not yet arisen. When animals have instead become natural resource commodities and objects of trade, they appear not to the gaze but to the eye. They are looked at. The gaze has been laid down and abandoned. Until the fur trade altered Indian-animal relations, animals were human equals.

Animals were lured by mimicking their erotic habits. The fat, passionate bull moose could be lured by men in canoes calling with a birch-bark cone that imitated a cow in heat. Muskrat were enticed with wooden calling instruments to canoes where they were hit on the head with paddles and skinned for their pelts and meat. Adult beavers could be lured with castoreum from the beaver's scent glands, imitating their sexual instincts. Or they could be tricked by stakes driven down through the ice around the beavers' food pile. As a hungry beaver entered, the Indian closed the tunnel by lowering another stake to trap and drown his prey. For the Abenaki (in contrast to the wider-ranging hunting tribes of southeastern Canada), beavers were an important source of food and clothing. Women cooked them in choice dishes, sewed beaver skins together to make robes, and even nursed young offspring.[29]

After the kill, animal remains were returned to their own elemental source for rebirth. The carcasses of land animals could not be thrown into a stream since the sight of the floating parts indicated a lack of respect for the particular animal that had submitted itself to be killed. Because the proper use of animals was for food, the gutted skeletons were hung on trees or bushes to indicate that they had been eaten. Mink carcasses had to be split down the center before being hung in a tree. The eyes of muskrat, an aquatic animal, were returned to the swamp to encourage a continual increase of young.

Reciprocity between humans and animals created taboos preventing a person or family from killing the animal it revered. Indian families not only took their names, but also derived their personalities from particular animals, often as a result of some personal encounter with them. A wounded porcupine, a beaver cub, a female bear, or a doe might inspire a feeling of kinship. The Bear family, for example, traced its origins to an ancestor raised by a female bear, and as a result the family members killed only male bears. Taboos on bird killing also served as ecological regulators. Swallows, as indicators of storms, were never killed; screech owls and barred owls were camp guardians, needed to warn of approaching danger.[30]

Shamans played a significant role in ecosystem regulation. Gluskabe was the model for human shamans, whose power was used to protect hunting territories from rival tribes and trespassers. Both men and women, usually the elderly, could become shamans. Abenaki women shamans were reputed to have especially strong powers. Shamans obtained their power from an animal helper who had given aid at some critical moment in their lives and into which they could be transformed at will. A shaman never killed his or her animal mentor nor ate its flesh. Many different animals served as favored helpers—rabbit, porcupine, woodchuck, deer, wolf, bear, chickadee, kingfisher, heron, loon, owl, shark, and eel.[31]

In times of scarcity and stress, the time and direction of the hunt were determined by the shaman. An animal might appear in a dream and offer hunting advice that could result in the capture of game. Shamans gave individual Indians manitous or fetishes (objects such as bones or stones endowed with life-giving power) to protect them from accidents and guide them in the hunt. The shaman could cause illness or bad luck if an individual violated tribal norms such as those governing the disposal of animal remains.

Divination by means of the shoulder blades and pelvic bones of muskrat and beavers or the breast bones of ducks or partridge (when randomly twirled or raised above the head and the lines or bloodstains interpreted), indicated the direction of the hunting ground. Such divination methods operated to statistically randomize the hunt within the larger territory when the prior locations of the animals were not known in advance, preventing overexploitation of particular hunting areas.[32]

The harsh winter environment in the area that became northern New England supported fewer numbers of individuals than did the southern part of the region. Nevertheless, sufficient food to sustain the several tribes of the region was harvested from the woods, lakes, and streams using techniques especially adapted for the northern climate. Nostalgia for the traditions of precolonial hunting and gathering still lingers among the twentieth-century Penobscot: "It was as easy for the Indians to pick up berries, game, and fish as it is for them to pick up snow outside tonight."[33]

New England Indian hunters thus inhabited an active spiritual world of maternal ancestry regulated through participatory consciousness. The natural and spiritual were not distinct nor were people denigrated by association with the wild. The lack of contradiction between human and animal precluded the nature-culture dichotomy that European settlers would impose on Indian lands. With overseas trade, the circulations of the life principle would be severed by commodity exchange. The beaver would be transformed from an equal subject outsmarted by the Indian's lure to a resource object. The beaver as commodity became the lure in which Indians themselves were entrapped.

The Breakdown of Abenaki Subsistence

The breakdown of the Abenaki way of life began with the mapping of their homeland onto geometric space by European explorers and mapmakers. In the domain of the geometric, space becomes structured as a distant image on a plane surface. The history of spatial changes is a history of power changes. Before colonization the northern gatherer-hunters lived within a web of human and animal movement in interlacing cyclical space-time. Space for these tribes was a world of movement through which humans and animals migrated in seasonal patterns within riverine homelands. Summers were spent on the seacoasts and lowlands, winters upstream in smaller hunting bands organized predominantly by matrilocal, but including patrilocal patterns.[34]

Space was active place—a fusion of natural characteristics with human needs. Not demarcated by the boundary between wild and civilized as it would be for Puritans, place was identical with the natural features of Indian homelands. Named places were power spaces often having ecological survival value: "clam place," "bad supply of game," "place of over-grown eels," "big dead-water," and so on. Each place was imbued with many levels of meaning from a person's own associated experiences, to the collective memory embodied in tribal myth, to the spiritual vitality that permeated the entire landscape. Every space was a familiar extension of home. What was wild and unfamiliar to the colonists was a multileveled place of meaning to Indian inhabitants.[35]

Time was measured by recurrent ecological phenomena. Not connected to money production and sexual abstinence as bourgeois time would be, Indian time was synonymous with the cyclical habits of animals. In September, the voice of the tree frog in the woods initiated the time of "still-hunting at night by canoe" for moose, deer, and caribou. February was "still-hunting and stalking" time when the beaver hunts took place. The spring bear hunt, which began with the emergence of the chipmunk, supplied meat and celebration for the whole village. Lightning bugs in late spring indicated that the spring run of salmon had begun, while July and August were the periods of seal hunting along the coast.

The mapping of space by explorers with the aid of Indian informants began the process of its devaluation from an active place of power to a fixed, inert, geometric surface. Mapped space distances the observer, breaking down participation through the imposition of perspective. Through the scrutiny of the surveyor, the land is seen as a bounded object. A spatial perspective leads to its management and control.[36]

The earliest extant globe constructed in 1492 was an "earth apple" (*Erdapfel*), a sphere imprisoned within a grid on which natural objects such as forests, animals, fish, and human hybrids—mermaids and mermen—were painted in different colors. Constructed by Nuremberg mapmaker Martin Behaim and an artist named Glockenthon from strips of parchment on a spherical shell, the equator, ecliptic, zodiacal signs, tropics, and Lisbon meridian constrained the sphere like rigid bands. Mathematical rules governed the construction of this "world picture."

Mapping the globe onto a flat surface required perspective, or "seeing from a point of view." Gerardus Mercator's projection of the world globe onto a flat surface in 1569 converted the mariner's great circles into meridians of longitude that intersected at right angles with progressively spaced latitude parallels. Soon after, logarithmic tables were introduced to construct the Mercator projections. Abraham Ortelius's atlas of seventy maps called the "Theater of the World" (*Theatrum Orbis Terrarum*) published in 1570 created a stage for viewing space. Like the Greek giant Atlas, human beings could now carry the world in their arms and see it from a distance.[37]

The illustrated maps and catalogs of coasts, rivers, forests, fauna, and Indians used by the seventeenth-century explorers began to impose spatial patterns on the New England land that allowed it to be "seen" as object and commodity. Samuel de Champlain's map of Gloucester (named in 1642 by the English) contained a legend denoting Indian villages and natural features such as rocky headlands, fields, meadows, and "wooded peninsulas." Captain John Smith delineated bays and coastal rivers and showed fauna as sea monsters and leopards on his 1616 map, and listed plants and animals useful for trade. Willem Janszoon Blaeu's map of New Belgium and New England of 1635 depicted Indians in canoes along with forests and realistically illustrated beaver, foxes, bear, deer, elk, turkeys, and herons (Figure 2.2). By 1672 John Josselyn had published his *New England's Rarities*, a long list of native and introduced plants, animals, and minerals useful for commodities and trade. Over the ensuing century this process of mapping and cataloging supported the process of reconstructing both environment and human consciousness.[38]

Production and Reproduction

The breakdown of Abenaki subsistence was a process of interaction between the fur trade that disrupted traditional gathering and hunting production and introduced diseases that disrupted biological and social reproduction. Externally caused by ecological additions and withdrawals, it opened the way for a new symbolic system in which the transcendent God of Christianity replaced Abenaki animism.

The fur trade of New England that would devastate beaver and Indian began inauspiciously as an extension of regular fishing expeditions from Bristol, England, to the Newfoundland coast around 1480. The cod banks also attracted fishermen from France and Portugal as well as coastal explorers such as John Cabot (1497), Giovanni da Verrazzano (1524), and Jacques Cartier (1534). The Indians of Narragansett Bay received Verrazzano in the tradition of native reciprocity exchange patterns, trading mainly for decorative copper earrings and necklaces.

In the north, however, early exchanges involved tools and utensils. The shrewd Abenaki of present-day Maine, whose experience of the fur trade had included kidnappings by Portuguese and Spanish explorers, traded only off treacherous coastal rocks and demanded

Figure 2.2

Willem Janszoon Blaeu's Map of New Belgium and New England of 1635 used animal images to convey the richness of New World resources. On this map, north is to the right.
Source: Le Grand Atlas, Douzième Volume de la Géographie Blauiane, Contenant L'Amérique Qui est la V. Partie de la Terre. Amsterdam: Chez Jean Blaeu, 1663, between pp. 17 and 18.

from Verrazzano "knives, hooks for fishing, and sharp metal" for tools more durable than their own. To their north Micmac Indians on the Saint Lawrence Gulf, who waved sticks with furs to attract Cartier in 1534, also wanted the metal tools that would facilitate hunting, fishing, cooking, and sewing. Far from being passive pawns at the hands of unscrupulous traders, these Indians recognized the advantages of the new tools for their own subsistence. But as iron arrowheads, axes, knives, and kettles gradually replaced decomposable bone hooks, wooden arrows, and bark baskets, the material base of the gathering-hunting economy was transformed by a technology the Indians themselves did not control. The adoption of utilitarian technologies absorbed into gathering-hunting production initiated a transition that would ultimately become an ecological revolution in northern New England.

In the mid-sixteenth century fishermen established salt-processing stations on shore in order to increase and lighten their cargoes, and began bargaining for pelts with Indians of Labrador, Newfoundland, and Nova Scotia. Trade quickened in the 1580s when the Indians of the Saint Lawrence River provided sufficient furs to lower the price of the new beaver hats described by Philip Stubbes.[39]

While the earliest exchanges of commodities for furs were a byproduct of fishing expeditions, mercantile capitalists financed explorers who scouted the New England coast for profits from the beaver trade. Martin Pring, who set out to look for fish, furs, timber, and sassafras (a reputed cure for syphilis) explored the Massachusetts coast in 1603 and enthusiastically envisioned profits from the furs of the many "wild beasts" he saw there. In the year 1604 alone, Pring reported, the French had imported from Canada beaver and otter skins amounting to 30,000 crowns. On his visits to the Maine coast in 1604, 1605, and 1606, Samuel de Champlain offered the Penobscot Indians the opportunity to "hunt the beaver more than they had ever done, and barter these beaver with us in exchange." Captain John Smith identified New England's potential for furs, as well as fish and timber, on his voyage of 1614 from the Penobscot to Cape Cod. Here he "got for trifles near eleven hundred beaver skins, one hundred martins, and as many otters." He estimated "of beavers, otters, martins, black foxes, and furs of price may yearly be had 6 or 7000 [pelts] and if the trade of the French were prevented, many more: 25,000 this year were brought from those northern parts into France."[40]

English exploitation of Abenaki furs commenced in earnest with George Weymouth's expedition to the coast of Maine in 1605. When 3 Abenaki dressed in beaver skins approached his ship, Weymouth signaled his desire to trade for pelts. Twenty-eight Indians returned the following day with forty beaver, otter, and sable pelts which they exchanged for "knives, glasses, combs, and other trifles to the value of four or five shillings." Seemingly eager for additional trading, an assemblage of 283 Indians with bows, arrows, and dogs encouraged the crew of 15 to proceed farther up the river where more furs were allegedly stored. Instead, the now suspicious Weymouth kidnapped 5 Indians as insurance against future mischief and soon afterward set sail for England with glowing reports of abundant timber, fish, and furs in the new land.[41]

Two years later the English colonists George Popham and Raleigh Gilbert returned to establish a trading center at the mouth of the Kennebec, bringing with them one of Weymouth's Indians as a guide. Indian women, barely visible during Weymouth's visit, were now actively engaged in trading beaver. Having received higher prices from the French, the women demanded more than the English were willing to pay and were rejected. By spring, however, the colonists had traded a fairly good supply of furs and completed a fort. They were enthusiastic about the fertility of the land, the abundance of spruce trees for masts, and the "goodness" of the oak and walnut trees that grew open and free of thickets as in "our parks in England." Despite these successes and the eagerness of the Abenaki to trade, the harsh winter forced the colonists to return home. Nevertheless, both the English and the French continued to send trading vessels every year, exchanging iron knives, fishhooks, hatchets, kettles, and food for pelts. Faced with attacks by the Micmac to the north, who had greater access to European weapons and tools, and fated with a short growing season with sparse crop yields, the Abenaki soon came to depend on the Europeans for bread, peas, beans, and prunes and on the southern New England tribes for corn. Furs provided the exchange values needed for the European tools and food required for subsistence. What had begun as adaptation and absorption became dependency.[42]

Indians, with their access to a resource in demand as a symbol of status by upwardly mobile Europeans, were thus drawn into a system of worldwide mercantile exchange. Mercantile capitalism soon linked European capital with American natural resources and African labor in a pattern of money-mediated trading relationships often involving triangular voyages. The integral components of balanced ecosystems in the colonies became natural resources yielding fish, furs, and timber. Enslaved Africans were transported to the New World to become human resources helping to produce the profitable monocultures of tobacco, rice, sugar, and eventually cotton. Gold and silver extracted from the American earth fueled the process and financed the voyages of the adventurers. The dependency of native

American production on mercantile capitalism was the first phase of the colonial ecological revolution in northern New England.

While the first impact of Europeans had affected the relations of production, offering the Indians the means to hunt beavers and other animals more efficiently for subsistence and exchange, the second altered the relations of reproduction. In 1616 disease struck the villages. From a population of about 10,000 in 1605, the Abenaki were within a few years reduced to 3,000, resulting in abandonment of over half the villages. The disease was probably either smallpox or a type of bubonic or pneumonic plague, originating along the shores of Massachusetts Bay in 1616 and spreading northward over the next four years to the Kennebec River and Penobscot Bay, leaving fields and villages barren in its wake. Plague is transmitted by rats and fleas as well as human contagion. By the time of Champlain's voyages of 1603–6 rats had been observed leaving European ships, while infestations of fleas in Indian summer wigwams were noted in colonial accounts. A letter of 1619 describes the epidemic's effect on the peoples of the Maine coast: "in other places a remnant remains, but not free from sickness. Their disease the plague, for [so] we might perceive the sores of some that had escaped, who described the spots of such as usually die."[43]

The impact of this crisis in reproduction on Indian subsistence was drastic. Women too weak to plant or gather and men unable to hunt lay helpless in their wigwams. Hunting band cohesion on which the success of the hunt depended was destroyed. Family hunting grounds evolved into trapping territories as tribes gave up winter hunting in small family bands and remained in permanent villages near the coast. The regulatory role of chiefs and shamans was also undercut. By 1624 only seven Abenaki sagamores remained to lead their people. The traditional power of shamans to assign rewards and punishments was rendered ineffective in the face of the unknown illnesses. A second major epidemic in 1638, this time smallpox, accentuated the changes initiated by the devastations observed in 1619.[44]

The demographic catastrophes that rendered the Abenaki more dependent on exchange for their own subsistence afforded the colonists an opportunity for trading expansion. The Plymouth Pilgrims, who themselves needed a resource to exchange for European merchandise, turned to the fur trade. By 1621 they had already obtained from the Massachusetts Bay Indians two hogsheads (each weighing 400 pounds) of beaver and other skins worth £500. Expanding northward, they traded a boatload of corn to the Abenaki for 700 pounds of beaver pelts. After the discovery by the Dutch in 1628 of the value of wampum (strings of white and purple shell beads produced by the Pequot and Narraganset for religious ceremonies) among the more distant tribes, the Pilgrims, aided both by their easy access to wampum and by their corn surpluses, established successful trading houses on the Kennebec River. In 1636 Pilgrim exports to England since the time of settlement had reached some 12,000 pounds of beaver pelts and 1,000 pounds of otter.[45]

Meanwhile, the Piscataqua River at present-day Portsmouth, New Hampshire, was being developed as a possible route to the beaver sources of the Great Lakes. The Laconia Company of Ferdinando Gorges and John Mason failed to find an east-west route into the interior, but in the process it spent large sums of money outfitting the post for trade. By 1633 as many as one hundred Indians at a time gathered there to exchange pelts for food and tools.[46]

The devastating changes in biological reproduction were soon followed by equally momentous changes in social reproduction that altered land tenure. In place of the Indian view of the habitat as tribal home, the English imposed a legal concept of private property that would convert Indian lands to trapping territories. To the Indian, white pressure to cede territory meant extending hunting and fishing privileges on tribal homelands to the newcomers. To the English, however, it meant release of all tribal rights. Thus, two different interpretations of land tenure were operating when, in 1646, Nutahanada, son of the sagamore of the Kennebec River, transferred his lands to William Bradford, "to have and to hold to them and their heirs forever with all the woods, waters, soils, profits, liberties, and privileges any way belonging thereunto or arising from the same for and in consideration of two hogsheads of provisions, one of bread, and one of peas, two coats of cloth, two gallons of wine and a bottle of strong waters."[47]

Home to the English would mean the family farm on which colonists reproduced the family's subsistence through property inheritance by male sons and on which resources such as potash and lumber could be obtained for exchange. Massachusetts Bay merchants who bought land from the Maine Indians in the 1640s began cutting pines and shipping them to England. English settlements appeared at the mouths of rivers along the Maine and New Hampshire coasts where white pine masts, yards, spars, bowsprits, and naval stores could be cut and shipped to England. Sawmill owners soon realized lucrative profits and were able to add general stores and gristmills. The estate of Major Nicholas Shapleigh of Kittery, Maine (d. 1682), for example, included an elaborately furnished farmhouse with several Irish and black servants, farmlands with outlying marshes and fields, a gristmill, a blacksmith shop, a sawmill, 10,000 feet of boards, timber chains, mast wheels, mast chains, shallops, canoes, eleven oxen, and yokes all related to the timber trade. Henry Sayword, who died in 1679, owned a sawmill valued at £150 and 347 acres of land at £314, for a net worth of nearly £600. Less wealthy men such as John Batson (d. 1685), with holdings worth £130, claimed half a sawmill. The estate of Sarah Tricky and her deceased son, whose total worth was £153, revealed two handsaws, a whipsaw, and a crosscut saw—all items of use in the lumber trade.[48]

By the 1640s, the relations of production and reproduction in Abenaki subsistence had been drastically altered. Withdrawals of animals and trees as commodities changed the ecology of ponds, rivers, and forests. In turn, the loss of traditional habitats in the Indian homeland meant fewer resources for subsistence production. Moreover, additions of European pathogens and people undercut patterns of biological and social reproduction, further disrupting the relations of production. These dialectical processes between production and ecology and between reproduction and production changed material life for Indians. With these changes traditional forms of consciousness also began to break down. The myths, rituals, and taboos inherited from Gluskabe and his animal ancestors that had regulated a viable gathering-hunting economy were now vulnerable to replacement.

Transcendence

Transcendence undermines the epistemological equality of the senses through its emphasis on the visual. Here truth is the light of God, knowing is seeing, and knowledge is illumination. Vision as the primary source of knowledge creates an observer distant from nature. Knowledge gained through the body by touch, smell, and taste is degraded in favor of knowledge modeled on perspective. A distant God is substituted for the spirits within animals, trees, and fetishes. How did this process of replacement occur?

In 1646 the bearer of transcendent religion, French Jesuit, Gabriel Druillettes, arrived in the Kennebec region at the request of Abenaki who had sought refuge from the devastations of the smallpox epidemic of 1638 at the mission of Saint Joseph at Sillery on the Saint Lawrence River where nuns operated a hospital. Accompanied by already converted tribesmen who had taught him their language, Druillettes visited sick Indians along the Kennebec River, baptizing only those who were close to death. At English coastal trading posts, he offered food to the sick and won the souls of those who happened to recover. Provided with letters of introduction to the English that asserted his lack of interest in the fur trade, he seemed to represent no immediate threat and was received cordially.

Druillettes's visitations initiated the process by which the transcendent God of the Christian superseded the animate cosmology of the Abenaki. When a shaman who was ill and sought help recovered, Druillettes asked him in the presence of witnesses to give up his drums and charms. When a woman tried Christian prayer as a help for her sick baby, she became a ready convert if her child survived. If a man died after entrusting himself to the ministrations of the shaman, he was held up as an example of the Devil's work. The priest's own immunity to the European-introduced diseases rendered him and his God more powerful in the eyes of the Abenaki than their own manitous.

Druillettes, one of the shrewdest and most deliberate of the Jesuit missionaries, used these converted Indians to challenge the power of the shaman and to introduce Christian concepts and morals. He asked his initiates to give up three things—liquor, warfare, and their manitous. Manitous, or the spirits embodied in stones and other objects, were given to braves by the tribal shaman to bring them good fortune during the hunt. Many of the converted complied with Druillettes's demands according to his chronicler: "Those who had some of these charms, or manitous, drew them from their pouches.... Some sorcerers or Jugglers ... burned their drums and other instruments of their trades.... One no longer heard in their cabins those howlings, those cries, those commotions which they raised about their sick, because most of the people loudly protested that they would have recourse to God. I say the most part and not all; some did not relish this change."[49]

The French missionary replaced the gifts offered to the shaman in reciprocity for dream interpretation, cures, or manitous with visitations to the sick, the confessional, and the Sacraments of the Mass. The converted compared the priest with the shaman: "This man is very different from our Jugglers. The latter are always asking, the former never asks anything; the latter are almost entirely absent from our sick, but the former spends days and nights with them. The latter seek nothing but the robes of otter, of beaver, and other animals; the former does not so much as look at them from the corner of his eye." The tributes to the shaman of the furs of animal spirits, through which the ecosystem had been functionally maintained, gave way to prayers to a God above nature.[50]

Druillettes used the hunt to further undermine the power of the shaman. When the bands assembled for the communal hunt in January, he gathered his followers around him. The shamans were warning that the praying Indians would be captured by Iroquois while on the hunt. "Having separated into several bands," wrote the Jesuit chronicler, "they declared war on the Deer, the Elks, the Beavers, and other wild beasts. The Father constantly instructed his band, following it in all its expeditions." The success of the hunt proved the shamans wrong, for the praying Indians did not encounter the Iroquois or fall into disaster. Moreover, "some sick people, at a distance from the Father, having had recourse to God in their sufferings, had received the blessing of very unexpected health."[51]

By the end of the seventeenth century, the Abenaki, who were now almost entirely converted to Catholicism, found themselves caught between the French who provided them with a religion that seemed to offer help for their illnesses and the English who supplied the food and trade items on which they now depended. An Abenaki spokesman put it to the English thus: "Thy Ministers, [never] spoke to me of prayer or of the Great Spirit. They saw my furs, my beaver- and elk-skins, and of those alone did they think. . . . I was not able to furnish them enough. On the contrary, . . . one day I landed at Quebec, . . . I was loaded with furs, but the French black Robe did not deign even to look at them; he spoke to me first of the great Spirit, of Paradise, of Hell, and of Prayer, which is the only way of reaching Heaven. . . . I asked for Baptism, and received it."[52]

The substitution of the Christian ethic for the Abenaki ethic altered the symbolic superstructure of the Indians' economy. An ethic of moral obligation between human and God replaced the ethic of reciprocity between human and animal. While the older practices of divination, taboos, and disposal of remains continued, they ceased to function as a restraining environmental ethic in an economy in which survival now depended on the sale of animal furs in the marketplace. The Abenaki could now combine the teaching of both European cultures they had adopted. By convincing the Indians to give up manitous and fetishes endowed with life and spirit and to embrace instead a transcendent God above nature, the Jesuits prepared the way for the fetishism of commodities. Under capitalism, the properties of life, growth, and development associated with organic life would be transferred to money and the products of the market. The market would exhibit strength, weakness, depression, and death, obscuring the underlying death of the animals and their Indian equals.

The process of ecological breakdown began at the level of material culture. Production relations were altered as tools and utensils obtained in the fur trade created inequalities among neighboring tribes, and dependency relations were substituted for reciprocity. The relations of reproduction were altered by diseases and property rights that further destroyed traditional patterns of subsistence. Finally, a new religion injected by Jesuit missionaries, who consciously set out to undermine Indian animism, seemed to offer rational explanation and solace in a time of crisis and confusion. The colonial ecological revolution in northern New England that began with the fur trade was essentially complete by the end of the seventeenth century.

Denouement

During the eighteenth century ecological disruption continued with further depletion of fur-bearing animals and trees and more land acquisition by whites. By the early eighteenth century, the Abenaki were becoming more destitute of the resources desired by the English and of the game they needed for their own subsistence. Their priest, Father Rasles, reported in 1723: "Our savages have so destroyed the game of their country that for ten years they have no longer either elks or deer. Bears and beavers have become very scarce. They seldom have any food but Indian corn, beans, and squashes."[53]

The English continued their policy of settling the lands to which they had laid claim. The Proclamation of 1763, which ended the French and English conflict in the Northeast, ostensibly halted encroachment on lands assigned to Indian tribes. By this time, the Abenaki, responding to depletion of their main trading resource, had introduced a new ethic that reflected conservation and resource management. When the surveyor Joseph Chadwick journeyed up the Penobscot River the following year, he found that "Their hunting ground and streams were all parcelled out to certain families, time out of mind; that it was their rule to hunt every third year and kill two-thirds of the beaver, leaving the other third part to breed, and that their beavers were as much their stock for a living as [the] English-man's cattle was his living; that since the late war English hunters kill all the beaver they find on said streams, which had not only impover-ished many Indian families, but destroyed the breed of beavers, etc."

"The Governor's response," continued Chadwick, "was that the En-glish should not extend their settlements above the Falls ... and or-dered me to go up and mark out a line, and acquaint the people that they were not to make any settlement above said Falls. In obedience to the above orders I mark[ed] out a line and acquainted the people and gave the Indians a sketch." Shortly afterward the General Court of Massachusetts, having jurisdiction over what is now the state of Maine, passed an act forbidding anyone but Indians to hunt beavers, sables, or other fur-bearing animals in the area north of Saco.[54]

By 1808, however, the traveler Edward Kendall announced the death of the Indian hunting economy: "Fisheries are now unimpor-tant, the fur trade can scarcely be said to exist; the native animals like the native inhabitants are destroyed, but the silent and solitary forest that they have left remains to be subdued." Ten years later the Abe-naki relinquished their trapping territory and last two islands. The Indians who remained supported themselves first by lumberjacking and later by craft articles produced for tourists.[55]

Colonial Denigration of Animals

Colonial attitudes toward wild animals and meat, similar to those evolving in Europe in the sixteenth and seventeenth centuries, legiti-mated the dissolution of the wild initiated by the fur trade. The early settlers, who saw themselves as a small minority struggling for sur-vival in an unfamiliar wilderness, sharply dichotomized the differ-ences between good and evil, wild and cultivated, red and white, and animals and humans. Degrading the wild, those who settled in emerging urban areas and towns defined themselves as "civilized" in accordance with European standards.

In the continuum between wild nature and human culture, colonists saw their new lands as "wastes" (barren rocks and swamps), "unbroken" (fields unfenced and untouched by plows), "broken" (plowed lands lying in fallow), or "improved" (cultivated or fenced "dressed" land). Stones and trees from the realm of wild nature became instruments of culture when converted to fences that ordered the land. Culture itself was the nurturing of food and fiber. Farmers separated their "unimproved" animals and "raw" grains by placing them in barns at some distance from their own "improved" houses. The house likewise revealed a continuum of order from the garrets, cellars, and lean-tos in the rear where raw foods and fibers were stored and broken, to the kitchen where broken foods and fibers were improved, to the chambers and parlors where improved fibers were stored and displayed.[56]

In the struggle to set humans apart from nature, Puritans, like Europeans, soon outlawed human sex with animals, making "bestiality" (or buggery) a capital crime for males. The fear that human copulation with animals could produce half-human monsters, degrading and dehumanizing supposedly civilized Europeans, may have provoked the severe punishment. Upon conviction, the animals were killed before the eyes of the accused and the individual was hanged as mandated in Lev. 20:15. In New Haven in 1638, for example, a poor man with a white deformed eye was put to death when a sow on the farm where he had worked gave birth to a monstrous fetus with a similar white eye. Two decades later a sixty-year-old man was executed for sexual relations with a cow, two heifers, three sheep, and two sows. In Plymouth, in 1642, a seventeen-year-old boy was put to death after being accused of bestiality with a mare, a cow, two goats, five sheep, two calves, and a turkey. After 1673 execution ceased to be a punishment for buggery as religious frenzy slowed, the state became more secular, and wilderness became less threatening (or perhaps such sexual offenses were tolerated because they were actually too numerous to contain).[57]

The association of Indians with animals also helped to legitimate the extermination of the red race through warfare. When directly confronted with Indian ways of life, some white captives revealed their disdain for the "animal-like" appetites of Indians. Mary Rowlandson, the wife of a minister in Lancaster, Massachusetts, a frontier town north of present-day Worcester, was captured during the war with the Indian known as King Philip in 1675. Faced with marches "into the vast and howling wilderness," followed by rests in Indian campsites over a period of several weeks, Mrs. Rowlandson was forced to consume Indian food in order to survive. She ate horse liver and flesh, boiled peas and bear meat, venison, acorns, and boiled ground nuts cooked Indian style, food welcome under starvation conditions but which was ordinarily repulsive to her tastes. "I have sometime seen Bear baked very handsomely among the English," she commented, "and some like it, but the thoughts that it was bear, made me tremble: but now that was savory to me that one would think was enough to turn the stomach of a brute creature."[58]

Although the colonial army had cut down Indian corn and destroyed Indian food supplies whenever possible, Mrs. Rowlandson was amazed that God had not allowed one Indian to starve to death. "I did not see (all the time I was among them) one man, woman, or child die with hunger. Though many times they would eat that, that a hog or a dog would hardly touch. . . . They would pick up old bones and cut them to pieces at the joints, and if they were full of worms and maggots, they would scald them over the fire to make the vermin come out and then boil them, and drink up the liquor and then beat the ends of them in a mortar, and so eat them. They would eat horses guts, and ears, and all sorts of wild birds which they would catch: also bear, venison, beaver, tortoise, frogs, squirrels, dogs, skunks, rattlesnakes; yea the very bark of trees." The ability of native Americans to conserve and utilize every substance provided by nature was perhaps nowhere so graphically described—nor was white repulsion at their way of life.[59]

The reaction of the French Jesuit, Father Rasles, was similar to that of Mary Rowlandson. "The thing that shocked me most when I began to live among the savages," he exclaimed, "was being obliged to take my meals with them; for nothing could be more revolting. When they have filled their kettle with meat, they boil it, at most, three-quarters of an hour,—after which they take it off the fire, serve it in basins of bark, and distribute it among all the people who are in their cabin. Each one bites into this meat as one would into a piece of bread. This spectacle did not give me much appetite, and they very soon perceived my repugnance." His own food, he said, was simple and light. Because he could not stomach the Indians' meat and smoked fish, he made only a corn broth sweetened with a little maple sugar "to relieve its insipidity."[60]

The identification of the frontier with wildness and savagery was so powerful that it led commentators such as J. Hector St. John de

Crèvecoeur in 1782 to espouse a form of environmental determinism concerning wild animals as food. In his famous essay, "What is an American," he identified the formation of human personalities with their environments and diets. Men who lived on the "boisterous" seaboard on a diet of fish were "bold and enterprising." Those in the farming regions of the interior were "like plants; the goodness and flavor of the fruit proceeds from the peculiar soil and exposition in which they grow." The "simple cultivation of the earth purifie[d] them" and implanted sagacity, industry, and pride. The frontier, however, reduced people to barbarous animals, exhibiting "the most hideous parts of our society." "There men appear to be no better than carnivorous animals of a superior rank, living on the flesh of wild animals when they can catch them." The closer to the frontier and the farther from eastern urban centers an individual lived, the farther was he or she removed from European standards of the "civilized." Robert Thomas's *Old Farmer's Almanac* of 1807 reinforced this tradition with its advice to farming folk: "Animal food has a tendency, it is said, to make men ferocious like dogs, wolves, and tigers, whereas vegetables incline them to docility and kindness." Until the American wilderness began to be appreciated as a unique asset, its association with animals and wild men served to legitimate the removal of wild animals from New England.[61]

Ecological Repercussions

In their continuing campaign to remove wild animals from their immediate environments, New Englanders exterminated most of the large mammals near their settlements. Wolf and wildcat bounties, moose and deer hunts, along with the fur trade soon accomplished these objectives. In 1642 Plymouth Colony required its towns, under penalty for negligence, to make and bait wolf traps and to check them every day.[62] By the 1650s Edward Johnson, in his *Wonder Working Providence*, was able to boast, "Where wolves and bears once nursed their young" are streets "full of girls and boys sporting up and down ... [and] a continued concourse of people." "This remote, rocky barren, bushy, wild-woody wilderness" has "become a second England for fertileness in so short a space that it is indeed the wonder of the world."[63]

Beaver trapping, begun in the seventeenth century, continued throughout the eighteenth. Between 1700 and 1775 the beaver comprised over half of England's total fur imports. Eight other animals (bear, coney, otter, mink, marten, raccoon, fox, and hare in that order) totaled 40 percent. As beavers vanished, New England's share in English imports of beavers declined from about 15 percent in 1700 to 3 percent in 1775. Britain in turn reexported the beaver back to the colonies in the form of hats. By the American Revolution, 55 percent of the hats exported to the colonies were being sent to those colonies with the largest commercial elites—Virginia, Maryland, and New England. As in England, Americans were claiming social status through the beaver.[64]

In 1792, the American naturalist Benjamin Smith Barton predicted that the beaver would soon be extinct in the Northeast. "There is great reason to fear that the race of the Beaver will in a few years, be entirely extinguished in the greater parts of that large extent of the United States which is comprehended between the Alleghaney Mountains, on the west, and the Atlantic Ocean, on the east.... I have sometimes been so extravagant as to wish that the laws of my country were extended, in their influence, to the protection of this sagacious quadruped."[65]

As beavers, along with their dams and ponds, disappeared from the New England states, so did other associated species. Fewer black ducks, ring-necked ducks, hooded mergansers, and goldeneyes returned to breed on beaver ponds in Maine. With beavers no longer able to maintain their dams, muskrat and otters were either flooded or frozen out by fluctuating pond levels. Mink and raccoon, both of which ate frogs, snakes, and suckers in beaver flowages, found less food to sustain their numbers when ponds shrank into marshes and finally became meadows. Larger animals that used the beaver ponds also were affected in subtle but negative ways. Moose and deer had browsed on the leaves and roots of aquatic plants and escaped from flies by standing in the cool water. Tree stumps cut down by the beaver for food and dams had sprouted tender stalks and leaves which fed deer, rabbit, and snowshoe hare. Black bears had wallowed in the moist earth on the edges of beaver flows. Trees felled by beaver provided the brush that had protected rabbit and the drumming logs for the springtime mating of the ruffed grouse. Red foxes who depended on these mammals for survival now found fewer to stalk.[66]

By 1800 most game animals had dwindled, to vanish almost completely by mid-century. The white-tailed deer was exterminated in

Connecticut by about 1850 and in the rest of New England (except for Maine) by 1890. "Previous to 1878, to see a deer in Vermont was certainly a rarity." By 1895, "the rumor of a wildcat or a deer being seen anywhere in southern New Hampshire was hooted at."[67]

In Indian days buffalo had roamed the Connecticut Valley only to disappear with colonization. The American elk vanished from Massachusetts and Connecticut. At Massachusetts Bay in 1634, William Wood had observed a few moose, and the species may have survived in the southern part of the state until the early eighteenth century. Moose and caribou hung on in northern New Hampshire and Vermont until about 1900. In Maine, the Fisheries and Game commissioners reported in 1889, "We think moose and caribou have made no increase." By 1900 caribou ceased to be seen until 1914, when hunters spotted a small herd on Mount Katahdin. Under protection they began to return to the upper waters of the Saint John's River in 1924.[68]

As the deer, moose, and caribou on which they preyed decreased, cougars and wolves attacked cattle and sheep. Large bounties soon contributed to their rapid disappearance as well. Cougars, fairly prevalent even in southern Massachusetts and Connecticut, were gone by about 1800, remaining in New Hampshire and Vermont until 1888. Only three were spotted in Maine in 1906–7. The last wolf was killed in Connecticut in 1837 and in New Hampshire in 1887. Wolves disappeared from Maine in 1909.[69]

In colonial America few tears were shed over the demise of the wild. A nineteenth-century New England chronicler noted proudly that, where the shrieks of the "wild panther" had once rent the night, now resounded Sunday hymns and the busy hum of machines. A civilization illuminated by books and learning had superseded a race clothed in skins and nourished by wild beasts.[70]

Conclusion

The colonial ecological revolution completed in northern New England by the late seventeenth century was the first phase of a process of deconstructing the environment and reconstructing human consciousness. In the gathering-hunting economy, Indians, wild animals, plants, and rocks were all face-to-face material subjects in a space-time web. Exchanges between subjects—Indian and beaver—had been reciprocal, based on mutual give and take. Objects of human production (wigwams and bark baskets) became one with the habitat again when their usefulness ceased. The introduction of European commodity exchange wrenched Indians from their relations with beavers and pine trees as equal subjects. The latter became objects of extraction, natural resources mapped onto voyage collection points to be transported far from "home."

The mimetic consciousness of native Americans based on the epistemological equality of all the senses gave way to the domination of the visual as the transcendent God of the Europeans replaced the Indians' animism. The erotic relations between Indians and animals and the lack of sharp distinctions between them reinforced the colonists' own separation between the human and animal worlds. The "civilizing" process introduced by European explorers, fur traders, and timber merchants distanced Indian subjects from resource objects, placing in the hand for examination what the eye had confronted directly. The gaze had shifted from "thou" to "it."

3

· · · · · · · · · · · · · · · · · ·

From Corn Mothers to Puritan Fathers

Seeing the world through the "eyes" of a plant is an agricultural people's vision. The Indians of southern New England had been a horticultural people since approximately A.D. 1000. Extending inland from the coast, the Wampanoag, Narraganset, Massachuset, and Nauset, the Pequot-Mohegan, the Nipmuck–Connecticut Valley tribes, the Wappinger Confederacy, and the Mahican (see Map 2.4) depended on the corn, bean, and squash complex for their sustenance. Tapering off in the area between the Saco and Kennebec rivers in Maine, corn cultivation extended as far north as the Saint John's River where green or milk corn could be harvested. In contrast to the animal mythologies that focused the culture of northern gatherer-hunters, the cosmology, mythology, and rituals of New England's southern Indians centered on the cultivation of maize, supporting a system of production largely in the hands of women. The home of the corn plant and its female cultivators was a clearing in the lowland woods that gradually shifted to upland hunting forests where wood gathering and local hunting radii tapered off. As in farming villages of old Europe that clustered around a tree of life, the vegetable world was the center of vitality and seasonal ritual.

The colonial ecological revolution changed the Indian way of life in southern, as well as northern, New England. The European complex of animals, plants, pathogens, and people that arrived on New England shores in the 1620s disrupted the southern Indians' patterns of subsistence. Pilgrim and Puritan settlers, abrogating their own ancient heritage of reverence for trees, tamed the vegetative world by clearing forests and confining crops within fenced-off fields and gardens. Cutting trees for the timber trade and extracting beavers for the fur trade removed ecological components of the Indians' homeland for export. Their vision of fruitfulness originating from a God above rather than the earth below, the Puritans recreated in the "new Canaan" a home formed in the image of the Garden of Eden.

By roughly the end of the 1675–76 war between the settlers and the coalition of southern New England tribes under the Indian known as King Philip, an ecological revolution had taken place (Map 3.1). What was the southern New England Indian vision of the vegetative world, what were the methods through which these tribes produced and reproduced daily life, and how did their way of life break down under the advent of European ecologies and consciousness?

Cosmology, Mythology, and Ritual

A worldview is a synthesis of a particular people's beliefs about the place of self within society and cosmos. As such it has a value system inherent within it: sacred symbols link cosmology with ethics. Meanings embedded in the symbols are stored in tribal memories through myth and acted out through ritual. Through their own cosmology and mythology, the southern New England tribes expressed their worldview, translating it into daily behavior. As for other woodland cultivators along the Atlantic seaboard, their entire cosmos was alive, their mythology centered on the origins of corn, and their calendar revolved around planting rituals.[1]

The cosmology of the Narraganset tribe of present-day Rhode Island designated some thirty-eight deities whose superior powers were acknowledged through propitiation and festivals. A manitto (or manitou) referred to any being superior to or surpassing humans, the word meaning literally "God (*manit*) exists." Kiehtan or Kautantouwit (Cautantowwit), god of the southwest, was also the creator of the other deities. Individual gods had power over animals and plants, the heavenly bodies, spatial directions, and the weather.

The animate cosmos was expressed through interlinked words of action. Father (*oosh*), mother (*ookas*), and earth (*ohke*) were all related to the verb of motion "oo": The verb "oosh-oh" was the active animate producer, meaning "he comes from him." The word "ook-as" signified a passive animate producer, while the noun "ohke" meant earth. In contrast to the northern hunters whose ancestors were animals, the Narraganset were generated from plants. When told the European creation story that Adam was made by God of red earth and Eve from Adam's rib, they related their own origin story. Kiehtan had made a man and a woman from a stone, but, not liking the result, broke them apart and made another man and woman, their ances-

Map 3.1
Colonial New England, ca. 1675

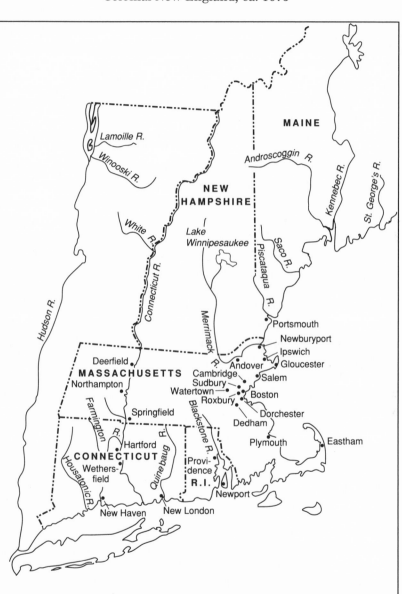

Source: Kenneth A. Lockridge. *A New England Town: The First Hundred Years* (New York: W. W. Norton, 1970).

tors, from a tree. As a result, they believed that they themselves had "sprung and grown up in that very place, like the very trees."[2]

Myths also accounted for the origin of corn. For the Massachusetts and Narragansett Bay Indians, the source of the gifts of corn and beans was their southwestern god Kiehtan. His crops grew better as one proceeded toward the southwest and more poorly toward the northeast. Roger Williams also reported the Narrangaset's belief that a crow had brought a grain of corn in one ear and a bean in the other. Other Indians held that, whereas the crow had brought the bean, a blackbird deposited the first corn seed. Ritual prevented the killing of both these sacred bearers.[3]

For most of the tribes of the eastern American woodlands, however, corn was the gift of the Corn Mother, a mythical female from whose body had come the corn plant, maize. A Penobscot Indian myth from northern New England explained the origin of both corn and tobacco and instructed the Indian to plant them in the woods. A great famine had deprived people of food and water. A beautiful Indian maiden appeared and married one of the young men, but soon succumbed to another lover, a snake. Upon discovery she promised to alleviate her husband's sorrow if he would plant a blade of green grass clinging to her ankle. First he must kill her with his ax, then drag her body through the forest clearing until all her flesh had been stripped, and finally bury her bones in the center of the clearing. She then appeared to him in a dream and instructed him how to tend, harvest, and cook the corn and smoke the tobacco. Thereafter corn nourished the Indians' bodies and tobacco eased their minds. This origin story taught the Indians not only to plant their corn in forest clearings, but also that the earth would continue to regenerate the human body through the corn plant.[4]

A related myth from the Penobscot and the Saint John's River Malecite told of a woman who could produce corn from her body. She told her husband to clear land and drag her body over it after her death. Corn grew in the clearing. While legends for the Connecticut Valley Indians and other central New England tribes have not been transmitted through historical sources, neighboring tribes in the New York and Pennsylvania areas had Corn Mother traditions.

The two types of corn origin stories were variants of similar myths of other eastern tribes such as the Cherokee, Creek, and Natchez of the south, and the Iroquois of the New York area. The bird and Corn Mother stories were linked in Creek versions. In them, the Corn

Mother shook the corn and beans from her body and stored them in a crib, but her disobedient son took some and hid them. Crows discovered the son's crib and ate the kernels, dropping a few which were found and planted by the Indians. In related Creek stories the Corn Mother told her son (sometimes an orphan born from her discarded blood) to kill her and drag her body on the ground, from which corn grew.[5]

Symbols expressed in tribal myths instill moods and motivations within individuals, influencing their behaviors toward nature and other humans. In southern New England, corn planting, ripening, harvesting, and first seasonal uses of major plant and animal foods were celebrated by gift offerings to the appropriate spirits, reciprocating the gifts of these deities to the Indians. Some ceremonies were propitiation rituals, others were distribution rituals. The sachem, who granted rights to hunt and plant the land, collected the first fruits of the harvest and hunt. The festival celebrating the green corn ripening in August was more significant than those of planting and harvesting. In a rectangular longhouse, symbolic of the four directions of the cosmos, hundreds danced and presented gifts to the poor. Although practiced differently among the eastern woodland tribes, the ceremonies included ritual dances with separate as well as mixed roles for the sexes. By propitiating the corn spirit and offering gifts to those whose harvests were poor, the feasts reinforced an environmental ethic that maintained survival relationships between the animate world and the interdependent community of humans.[6]

Only a few references to the green corn festival in New England survive. Roger Williams described what seems to have been the Narraganset's green corn festival: "toward harvest ... they set up a long house ... sometimes a hundred, sometimes two hundred feet long upon a plain near the Court ... where many thousands, men and women meet, where he that goes in danceth in the sight of all the rest; and is prepared with money, coats, small breeches, knives ... and gives these things away to the poor." A Hartford, Connecticut, manuscript mentions "the great dance at Ninecrafts, which would be held when 'green Indian corn was high enough to make their bread of.'" An old man told Ezra Stiles in 1790 he had attended a Mohegan "new corn feast at which ... they danced all night." In the early twentieth century, Mohegan descendants still celebrated a modified form of the green corn dance every September. The women of the tribe determined when the corn was ripe enough to begin the festival.[7]

Corn Mother mythology, sacred corn bearers, and green corn rituals were manifestations of a religious ethos centered on the animate vegetative world. As cultural symbols they instilled tribal survival values in those who produced the food that sustained the daily life of the tribal whole.

Female Farmers

The southern New England tribes produced their subsistence primarily through the planting of corn, beans, and squash by women, supplemented by male hunting and mixed-gender fishing (Table 3.1 and see Appendix A). Horticulture modifies the habitat more than does gathering-hunting. It reconstructs nature by simplifying ecological patterns into food crops and herbs as objects of production. But shifting cultivation as practiced by most indigenous peoples mimics natural patterns. It consists of polycultural groupings of food plants in woodland clearings that are allowed to revert to forest after a few years of cultivation. Today interest in traditional agriculture has been rekindled owing to problems of maintaining high-yield, high-acreage monocultures through the use of artificial fertilizers and pesticides that leave long-lasting residues and often result in pesticide-resistant strains of insects. The Indian women of southern New England left a legacy of agricultural traditions that are beginning to be appreciated by scientists interested in sustainable agriculture.

Compared to settled agriculture, shifting systems had certain positive ecological features. Here the required soil nutrients were obtained from periodically burning the secondary forest, supplying potassium and phosphoric acid as fertilizer. Additionally, the stalks and weeds in the fields were burned in early spring. Some fields were left fallow to regain fertility, the cycles being shorter in the poorer, sandier soils of the Narraganset than those of the Massachuset Indians. Throughout New England, the brown podzolic soils required more frequent shifting than did those cultivated by the Middle Atlantic tribes.[8]

New fields were cleared from the surrounding forest by fire. Since the resulting ash rather than the soil itself was the primary source of the required minerals, burning needed to be as thorough as possible. Fires were set at the base of the trees in the fall, killing them and thereby preventing new leaves from appearing the following spring.

Table 3.1
Approximate Food Intake per Capita of
Southeastern New England Indians, 1605–1675

Item	Average Calories per Day	Percentage of Total	Gender Division of Labor
Animal Products			
Animal and bird carcasses	250	10	M
Fish and shellfish	225	9	F + M
Eggs	25	1	F
Vegetable Products			
Grain products	1,625	65	F
Grain alternatives	50	2	F
Nuts and leguminous seeds	200	8	F
Vegetables and fruits	100	4	F
Vegetable fats	25	1	F
Totals	2,500	100	85.5% + 14.5%

Sources: Adapted from M. K. Bennett, "The Food Economy of the New England Indians, 1605–75," *Journal of Political Economy* 63, no. 5 (October 1955): 392. Data based on Daniel Gookin, "Historical Collections of the Indians in New England (1674)," in *Collections of the Massachusetts Historical Society*, 1st ser., 10 vols. (Boston: Massachusetts Historical Society, 1792); Thomas Morton, "New English Canaan (1632)," in *Tracts and Others Papers Relating Principally to the Origin, Settlement, and Progress of the Colonies in North America, From the Discovery of the Country to the Year 1776*, 2 vols., ed. Peter Force (Washington, D.C.: Peter Force, 1838); Roger Williams, *A Key into the Language of America: Or, An Help to the Language of the Natives in that Part of America, called New England* (London, 1643; reprint, Providence, R.I.: Narragansett Club, 1866); John Smith, *A Description of New England* (London: Humphrey Lownes, 1616); John Josselyn, *An Account of Two Voyages to New England Made During the Years 1638, 1663*, 2d ed. (1675; reprint, Boston: William Veazie, 1865); Mary Rowlandson, "The Captivity of Mrs. Mary Rowlandson (1682)," in *Narratives of the Indian Wars, 1675–1699*, ed. Charles H. Lincoln (New York: Charles Scribner's Sons, 1913). "Gender division of labor" added to Bennett's table.

The ash from the brush and trees served as fertilizer for the crops planted among the standing trees. After the burned trees fell, they were further burned into segments, rolled into piles, and burned again to clear the field. "A smart woman among a large number of fallen trees, would burn in pieces as many as an expert axe-man could cut in two or three days." With a stone ax "they rubbed off the coats of the burning logs to hasten their consumption."[9]

In the cultivated fields, burning the field stubble of the previous year (since only the edible portion of the plant was harvested) released nutrients into the soil. The secondary stubble from the fields yielded less ash than the original forest. Therefore, every eight to twelve years the abandoned fields were allowed to recover their nutrients by returning, through ecological succession, to the original forest. If the periods of field fallow and forest fallow were well managed, crop productivity could be sustained.[10]

This system required spring and summer encampments near rivers and seashores where the soil was sufficiently fertile for horticulture. The round wigwams occupied during the spring and summer planting season were easy to transport. The walls of close-woven mats fabricated by the women and the deerskin doors could be quickly disassembled, leaving the pole framework behind for future occupancy. During the winter the summer groups gathered together in more permanent longhouses in sheltered inland areas.[11]

Women's horticulture was the major source of food, corn alone providing the Indians of southeastern New England with about 65 percent of their caloric intake (see Table 3.1). Through production practices, women had a direct impact on the environment. Most eastern woodland traditions attributed to women the major roles in planting, weeding, harvesting, and distributing the corn, beans, squash, and pumpkins. Several varieties of each were planted. Corn was black, red, yellow, blue, and white, speckled and striped. Bush and pole beans were red, white, yellow, and blue. Crane and crooknecked squash and pumpkins appeared in several colors and varieties as well.[12]

Since horticulture was the domain of women, it is probable (although the archaeological record cannot speak with certainty) that over time women selected the seed types that would mature early in New England's short northern summers and developed the technology for cultivating the soil. The women who hoed the fields, planted seed, and weeded the plots had an intimate understanding of the labor requirements. They may well have chipped the tools they needed from the easily flaked sandstone, schist, and pegmatite, notching them for attachment to wooden handles. Little time seems to have been spent in perfecting implements or making them durable, presumably because they were not transported from site to site. Archaeologists have identified several types of hoes—large blades for breaking the ground, medium blades for hilling up the corn, and small blades for weeding. Spades were pointed, straight, or convex; corn planters were long and narrow with notched sides for attachment to a stick. After the women had dug up the corn hills from the previous year with triangular stone hoes or with hoes fashioned from a large clam shell attached to a stick, they pulverized the soil with medium-sized hoes and piled it into hills.[13]

Planting time was measured both by the stars and by annual natural events. According to Verrazzano who visited Narragansett Bay from April 21 to May 6, 1524, the time for spring planting was governed by the Pleiades. The seven stars of the Pleiades, located in the head of the constellation of the large horned animal (known to Europeans as Taurus the bull) disappeared from the twilighted western horizon from early May to mid-October, their absence coinciding with the frost-free season of 153 to 163 days in southern New England.

In the Hudson River Valley just to the west, "on seeing the head of the bull, . . . the women know how to explain that it is a horned head of a big, wild animal . . . and when it rises in a certain part of the heavens, at a time known to them, then is the season for planting." "The women there are the most skillful star gazers; there is scarcely one of them but can name all the stars; their rising, setting; the position of the Arctos, that is the Wain, is as well known to them as to us, and they name them by other names."[14]

Other ecological indicators of planting time were the spring runs of alewives up the rivers and the spring growth of the leaves of the white oak to the size of a mouse's ear. When the signs were right, the women planted each hill with four grains of maize and two of pole beans that would climb and twine around them. Squash and pumpkins planted between the hills would achieve sufficient height in time to provide a broad canopy of leaves to smother late growing weeds by reducing the light reaching the soil below. This two-tiered system allowed the corn and beans to find their place in the sun at the top of the crop system, while the spreading squash and pumpkins on the lower level formed an umbrella, shielding the soil from excessive sun and rain. Fields were probably planted over a period of several weeks, spreading out both the planting and harvesting labor, and reducing the impact of late spring or early fall freezes and other climatic disasters. Some accounts indicate that the beans were planted in the "middle of May when the maize is the height of a finger or more."[15]

Historians disagree on the extent to which the Indian women used fish as fertilizer. Only three of the many explorers and colonists who described early agriculture comment on the Indians' use of fish—William Bradford in *Of Plymouth Plantation*, Edward Winslow, and John Winthrop, Jr. Both Bradford and Winthrop, however, mentioned its use in worn-out or "old grounds," indicating that Indians may have used fish only in dire necessity or at the end of the cycle of shifting agriculture before moving the whole village to a new site.[16]

Other early writers claim that the Indians did not use fish, among them John Winthrop himself in a letter of 1636 describing the Narraganset of Rhode Island and William Wood who stated that "the Indians who are too lazy to catch fish, plant corn eight or ten years in one place without it, having very good crops." The Indians' field fallow system of resting each field every third year combined with a longer forest fallow system of shifting villages to new sites every eight to twelve years reduced labor and the need for fertilizers. Some historians argue that the colonists rather than the Indians used fish because the former established permanent farms rather than shifting villages.[17]

The labor of fertilizing even 1 acre of land containing some 360 hills of corn with 2 or 3 one-pound fish would have been considerable, requiring that up to 1,440 fish be carried from stream to field. Based on Roger Williams's report that an Indian woman produced 24 to 60 bushels of shelled corn and an assumed yield of 18 bushels per acre, each woman would have planted 1.3 to 3.3 acres a year. Each would therefore have had to carry 960 to 2,400 pounds of fish to the fields during planting time. Indians were most dependent on fish for food in the spring when grain stores from the previous harvest were lowest but a surplus of fish was available. The 40 bushels per acre Daniel Gookin reported for a village in northern Connecticut might have been achieved only with the addition of fish fertilizer. It would seem therefore that Indians, especially those along the southern coast of New England, knew of the value of fish as a fertilizer, but because of the added labor used it only as needs required.[18]

The corn, bean, and squash complex had evolved intricate, highly successful interdependencies during the centuries that it had diffused northward from its Mexican birthplace. In addition to the sun-moisture microclimates achieved by this three-plant polyculture, biological interactions among pests, natural enemies, weeds, and crops had been optimized. The increased diversity in the mixed system not only created microclimates unfavorable to some insect pests, but also reduced the likelihood of devastating outbreaks of pests. Mixing several crops in one field made each less visible to its associated insect pests and provided physical barriers to insect dispersal. The cultivated plots were surrounded by fields and forests that harbored birds and other insect enemies of the crop pests. Experiments on corn, bean, and squash polycultures show that the numbers of leaf-eating beetles attacking beans and squash are significantly lower when the three crops are planted together than when grown singly. The beetles seem to prefer to feed on plants well exposed to the light, rather than those shaded by the corn, and are thus more likely to leave the plant. Additionally, the mix of species makes it more difficult for the pest to find its own host.[19]

But pest control also required active labor. Children stationed in the fields or on the platforms of watch houses among the corn rows drove away blackbirds, crows, and chipmunks from the seed and young plants. Seed soaked previously in hellebore caused drunkenness in the marauding birds. Women and children removed cutworms from the base of the corn, a difficult task since the worms were almost invisible against the green stalk.[20]

By late May the fields required the first weeding. Early accounts praise the Indian women for their meticulous weeding, "not suffering a choking weed to advance his audacious head above their infant corn or an undermining worm to spoil his spurns." So important was weeding that an entire month of the Indian year (May) was named the "weeding month." John Winthrop described two weeding periods during the growing season, the first after the corn began to emerge, the second when the stalk began to grow high.[21] In polyculture systems such as the corn, bean, and squash complex, the most important time for labor-intensive weeding occurs during the first four weeks after the crop emerges. After this the squash and pumpkins planted between the corn rows reach sufficient height to form a canopy that inhibits weed growth beneath it, reducing labor. Polycultures kept weed free for the first four weeks are more productive than corresponding monocultures.[22]

In July, the women hilled corn by piling earth around the base of each stalk with hoes, forcing it to grow support roots for stability against the summer winds. After this the fields required no additional attention until August, when the green or milk corn was ripe enough to begin harvesting. The main harvest took place in September while the men were away on the autumn hunt. The fresh corn was cooked with the harvested beans to produce a succotash seasoned with fish, ground nuts, and Jerusalem artichokes. The combination of corn and beans in the diet had a nutritional advantage. Maize supplied zein, the protein in corn, but lacked lysine and tryptophan which were contributed by the beans. The synergistic effect of these amino acids resulted in a highly desirable protein combination.[23]

Roger Williams reported on the amount of the Rhode Island Indians' corn yield after it had been dried for storage: "The woman of the family will commonly raise two or three heaps of twelve, fifteen, or twenty bushels a heap which they dry in round broad heaps; and if she have help of her children and friends, much more." This would mean somewhere between twenty-four and sixty bushels of shelled corn per woman for the ensuing winter and spring. Indians of Pennsylvania were believed to have planted one to one and one-half acres of corn and harvested forty to sixty bushels. Assuming that Williams's Indians also planted one to one and one-half acres per family, their yields would have been sixteen to twenty-four bushels per acre at the lower range and forty to sixty at the higher. Daniel Gookin reported yields of forty bushels per acre in a northern Connecticut village. These high yields of corn afforded each person in a household of five to six persons about 1,625 calories of corn per day (with a range of 1,150 to 2,900 calories), more than adequate to supply nutritional needs from grain products. The annual corn crop probably provided about 65 percent of the caloric intake of the adult Indian (see Table 3.1).[24]

The yields of polyculture systems such as the corn, bean, and squash complex of the New England Indians are traditionally high, often outperforming monocultures of the same crops on comparable acreages. Where crops are planted in areas previously left fallow or brought into new cultivation through slash and burn, the combination of adequate fertilizer and weeding reduces competition for nutrients. Even if only one of these treatments is used, no significant decrease in yield results.[25]

Women controlled the storage and distribution of the dried shelled corn. They placed it in large grass sacks or baskets and buried it in holes dug five or six feet into the ground, "covering it from the inquisitive search of their gormandizing husbands, who would eat up both their allowed portion and reserved seed, if they knew where to find it."[26]

Men's participation in the agricultural branch of production, in addition to the help they gave women in breaking up fields and occasionally in weeding and hoeing, centered on the production of tobacco. In April they planted a small round-leafed variety called poke used for aiding the digestion, preventing infection, calming toothaches, and raising their spirits. Tobacco played an important role in shamanism and male rituals in council and decision making. "They generally all take tobacco," noted Roger Williams, "and it is commonly the only plant which men labor in; the women managing all the rest: they say they take tobacco for two causes; first, against the rheume, which causeth the toothache, which they are impatient of: secondly to revive and refresh them, they drinking nothing but water."[27]

Indian women thus held the dominant role in horticultural production. This contrasts with the colonial division of labor between men in the fields and barn and women in the home and farmyard. The colonial ecological revolution would undercut female power, imposing European roles on Indian men and women.

Gathering, Hunting, and Fishing

Women were responsible not only for horticulture, but also for gathering nuts, berries, and probably birds' eggs. Feminist anthropologists suggest that gathering may have been the quintessential process through which human evolution originally took place. Woman the gatherer may have invented digging tools from sticks; bone tools for extracting roots, nuts, and berries; stone grinders for pulverizing them; mats and thatching for shelters; and slings for carrying infants. In New England, Indian women gathered strawberries, raspberries, blueberries, blackberries, grapes, wild plums, and cherries as each species ripened over the summer months. Eaten fresh or ground into mush to be baked into bread or sweet cakes, berries contributed essential vitamins to the diet. In the fall the women collected and roasted walnuts, chestnuts, and acorns or ground them into meal. Indians had access to sugar only as far south as the sugar maple ranged, women tapping its sap into bark baskets in the spring and boiling it into sugar. Women's gathering contributed about 16 percent of the total caloric value of the diet.[28]

Male labor predominated in hunting, an activity both cooperative (as in deer drives) and individual. Men obtained animal proteins and clothing for the community by hunting larger mammals—deer, moose, and bear—along with smaller animals—beavers, otters, wildcats, and foxes. Partridges, pigeons, turkeys, and quail were abundant in the forests, and cranes, geese, mallard, and eider ducks bred on lakes and beaver ponds. Hunting contributed about 10 percent of the Indian diet. Male leisure alternated with periods of hard labor and long-distance travel; women's labor was continuously paced, but not all of it was of equal physical demand.[29]

Both men and women participated in fishing and seafood gathering. In April and May, during the spring runs of salmon, eel, shad, and alewives, Indians moved from their winter longhouses in sheltered valleys to the edges of fresh-running rivers. A river such as the Merrimac in northern Massachusetts provided a variety of ecological niches. Alewives, migrating upstream to spawn, turned off at the small side streams, seeking warm lakes free of larger fish predators; shad returned to the larger warm lakes; salmon swam up the cold fast-flowing streams filled with rocks, falls, and rapids. Across the streams men set brush fish weirs and stretched hempen nets between saplings. On larger lakes they attracted fish by night with torches and speared them from canoes. On the seacoasts they set weirs in tidal rivulets to net fish carried in on the floodtide. Women gathered clams and other shellfish on the coasts, dove for lobsters, and fished with hooks for cod and bass. They cleaned, scaled, and cooked the fish, drying and smoking the surplus for future consumption. Fish and shellfish contributed about 9 percent of the Indian diet.[30]

Much of the summer's food production was thus in the hands of women and the Corn Mother. Female horticulture, gathering, and fishing contributed approximately 85 percent of the total caloric intake. Male hunting supplemented the stores of dried corn during the winter, while fish helped to bring the tribe through the spring "starving time" until the berries ripened and grain crops were ready for harvest (see Table 3.1).

Women as Reproducers

In subsistence systems such as those of native Americans, production existed for the sake of tribal reproduction. Reproduction was both biological and social. As biological reproducers, Indian women gave birth to and suckled the next generation of cultivators and hunters. As social reproducers, they taught girls the gathering and planting skills needed for daily survival and assigned both boys and girls weeding and pest control tasks. Boys learned hunting by imitating their fathers. The reproduction of daily life was thus synonymous with production.

As reproducers of daily life, women created bark baskets and earthen pots for cooking and wove rush mats for the walls and floors of shelters. They fashioned the deerskin clothing and moccasins that conserved body heat, and prepared, cooked, and distributed the food that supplied daily energy. They roasted and broiled corn on cleft sticks or in hot ashes, created corn paste from the milk ears, dried and parched the kernels to make porridge, crushed them for flour and loaf cakes, or boiled them with beans, fish, and meat in earthen pots. They broiled and roasted venison and served it with ground nuts, boiled bear meat, and boiled deer blood in deer's pouches. They made cakes of meat, beans, and ground nuts; boiled chestnuts; and prepared boiled puddings of beaten corn and blackberries. They had no salt except that from clam liquor and animal blood, no sugar in the southerly regions, and no wine, beer, corn whiskey, or cider, water sufficing for drink.[31]

While reproduction of the social whole through tribal governance was primarily a male function, women could and did assume significant roles. Succession to the office of sachem, the tribal ruler, followed patrilineal lines, but, where there was no male successor, a wife or sister could hold the office of squasachem or sunksquaw. Several examples from colonial times indicate the historical continuity of the practice.

The Massachuset Confederacy, for example, was governed by Squa-Sachim, "the Massachuset Queen," who assumed leadership after her husband was killed by the Abenaki in 1619. The Narraganset sunk-squaw, Quaiapan, took over in 1667 and defended her tribe by launching an attack of three hundred warriors on the Nipmuck who had defied her rule. She defended the Queen's Fort in the Rhode Island swamps during the retaliatory war organized by King Philip in 1675 until she was killed by English forces the following year. Wheetamoo, who became the Pocasset's sunksquaw in 1662, was an ally of King Philip and commanded a force of three hundred men. Awashonks, squasachem of the Sakonnet (of the Wampanoag Confederacy), defended her people against the English and, after being forced to surrender in 1676, saved them from being sold into slavery in the West Indies.[32]

The shaman's power to regulate the body and the ecosystem could also be wielded by women. A number of female shamans in southern New England were reported by early colonists. Daniel Gookin wrote in 1674 that "there are among them certain men and women, whom they call powwows: These are partly wizards and witches ... and partly are physicians, and make use at least in show, of herbs and roots, for curing the sick and diseased." Both male and female shamans attempted to cure the Wampanoag sachem Massasoit in 1623. Another Wampanoag sachem, Waban, had a son whose wife was a "great powwow." The Narraganset women also are said to have worshiped a woman's god, Squauanit.[33]

The sexes thus played complementary roles in survival. But considerably more interaction and blurring of sex roles occurred than a strict sex-gender division of labor would imply: Older men and children assisted in planting and weeding, and mixed groups of adults helped to break up fields and harvest crops. Women as well as men wielded axes in forest clearing; cut, gathered, and carried firewood; and probably chipped planting and hoeing tools. Men planted and tended tobacco plants. Women and children accompanied men on nearby hunts, and women fished with hooks and lines. Women wove mats and cleaned and prepared skins for wall hangings that completed the longhouse and wigwam frames men had constructed. Women shared decision making and leadership roles in tribal governance, warfare, medicine, and religion.[34]

Power was balanced between the spheres of production and reproduction. In the sphere of production, power was in the hands of women who produced most of the caloric energy of the tribe, although men had a complementary function in hunting, fishing, tool and boat construction, and field and forest clearing. In the sphere of reproduction the locus of power lay in governance, primarily in the hands of men, while women's role as reproducers of the species and daily life was also an essential function. By the end of the seventeenth century, the productive-reproductive balance was undermined by the colonists' exogenous ecological introductions, their extraction of commodities for overseas trade, and a consciousness that gave precedence to European culture over "wild" nature. Indian men were forced into farming roles, undercutting female power in production, and were recognized by the colonists as the tribal decision makers, solidifying their locus of power in governance.

The Collapse of Corn Mother Farming

The colonial ecological revolution was externally caused. European systems of production, reproduction, and consciousness directly conflicted with the corresponding systems of native Americans (see Figure 1.1 and Table 1.1). For Indians, production existed for the sake of tribal reproduction, while, for coastal and Connecticut Valley colonists, production was oriented both toward subsistence and mercantile trade. Colonial production altered the local ecology which in turn undermined native American production. The collapse of production was further reinforced by changes in biological and social reproduction brought about by introduced pathogens, warfare, and disputes over land titles. The form of consciousness introduced by colonial elites—vision and its cultural symbols (records, treaties, accounts, maps, and the Bible)—was the mode of knowing "reality" that facilitated control over land and natural resources. In the process of breakdown, Indians adapted to colonial ways and colonists appropriated many techniques of Indian subsistence. Yet a major transformation in the southern New England habitat had occurred by the time the dust settled from the devastating 1675–76 war between colonial settlers and the Indian sachem King Philip (see Map 3.1). What was the process by which the colonial ecological revolution took place?

The Indian production system of horticulture, gathering, and hunting had evolved in symbiosis with the local ecology. Into southern New England, the Plymouth Pilgrims (after 1620) and the Massachusetts Bay Puritans (after 1629) introduced a European ecological complex of animals, plants, pathogens, and people (Figure 3.1). This exogenous complex had an immediate impact on New England's ecology and native American production. Some of the intrusions were planned, others inadvertent. The most visible impact was created by people and their large domestic animals. Horses, goats, sheep, cows, oxen, and pigs arrived on the ships that brought the colonists. Pigs rooted for acorn mast in the woods, while cattle, horses, and sheep chewed their way through native grasses—wild rye (*Elymus* sp.), broom straw (*Andropogon* sp.), and carex. The first two had too high a ratio of bulk to nutrients to maintain the animals' weight, and carex was rapidly depleted. So the English soon seeded bluegrass and white clover.[35]

With them the colonists also brought the European tetrad of grain crops—rye, barley, oats, and wheat—along with root crops and vegetables—carrots, red beets, radishes, turnips, peas, cabbage, lettuce, garden beans, cucumbers, and naked oats (silpee). Garden herbs included sorrel, parsley, marigold, French mallow, chervil, burnet, winter and summer savory, thyme, sage, spearmint, fetherfew, coriander, and dill. Flowers and garden plants comprised ground ivy, houseleek, hollyhock, garden sorrel, patience, English roses, and tansy. While establishing these European crops, the colonists depended on the Indian corn, bean, and squash polyculture. In appropriating these plants, however, they substituted the ox and plow for the hoe and the male for the female in the field.[36]

But the ships also contained some uninvited stowaways that took hold in the New World soil, augmenting the inventory of weeds common to both continents. Shepherd's purse seeded itself in cornfields and around barns accompanied by giant burdock. Dandelions, groundsel, sow thistles, stinging nettles, and field mallows settled in as weeds on disturbed ground, and white garden nightshades sprang up around rubbish heaps. "Where a European had walked," plantain or Englishman's foot "grew in his footsteps." Black henbane, mayweed, and wormwood (or ironwort) appeared along roadways.[37] The lethal pathogens of the "virgin soil" epidemics of bubonic plague (or smallpox?) in 1616 and smallpox in 1637 were followed by others to which Indians also lacked immunity: syphilis, measles, diphtheria, scarlet fever, and typhoid.[38]

Indians' shifting agriculture left them particularly vulnerable to colonists practicing settled agriculture. Indians already occupied the most arable 20 percent of New England along the coast and river valleys. Most English settlements, therefore, bordered and encroached on Indian planting grounds, especially those left in twenty- to fifty-year fallow.

Indian and colonial land requirements for vegetable crops were similar, but diverged widely for meat products. Based on Indian corn yields of 16–24 bushels per acre (drawn from estimates of Roger Williams and Daniel Gookin) and an individual consumption of 8 bushels of corn per year, an Indian village of four hundred persons would require 133–200 acres of tillage for an eight- to ten-year planting cycle and five times as much or 665–1,000 acres over a forty- to fifty-year-long fallow cycle. By comparison, a sample of fifteen inland colonial towns in 1771 with grain yields ranging from 5.2 to 14.2 bushels per acre showed a similar range of 155–1,244 acres in tillage (see Appendixes C-3 and C-5).[39]

Acreage requirements for meat production differed because settled agriculture used land more intensively than did Indian hunting. Colonists used outlying fields and uplands for grazing livestock. A sample of fifteen inland towns in 1771 showed a range of 843–5,580 improved acres (tillage, pasture, and meadow [see Appendix C-3]). By contrast, Indians needed thousands of upland and forest acres for hunting. Ecological changes from colonial livestock introductions undermined Indian game production. English cattle and pigs, grazing in forests and marshes, altered the habitats that supplied Indians with animals for clothing and food. The English demolished beaver dams to create fertile meadows and drained marshes that had supplied rushes for baskets and mats, increasing competition for vegetative resources. A dialectic thus existed between colonial production and native habitats that fed back to undercut Indian subsistence. Nature as ecological actor responded to colonial introductions, in turn causing scarcity for Indians.

Resource extractions for colonial trade further disrupted the ecological base. The timber trade cut down foraging sites for deer, elk, and moose. Sawmills, gristmills, and fulling mills dammed streams and polluted waters where fish had run and spawned. The fur trade removed beavers, muskrat, foxes, lynx, bear, and other animals that had supplied Indian meat and pelts. In the lower Connecticut Valley between 1623 and 1633, Dutch traders extracted an estimated 10,000 beaver pelts. Then Plymouth sea captain William Holmes sailed up the Connecticut River to intercept the trade at the present site of

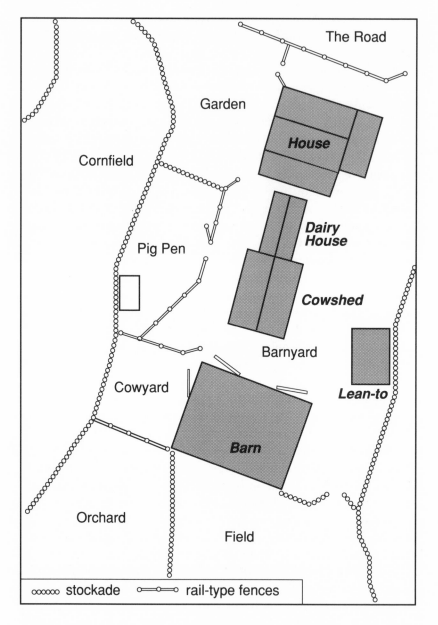

The Road

Garden

House

Cornfield

Dairy House

Pig Pen

Cowshed

Barnyard

Cowyard

Lean-to

Barn

Orchard

Field

ᴏᴏᴏᴏᴏ stockade   o═o═o rail-type fences

Figure 3.1

Plymouth Colony Home Lot. Pilgrims and Puritans introduced an ecological complex of animals, plants, weeds, and diseases into the New England environment. Their fenced farm spaces included sheds, yards, and pens for domestic animals—pigs, cows, horses, sheep, oxen, and goats—as well as fields

Hartford, Connecticut, and Massachusetts Bay fur trader John Oldam, whose death would spark the bloody Pequot war in 1637, brought settlers to Wethersfield a mile below Hartford.[40]

William Pynchon, the Bay colony's most successful fur trader, exchanged wampum, hatchets, hoes, knives, and coats for the deed to Agwam lands at Springfield, Massachusetts. The Indians received the right to retain the grounds then planted and the "liberty to take fish and deer, groundnuts, walnuts, acorns, and sasachimmeph or a kind of pease." If cattle trampled their fields, the Indians were to be compensated, and hogs were not to be allowed on the Indians' side of the river except after the acorns had fallen. Soon Indian hunters were bringing beaver, otter, mink, and moose skins to Pynchon's traders from a vast network of streams extending northward to New Hampshire and Vermont and westward where they intersected the Dutch trade at Albany. At his warehouse in Springfield, Pynchon stocked brass kettles, cloth, scissors, thimbles, needles, pins, combs, and mirrors for Indian women. For Indian men he provided knives, awls, and hatchets. Between 1652 and 1674, John Pynchon, who took over his father's business, shipped over 15,000 beaver pelts as well as pelts of moose, otters, muskrat, marten, mink, foxes, raccoon, lynx, and fishers. By 1675 not only had the beaver been depleted, but also the outbreak of King Philip's War ended Indian-white fur trading relations. With the combined failure of Pynchon and the Boston merchants to extend the fur trade to the Mohawk Valley, it fell into decline leaving John Pynchon among the richest men in New England (see Appendixes B-1 and B-2).[41]

The Narraganset sachem, Miantonomo, predicted the outcome of the clash between Indian and colonial production needs in 1642: "Our fathers had plenty of deer and skins, our plains were full of deer, as also our woods, and of turkies, and our coves full of fish and fowl. But these English having gotten our land, they with scythes cut down the grass, and with axes fell the trees; their cows and horses eat the grass, and their hogs spoil our clam banks, and we shall all be starved."[42]

While the exogenous ecological complex disrupted native Ameri-

---

for rye, barley, oats, wheat, and Indian corn; orchards for fruit trees; and gardens for vegetables.
Source: Darrett B. Rutman, *Husbandmen of Plymouth: Farms and Villages in the Old Colony, 1620–1692* (Boston: Beacon Press, 1967), p. 35.

can subsistence production, biological reproduction and social reproduction were altered by Indian depopulation, the growth of colonial
population, and an introduced system of property ownership that put
increasing pressure on Indians to cede more land. Intragenerational
reproduction of daily subsistence depended on the intergenerational
reproduction of human populations at a level that would provide a
continuing supply of hunting and planting labor. But epidemics and
warfare undermined each tribe's capacity for biological reproduction
of its members. The aboriginal population in 1610 in southern New
England has been estimated at upwards of 65,000. The Indians near
Massachusetts Bay and Plymouth colonies were virtually annihilated
by the epidemic of 1616, making colonial settlement of Indian old
fields along the coast relatively easy. The population of the Nipmuck
and central Connecticut Valley Indian tribes was about 5,300 in 1610.
To the south the Pequot and Mohegan Indians of eastern Connecticut
numbered about 3,500 (see Table 2.1). Smallpox epidemics in 1633
substantially reduced the Connecticut Valley Indians.[43]

The smallpox epidemic, the second major disease to decimate the
New England Indians, had spread west from the Massachusetts Bay
area where it broke out in November 1633. "This spring," wrote William Bradford, "those Indians that lived about their [Oldam's] trading
house . . . fell sick of the small pox, and died most miserably . . . they
die like rotten sheep." Kinship bonds and tribal loyalties held the
afflicted households together long enough for the disease to take its
toll on parents, grandparents, and children alike, leaving no one well
enough to care for the sick. As Bradford observed: "They were in the
end not able to help one another, no not to make a fire nor to fetch a
little water to drink, nor any to bury the dead." In the Hartford area
950 out of 1,000 Indians died that winter.[44]

Warfare helped to finish what disease had begun. In the Pequot war
of 1637, about 700 Pequot males of hunting and reproductive age
were lost in two major battles. In 1675–76 the Wampanoag sachem
King Philip united his people with the Narraganset, Nipmuck, and
Massachuset groups in the Connecticut Valley. Nearly 8,000 warriors
were killed in battle, died of wounds, or were sold into slavery. In 1674
Daniel Gookin estimated that only 2,150 warriors remained in southern New England, implying a total population of 8,600–10,750 Indians. Disease and warfare had thus reduced the population from over
65,000 to 10,000, a sixfold decrease.[45]

Reproduction required not only the biological maintenance of individuals, but also the retention of tribal rights to enough land to assure hunting and planting success. Legal and political disputes over Indian property rights accompanied the continual erosion of tribal territory. In theory, Indians who ceded their lands to whites received the same protection under English law as the English immigrants. A 1652 document from the Massachusetts General Court asserted that Indians within its jurisdiction had rights to the land "by possession or improvement, by subduing of the same . . . according to Genesis 1 and 28, chap 9:1, and Psalms 115:16." If any English were to drive "Indians from their planting grounds or fishing places," the Indians would have the same recourse as the English.[46]

While Indians remained numerous and powerful, their rights under the law were at least respected. In 1662, the General Court of New Plymouth sought to prevent the English from pasturing their cattle on lands adjacent to Indian cornfields. In Providence, Rhode Island, Indians who lived within the town limits were granted the same privileges as the English, but outsiders—"to wit Indians"—who went into the township to hunt or fish did so illegally.[47]

But as the English appropriated more territory and Indians became weaker, such protection broke down. In Farmington, Connecticut, the English settled more land than Indians believed they had deeded. The native farmers petitioned the General Assembly at Hartford in 1672 that their ancient rights to meadow and upland, "never sold to the English," had been encroached on. Reduced to small numbers with little power, they hoped that "there is yet justice to be had from the English."[48]

By 1676, at the end of King Philip's War, Indian populations had been reduced to the point where they were no longer threats to the colonists. The differences between each culture's requirements of production and reproduction were now clear. Indians in the New World and English in the Old World had evolved different subsistence systems that competed for the same habitats. The elements of the two systems differed at the level of production in their extractive technologies (hoe versus plow, fire versus saw, arrow versus gun), production of subsistence (shifting versus settled agriculture, hunting versus animal husbandry), and gender relations of production (females versus males in the field). But in addition to subsistence, colonial production was also oriented toward mercantile trade in the international market, causing added ecological stress.

At the level of reproduction, the two systems conflicted in the needs of the intergenerational reproduction of laborers (equilibrium versus growth) and in the reproduction of the social whole (tribal territories versus private property). The rapid decline in Indian reproductive capacity meant a consequent inability to retain territory for the tribal whole. Conversely, the colonists' need to expand their own labor force led to population growth and continual appropriation of land for individual male ownership.

The downfall of Indian subsistence in southern New England was the result of the exogenous impacts of the colonial ecological revolution. The dialectic between colonial production and local ecology weakened Indian production. Changes in reproduction conspired to further erode production. Thus, critical processes at each structural level destroyed the Indians' productive-reproductive balance and brought about the collapse of Corn Mother cultivation.

Denouement

With the ecological revolution in southern New England essentially complete by the end of King Philip's War, the surviving Indians struggled to adapt to reduced numbers and land acreages. Although Indians were successful in retaining much of their own tribal culture and consciousness, in external dealings with dominant whites they adopted new methods. Subsequent events dramatized the conflict between Indians and whites over subsistence production, legal reproduction, and consciousness.

To colonists, "civilizing" the Indians meant converting their female-dominated shifting horticultural production into male-dominated settled farming. Despite the power of women in production, colonial fathers dealt only with Indian males. As time progressed, many Indian men, unable to take sufficient game on their shrinking hunting grounds, turned to raising cattle and sheep. Tribal reproduction changed from oral negotiation and warfare among neighboring sachems to a struggle to retain legal titles written in the language of English common law and recorded in colonial courts. An oral consciousness in which negotiations between skillful male orators in tribal councils were transmitted through exact female memories gave way to one in which men scratched a sign on lengthy English legal documents they were unable to read.

In land disputes that continually plagued the survivors, Indians enlisted whites to represent them to courts and commissions, but their champions often had their own interests at stake. Powerful magistrates and governors vied against each other and against those of adjacent colonies in the great land-grab scams of the colonial era. Both the Pequot, who had already been vanquished in the war of 1637, and the Mohegan, who had seceded from the Pequot and allied themselves with the colonists, brought complaints against the farmers and officials of Connecticut.[49]

In 1735, twenty-seven surviving Pequot Indian men complained to Governor Joseph Talcott of Connecticut. They were now dependent on cattle and corn since so little hunting land was left. The previous spring their corn had been destroyed by English cattle and their apples eaten by English swine. The English had taken additional apples for cider, erected houses, and sowed wheat on Indian lands. Some of the Englishmen routinely let their cattle into Indian cornfields at night, removing them in the morning and threatening to "beat their brains out" if the Indians complained. They dismantled fences the Pequot had built to keep English animals out of their crops and used the wood to construct their own fences. English fences and houses had so depleted the Pequot's timber that little remained for firewood. "We see plainly," mourned the angry Indians, "that their chiefest desire is to deprive us of the privilege of our land, and drive us off to our utter ruin."[50] Captain James Avery, a justice of the peace in New London County who investigated their complaint, concluded, "I have enquired of said Indians, and can't find that there has been any real damage done them."[51]

The following year, in 1736, culminating years of bitter dispute, the Mohegan, who by now had been reduced to 400–500 individuals, petitioned King George II for return of their hunting and planting grounds. Sachem Mahomet's (called Mamohet by the Indians) petition protested that the Mohegan had been reduced to two square miles of land so rocky they could barely eke out a subsistence and that they would soon be forced to flee westward to join tribes friendly to the French. English settlers had ignored the agreement reserving "hunting and planting grounds," encroached on their town lands, and threatened them with death should they retaliate.[52]

In both confrontations, the Indian production system of separate planting and hunting grounds came into direct conflict with the colonists' system of settled agriculture and animal husbandry. Whites based their arguments on the smaller acreages required for settled agriculture, while the Indian cases rested on the need for additional hunting lands and shifting planting sites. The English argued that their system was superior inasmuch as they had worked hard for many decades to subdue the wilderness.[53]

The Mohegan dispute, one of the longest in Connecticut legal history, also illustrates the way in which failures in legal reproduction reinforced problems of production. The dispute originated in the conveyance in 1640 of eight hundred square miles of land to Connecticut Governor Hopkins by Mohegan sachem Uncas (d. 1682 or 1683) for five and one-half yards of cloth and a few pairs of stockings. Believing that Major John Mason (d. 1672) knew better how to deal with the English and with English law than did the Mohegan, Uncas had also deeded lands to him in 1659 and 1665. Mason in turn, in 1671, had reconveyed a tract of land between New London and Norwich to the Mohegan for planting and had further provided that none of these lands should be disposed of in the future without his consent or that of his heirs.[54]

Supporting the Mohegan's 1736 petition, Mason's descendants, John Mason and his son Samuel, acting as trustees for the tribe, complained that, despite the Indians' long history of friendship and wartime aid to the English, the Connecticut General Court had taken from them "that small tract of land that they had reserved to themselves." Thirty-two square miles of their planting land had been given to New London, eighteen square miles to the town of Lyme, and a large tract of hunting land to Colchester. Moreover, a commission appointed by Queen Anne in 1704 had already determined that the land should be restored.[55]

Mahomet, great-grandson of Uncas, and John and Samuel Mason, who had their own personal financial interests at stake, traveled to London to present the case directly to George II. Unfortunately, however, both John Mason and Mahomet died while in London, and the question of the latter's successor, whether John or Ben Uncas, became a matter of legal dispute, dividing the tribe into two uneven factions. The overwhelming majority supported John Uncas, who had descended from the royal line that went back to the second son of old Uncas. By contrast, Ben Uncas was a descendant of the youngest son, Ben Uncas, who was illegitimate. Descent was determined by the female line and Ben's mother was not of royal blood.[56]

Nevertheless, a new commission, appointed in 1738, questioned the legitimacy of John Uncas, asserting instead that the rightful ruler was

Ben Uncas, a man who favored giving up the Indian lands to Connecticut. A majority of the commissioners, who included the governor of Rhode Island and six of his assistants, supported Connecticut's case by declining to hear the testimony of the Indians' representatives. Several other motions made on behalf of the Indians were also denied. The decision was protested by the two commissioners from New York and the two counsels for the tribal majority, one of the grounds being that the state of Connecticut had no right to determine who was the sachem of a free and independent people.[57]

Governor Talcott, looking through the spectacles of settled agriculture, defended his colony's action, stating that about one hundred Indians (men only) occupied some 4,000 fertile acres, 100 of which had already been improved and the rest were "all suitable for planting, mowing, and pasture." The pleasant New London River abounded in fish, oysters, and clams. Furthermore, after the death that year of Mahomet, the new sachem, Ben Uncas, had retracted the complaint.[58]

Fifty-seven Mohegan males then scratched their marks on a new petition stating that Ben Uncas was not their lawful sachem, but an impostor set up by the governor who had bribed him into signing a quitclaim for the lands. Moreover, title to the lands was vested in the tribe, not the sachem, and hence the initial conveyance of lands by Uncas to Major Mason in 1659 was invalid.[59]

Talcott now responded that there were only 41 Mohegan over sixteen years of age and their numbers were declining. Their 4,000 acres of good land were more than they could improve anyway. On the other hand, the 367 English families who had settled on the land originally granted by Uncas had "subdued the country from a wild wilderness to a fruitful field," conquered the Pequot, and now had their farms as their sole means of subsistence. He trusted that the king would not allow half his colony to suffer at the rebellious hands of "seventeen Mohegan subjects signing the Memoriall . . . who never had nor pretended to have any title to the land till now." Ben Uncas had the right to the sachemship by descent; John Uncas had never before made any claim to being sachem, and the Masons had set him up as an impostor.[60]

Because of complaints by the two New York commissioners of the irregular proceedings of the 1738 hearing, a new five-member commission was appointed in 1743 that included the two New Yorkers as well as Cadwalader Colden, historian of the Six Nations. The counsel for the Mohegan majority argued that all the documents conveying land to the English were unfair because they had been written down by whites in a way most favorable to themselves. Moreover, the Indians were a free and independent people not subject to English law. New York commissioner Daniel Horsmanden (a chief justice of the colony of New York), who had been one of the dissenters on the 1738 commission, questioned the mark of Uncas on the original deed of 1640. He suggested that it was the fabrication of Governor Hopkins of Connecticut and because of the subsequent events the entire conveyance should be invalidated. By a vote of three to two, however, the commission decided in favor of Connecticut, revoking the 1704 land restoration and allowing the Mohegan to retain only their 4,000 acres. Horsmanden's lengthy opinion on the decision was of such a nature that the commissioners voted three to two not to record it (which he likewise protested). His opinion and the appeal of the Indians were sent to England where the case was again heard and finally disposed in favor of Connecticut in 1766.[61]

The problems associated with legal reproduction thus reinforced those of production. Indian failure to retain title to their lands increased the difficulties of producing subsistence through traditional hunting, gathering, and horticulture, pushing them toward settled farming and cattle raising. Simultaneously, English modes of consciousness were reinforcing the dominance of the visual sense in law and religion.

The Indians' face-to-face, oral-aural mode of transactions had been fully integrated with the other senses in daily survival. Thomas Morton believed Indians to be superior in all of their senses to Europeans. Their "sense of seeing was so far beyond any of our Nation," Morton wrote, that they could see a ship at sea one to two hours before an Englishman. In smell they excelled even beyond that of sight. In pursuing a deer, an Indian "digs up the earth of one; and by smelling, says, that was not of the fresh deer: then digs up the other; and viewing and smelling to that concludes it to be the . . . fresh deer which he had pursued and thereby follows the chase and kills that deer . . . such is the perfection in these two senses."[62]

As the Puritans began to "civilize" Indians, this perfection in integration of the senses so admired by Morton began to erode. As early as the 1640s, the Puritans had been converting the Massachusetts Indians to Christianity and resettling them into praying towns where they were taught reading and writing along with farming and trades. Visual dominance was manifested through a transcendent God whose

Word was known through reading the Bible. Print emphasized vision in a form that distanced the Indian from nature. Indians exposed to the Bible were awed by the power of print and the power of the Christian God to use it. Puritans took full advantage of this in converting them to English ways.[63]

In organizing the praying towns, John Eliot used the Bible to institute its laws, rules, and directions in earthly communities. He translated the Bible into the Massachuset dialect and prepared an Indian grammar that set out the rules of the Indian language. In 1654 he founded an Indian college at Harvard (although it educated only five students before its demise in 1692) and promoted English-style education for Indian children. Eliot's attempts to introduce English reading, trades, farming, and the wearing of English clothing and his forbidding of furs and bear grease left the converts stranded between two cultures. Despite these efforts at instilling literacy, however, the assimilation of English ways was incomplete and cultural differences militated against reading and theorizing. Indians memorized and repeated biblical passages during the religious conversion experience and appreciated church services more for their participatory rituals than for the intellectual lessons of the Bible, sermons, and Puritan theology.[64]

By the end of the devastations of King Philip's War only four of the fourteen Massachuset's praying towns remained. Nevertheless, the conversion campaign continued. In 1727 the colony of Connecticut ruled that all Indians were to be taught English and the Christian doctrine. Until his death in London in 1736, John Mason taught the Mohegan in a schoolhouse built for them by the colony, and in the 1730s and 1740s minister John Barber preached the Bible to them. When Ben Uncas declared himself a Christian, he was rewarded with an English hat and coat. During the Great Awakening of the 1740s, Indians like whites turned toward the Christian God in large numbers.

Despite their vast reduction in numbers and lands and their acculturation to European ways, the surviving Indians maintained much of their tribal heritage, mythology, customs, and spirit. Shamans continued to effect cures, divine the future, and conduct hunting rituals, but they also called on the Christian God when their own methods failed. Sachems still hosted feasts, conducted first-fruit rituals, and maintained life-cycle rites. Indian folklore, mingling with English traditions, was passed down through the generations. Indian mimetic consciousness survived within the wider constraints of the now dominant visually oriented colonial consciousness.[65]

Colonial Production

The ecological complex of animals, plants, pathogens, and people that invaded the New England coast and the Connecticut Valley was embedded in a European production system of settled farming integrated with mercantile trade. In the towns of the Puritan fathers, power and prestige lay in the hands of ministers, magistrates, and merchants. The early Boston merchants rose from upstart London businessmen, tradesmen, and East Anglian cloth workers who had joined the ranks of persecuted Puritans fleeing England. They accepted the Renaissance framework of organic community in which each individual was subservient to the whole and the medieval business ethic that a just price and minimal interest must be charged for commodities. Commodities were products of nature, such as pastures, waters, or beasts, or articles produced for use or trade. Puritan ministers such as John Cotton set the standard for New England merchants: "A man may not sell above the current price . . . as is usual . . . and as another (who knows the worth of the commodity) would give for it."[66]

The early merchants traded natural resources—furs, lumber, and fish—for necessary manufactured items from England—cloth, blankets, stockings, leather goods, iron pots, pottery, weapons, gunpowder, and salt. They obtained goods from English merchants on credit and sold them on credit to farmers, lumberers, fishers, and artisans in exchange for agricultural commodities—cows, sheep, wheat, corn, or oats—which they resold at a profit. With the settlement of the Massachusetts Bay colony in 1629, Plymouth farmers found ready markets for agricultural produce and many increased their production of surpluses accordingly. Other towns that were tied into the agricultural, fishing, fur trading, lumbering, and mercantile networks spearheaded by the merchants sprang up in the Bay and Cape areas and along the New Hampshire and Maine coasts and the Connecticut River. During the depression of the 1640s, as fewer ships arrived from England owing to the Puritan revolution, the merchants established trade routes with Spain, Madeira, the Azores, the Canary islands, Newfoundland, and the West Indies. With the decline of the fur trade in the Connecticut Valley in the 1660s, John Pynchon shifted his exports to wheat and livestock and his imports to sugar, molasses, and rum.

As the merchants increased their power in trade, they gained control over more natural resources, investing profits in gristmills, sawmills, timber, and pastures. Land was a more secure form of investment than exchangeable commodities and fulfilled their Old World aspirations to become country gentlemen. By the Restoration of the 1660s, many of the new-generation merchants had moved away from the ethic of early Puritanism toward the Anglican religion and Royalist politics. They created debtors among those who were unable to make payments on their accounts and took over their lands and homes as payment. Fishermen, observed John Josselyn in 1675, "must enter into the Merchants books for such things as they stand in need of, becoming thereby the Merchants slaves, and when it riseth to a big sum are constrained to mortgage their plantation ... and stock of cattle, turning them out of house and home." John Pynchon had a substantial group of debtors, many of whom were forced to forfeit their lands, livestock, and homes when no longer able to negotiate extensions on their payments. With increasing scarcity of coin at the century's end, coin valuation became an issue. By then not only had New England's natural resources become commodities, but also "the design of the Merchants [was] to [consider] money a commodity," fluctuating as did the value of other commodities.[67]

Despite this emphasis on the extraction of commodities from nature, within the interstices of the coastal mercantile economy, a production system oriented primarily toward subsistence farming also found expression. While settlers whose primary objective was obtaining subsistence from the land lived in all the coastal towns, in some cases whole towns existed largely outside the bounds of mercantilism. Founded in 1636 just ten miles from Boston, the town of Dedham for over one hundred years developed as a closed corporate community of subsistence-oriented farmers. While small quantities of grain, wood, beef, and hides were traded in Boston to obtain necessary manufactured goods, no particular cash crop or livestock dominated town production. The inventories of most farmers showed five or six sheep and hogs, one or two horses, a few cattle, and several bushels of grain. While wealth differentials existed, the spread was not wide and most farmers lived in comfortable abundance. Even five generations later in the mid-eighteenth century as grandsons inherited smaller farms, they did not rush to join the market system. Although some townspeople began to specialize in trades, the vast majority of farmers did not adopt the specialized agricultural techniques that could have propelled them through the circle of closer towns into the center of Boston trade.[68]

During the eighteenth century the Dedham model moved inland. Many towns too distant from the rivers and coasts to gain easy access to markets were settled in upland New England. While some products such as potash made market journeys profitable and others such as cattle could be driven to market on the hoof, most products were too heavy and bulky to make long journeys over poor roads profitable. During the eighteenth century, therefore, a subsistence-oriented economy developed in the inland towns (see Chapter 5).

These dual economies of mercantilism and subsistence-oriented farming coexisted until after the American Revolution, when the combined market and transportation revolutions of the early nineteenth century drew inland New England into the dynamism of capitalist development. Whereas the colonial ecological revolution was based on mercantile trade, the capitalist ecological revolution was grounded in industrial production and capitalist agriculture.

Puritan Consciousness

Facilitating the colonial ecological revolution in the coastal and Connecticut Valley towns were forms of consciousness and symbols of nature that differed in important ways from those of native Americans. The antianimality of Pilgrims and Puritans was only one aspect of the subordination of wild nature to human culture sanctioning the ecological takeover. Puritan fathers also brought with them ideas that legitimated the subjugation of wilderness and the subjection of women. Assumptions about generation, virginity, and marriage supported the Puritans' treatment of nature and their cultural superiority over it. In contrast to native American men and women whose ancestors had been generated from the earth, animals, or trees, Eve was generated from the body of a man by a male God who had created nature ex nihilo. In opposition to Indian female farmers who tended corn, beans, and squash, the Puritans assigned male farmers the task of restoring the garden lost by Eve.

While native Americans had venerated Grandmother Woodchuck,

corn maiden, and earth mother, Puritans saw the creator as transcendent Father and the land as virgin. William Strachey, in his 1609 account of the colony of Sagadahoc in Maine, described the land as a female whose "fertility and pleasure," tender to the surveyor's eye, would be enhanced by "cleansing away her woods" and converting her into "goodly meadow." Thomas Morton in his *New English Canaan* (1632) argued that the introduction of art and industry into New England was required to make a virgin Nature fruitful. Decked out in rich ornaments, she was like "a faire virgin, longing to be sped, / And meete her lover in a Nuptiall bed." At present, however, Canaan's "fruitful wombe, / Not being enjoy'd is like a glorious tombe." These virgin land metaphors implied not rape, but marriage. The pure virgin land when married to the industry and art of men could be recreated in the image of the garden Eve had lost. From this union, the fruits of the earth would be produced.[69]

For the small communities of Pilgrims and Puritans struggling to survive in a land of forests and Indians, the dualities good and evil, male and female, civilization and wilderness, white and red were more sharply accentuated than for Europeans. The evil of wilderness contrasted with the goodness of salvation. Wilderness tested the strength of one's faith in God and defiance of Satan. In the biblical Exodus, Moses had led the children of Israel out of Egypt through the Red Sea into the wilderness of Sinai. After this trial, God had provided bread called manna which they ate for forty years until they reached Canaan, a land flowing with milk and honey. The book of Numbers or "In the Wilderness" described the experiences and tests undergone by the chosen people during those forty years of wandering.[70]

Colonists saw the forests of New England through these biblical glasses. William Bradford, landing on the shores of Cape Cod in 1620, exclaimed over the "hideous and desolate wilderness, full of wild beasts and wild men." Unlike their Judaic counterparts, they could not climb to the summit of Pisgah to obtain a more hopeful view of the land, "the whole country [being] full of woods and thickets, represented a wild and savage hew." They were "ready to perish in this wilderness." But Morton's *New English Canaan* soon held out hope of fruitfulness and prosperity to potential settlers in the new land of milk and honey.[71]

The symbolic wilderness functioned as an environmental ethic, helping Pilgrims and Puritans to facilitate the ecological takeover in New England. A related set of symbols legitimated the cultivation of the new lands. Improving wilderness wastelands meant introducing settled agriculture and artifact. Quoting Gen. 1:28, "encrease and multiply and replenish the earth and subdue it," before sailing for Massachusetts Bay in 1629, John Winthrop argued that Puritans could legitimately expel the Indians because they "enclose no land, neither have they any settled habitation nor any tame cattle to improve the land by." According to John Cotton, the epidemics of 1616–19 were a sign from God to the English because "when the Lord chooses to transplant his people, he makes a country though not altogether void of inhabitants, yet void in that place where they reside."[72]

The first settlers' dualistic perception, filtered from senses through symbols to ideology, helped the next wave of immigrants to justify their journey and to survive the early years of settlement. Puritan fathers compared Old England to the fleshpots of Egypt and New England to the promised land. Thomas Hooker (1586–1647), shortly after the settlement of Hartford, Connecticut, likened the trials of New Englanders to those of the children of Israel. Puritans "must come into and go through a vast and roaring wilderness ... before they could possess that good land which abounded with all prosperity, and flowed with milk and honey." In 1646, Peter Bulkeley preached that "God hath dealt with us as his people Israel," for "we are brought out of a fat land into a wilderness." But "the hardships which Israel suffered for awhile in the wilderness were recompenced with a land flowing with milk and honey."[73]

Wilderness symbolism abounded in New England as nowhere else in the colonies. In contrast to the native American environmental ethic, which restrained exploitation to ensure survival, the Protestant wilderness ethic sanctioned subjugation for the same purpose. Yet as forests and uncultivated wilderness vanished into farmland, as trade in furs, fish, and lumber flourished, and as Puritans began to live comfortably and profitably, the rhetoric of "a wilderness condition" persisted. A society now in economic prosperity and in danger of spiritual decline needed the symbolic wilderness to recall its former religious values. Roger Williams preached of a "wild and howling" land as a reminder that human beings had fallen from grace and that their souls were spiritual wildernesses. The Puritan wilderness was a cultural metaphor, at odds both with the parklike forests they beheld on arrival and the meadowed landscape they created soon afterward.[74]

Formal Puritan doctrine as promulgated by elite divines and heard by local congregations was fully compatible with the ecological take-over of Indian lands and the trade of its plants and animals as resources. Yet the texts of sermons and the interpretations of biblical passages were only the most visible forms of colonial religion. A different consciousness lay just beneath the surface of literate society, one that would find fuller expression in the inland subsistence culture of the eighteenth century.

Popular Consciousness

While the writings of Puritan divines and merchants record ideas about the nature of literate elites, folklore offers clues to the culture of ordinary people. Contrasting with the biblical interpretation of nature was an ancient heritage of folklore and folk religion. These sources reveal an animate world permeated by spirits, ghosts, witches, and apparitions reflecting the rewards and punishments of God and the Devil, as well as pagan rituals performed for centuries by English ancestors. Vernacular traditions, learned mimetically in childhood and passed down through generations, were embedded in religion, festivals, songs, stories, superstitions, and cures. They reveal a consciousness about nature rooted in the realities of daily subsistence, similar in form to the oral-aural culture of native Americans.[75]

Popular religion offered a counterpoint to Christian doctrine and congregational life. Many immigrants neglected or refused to join a church or attend services on a regular basis. Dispersal of the original communities, interest in earthly rather than heavenly gains, and the insistence of the original congregations on the conversion experience as a requirement for admission led to a decline in membership and piety. After 1650, only about a third of New England's adults belonged to churches. Some of the alternatives to organized Puritan religion can be found in Old World pagan beliefs concerning nature.[76]

English country life had emphasized the organic community of open field farming, opposing the village and its outlying fields to wilderness. Each cluster of houses formed its own ordered world, centered around a tree of life or hewn staff, frequently replaced in Christian times by a large cross. Rings of fields conforming to local topography surrounded each village center, with those requiring the most attention such as orchards and vegetable plots closest, grain fields next, hay fields cut once or twice a summer beyond, and pasture on the periphery. Walking time determined spatial construct; when time increased too much, the young moved on to create new spaces.

Medieval pagan religions had worshiped trees and spirits through fertility rites, sexual license, and Maypole frolics. Familiar places, vested with spirits and steeped in village traditions, enriched the home landscape. On the fringes dwelt woodcutters, charcoal burners, and hunters. Beyond the village bounds lurked wild folk, exiles, criminals, ghouls, witches, and half-human beasts. Christianity had unified village with heaven, arraying against satanic wilderness the little enclaves of fields and farms. But only with difficulty, and not always successfully, had the church undercut the power of pagan rites.[77]

The medieval church had Christianized many pagan customs and festivals geared to the agrarian cycle of solstices and equinoxes. Although the Protestant Reformation had attempted to purge the magical aspects of Catholic ceremony, vestiges of the old English country traditions remained embedded in New England festivals. In England Christmas had been a day of games and feasting at the time of the winter solstice, and non-Puritan immigrants had attempted to keep it that way in the 1620s. Plymouth's Governor Bradford had other ideas, however, and eschewed "revelling in the streets" in place of labor on Christmas Day. But this may only have driven the old celebrations underground for, as Bradford noted, "since that time nothing hath been attempted that way, at least openly."[78]

More overtly pagan in its celebration of the ancient tree of life and fertility was the Maypole tradition that Thomas Morton attempted to introduce at Merry-Mount in 1627. May Day, a public holiday in medieval and Tudor England, was an anathema to Puritans. Bradford decried Morton's excesses: "They also set up a May-pole, drinking and dancing about it many days together, inviting the Indian women, for their consorts, dancing and frisking together, (like so many fairies, or furies rather,) and worse practices. As if they had anew revived and celebrated the feasts of the Roman Goddess Flora, or the beasly [sic] practices of the mad Bacchinalians." Morton selected an eighty-foot pine tree and lashed buck antlers, colored ribbons, and flowers to its top. Amid drumbeating, singing, and drinking, the revelers planted it on the hill and Morton affixed a poem: "With proclamation that the first of May, / At Ma-re Mount shall be kept hollyday." He composed a song to the Greek maiden Io and to Hymen, the god of marriage and son of Bacchus and Venus.[79]

Although, as Bradford intimated, such nature rituals may not have been practiced openly, an animate world of spirits, apparitions, and occult powers filled the world of even the most devout Puritans. Increase Mather believed there were "marvelous sympathies and antipathies in the natures of things," especially the sympathy between the lodestone and iron. He observed that people took apparitions, possession by the Devil, and witchcraft, along with natural disasters such as earthquakes, floods, tempests, and thunderstorms, as evidence of God's judgment. Specters in the sky, sea serpents, noises from subterranean caverns, infestations of caterpillars, and appearances of strange wild birds and beasts all had supernatural meaning. Sometimes they were signs from God, sometimes instruments of the Devil, sometimes the extraordinary powers of witches.[80]

Witchcraft as a form of popular consciousness about nature was closely associated with women. In its pagan form, it was a natural religion that worshiped fertility and sexuality within the regularity of the lunar cycle. To the Christian, the witch symbolized wild and uncontrolled nature, and witch trials persecuted women as the causes of natural disasters and of evil. In New England both pagan beliefs and Christian perspectives about the closeness of women to nature underlay the presumed practice of witchcraft as well as the persecutions of women as witches.

The reproductive cycle of nature as female was central to pagan beliefs and practices. Women's reproductive cycle was tied to nature's and reinforced by sexual practices. Women could enter caves leading to the womb of the earth mother or lie down on the soil to initiate pregnancy. Hills took on the form of breasts and springs were evidence of the earth's fertilizing fluids. Throughout the British Isles, on churches and castle walls of the late Middle Ages, are hundreds of striking remnants of pagan beliefs about female sexuality. Fertility symbols, known by their Irish name as *sheela-na-gigs* (nude frontal females with vulva held open by the hands and barely visible breasts), are reminders of the divinity accorded to procreation. Together with the young virgin, the universal pregnant mother, and the old hag, image of impending death, these fertility figures symbolized the life cycle of nature as woman.[81]

Witch trials replaced the fuzzy boundary between women and nature with an impermeable wall. Church persecutions of women as witches broke the pagan nature-oriented life cycle, suppressing sexuality and death while elevating virginity and marriage. According to the *Malleus Maleficarum* of the German Dominicans Heinrich Institor and Jacob Sprenger (1486), women, especially the old and the widowed, were more inclined than men to satisfy carnal desires in base ways. In the witch trials of Renaissance Europe and Puritan New England women were accused of yielding to sex with the Devil, often in the form of a goat; of being sucked by animal familiars such as cats, dogs, or toads; and of turning themselves into animals to carry out evil deeds. The crime of witchcraft was the female counterpart of male bestiality. The trials increased the distance between humans and nature by penalizing those who succumbed to nature's "base" inclinations.[82]

A second basis for the trials lay in witches' presumed power over nature. They were suspected of controlling and subverting natural processes by causing storms, killing cattle, blighting crops, spoiling cheese, causing impotency in men, aborting fetuses, and killing infants. Cotton Mather attributed storms, hurricanes, plagues, winds, and tempests to the Devil acting through witches. "It is not improbable that Natural Storms on the World are often of the Devils raising," he asserted in *On Witchcraft, Being Wonders of the Invisible World* in 1692. "Undoubtedly the Devil understands as well the way to make a tempest as to turn the winds ... perhaps it is, that thunders are observed oftner to break upon churches than upon any other buildings." Acting through witches as agents, he caused them "to do all sorts of mischief to the neighbors." John Kemble's cow was found stark dead after being threatened by Susanna Martin. John Louder's apple tree shook all its fruit to the ground after Bridget Bishop unleashed a devil in his yard. At "prodigious witch-meetings," Mather pronounced, the Devil used witches as "methods of rooting out the Christian religion." One of the women accused of witchcraft in the Hartford trials of 1662–63 testified that "there was a meeting [of witches] under a tree in the green ... and there we danced and had a bottle of sack." Fear of the revival of pagan nature religions in New England was one of the reasons for Puritan repression of witchcraft.[83]

Women's roles as both biological and social reproducers were at stake in the witch trials. (On women's roles in production, see Chapter 5.) In New England, as in Europe, most persons accused of witchcraft were women. In the witch accusations, trials, convictions, and executions that took place in New England between 1620 and 1724, including the three major outbreaks in Hartford in 1662–63 and in Salem and Fairfield in 1692–93, 80 percent were women (259 of 322 accused, 29 of 36 executed), with those over forty (about 60 percent of the accused) being more vulnerable than younger women. Most had thus ceased to bear and care for children and many were now dependents on their own children. While the majority of them were married, women over the age of thirty who lived alone as spinsters, widows, divorcées, or deserted women were almost twice as vulnerable as their representation in the population at large would predict (32–35 percent accused or executed compared to 20 percent in the general population).[84]

First, the failure of these accused postmenopausal and single women to bear children challenged needs and expectations for biological reproduction. New England women were at a premium to assist in populating the new land. Puritan divines such as John Cotton and Samuel Willard emphasized the necessity of virginity for single women and fidelity for married women in generating and reproducing families. While sexual expression within the marriage was condoned and outside it condemned, a double standard was applied to the sexes. For a man adultery was defined as sex with a married woman, fornication as sex with a single woman. For a woman, however, any sexual relationship outside of marriage was adultery.[85]

Second, the control of certain accused women over property threatened social reproduction. In patriarchal agricultural societies, such as colonial New England, land inheritance was the primary means of the continued reproduction of family subsistence. Title to land and homestead passed from fathers to sons, widows having the legal right to the use of one-third of the estate during their lifetimes only. Women who inherited title to property by the choice of fathers or husbands or through lack of male heirs stood out as anomalies in their communities. Of 110 New England witchcraft cases in which families can be reconstituted, 64 percent of those accused (71 women) had no male heirs in contrast to 25 percent of the general population. Twelve other women accused of witchcraft had gained control of property despite the presence of sons or brothers in the family.[86]

As social reproducers in New England's patriarchal society, women played important roles in upholding social values in home and church and in the transmission of property from father to son. Their marriages were arranged by their fathers and they were subordinate to their husbands. Inasmuch as Eve had entered into motherhood only after the fall from grace, Puritans emphasized the position woman had held in paradise as helpmate and downplayed her role as mother. They honored married women as worthy, faithful, and loyal wives who voluntarily subjugated themselves in the marriage relationship. Women, like animals, had been specifically created as helpmates for men. They were expected to be hardworking, obedient, and frugal. In church, where female membership predominated, Puritans accepted women as spiritual equals in the priesthood of all believers because they had souls that could be preordained for salvation and minds that could read and interpret the Bible. But women, unlike men, could be more easily tempted by the Devil as was Eve originally.[87]

Although the Salem witch trials in 1692 were among the last trials in the English-speaking world, belief in witches, astrology, medicine, fortune-telling, divination, treasure hunting, water witching, and prognostication continued in the popular culture of the eighteenth century. The fatalism of Calvinist predestination in official church religion and the fatalism of signs in the stars, earthquakes, and floods in the popular belief system had similar foundations: Nature, acting on behalf of God, dealt rewards and punishments. Fate, not people, controlled the world. Among elites in the coastal towns, the Arminian heresy that humans could control their own destiny and salvation began to move religion toward Deism and Unitarianism. But until the perception that humans could control and dominate nature began to permeate the lives of ordinary farmers during the capitalist ecological revolution, most people lived within the necessities imposed by Fate.[88]

Conclusion

The agriculture of southern New England imposed new patterns on the land that prefigured machine production. The horticulture of Indian women began to reconstruct the environment, but their production system mimicked natural patterns. By utilizing star motions and leaf growth as indicators of planting times, long-fallow restoration, companion plantings, and labor-intensive weeding practices, they minimized ecological depletion and optimized yields. In contrast to the animal mythologies of the northern hunters, their vegetative world focused on ancestral trees and the gifts of the corn maiden.

Into this open, shifting homeland, Pilgrim and Puritan settlers introduced livestock and grains, confining them within the geometric spaces of rectangular fields outlined by fences. Their patriarchal homes were constricted domains mapped onto space as private property. Here the colonial family reproduced its own subsistence, and entrepreneurs extracted resources for the triangular mercantile trade. But although their New World gardens were framed and farmed in an Old World image, the surveyed distances between marker trees and stone walls, needed to transmit inherited property, foreshadowed the Cartesian grids later imposed by the land survey system.

The colonial ecological revolution in the New England homeland was externally caused and resulted in the erosion of Indian modes of relating to nature. Local ecology on which Indian gathering-hunting and agricultural production depended was disrupted by plant and animal introductions and by fur and timber extractions. Biological reproduction was devastated by disease and war, social reproduction by colonial land treaties that continually reduced tribal territories. The weakening of production was thus reinforced by radical changes in reproduction. With the balance between them destroyed, the ecological core of the Indian way of life collapsed. Although many surviving Indians resisted white culture, land hunger, and settled farming, they also adapted to the new ecological conditions and where possible used whites as allies in dealing with the now dominant English system.

As the older ways of life became less viable, mimetic consciousness was also undermined, giving way to transcendent religion and ultimately to a new analytic mode of knowing. Benjamin Franklin's bagatelle, "Remarks Concerning the Savages of North America" (1777–85), characterized the way in which European learning challenged the oral-aural tradition of Indian public councils: "The old men sit in the foremost ranks, the warriors in the next, and the women and children in the hindmost. The business of the women is to take exact notice of what passes, imprint it in their memories, for they have no writing, and communicate it to their children. They are the records of the council, and they preserve tradition of the stipulations in treaties a hundred years back, which when we compare them with our writings, we always find exact."[89]

Indians, according to Franklin, had much time for improving the art of conversation but resisted the introduction of European science and education. Indian parents deemed "frivolous and useless" the way of thinking taught to the few sons who had attended New England colleges. When in 1744 they were offered a special fund for educating their youth at William and Mary College in Williamsburg, Virginia, they politely considered the matter before declining:

> We are convinced . . . that you mean to do us good by your proposal, and we thank you heartily. But you, who are wise, must know that different nations have different conceptions of things; and you will therefore not take it amiss if our ideas of this kind of education happen not to be the same with yours. We have had some experience of it: several of our young people were formerly brought up at the colleges of the northern provinces; they were instructed in all your sciences; but when they came back to us they were bad runners; ignorant of every means of living in the woods; unable to bear either cold or hunger; knew neither how to build a cabin, take a deer, or kill an enemy; spoke our language imperfectly, and were therefore neither fit for hunters, warriors, or counsellors; they were totally good for nothing. We are, however, not the less obliged by your kind offer, tho' we decline accepting it; and, to show our grateful sense of it, if the gentlemen of Virginia will send us a dozen of their sons, we will take great care of their education, instruct them in all we know, and make men of them.[90]

The downfall of the Indians' memorized oral tradition and its replacement by a European system of thought, science, and education was a major epistemological transformation. It was the same process that took place in Greece with the defeat of the mimetic oral mode of knowing of the Homeric era by the Platonic visual analytic tradition. The legacy of the Platonic mode of thinking and knowing, when brought to American shores by European colonists, ultimately transformed American Indian mimetic consciousness.[91]

The abandonment of the ear by elite society as the key to preserving group identity through the collective memory and the emergence of the self as knower depended on a new epistemological supremacy associated with vision and transcendence. Seeing the written word provided the opportunity for individual recall without the emotional associations of song, rhyme, or rhythm of speech. Not recalling, but problem solving was what mattered; not repetition, but seeing and creating anew.[92]

It is small wonder that Indians sent to elite New England colleges rebelled against this "frivolous and useless" mode of knowing. The educational process by which aural learning becomes abstract conceptual knowledge wrenches the student out of a participatory consciousness based on hearing, touching, bodily imitation, and intuition and catapults him or her into an objectified world dominated by vision. The objects of knowledge (gnosis) are concrete images of the abstract forms. The concepts are invisible, but their manifestations can be studied. In being dragged out of the becoming of story recollection into the being of arithmetic and science, the psyche itself must emerge and clothe itself in new garments.

Rather than an extended consciousness merging with its environment, an autonomous psyche confronted objects outside itself. The mental visions that accompanied the aural rendering of the myth or saga became invisible abstractions or objects of thought. The preservation of tribal treaties by mnemonics and face-to-face transactions was replaced by the abstractions of law. The legal, commercial, and educational documents of merchants and gentlemen, cast in the language of numbers, measurements, and the common law, governed the form of treaties, land titles, inheritances, and money exchanges through which the larger society reproduced itself. The tribal narrative with its temporal sequences of events in past, present, and future tense was replaced by the logic of connections among objects. The syntax of process was taken over by the analytic of statement, making systematized knowledge sovereign. Mythos had become logos.[93]

While Indians now had to relate to colonials within this formal framework dominated by the written word and abstract logic, everyday life continued within the traditions of oral culture and mimetic consciousness. For Indians as for most colonial settlers, transactions within the community were face-to-face communications. Family relationships, work sharing, bartering with neighbors, participating in festivals, dances, and games produced and reproduced daily life, passing on its traditions to new generations.

. . . .

The Animate Cosmos of the Colonial Farmer

Eighteenth-century New England represents both the expansion of the elements of the colonial ecological revolution and the starting point for the capitalist ecological revolution. The continued development of the mercantile, exporting sector of the economy coupled with the inland expansion of the subsistence-oriented sector was an evolution of patterns created by the colonial ecological revolution. But the intellectual framework of eighteenth-century New England that supported this evolution reflected a more benign view of nature and God than did that of the seventeenth-century Puritan fathers.

As settlers moved inland to found towns without easy access to coastal harbors and navigable rivers, communities of rural farmers were generated. Ideas about nature that permeated rural culture formed a continuity with the popular consciousness of seventeenth-century settlers and their English forebears in Renaissance England. Like the cosmos of the precolonial Indian, the eighteenth-century cosmos was alive and animate. But unlike Indian animism with its many deities within animals, plants, and rocks, the English God was transcendent, Nature acting as his vice-regent in the mundane world. Like the consciousness of the Indians, the consciousness of most rural farmers was participatory and mimetic. But unlike that of Indians, it was a participatory consciousness dominated by vision. The oral culture of folk traditions was reinforced by a mix of astrological and alchemic symbols conveyed by elites through the world of print.

The animate cosmos of Old England and New England, however, was not a unified fabric of ideas and symbols. In England, by the late seventeenth century, the mechanistic worldview of the scientific revolution was challenging Renaissance animism. Elite philosophers and scientists questioned the geocentric theory and increasingly accepted the Copernican heliocentric hypothesis. Terrestrial and celestial motions were described by mathematical laws. The increasing use of machines such as waterwheels, iron and fulling mills, cranes, and pendulum clocks in daily life was reflected in the description of the cosmos as a vast machine regulated by a God variously depicted as clockmaker, engineer, and mathematician. Intellectuals themselves had a foot in each world. Their writings were often permeated by older Aristotelian, Neoplatonic, Stoic, alchemic, and cabalistic explanations and symbols, while also striving toward an emerging mathematical description of nature.

New England elites likewise drew on both the old and the new ideas, reflecting the emerging split in forms of consciousness. The market orientation of merchants and gentlemen farmers, however, required calculating, accounting, and quantification. As the century progressed, elites codified the newer scientific and agricultural ideas into mechanistic thinking consistent with the entrepreneurial perspective. Production and consciousness evolved in mutual support.

At the other end of the spectrum, the subsistence-oriented farming sector was expanding beyond the coast and Connecticut Valley into inland-upland New England. While these towns had a small market-oriented elite, most farmers were involved in a local bartering economy, producing for the sake of family reproduction (see Chapter 5). It was rural New England's failure to reproduce its system of production that initiated the capitalist ecological revolution (see Chapter 5). Pushed by ecological degradation and stimulated by market opportunities, ordinary farmers took up more quantitative methods of management during the nineteenth century. Urged by elite scientists, improvers, clergy, and doctors to abandon their old ways and become entrepreneurs, they were drawn into the mechanistic approach to nature. A participatory consciousness dominated by vision changed to the analytic consciousness required by capitalist agriculture (see Chapter 6). An understanding of the historical process by which ordinary farmers were brought into capitalist agriculture and consciousness first requires an immersion within the animate worldview of Old England and its extension into the farming communities of eighteenth-century New England.

Consciousness and Cosmology in Old England

The rural farming family of New England lived within a panoply of symbols similar in important ways to the animate cosmos of Renaissance England. Appreciating the other side of the great cultural divide that separates modern Euramericans from their colonial ancestors requires donning a colorful garb of symbolic clothing foreign to modern consciousness. Our premodern counterparts lived in a world of quality and spirit rather than physical causation and natural law. The mind was less like an inner world encased in the brain, as a movie projector is situated in a theater, and more like an extension of the imagination merging with the signs and symbols of the stars and planets. It was a world that people wore like an outer garment. Mind had not yet been severed from body; knowing was not yet synonymous with numbering.[1]

Natural phenomena were infused with symbolic meaning. Through signs and symbols, people participated in a common reality that assumed the existence of a transcendent God who created and directed animate nature, heavenly bodies that influenced the human body, and a living earth in which herbs, metals, and stones grew and had creative powers. A hierarchical cosmos ascended like a great chain in graded links from the lowliest stone upward to plants, animals, humans, angels, and finally God the creator. The microcosm-macrocosm theory depicted the body, soul, and spirit of humans as miniature reflections of the body, soul, and spirit of the larger animate cosmos.

In both Old and New England, two worldviews inherited from ancient civilizations underlay explanations for the phenomena of nature. The Egyptian and Greek views based on the circular cosmos and the eternal cycles within nature mingled with the Judaic and Christian schemes of an absolute God who produced catastrophes and dealt rewards and punishments to his earthly subjects. Both perspectives informed farmers' continuing efforts to predict weather, determine planting and harvesting dates, and maintain healthy soils.

Nature, personified as animate mother, carried out God's dictates in the phenomenal world. To the peasant and farmer, her signs and activities were often enigmatic and had to be accepted as God's will rather than challenged or analyzed. Presaged by comets, planetary conjunctions, or earthquakes, Nature inflicted God's rewards and punishments in the form of rain or drought, good harvests or crop failures, health or disease. But by understanding the celestial cycles and working within them, the land could be made to yield and the soil could be healed. Within this collectively experienced reality, English countryfolk encouraged the natural processes through rituals, while intellectuals developed explanatory theories about farming, weather, soils, and fertilizing salts.

Almanacs and agricultural treatises drew on the ancient traditions. Astrology and meteorology codified empirical observations into rules for prognostication. Aristotle (d. 322 B.C.) was the sage of meteorologic theory, while Theophrastus (370–278 B.C.), Virgil (70–19 B.C.), and Pliny (A.D. 23–79) offered observational rules for forecasting. Ptolemy's *Almagest* and *Tetrabiblos* were the sources for planetary positions and astrological predictions. Within these venerable traditions, almanac makers attempted to predict the weather while agricultural writers speculated about the chemical cycles that facilitated the circulation of fertilizing salts.

The farmer's macrocosmic role was to mediate between the influences of the heavens and the fertilizing salts produced in the bowels of Mother Earth. Sun and salt were the great life-giving principles. The sun was a creative agent whose light gave shape to matter. Salt was a formative principle (added to the Aristotelian principles of sulfur and mercury) and a universal balsam that glued the terrestrial world together. As creative powers, sun and salt produced the forms of objects in the natural world. But as Renaissance images of earth and sun evolved toward scientific concepts, sun and salt would be divested of their metaphysical meanings as producers of universal coherence to become manipulable physical forces.[2]

The sun symbolized the light of God and the soul of universe. To Nicholaus Copernicus (1473–1543), who revived the heliocentric theory, the sun was God's lamp at the center of the world. To Johannes Kepler (1571–1630), who endowed the sun with physical forces, it was the soul or *anima motrix* that swept the planets around in their orbits. To Renaissance Neoplatonists, the whole cosmos was enlivened by the world spirit (*spiritus mundi*) as it transmitted motion from the world soul (*anima mundi*) to the world's corporeal body (*corporea mundi*).[3]

The macrocosm or larger world directly affected the little world of the human body or microcosm. According to the doctrine of signatures, the planets imprinted their qualities on particular plants, animals, and minerals. As they moved through the twelve signs of the zodiac, the characteristics of the sign were combined with those of the planet. Especially important to the farmer was the moon, whose influence varied in accordance with its phase, from waxing to full and then through its decreasing or waning phase to new. Since each sign of the zodiac was also associated with a part of the human body, when the moon during its monthly journey around the zodiac was in a particular sign, the related bodily part was especially receptive to the sign's influence.[4]

The planetary influences were not physical causes, however, but mediative vehicles through which the human spirit merged with God's spirit in a connective fabric that clothed the soul. Each person participated in living spiritual manifestations of God. To know was to identify the meaning of the symbols expressed in the stellar phenomena. Through messages in the signs and signatures a person could apprehend the divine word within created nature.[5]

The astrological tradition, like the alchemic and magical traditions, exemplified a consciousness alien to most modern minds. Knowledge was a union of images rather than an act of analysis. Likenesses were expressed as sympathies or attractions, differences as antipathies or conflicts. Similarly, rituals were imitations of the cycles of nature. The farming rituals of English peasants and the weather forecasts of astrologers were the threads by which humans wove their lives into the cosmic fabric.

Farming Rituals

Land was a living thing that had to be nursed and humored. Mimicking nature's actions would produce a sympathetic response. Growing crops required rituals that would encourage the cooperation of the natural forces. The sun was beckoned to return northward, rain was called down from the heavens, seeds were cajoled into sprouting. Numerous customs and festivals oriented toward influencing the cycles of nature were practiced in the British Isles prior to colonization of the Americas. Rich details abound in the folklore of the English countryside: Somerset, Devon, Cambridgeshire, the Cotswolds, the Lake District, Hertfordshire, Warwickshire, and other areas.[6]

Keeping the soil fertile was the farmer's prime concern and the dung heap was symbolic of the farm's health. Near coasts and lakes, where seaweed was spread on the ground, offerings were made to sea spirits to produce more, and sprigs were hung over farmhouse doorways. The marling of fields with clay, dug from local marlpits, was followed by dancing and feasting. The lifeblood of cattle, wood ashes from bonfires, and handfuls of salt were broadcast on fields. Bonfires to encourage fertility were lit at the lunar and solar festivals that alternated throughout the year. Apple cider toasts were made to crops and cider-drenched bushes burned in the fields. When plowing, propitiation rituals were followed before disturbing the soil of the earth mother. The plow was rubbed with fennel or incense and blessed in the church on Plough Sunday. On Plough Monday, it was decorated and dragged through the village before the hard work commenced.

Planting time was determined by the size of elm leaves: when they reached the size of a mouse's ear, barley was sown, and when they were as big as a shilling, kidney beans were planted. To encourage crop growth, nature's energies were aroused by dancing and skipping in the fields to music. Energizing rituals included Maypole dances, heaving parties, and "beating the bounds" of the parish and its fields to ask for God's blessing on the crops. Cake with cider poured over it was buried in the fields, or the wheat fields were walked over and the cake was thrown into the air. To encourage a good apple crop, cider was poured over the tree roots and cake placed in the branches.

Once the seed had been sown, rain was needed. Sprinkling water on stepping stones, raising water crosses, and decorating wells with flowers encouraged the life-producing waters. At harvest time, the first wheat was taken to the church in an offering of thanksgiving. The last sheaves were often tied together in the form of an animal or woven into a corn dolly and transported with the last load to the harvest supper. More corn dollies from the last straw were kept in the home during the year to retain the wheat's spirit and fertilizing powers until spring.[7]

To foretell the weather was to survive another year. Observing the heavens, changes in plants, and the habits of birds and mammals might mean avoiding a killing frost or thunderstorm that could ruin the last supplies of seed or destroy a crop before its harvest. Lore passed down through the generations or preserved by ancient authorities formed the basis for prediction. For example, signs that fair weather was approaching included cranes flying out to sea and not returning, ravens crying, and an unclouded sun at rising or setting. Rain could be foretold by ants bringing out eggs from their nests and storing up provisions, cormorants crying loudly, solar halos, and an unusually red sun or clouds at dawn. Wind was indicated by dogs rolling on the ground, thunder in the morning, and sea birds flying in from the ocean.[8]

For ordinary countryfolk, mimesis was the mode of participation within the cycles of nature. By imitation, natural processes could be stimulated and sympathetic responses awakened. But as English agriculture was transformed from a process of sustaining peasant life to an enterprise for feeding cities and making profits, these fertility rites and harvest rituals would change from acts of participation to vestigial customs.

Contrasting with the farming methods used for centuries by peasants were the techniques and theories adopted by agricultural improvers interested in market production. During the sixteenth and seventeenth centuries many English yeomen and gentlemen farmers intensified crop production. They experimented with a new system of up-and-down husbandry that alternated a few years of crops with a few years in pasture. During the period of tillage, fields were manured and planted with oats, barley, peas, and wheat or rye in successive rotations over six to eight years. During the grass period, beef and dairy cattle were grazed on red and white clover and ryegrass for two years, followed by sheep, thereby dunging the land and building soil fertility. Cereals, meat, and wool were thus produced in succession.

Farmers increased crop yields by fertilizing arable and pasture, rotating crops, draining fens, and improving stocks and seed. They manured worn soils with sheep, cattle, pig, poultry, and pigeon dung collected in muck heaps. They composted vegetable matter from thatch, straw, rushes, bracken, leaves, seaweed, and vegetable wastes. They seeded fields with buckwheat and lupines and treated wheat seed with lime and brine. Lime, chalk, and marl were used to neutralize acid soils. Potash from soap makers, rotten bark from tanners, coal dust from miners, and street refuse and manures from towns were added as fertilizers.

Agricultural improvers such as Sir Hugh Platt (1594), Edward Topsell (1607), Gervase Markham (1614), William Lawson (1618), Gabriel Plattes (1639), Walter Blith (1652), Samuel Hartlib (1659), and Adolphus Speed (1659) disseminated the new methods to yeomen farmers involved in market-oriented improvement. They recommended ways to increase yields, improve soils, and increase profit.[9]

Fertilizer Theories

The Renaissance organic cosmos was the framework for theories concerning fertilizers and plant growth. The hydrologic cycle in the terrestrial world echoed the circular motion of the planets and stars in the realm above the moon. Water and fertilizing salts were cycled and recycled from earth to atmosphere and back to earth, renewing the life of soil, plant, and human.[10]

The importance of soil fertilization had been recognized since Greek and Roman times. According to Pliny, farmers knew the value of the manure of poultry, animals, humans, and plants, of growing legumes and plowing them under, and the importance of spreading fertilizing salts such as lime (calcium oxide), marl (calcium carbonate), and niter (sodium or potassium nitrate—saltpeter) on soils (Table 4.1). For metaphysical as well as practical reasons, niter, which supplied potassium and nitrogen, was the fertilizer most discussed by Renaissance and seventeenth-century natural philosophers.[11]

Alchemists and medical chemists speculated on the qualities of fertilizers and on nature's power to restore the health of soil—the living skin of the animate earth. Paracelsus's (1493–1541) influential theory of plant growth and fertilizers centered on his three principles—combustibility (the sulfuric principle), fluidity (the mercuric principle), and solubility (the saline principle). Plants absorbed organic materials (sulfur), water (mercury), and minerals (salt) from these same principles within soil and rain. Salt prevented decay, as could be seen by the preservation of dead meat with salt. Each had to be nourished by its own kind or its bodily health would be destroyed. Paracelsus's influence in New England was apparent in apothecary shops.[12]

English agricultural improver John Worlidge (fl. 1669–98) elaborated on Paracelsus's interpretation of fertilizers in his *Systema Agriculturae* (1668). Of the three principles, salt gave body to the seed or matrix of the plant, mercury was the spiritual or active part, while sulfur supplied its color, texture, odor, and form. Salt was the immediate cause of soil fertility and the growth of vegetation. Mercury provided animals and vegetables with their life, generation, growth, and motion; sulfur produced the heat of the haystack and the stink of the dung pile.[13] Worlidge's book aided literate New England farmers.

The earth "herself" perspired daily, Worlidge observed, emitting a universal spirit consisting of the unification of the three principles in equal proportions. The continuous exhalation of this *spiritus mundi*

Table 4.1
Source and Chemical Content of Fertilizers

Source	Chemical Content
Animal Manure	Nitrogen (N)
Legumes	Nitrogen (N)
Saltpeter/Niter	Nitrogen (N) ($NaNO_3$ or KNO_3)
Fish	Phosphorus (P)
Guano (seabird manure)	Phosphorus (P)
Potash/Ashes	Potassium (K) (K_2O or K_2CO_3)
Lime	Calcium (Ca) (CaO)
Marl	Calcium (Ca) ($CaCO_3$)
Gypsum	Calcium (Ca) ($CaSO_4$) (Plaster of Paris)

through the earth's copious breathing caused the generation of animals and vegetables. The spiritus was not only fertile, but also contained a vivifying warmth. Where "her" pores were open, the earth perspired freely, emitting cold water springs; where "her" pores were closed, hot springs oozed forth.

Several methods could be employed to encourage the natural fertility of the spiritus mundi. The salts extracted from vegetation would attract and condense the spirit, improving the soil's fertility. Sheltering land from the hot sun and desiccating winds would preserve it within the ground. Leaving fields fallow to attract the spirit would enrich and improve them. Burning limestone on the soil would evaporate the acidity, enhancing the fertilizing action of the spirit.

In America, Worlidge observed, the practice of burning wooded lands destroyed the acids that hampered fertility by liberating the salts and mixing them with the wood ashes. Burning stubble and weedy bushes further improved the land. But, in addition, lime mixed with the ashes and left to slake in the rains, as well as dung, urine, fish, seashells, and manures of all kinds, would enhance fertility.[14]

English alchemist Kenelm Digby in his *Discourse Concerning the Vegetation of Plants* (1660) wrote of the ancient poets whose knowledge of their "salt-begotten Goddess" was revealed only "under saline veils." Nitrous salts, said Digby, gave fecundity to all things, making seed soaked in it incredibly prolific. The niter acted as a magnet attracting like salts from the air which contained a "hidden food of life." Within nitrous salts were "the seminary virtues of all things."

Digby's comparison of the power of saltpeter to a magnet provided Concord naturalist Henry David Thoreau with his rationale that fallow fields could regain their fertility by absorbing vital spirits from the air.[15]

From the theory of fertilizing salts derived certain practical tips for farmers. When left untouched, nature would automatically heal and replenish fallow lands, but by art, or the imitation of nature, the process could be hastened. Because Earth herself was prolific, "before married to something of a more masculine virtue, which irradiates her womb," wrote English diarist and scientist John Evelyn in his *Terra* (1675), merely exposing her fields to the heavens allowed soils to become pregnant as the "seminal rudiments" flourished. The earth, said Evelyn, was nourished by "all that the air, dews, showers, and celestial influences can contribute." The fertility claimed by the "virgin earth" could therefore be replenished through natural aids like fallow, as when "our worn-out exhausted layfields . . . enjoy their sabbaths." Through sympathetic attractions the heavenly influences were brought down by the earth's magnetism. "The earth in the years of repose, recovers its vigor by the attraction of the vital spirits." Evelyn's recommendation provided Thoreau with his rationale that the soil in his bean field at Walden Pond had a magnetic power that attracted the life-giving salt.[16]

But Evelyn also offered numerous artificial methods for improving the land. Mechanical aids to fertility included pulverizing and breaking up the soil with a spade or plow so that it might receive the "natural impregnations." Animal and vegetable salts would attract the nitrous rains and dews that descended from the celestial atmosphere. Salt, the ingredient in all dungs and composts, revived the dead earth, its vigor being renewed as rain and dew melted into its bosom. Soils could be made fruitful by applying Aristotle's principle of the contraries—marrying opposites together like male and female. Thus, moist soils should be drained or treated with drying agents, dry soils should be given binding, cold soils needed a hot fermenting compost, while hot soils should be cooled and refreshed. Sand, ashes, chalk, lime, marl, air, sun, dew, rain, frost, snow, trenching, drilling, manuring, and composting were the agents needed to effect these changes.[17]

The treatises of these English improvers set out two basic approaches to fertilizing the soil. The first was a rationalization for the fallow field method. Here Nature, as earth mother, did the restoring herself through the cosmic cycling of fertilizing salts. This approach was widely used in colonial New England where the soils were sufficiently fertile that they could be restored through "naked" fallows. Using the medieval three-field system, one field each year was left in fallow to restore its fertility. Manure from grazing animals and ashes from burning trees and brush contributed their fertilizing powers. The second method was for humans to aid Nature by adding fertilizers to speed up her processes. This method required additional human labor and information. It was the approach of the agricultural improvement movements in seventeenth-century England and nineteenth-century New England. In the first approach humans were subordinate to Nature's cyclical processes, in the second they appropriated her powers through manipulating her processes.

The Cyclical Cosmos

The annual solar cycle, the monthly lunar cycle, and the cosmic meteorologic and hydrologic cycles were the basis of the farmer's worldview. From deep within the bowels of the earth, fluids and gases rose up to mingle with the air and spiritus mundi above its surface. As depicted in Athanasius Kircher's *Mundus Subterraneus* (1678), the earth's interior was filled with fiery chambers, volcanic holes, subterranean waters, underground springs, and deep reservoirs of water. Its fires broke through the surface as volcanic eruptions, its waters as springs, rivers, and lakes that circulated back to the underground caverns. Above the earth, God's hand released the Great Chain of Being on which the earth hung suspended between a fiery, cloudy sun and a crater-pocked moon.[18]

Isaac Newton's alchemic speculations of 1674 treated nature as a perpetual circulatory worker. Gross matter, exhaled from the bowels of the earth, ascended to the atmosphere where as vapor it was buoyed up by new air and vanished for a time into an ethereal spirit. There it was imbibed by the sun to "conserve his shining" before recondensing and descending again to feed the earth. "Nature is a perpetual circulatory worker," Newton asserted, "generating fluids out of solids, and solids out of fluids." Some things rose to "make the upper terrestrial juices, rivers, and the atmosphere." Others descended "for a requital to the former." Kept thus in perpetual circulation by hydrologic and chemical processes, matter and activity were conserved and nature's self-sufficiency and balance were maintained. In fact, the entire frame of nature, Newton speculated, may have been condensed by chemical fermentation from ethereal spirits and vapors "at first by the immediate hand of the Creator, and ever since by the power of nature, who by virtue of the command, *Increase and Multiply*, became a complete imitator of the copies set her by the Protoplast."[19]

To English medical chemist John Mayow (1643–79), who in 1674 came close to discovering oxygen, the elements were circulated through the earth to plants to air and back again. Niter was generated in the bosom of the earth from the living seed of nitrous salts. Air was the most important source of the growth and nourishment of crops. Circulating through both was the common principle, nitro-aerial spirit–cause of combustion (i.e., oxygen). Because plants contained nitrous as well as saline salts, they burned profusely when their nitro-aerial particles were moved by the sulfurous particles of fire. In soil on which plants grew abundantly, "no nitrous salt is to be found, the reason being that all the nitre of the soil is sucked out by the plants." To increase the production of niter, the soil needed to be manured.[20]

The English translation of Pierre Le Lorrain, Abbé de Vallemont's *Curiosities of Nature and Art in Husbandry and Gardening* (1707) was an important synthesis of the assumptions of the cyclical cosmos and the farmer's place within it (Figure 4.1). Although Vallemont's book may not have found its way to the American colonies, most of the ideas and assumptions expressed within it were sufficiently widely held that they can be taken as representative of the eighteenth-century belief system. These ideas and assumptions were reflected in the scientific treatises of Harvard professors, New England divines, and the authors of farmers' almanacs.

Like most agricultural writers, Vallemont held that stones and minerals, plants, animals, and humans constituted a hierarchically organized chain of being with the farmer as link and mediator between earth and heavens. The first garden, the author related, was given to humankind to keep and till. Farming was the joy of humanity, not a punishment for sin. The Golden Age had been spent, not in the city, but in the pleasures of the country. The farmer, like the alchemist, was the imitator and follower of nature. "The industry of husbandmen might always imitate and do by Art, what Nature sometimes

Figure 4.1

Curiosities of Nature and Art in Husbandry and Gardening. Nature in the seventeenth and eighteenth centuries was depicted as a woman. Here Nature (right), with six breasts, symbolizes fertility stemming from the multibreasted Artemis (Diana), Greek (Roman) goddess of wild untamed nature, fecundity, and secret knowledge. Art (left), also symbolized by a woman, holds a celestial sphere representing ordered nature. In the background, husbandry is symbolized by the farmer tilling his soil, while gardening is depicted as an does of her self. . . . When we have discover'd what could put her once in so good a humour; we need only treat her in the same manner, to make her act over again the same scene."[21]

The fruits and vegetables of the earthly garden lacked sensation, but had souls. The growth of leaves, flowers, fruits, and seed depended on the addition of niter produced by subterranean fires in the earth's bowels and released as steam and vapor into the atmosphere. Niter was Mother Earth's most wonderful treasure and the source of her fruitfulness. As the "universal spirit of the elementary world" it was the secret key to multiplication. As the Balm of Life, it "maintain[ed] the whole harmony of Nature." As the salt of fecundity, it held together the bodies of the elemental world.[22]

Vallemont extolled the role of niter in the great cosmic circulation that maintained life. When leaves fell in autumn, niter was being returned to the earth to be liberated. In the spring, the sun's heat reinforced the central exhalations that pushed the niter up into the roots of newly awakened plants. "By a perpetual and uninterrupted circulation, it ascends from below, and descends from above. . . . It never perishes but changes only its figure. If it enters into animals under the appearance of nourishment, it goes out from them under the veil of excrement." It thus moved in a perpetual circle from elements to aliments to excrements and back to elements.[23]

But each time the earth gave of itself to create vegetation, some of its production had to be returned to ameliorate its weakened condition. "How great soever are the magazines of provisions that Nature hides in her bosom for the nourishment of plants, in time they will waste and be consumed." He instructed farmers to compost all waste and return it to the soil. Straw, flesh, manure, urine, horses' hooves, nails, skin, wood, leaves, ashes, seed—anything corruptible—should be saved and combined with water to form a fertilizing liquor in which seed was to be soaked. When planted, the earth was "impregnated with nitrous salt . . . the salt of fruitfulness."[24]

The niter permeating the sown seed had a magnetic virtue that

---

ordered geometric garden with central fountain. On the hill, the muses preside over the arts and sciences.
Source: [Pierre Le Lorrain, Abbé de Vallemont], *Curiosities of Nature and Art in Husbandry and Gardening*, translated by William Fleetwood (London: Printed for D. Brown, A. Roper and Fran. Coggan, 1707), frontispiece.

attracted the atmospheric niter. When the rains fell, "the marriage of heaven and earth [was] consummated" and the seed was deposited in "the womb of the universal mother of all vegetable productions." Care must be taken not to sow it too deeply or it could not attract the nitrous vapors and exhalations that floated through the air.[25]

Like most seventeenth- and eighteenth-century writers, Vallemont assumed that stones, minerals, and metals were alive and grew within the bowels of the earth, making the whole cosmos animate. "The very metals form themselves into plants," he explained, "as if all Nature would have a hand in the affair of vegetation." When the earth was mined, the metals grew back again like the branches of trees reaching upward toward the earth's surface. Thus, nature produced pieces of gold shaped like tree branches that chemists could imitate by pouring the spirit of niter over silver, crystallizing it in the shape of a Diana's tree with branches and fruits. "Art mimics what Nature does, when she produces silver in the mines."[26]

Integral to the cyclical cosmos was the idea that Nature was an animate mother, subservient to God yet a powerful actress in the mundane world. As the mechanistic worldview began to replace the animate, Nature's power was gradually circumscribed. Rather than cajoling her by participating in the natural cycles, humans increasingly appropriated her restorative functions for the purpose of increasing yields and profits.

The Mechanical Philosophy

During the seventeenth century, important economic changes occurred in England. Overseas trade and internal economic development supported early capitalist industries such as shipping, mining, metallurgy, textiles, glass, soap, and paper making. Shippers depended on the forests to supply timber for houses, warehouses, docks, barges, locks, ships, and masts. Artisans needed charcoal for furnaces, forges, and soap and glass making. Farmers required wood for barns, sheds, plows, and farm tools. Expanding textile production provided incentives for gentlemen farmers to enclose land from the commons, drain marshes, and increase herds. Urban growth stimulated grain, fruit, and vegetable production. The new activities exploited the earth's resources on a scale not previously experienced in European history.

While many English writers continued to work within the ancient tradition that the earth was alive and active, the "moderns" were purging nature of animism and characterizing human beings, not as imitators who followed in nature's footsteps, but as masters of its processes. Francis Bacon (1561–1626) exemplified the transition. His *Sylva Sylvarum* (1626) advocated the four ancient helps for worn soil—dung, marl, ashes, and legumes. But farmers could also accelerate the earth's production of fertilizers by breeding niter in a pit filled with compost, pond earth, and chalk. They could speed up germination by soaking seeds in water mixed with cow dung, urine, wine, ashes, chalk, and soot. They could ripen fruits faster by applying heat to call "the spirits of the body outward." Such methods mixed human labor with nature's labor so that greater crop yields could be obtained.

Bacon's view of the garden was also consistent with the emerging mechanical philosophy of the moderns. Owing to the sin of Eve, the first parents were exiled from the Garden of Eden. Thereafter the objective of the human race was to recover its right to the garden lost in the fall. This could be accomplished through mastering nature and recovering the power originally assigned to humankind by divine bequest. We must "endeavor to establish and extend the power and dominion of the human race itself over the universe," he asserted.[27]

By the end of the century, a new philosophy of nature based on particles of inert, dead matter moved by external forces was adopted by elites working in France, England, and Germany. Philosopher René Descartes (1596–1650), mathematician Isaac Newton, and chemist Robert Boyle (1627–91), among others, developed a new science based on the analogy that God was a mathematician and the cosmos a machine. The new philosophy was consistent with an environmental ethic that nature was dead and could be exploited for human progress.

Descartes asserted that motion was put into the universe by God and passed from particle to particle. The human body was a machine within which the mind was a separate essence. Light was composed of tiny corpuscles of various sizes that impinged on the nerves of the retina, carrying images by way of the pineal gland to the unextended mind. Even animals were little machines that could be experimented on without feeling pain.[28]

Newton's *Mathematical Principles of Natural Philosophy* (1687) synthesized the laws of terrestrial and celestial motion into a mechanical science. His queries to the *Opticks* (1706) characterized the world in terms of hard, impenetrable particles that formed objects through separations and associations. Through his spokesperson Samuel Clarke in 1716, Newton depicted the cosmos as a clock, created, wound up, and kept in repair by a clockmaker God who intervened to keep his machine from running down when passing comets perturbed the planets' paths. For Leibniz, God's wisdom and foresight were so great that he need not intervene once the cosmic clock had been created. This clocklike mathematical cosmos, created and repaired by an external engineer, sanctioned the human domination of nature through machine technology, experimentation, and mathematical prediction and control.

Both animate and mechanistic symbols of nature and agriculture formed the intellectual background for colonial New England elites and almanac makers who offered agricultural advice to farmers. But through most of the eighteenth century, New England farmers were more receptive to the ideas associated with the animate cosmos than to those of the newer mechanical philosophy. Old World farming practices brought to New England by English immigrants and transmitted to their descendants formed the practical means for participating in the cycles of nature.

Consciousness and Cosmology in New England

The environmental ethic of eighteenth-century New England was more benign than the wilderness subjugation ethic of the early Puritans. While the biblical imagery of dominion had been preached by seventeenth-century Puritans as a justification for taking over the land, milder pastoral imagery accompanied the eighteenth-century's extension of the Garden of Eden into the New England landscape. In both elite and popular culture, the world was the expression of a benevolent deity. A God against nature shifted toward a God who expressed his goodness through nature.[29]

During the eighteenth century, Boston elites moved gradually away from Calvinism and toward the scientific rationalism of the mechanical philosophy. The universe was created by God as a manifestation of the harmony of Newtonian law. The orderly life of the merchant exemplified the logic of market trade. Control by the mind over the emotions and animal passions represented the ideal conduct for the rational person. Salvation was not preordained as for the Calvinist

Puritans but the result of a moral life on earth. The emergence of Unitarianism in Boston was rooted in the primacy of matter over spirit. Reality was material substance rather than the shadow of idea.

The Great Awakening of evangelical Christianity that swept rural New England in the 1740s, however, represented a shift from head to heart, from the intellectualism of Puritanism and the scientific rationalists to the emotions and love that were the basis of antinomianism. New light minister Jonathan Edwards (1704–58) perceived the threat to religion posed by Newtonian rationalism. God did not create the world as a clockmaker from outside it, but as an overflow of his own fullness. "It was not enough for Edwards to say, as John Cotton had done," wrote historian Perry Miller, "that God created the world out of nothing to show his glory; rationalists in Boston could reply that God's glory was manifested in the orderly machine of Newtonian physics, and that a man glorified God in such a world by going about his rational business: real estate, the triangular trade, or the manufacture of rum out of smuggled molasses. God did not create the world, said Edwards, merely to exhibit His glory; .... He made the world not by sitting outside and above it, ... but by an extension of Himself, by taking upon Himself the forms of stones and trees and of man." For Edwards, this was "a dynamic world, filled with the presence of God, quickened with divine life, pervaded with joy and ecstacy. With this insight he turned to combat the rationalism of Boston."[30]

Edwards's beneficent universe was infused by light, sun, and spirit, reminiscent of the Neoplatonism of the Renaissance. Light was an emanation from the sun, the world an expression of God's love. Yet Edwards was careful to preserve the Calvinist distinction between God and his creation. God was not within nature, as for pantheists, but transcendent above it. The result was a world in which natural objects and processes were an expression of God's goodness. Whereas Cotton Mather in 1692 had attributed natural disasters to the work of the Devil, Edwards in 1740 saw storms as evidence of the beneficence of God. Edwards's awakening took place in his father's (Father's) pasture. "God's excellency," he wrote in his "Personal Narrative,"

> seemed to appear in every thing; in the sun, moon, and stars; in the clouds, and blue sky; in the grass, flowers, trees; in the water, and all nature. ... Before, I used to be uncommonly terrified with thunder and to be struck with terror when I saw a thunder storm

rising; but now, on the contrary, it rejoiced me. I felt God, so to speak, at the first appearance of a thunder storm; and used to take the opportunity, at such times, to fix myself in order to view the clouds, and to see the lightnings play, and hear the majestic and awful voice of God's thunder, which oftentimes was exceedingly entertaining, leading me to sweet contemplations of my great and glorious God.[31]

The religious fervor that spread in waves through the countryside during the eighteenth century was an awakening of the heart to God's love. The stern retribution felt by the seventeenth-century Puritan was replaced by an outpouring of emotion. Transcendent vision was infused with bodily feeling. God was still known by his signs and symbols in the everyday world, but they were now perceived less as the work of the Devil and witch and more as that of a benevolent deity. The existential concerns that encouraged people to project their fears onto an evil wilderness in the seventeenth century led them to emotional religious expression through evangelical ministers in the eighteenth century.[32]

The cosmology of eighteenth-century Boston elites was a mixture of Renaissance and Newtonian natural philosophy. As in England, the physical cosmos was structured by the microcosm-macrocosm theory and the Great Chain of Being in which each species found its proper place between two other links from earth upward to God the creator. Within this system the farmer played the important role of restorer of the garden lost in the fall of Adam and Eve.

Charles Morton's (1627–98) *Compendium Physicae*, used at Harvard until 1728, discussed the farmer's place in a cosmos that ascended from inanimate stones, metals, and minerals to animate plants, sensible animals, rational humans, and invisible angels until it reached God, the "First Cause" of the universe. Owing to the sin of the first parents, Morton wrote, agriculture and husbandry must be used to combat soil sterility and the overproduction of weeds through fencing, tilling, manuring, and draining the land.[33]

Morton, who was installed as pastor of the First Church in Charlestown just outside Boston in 1686, had studied natural philosophy at Oxford during the period of the evolution of the new science and wrote his *Compendium* about 1680. He based his text on Aristotle's logic, physics, meteorology, and biology, while also introducing the newer cosmologies of Copernicus, Tycho Brahe, and Descartes. He rejected the Platonists' concept of a world soul diffused throughout matter, and followed Aristotle in the belief that each body had its own form (or soul) associated with its matter. Of the four elements (earth, air, fire, and water), earth had both an upper and a lower region. The upper received the heat of the sun and rain, and formed the vegetables that supported human life. The active lower region below the surface was the source of the alchemic principles sulfur, mercury, and salt. It produced the metals and minerals that rose to the passive upper level. This process generated the all-important substance, niter, which ascended to the earth's surface to fertilize the growing vegetables.[34]

Samuel Willard (1640–1707), a Harvard graduate and its vice-president from 1701 to 1707, joined the husbandman with the heavens in the Great Chain that originated with God. A series of second causes tied the farmer to the other links in the chain: the heavens first distilled their influences, the earth received them, the farmer manured the ground, and finally the seed drew in the life-giving moisture.[35]

Boston minister Cotton Mather (1663–1728), in *The Christian Philosopher* (1721), affirmed his belief that "there is a scale of nature wherein we pass regularly and proportionably from a stone to a man ... yet man is, as one well expresses it, but the equator of the universe ... 'there are several orders of imbodied intellect before we come to pure mind.'" Or as Newport minister Ezra Stiles put it in his creed in 1752, "I believe the moral world is composed of intelligences, of various orders, succeeding in a most beautiful gradation in the scale of being from infinite to nothing."[36]

But Mather was more sharply divided in his allegiance to the Renaissance cosmos than his contemporaries and represented the cutting edge of the mechanistic worldview in New England. Although he believed in a higher order of spirits than man, he firmly disagreed with the idea of a Platonic world soul animating the entire cosmos. He also rejected the substantial forms, plastic virtues, radical heats, and hylarchic principles of the Aristotelians, naturalists, and Neoplatonists. Such concepts, he believed, had been cast aside by the Newtonian revolution and replaced by a world machine operating according to divine law set down by God, the first mover, who by his will continually upheld the whole creation. But God retained the power to abrogate his laws should he so desire. He likewise sustained the inertial motion and rest of bodies, matter being incapable of moving itself.[37]

Nevertheless, his philosophy of agriculture was still permeated with the terminology of the cycle of niter and the organic rebirth of nature. According to Mather, soil fertility derived from the action of rainwater on the land. Water mixed with terrestrial matter was drawn up through the stems of plants and exhaled through the leaves into the atmosphere. The water vapor carried this fine vegetable matter upward and returned it to the earth as rain, leaving the coarser mineral matter that could not enter the roots in the soil. Unless the soil was first stirred, loosened, and then aided by niter and other salts, it could not receive the fertile water. After it had remained fallow for some time, replenishing itself from the rains, the husbandman could grow wheat for a few seasons. When exhausted for wheat, another crop such as barley could be planted, then oats, and finally peas. "The care of the tiller in manuring of it, lays upon it such things as are most impregnated with a supply for vegetation."[38]

In 1731, upon the death of Thomas Hollis who had endowed his Harvard chair, the natural philosopher Isaac Greenwood delivered a lecture relating life and death in the human microcosm to the same processes in the macrocosm. In the world below the moon, the vegetable soul of plants grew under the influence of the sun to a ripe plant that bore fruit, then decayed and died. Similarly, the body and soul in the mundane world were like the moon, lowest of the heavenly bodies in the macrocosm. The soul, like the moon, remained the same throughout its course through life, but the human body like the moon's apparent body grew to maturity and then decayed until reborn in a new life.[39]

Greenwood extended the organic analogy between microcosm and macrocosm to include Nature, whom he personified as a mother. Like an indulgent parent, she sometimes improved her original plan and conception on earth, while at other times she altered and dissolved her handiwork. She was not only frugal, but active—uncertainty and mutability characterized her entire animate world. Below her surface, earthquakes, "fulminating damps," and volcanic eruptions produced continual change. Above it, vapors from the tails of comets supplied the water, heat, and light that restored the fluids used daily by vegetation. The air, impregnated with these exhalations and vapors, was "the chief agent that Nature use[d] in most of her secret processes." Respiration could produce death when the vapors were unwholesome and pestilential, or life and health when they

were refreshing. Sometimes the cosmic exhalations destroyed vegetation, while at other times they promoted growth and increase.[40]

Like the earth, man the microcosm was filled with even smaller
organisms. As had been revealed by English microscopists, humans
were composed of numerous changing inhabitants, "tribes of animals
which live in and upon us," carrying on the daily business of life and
death. But people do not notice them any more than the earth is
"conscious of . . . the birth, life and burial of one of us."[41]

This mixture of ancient and Renaissance organic cosmology, together with the concepts of the newer Copernican and Newtonian
science, was taught to elites who attended New England colleges and,
embroidered with astrological symbolism and earthy verses, disseminated through almanacs to farmers and "lesser sorts" of folk.

Almanacs as Symbol Systems

The farmers of eighteenth-century New England were intellectually united to the organic cyclical cosmos inherited from Renaissance
Europe. As for their European counterparts, the stars and planets
were thought to affect life on earth in accordance with the adage, "As
above, so below." Astrology and religion both revealed God's purpose
and will. The astrologer's predictions based on the motions of the
conjunctions and oppositions of planets could be coordinated with
Sunday sermons on the meaning of comets. The beliefs and practices
about the sun, moon, and soil carried to America were a venerable
tradition not easily challenged and one that was upheld by the farmer's main printed source of information about the natural world, the
astrological almanac.

Along with the Bible, the almanac was the most prevalent book in
colonial households. For either the meagerly or well-educated farming family, the almanac served as a set of mediating symbols that
connected the individual to the larger cosmos through diagrams,
woodcuts, verses, tables, and advice columns. On the inside cover
was the zodiacal "Man of the Signs" (Figures 4.2 and 4.3), along with
a table of symbols of the signs of the zodiac and the seven planets.
This information was critical to maintaining health. The user was
instructed to find the day of the month and note the sign of the zodiac
in which the moon was located. By comparing the sign with the man

in the woodcut, the part of the body affected on that day could be determined. If the moon was in Leo, the heart was vulnerable, if in Aquarius the legs could develop problems. Each month was heralded with a proverb or verses often accompanied by an illustration embedded with symbolic meaning. Finally, the endpapers reported the latest agricultural discoveries and planting tips. Since almanacs were among the few books a family possessed, these verses and articles received intensive use, conveying guidelines for agricultural decisions and daily behavior. The almanac was, in effect, the colonist's "weekday Bible."[42]

The pages of these slim, four-by-seven-inch pocket volumes contained the elements of the farmer's cosmic belief system. While sometimes complaining of the necessity of including the old folklore that related the zodial signs to the human body, the college-educated almanac maker knew that his audience would not purchase the guide without it. Printed in the endpapers of seventeenth- and eighteenth-century almanacs and their monthly verses was a marvelous mix of ancient assumptions about the organic character of the cosmos, the earth, the soil, the weather, and the human body along with the latest developments in Newtonian science, the new mechanical metaphor of the body, and experiments in scientific agriculture.[43]

When the printer interleaved blank pages between the tables of monthly events or the farmer personally inserted them and restitched the almanac, it became a diary for recording short line-a-day entries, planting and marketing records, and accounts. Such almanac diaries provide historical records that unite the farmer's cosmology with daily activities. Together with folklore, farm journals, newspapers, technological relics, and colonial textbooks, almanacs can be used to reconstruct the set of Old World beliefs and practices that guided the New England farmer. Using these tools, the adoption and diffusion of scientific agriculture and technology can be measured against the resistance to innovation derived from centuries of harvests based on old practices and beliefs.

The seventeenth-century almanacs had been written by Harvard tutors and contained scholarly essays on Ptolemaic, Copernican, and Tychonic astronomy; eclipses, comets, and planets; and the discoveries of Robert Hooke and Isaac Newton on gravitation, comets, and the tides. Of the forty-four almanacs published in Massachusetts by 1687, forty-one were prepared by Harvard graduates, including Nathaniel Chauncey (son of Harvard president Charles Chauncey), Joseph Dudley (one of the colony's governors), well-known ministers such as Cotton Mather, his younger brother Nathaniel, Harvard astronomer Thomas Brattle, his logician brother William, and Edward Holyoke who later became president of Harvard.[44]

But by the end of the seventeenth century, almanacs containing information specifically for farmers had begun to appear, and by the early eighteenth century they had replaced those of the Harvard scholars. The new authors were educated printers, physicians, and public-minded entrepreneurs. Harvard graduate and printer John Foster included weather information for farmers in his almanac of 1676, the first woodcut of the Man of the Signs [entitled "The Dominion of the Moon in Man's Body (according to astronomers)"] in 1678, and an illustration of the Copernican system in 1680. Daniel Leeds of Philadelphia edited an agricultural almanac in 1693 that reminded farmers of each month's tasks and advised them of the effects of eclipses. Continued by his sons Titan and Felix, over its fifty years of publication it provided farmers with information on astronomy, weather, agricultural improvement, homemaking, roads, and currency conversion.[45]

John Tulley, a British teacher of mathematics, astronomy, and navigation who settled in Connecticut and published between 1687 and 1702, included popular astrology, weather predictions, advice for farmers, and bawdy verses having a popular appeal beyond that of the Harvard tutors. Known as a skillful weather forecaster, Tulley included a "Prognostica Georgica: Or a Country-mans Weather-glass" on the end cover of his almanacs. Nathaniel Whittmore, an assessor of Lexington, published a *Farmer's Almanac* beginning in 1714. Nathaniel Ames of Dedham, Massachusetts, a physician and astronomer, and his son (a Harvard graduate of the same name) compiled almanacs from 1725 to 1775. Highly educated popularizers of learning, they not only wrote essays on astronomy, science, and politics, but also disseminated European popular beliefs about the earth, the cycles of nature, and the Great Chain of Being. In 1764, responding to the needs of Massachusetts farmers for details on soil improvement and crop yields, Ames began to include formal essays on agriculture in the endpapers. As the most successful of the New England almanacs, the Ames' had achieved a circulation of 50,000 copies by the time publication ceased.[46]

In 1793, Robert B. Thomas's *Old Farmer's Almanac* began its unbroken history of publication, maintained to this day under the deceased

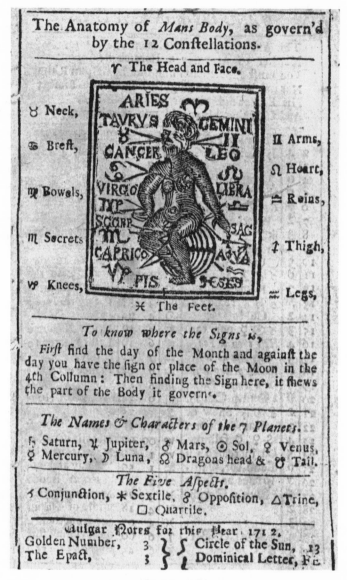

The Anatomy of *Mans Body*, as govern'd
by the 12 Conſtellations.

♈ The Head and Face.

♉ Neck,

♋ Breſt,

♍ Bowels,

♏ Secrets

♑ Knees,

♓ The Feet.

♊ Arms,

♌ Heart,

♎ Reins,

♐ Thigh,

♒ Legs,

To know where the Signs is,

Firſt find the day of the Month and againſt the
day you have the ſign or place of the Moon in the
4th Collumn : Then finding the Sign here, it ſhews
the part of the Body it govern*s*.

The Names & Characters of the 7 Planets.

♄ Saturn, ♃ Jupiter, ♂ Mars, ☉ Sol, ♀ Venus,
☿ Mercury, ☽ Luna, ☊ Dragons head & ☋ Tail.

The Five Aſpects.

☌ Conjunction, ✱ Sextile, ☍ Oppoſition, △ Trine,
☐ Quartile.

Vulgar Notes for this Year 1712.
Golden Number,   3 ⎱ ⎰ Circle of the Sun, 13
The Epact,   3 ⎰ ⎱ Dominical Letter, F ⅃

Figure 4.2

The Anatomy of Man's Body, 1712. The Man of the Signs symbolized the influence of the moon as it moved through the twelve signs of the zodiac (or
macrocosm) on the human body (or microcosm). The user found the day of
the month in the almanac, looked in the fourth column for the zodiacal sign
in which the moon was found, and then using the diagram found the part of
the body most vulnerable on that particular day.

author's name. Complete with the standard almanac features, it also included monthly tips on planting, harvesting, and husbandry in the "Farmer's Calendar" section and articles on agriculture and horticulture in the end essays. Nathanael Low's *Astronomical Diary* for the meridian of Boston beginning in the early nineteenth century featured articles on modes of increasing manure, hints on planting and propagating fruit trees, and the improvement of soils with manure.[47]

In setting out their cosmology the almanac makers drew on a variety of popular American and European distillations of scientific learning. The lectures of Harvard professors and the writings of Puritan divines merged cosmology, astrology, and Renaissance naturalism with the latest discoveries of English scientists such as Robert Boyle, Robert Hooke, John Mayow, and Isaac Newton. Textbooks used at Harvard and later at Yale (founded in 1702) drew on the older agricultural theories of Aristotle and Paracelsus as well as early agricultural improvers such as John Evelyn, Walter Blith, and John Worlidge. For the ordinary farmers of colonial New England, the Bible and the almanac were the chief intellectual sources of their cosmology, while folklore and ritual were handed down orally and manually. Not until the early nineteenth century would these older traditions be augmented by farmers' journals, societies for promoting agriculture, and agricultural fairs.

Almanacs and Farming Practices

The almanacs popularized the learning of the Harvard and Oxford lecturers and the European improvers in flowery, often humorous, verses that featured the cyclical nature of the seasons and the place of the farmer within the Great Chain of Being. Nature transmitted the immutable laws of God to the fleeting and changeable mundane world and fragile human substance. Rising vapors, unwholesome airs, circulations, the wrack of falling elements, the womb of chaos, the breaths and expirations of universal nature, vital airs, pestilential heats, and gaping earthquakes characterized the annual activities of

---

Source: [Daniel Leeds], *The American Almanac for 1712* (New York: William Bradford, 1711), DD Drake 5551. Courtesy of the John Carter Brown Library, Brown University, Providence, Rhode Island.

The Anatomy of Man's Body, as governed by the 12 Conltelat
♈ Aries, head and face.

♉ Taurus,
neck and
throat.

♊ Gemi-
ni, arms &
fhoulders.

♋ Cancer,
breaſt, ſto-
mach and
ribs.

♌ Leo,
heart and
back.

♍ Virgo,
bowels
and belly

♎ Libra,
reins and
loins.

♏ Scorpio
ſecrets,

♐ Sagi-
tarius,
thighs.

♑ capricor-
nus, knees,

♒ Aqua-
ries, legs,

♓ Piſces, the feet.

Figure 4.3

The Anatomy of Man's Body, 1782. Even into the late eighteenth century, almanac makers, although expressing skepticism over the mechanism by which the moon—merely by passing through certain zodiacal signs—could influence one part of the human body more than another, included the Man of the Signs in their publications because their clientele demanded it.
Source: Russell's *American Almanac for... 1782* (Danvers: Printed by E. Russell), DD Drake 3310. Courtesy of the John Carter Brown Library, Brown University, Providence, Rhode Island.

Mother Earth in language that harkened back to the animate cosmos of Renaissance Europe.[48]

Almanac makers and agricultural writers employed earth mother imagery in profusion in their discussions of agricultural methods and the relationship of the farmer to nature. The husbandman was instructed to learn from and imitate nature's cycles and to follow the advice of Virgil in his *Georgics*:

Borrow part of Winter for thy Corn
That while the Turf lies open, and unbound
Succeeding suns may bake the mellow ground.
But if the soil be barren, only scar
The Surface and but lightly print the share.[49]

The pulsating sexuality of a laughing, vital Mother Earth and virile
sun was captured in the colorful verses and graphics heading each
calendar month. The sun's gentle heat brooded over the female Earth
in dews and rains, defending her from harm. The signs of the zodiac
were personified and assigned human needs and desires. During August, when the sun moved from the sign of Leo the Lion into that of
Virgo the Virgin, Nathaniel Ames wrote:

The Virgin lends her bosom to aswage
And pacify Sol's burning furious Rage,
They embrace, and down to Thetis' Bed descend
Cool Nights arise, and all the World befriend.[50]

Almanac makers worked within the Renaissance tradition that the
earth was a human being writ large with whom the farmer had an
intimate, personal relationship. Ames's summer verses assumed a
direct parallel between the earth's anatomy and reproductive processes and those of the farmer. In June, he wrote, man joined the
"general smile of Nature," as "fierce passions vex[ed] his breast."
In July, mowers were cutting the humid hay as "distressful Nature
pants" with "hot ascending steams." Or as John Tulley put it, "wanton
Lads and Lasses do make Hay, / Which unto lewd temptation makes
great way." The August verse in a 1709 Boston almanac depicted the
earth's hair as needing cutting and grooming: "Terra's rich tresses
that hang dangling down / Are by the bending Reapers daily mown."[51]
Colonists interpreted natural events as evidence of God's power
and omniscience. Acting through nature, God could convey his pleasure or displeasure with humankind or deliver rewards and punishments:

By threatning Stars and Prodigies He shows
A shinning People their impending Woes
Earthquakes sometimes the trembling Ground do tear
And blazing Comets rule the troubled Air.

Verses warned of the wrath that Mother Earth could render—sometimes with a precaution that the lines were descriptive, not predictive:

> The Earth convulsed, her jaws are open'd wide
> Churches and all their lofty spires subside
> To Nature's Womb they sink with dreadful throws
> And on poor screaming souls the chasms close.

Tulley's almanac for 1693 explained earthquakes as part of the earth's elimination system, as "plenty of winds gotten in the bowels, holes, and corners of the earth bursting out of the earth and closing again."[52]

Most astrologers asserted the validity of natural astrology, or the action of the planets on the natural world and human body, but rejected, as superstition, judicial astrology, which dealt with their influences on the will. Natural astrology provided a "rational and philosophical" foundation for planetary influences on the environment.

Ptolemy's *Tetrabiblos* supplied the theory on which astrologers based their weather predictions and farming advice. John Foster's *Almanack* for 1680 elaborated the qualities assigned to each planet by Ptolemy. Each planet, in accordance with its distance from the earth (in the old geocentric cosmos), assumed two of the qualities. The moon being closest absorbed the moist, cold exhalations of the earth, whereas the sun had the hot, dry characteristics of fire. Saturn was cold and dry because (of the seven ancient planets) it was farthest from the sun. Because of its extreme cooling power, Saturn was an evil planet, whereas the moon was beneficent owing to its life-giving qualities of warmth and moisture.[53]

Each sign of the zodiac was associated with one of the four elements and hence with two of the four qualities. For example, planets moving through, or celestial events taking place in, the water signs (the trigon of Cancer, Scorpio, and Pisces) meant that the qualities of cold and moist would act on the earth. Ames used this framework to explain ecological events such as the massive destruction of fish and waterfowl that had occurred in Rhode Island in 1737, when two eclipses took place in the watery trigon. In another example, great floods and inundations occurred when a comet had appeared in the water sign of Pisces.[54]

By the eighteenth century, most almanac makers accepted Newtonian gravitation as the explanatory framework for astrology. The decrease of gravitational force, according to the square of the distance, was the cement that held the creation together. Without it the planets would fly off into infinite space. But the planets and moon also emitted effluvia and radiations that operated according to strict, albeit unknown, laws of nature. The effluvia were conveyed through the earth's most important appendage, the air, an elastic medium that was both a receptacle for vapor and a medium for sound. Through these effluvia the moon's action on the tidal waters could be augmented by planets such as Saturn or Venus when favorably situated.[55]

Farmers organized many of their activities according to the astrological theory conveyed by the almanacs. Because of the pull of the moon on water, a full moon would encourage the upward movement of plant fluids. They therefore planted seeds of upward-growing plants, such as corn, rye, and wheat, in the moon's waxing phase and root crops such as carrots and beets in the wane. Similarly, grafting or transplanting trees under a waning moon helped them set their roots downward. Tanners testified that oak bark peeled off readily in the new of the moon, but stuck closely to the trunk after the moon was full. Animal breeders followed the rule that horses should be gelded in the wane of the moon, while sows should be bred during its increase.[56]

Nathaniel Whittmore's *Almanack* for 1713 advised farmers that "the best time to cut timber for lasting sound and good is in the old of the moon; in December, January, and February, especially when the moon is in Pisces." Daniel Staples, a Maine farmer who was born in 1750, shared his observations on the moon's effect on tree sap with other readers of the *New England Farmer*. Trees cut in the "wane of the moon," when the sap was not flowing, would rot and decay more quickly, producing a better burn. Similarly, fruit trees should be pruned under a waning moon, since the cuts would heal more rapidly. He advised farmers to prune their orchards in May at the end of the waning phase, one to two days before the new moon.[57]

Nathanael Low's *Astronomical Diary: or Almanack* for 1807 reported the results of tests made by physician and clergyman Jared Eliot, Connecticut's first writer on agricultural improvement. Following the advice of old farmers, Eliot, in his *Essays Upon Field Husbandry* (1760), had suggested cutting brush and girdling trees on a cloudy day in the old (or wane) of the moon. If put to successful experiment, he believed, this could help in clearing the land. When he later performed the experiment, he found that the best time was in

July or August in the old of the moon when the sign was in the heart (i.e., Leo, July 23–August 22). "In every place it killed so universally, that there is not left alive, scarce one in a hundred; the trial was made in three or four places on the same day." His recommendation that the sun be in Leo can be explained because the augmentation of their mutual hot, dry qualities would aid in drying up the brush.[58]

Following English theories, Eliot relied on the circulation of fertilizers and nitrous salts in his recommendations for improving the health of soils. The dew that fell on fallow land was impregnated with nitrous particles that fertilized the soil. Prior plowing, however, was superior to weed fallow since it prepared the soil particles to receive the dews and salts. He advised farmers to plant cabbages, turnips, and peas before winter wheat so that the shade would increase the air motion and sweep in the nitrous particles from the atmosphere. To restore worn-out fields, dung, composed chiefly of nitrous salts, should be added, followed by green manures such as buckwheat, oats, or rye that could be planted and plowed under.[59]

To ward off crows, which ate corn seed, Eliot advised soaking the seed in a boiled liquor made from hellebore, a practice of the New England Indians. A farmer he knew, who had planted part of his field with soaked seed and the rest with untreated seed, found that crows pulled up the unsoaked corn, destroying his crop, but left the treated corn to mature.[60]

The farmer's astrological cosmos was an integral part of a more comprehensive organic framework. Not only did the animate earth produce and recycle nitrous salts to fertilize the soil, it also gave birth to the minerals, stones, and metals beneath its surface. While some American writers believed minerals to be God's direct creations, most concurred with European views that minerals grew and developed from the exhalations of sulfur, mercury, and salt or from the seed of the minerals themselves. The earth's interior heat fostered their growth or an internal "plastic virtue" imprinted a mineral's form on its matter. The animate and the inanimate, the organic and inorganic were thus blended into many gradations of the living.[61]

Charles Morton, in his *Compendium*, assigned stones, metals, and minerals to the inanimate world, but supposed that stones were generated from the moist first matter in which was dissolved some "nitre of the earth." The mixture then became hard through the action of cold and the subsequent evaporation of water. Not possessing vegetative souls, stones grew by adding matter to their outsides, whereas plants grew from the inside. He related the alchemists' belief that the soul and life of a metal could be separated from it, leaving the brittle, drossy, useless matter. When silver ore lay close to the earth's surface, "it sometimes sends forth branches (like white moss) of pure silver, called the silver tree."[62]

Edward Taylor, poet and minister in Westfield, Massachusetts, described "Nature's Tree" in a poem of 1705. Through her tree, she caused ore to rise from the roots through the branches to the leaves, producing fruits. The roots gave rise to the stones and lower metals— iron and lead. Higher up, the warmth of the earth "hatch[ed] silver bright and gold more fine / And sparkling gems that mock the sun and 'ts shine."[63]

Samuel Willard of Harvard believed that minerals "were at first made in the earth, and its womb was then impregnated, and made fruitful of them." Yale used as a textbook Benjamin Martin's *Philosophical Grammar* (1735) which asserted that "divers mines, when emptied of stone, metal, &c. have after a while recruited again."[64]

James Thacher who wrote on the production of iron ores in Plymouth, Massachusetts (1804), believed that bog ore, after it had been mined, took about twenty-five years to grow back, provided that the miners covered their excavations with leaves and other organic debris. These bogs beautifully illustrated nature's generating principle and process. "In a short period ... vegetable substances, even branches of trees suffer a complete transition to a metallick state. Does not this indicate an analogy between metallick and organick substances?"[65]

Like native Americans, many colonial elites and ordinary farmers thought of rocks and minerals as living, growing things. Filled with streaks, fissures, veins, and cavities, they were often difficult to distinguish from leaves, shells, mollusks, and other living or dormant organisms. As late as 1787 Thomas Jefferson was still describing the caves of Virginia as "impregnated with nitre." After extracting the niter, he complained, miners did not try a second time to see how soon the "earth they have once exhausted ... receives another impregnation." Such ideas persisted through the eighteenth century until microscopic techniques and experiments began to separate the animate from the inanimate world.[66]

Conclusion

Until the introduction of agricultural improvement in the late eighteenth century, the concept of the animate cosmos formed the ethical framework for the life and labor of most farmers. The Renaissance theory that water and fertilizing salts circulated from earth to atmosphere and back again, nourishing and restoring the health of fallow fields, legitimated a system of "naked" fallows through which the soil recovered its fertility unaided. Although knowledge of many kinds of fertilizers and their beneficial effects on worn-out soil was available in European texts, such information did not receive much dissemination in colonial America until the late eighteenth century.

Participatory consciousness dominated by religious vision was the framework for colonial engagement with the natural world. An abstract God known through transcendent vision was experienced through signs and symbols manifested in the everyday world. Light and truth were revealed from above, but interpreted in the concrete and mundane. Knowing was seeing, knowledge was illumination, and truth was light.

Yet a wide spectrum of forms of bodily and sensual participation was possible in eighteenth-century America. For antinomian "born agains" the heart awakened to the body's own knowledge. For Shakers the body responded to its own inner music. Elites, on the other hand, moved closer to deistic and Unitarian beliefs in a rational, calculating God who had created a mechanical, clocklike universe. But for most ordinary people, educated in local schools and working with hands and tools, the mental and physical were not yet severed. The mind had not become the disembodied intellect of scientific rationality; the physical eye was not yet the passive lens of empiricism. In colonial communities, the spoken word governed most face-to-face transactions. Oral-aural culture tied individuals, places, and times together.[67]

The colonial ecological revolution had transformed native American ecology and consciousness while also producing a synthesis of European and Indian methods of production. This colonial form of production was an "extensive system" of agriculture adopted by farmers settling inland-upland towns during the eighteenth century (see Chapter 5). Concurrently, Puritan attitudes toward nature softened as "wilderness" was "civilized," generating an organic cosmology and participatory consciousness that informed rural farming practices.

But the culmination of the colonial ecological revolution was also the starting point for the capitalist ecological revolution. Among eighteenth-century elites in rural as well as coastal and Connecticut Valley towns, a movement toward agricultural improvement coupled with a mechanical philosophy and an analytic consciousness was beginning to take shape. As a patriarchal system of land inheritance put pressure on the "extensive system" of production, in turn degrading the region's ecology, and a national market economy offered increased opportunities for profit making, ordinary farmers adopted agricultural improvement and specialization (see Chapter 5). In taking up more calculating quantitative methods of accounting and responding to pressure from elite improvers, their consciousness was also transformed. A literate populace became a calculating populace, nature a calculable order of forces (see Chapter 6). This transition to modernity constituted the capitalist ecological revolution.

PART TWO

. . . .

The Capitalist Ecological Revolution

5

. . . .

Farm Ecology: Subsistence versus Market

Mimesis, the process of imitation, linked the farmer's worldview to practice. The animate earth replicated the cycles of the larger cosmos, translating God's will into daily weather, annual harvests, and generational births and deaths. Following nature's cycles and imitating its patterns in fields, orchards, and gardens, farmers reproduced and maintained human life. As daughters learned milking and sons learned plowing, they were incorporating the values and techniques that had allowed their parents and grandparents to survive. A myriad of daily activities were imitated and passed on from generation to generation.

During the capitalist ecological revolution, imitation was subverted by analysis. No longer merely wooed for survival, nature was mastered for wealth. Production was oriented, not for subsistence, but for profit. Although the cutting edge of this future appeared among New England's eighteenth-century commercial elite, most farming families were still embedded in the traditions of the past.

New England's transition to modernity began in the late eighteenth century. Tensions between the requirements of production and reproduction forced the ecological transformation. Over the succeeding decades the majority of New Englanders were drawn into new forms of production, new gender relations of reproduction, and new forms of environmental consciousness.

During the eighteenth century, the subsistence sector of the colonial economy expanded as families founded towns in inland-upland New England—areas too distant from seaports to participate fully in the exchange economy of the mercantile sector (Map 5.1). In 1810, 67 percent of the inhabitants of the southern New England states lived in 385 townships (forty square miles) that numbered only 1,000–3,000 people. Towns in newly settled areas contained 500–1,500, while those in older coastal or fertile river valleys had typically 2,500–3,000. Only 3 of the 437 townships had populations over 10,000 (Boston,

33,250; Salem, 12,600; and Providence, 10,000); 11 held 5,000–10,000, and 38 had 3,000–5,000 inhabitants.[1]

Two economic extremes—the first oriented toward production for use, the second for market exchange—coexisted in coastal towns and inland villages. Mercantilism, with its focus on exchange values, was prevalent in four regions: a strip of land along the coasts of Connecticut, Rhode Island, and Massachusetts, extending northward into coastal New Hampshire and Maine; the Connecticut Valley for about sixty-five miles north to the falls at Enfield near Hartford; the western dairy region of Litchfield and Berkshire counties; and harbor towns such as Boston, Providence, New Haven, and Norwich. These areas represented 20–25 percent of the population. Yet even here a spectrum of commercial orientations existed, with many farmers still producing primarily for subsistence.[2]

At the opposite extreme, most inland towns beyond a twenty- to twenty-five-mile radius of urban centers and navigable rivers had limited access to commercial markets and produced primarily for use, extra income from crop surpluses being limited by bad roads, the capacity of sleighs and oxcarts, and unpredictable weather. But even here no farms were totally self-sufficient. All were involved in a network of community bartering, while participating in varying degrees in outside markets. Surpluses from cattle, potash, cordwood, or maple sugar raised cash for taxes and items such as coffee, tea, salt, and ammunition sold at the local store. During some years weather allowed more surplus than in others. But these "subsistence surpluses" did not necessarily indicate a profit-oriented mentality in which the farm was planned, planted, and managed for the commercial market, as would be the case in the nineteenth century. While every town had its market-oriented elite, the balance was tipped toward subsistence in the inland-upland towns of the eighteenth century. A sample of fifteen such towns in Massachusetts in 1771 (Map 5.2) is representative of the subsistence-oriented sector of the colonial economy.[3]

Family security and preservation were farmers' prime objectives. Food for the present and land and goods for future inheritance focused home life. In addition to producing or bartering most of the food needed for subsistence, many farmers practiced a local trade, exchanging goods and services with their neighbors as carpenters, tanners, wheelwrights, joiners, cobblers, coopers, storekeepers, doctors, and innkeepers. Farm women were not only wives, mothers, and grandmothers, but also vegetable and poultry producers, food proces-

Map 5.1
Isochronic Map of Settlement in New England

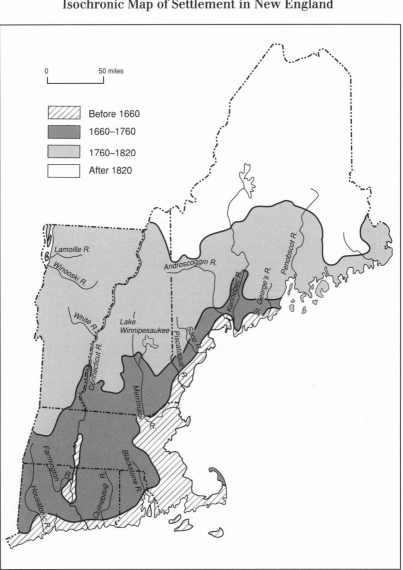

0   50 miles

Before 1660
1660–1760
1760–1820
After 1820

Lamoille R.
Winooski R.
Androscoggin R.
Penobscot R.
St. George's R.
Kennebec R.
White R.
Lake Winnipesaukee
Saco R.
Piscataqua R.
Connecticut R.
Merrimack R.
Farmington R.
Blackstone R.
Housatonic R.
Quinebaug R.

Source: Stanley D. Dodge. "The Frontier of New England in the Seventeenth and Eighteenth Centuries and Its Significance in American History," *Papers of the Michigan Academy of Science, Arts, and Letters* 28 (1942): 437

Map 5.2
Fifteen Inland Massachusetts Towns, 1771

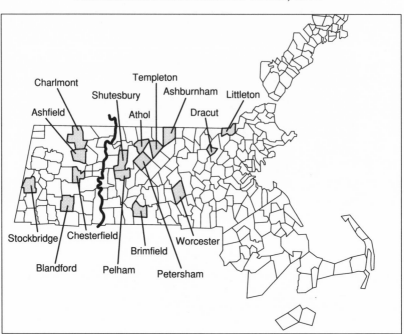

Source: Bettye Hobbs Pruitt, "Agriculture and Society in the Towns of Massachusetts, 1771: A Statistical Analysis" (Ph.D. dissertation, Boston University, 1981), Map. 1.

sors, cheese and butter makers, spinners, carders, weavers, sewers, herbalists, healers, and sometimes teachers or midwives as well.[4]

Between 1700, when the inland towns were being settled, and 1790, when ecological crisis and European markets stimulated agricultural intensification, an economy oriented to subsistence and family preservation flourished in inland-upland New England. This form of production differed from traditional European agriculture in that farmers held fee simple titles to their own land, rather than ancestral grazing, tilling, and woodcutting privileges on the commons. And it differed from nineteenth-century capitalist agriculture in that most males owned (or would soon inherit) their own farms, rather than supporting themselves wholly through wage labor.[5]

Agricultural Ecology

Agricultural ecology views the farm, not from the perspective of crop yields and the short-term maximizing of production, but as a totality of interdependent crops, animals, humans, soils, and woodlands. United by the patterns of nutrient cycling, energy exchanges, population maintenance, and ecological sustainability, a particular agroecosystem reflects both ecological and economic interdependences. Traditional small-scale farming relies on human and animal power and on local knowledge that has evolved over generations in good as well as marginal conditions. The synthesis of American Indian and medieval European agriculture achieved by the eighteenth century in New England was ecologically adapted to local habitats. But as traditional farming gave way during the nineteenth century to intensive agriculture and specialized production, the ecological stresses would increase, requiring greater management and control.[6]

The New England agroecological unit comprised a farm homestead (with space and technology for both agricultural and nonagricultural production); fields, orchards, and gardens for plant production; pastures, meadows, barns, and dairy for animal production; and a woodlot for fuel (Figure 5.1). Farm and household products moved off the farm to neighboring farms or more distant markets; purchased or bartered goods entered from outside. Within the farm boundaries, energy (food and fuel) and nutrients moved from one space to another. Forest and pasture provided feed for grazing animals and in turn received animal manure, while meadows supplied fodder to the barnyard for animals during snowy winters. Woodlots transmitted fuel to the homestead and ashes to the soil. Tillage, orchards, and gardens supplied grain, fruits, and vegetables while receiving manure from cattle, pigs, and poultry. Fields and gardens provided flowers for bees and other beneficial insects and birds, but also harbored pests. Whether the farm was a self-sustaining ecological unit depended on the extent to which energy and nutrients were circulated within or moved off the farm. The smaller the farms became and the more their market orientation increased, the greater were the ecological repercussions.

The availability of male and female labor as well as farm sizes and layouts governed the way time and space were used. Whether markets, credit, and outside information were readily available helped to determine a farm's orientation toward production for community

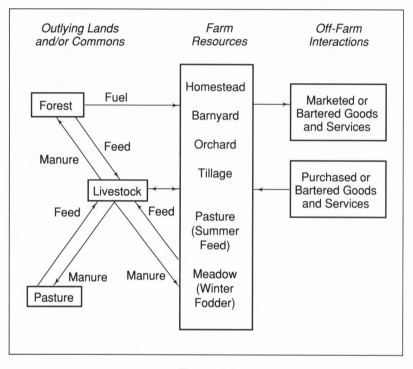

Figure 5.1

Agricultural Ecology of a New England Farm. Nutrients and energy (food and fuel) are transferred within a farm's boundaries among woodlots, pastures, meadows, tilled fields, orchards, barnyards, and homesteads. Purchased goods are brought in from outside, while farm and home products may be used by the family, marketed, or bartered.

Source: Adapted from Richard C. Harwood, *Small Farm Development* (Boulder, Colo.: Westview Press, 1979), p. 18.

subsistence or for commercial markets. A family's needs, goals, and values might tip the balance if choices were available.

Climate, soil, and plant and animal species set the ecological context. In crop-animal agriculture, soil is integral to the cycling of nutrients. The nutrient cycles are geared to the hydrologic (water circulation) cycle; the atmospheric cycles of carbon, oxygen, hydrogen, and nitrogen; and the cycling of minerals through the soil. Like all farms, New England farm soils needed nitrogen (N), phosphorus (P), potassium (K), calcium (Ca), and magnesium (Mg). Nitrogen is cycled through animal manure and legumes (green manure). Phosphorus is supplied by bones, fish, and poultry and bird manure (guano). Potassium comes from the ashes of burned vegetation (potash) and animal manure. (These three elements are the NPK of commercial fertilizers.) Calcium and magnesium are essential to counteracting the acid soils of the humid eastern states (western arid soils tend to be alkaline) and are especially important in New England. Farmers add calcium by spreading lime, marl, or gypsum (plaster of Paris) on their fields, magnesium by adding dolomitic limestone (see Table 4.1).[7]

Most soils in southeastern New England are brown forest soils—podzols and brown podzols (see Map 2.1)—that have a mat of organic material (or humus) on the surface and a thin, leached mineral layer just below it. When used for farming, the humus from decaying vegetation is quickly depleted. Because of high rainfall (forty to forty-five inches), the necessary salts of the neutralizing bases of calcium, magnesium, potassium, and sodium are easily leached out, leaving the soil quite acid. In the eastern coniferous areas and the western highlands are found the even more intensely leached, more acidic true podzols. In these cattle and dairying areas, adding lime is particularly important to maintaining the fertility of pastures and meadows. The soil of the coastal plain is light, sandy, and poor in potassium and phosphorus. Here fish fertilizers are especially needed.[8]

Before human settlement, the strong leaching of the mineral portion of the soil was counteracted by the buildup of humus, the real source of soil fertility. Humus is the organic layer of decomposed plants and animals at the soil's surface, whose particles mix with the minerals and plant roots. The leaves and fibrous roots of trees and plants decompose and are incorporated into the soil by insects, worms, and microbes to be taken up by plant roots before being washed away. With the introduction of agriculture by Indians and colonists, fertility was diminished since farm crops did not supply as much organic matter as forest plants. When humus is reduced and soils are also plowed, clods and crusts begin to form.

Farmers in the inland areas of New England used an "extensive system" of land use that synthesized native American and European methods of agriculture. It consisted of (1) a long-fallow system of clearing woodlands using the Indian method of girdling trees or cutting and burning; (2) adoption of Indian corn, bean, and squash polycultures; (3) the medieval three-field crop rotation system; and (4) upland pasturing. These were successful elements of subsistence agriculture until the late eighteenth century.

Subsistence-oriented farming practices may not have wasted the soils as much as historians have previously assumed. A "girdle and burn" long-fallow system of land clearing and crop production was practiced by Indians and pioneer farmers in new lands that allowed soils to recover their nutrients over periods of eight, twelve, or twenty years. The ashes provided by the burn, if all were not removed for potash, supplied potassium which helped to neutralize the acidity of forest soils, providing adequate fertilizer in the first year, while brush burning accomplished the same in the second year. Buried fish, where available, supplied phosphorus and was a good fertilizer in subsequent years.[9]

The small amounts of potassium and phosphorus in the manure of the colonists' livestock as they grazed in pastures, orchards, and harvested fields were easily leached out, but manure was important in adding nitrogen. More manure was supplied when carted to the fields or spread during communal dung frolics, but labor for this was scarce. Peas and beans planted in tilled plots were also good nitrogen restorers. Nitrogen depletion would have been delayed, but not entirely prevented, had colonists regularly planted clover on fallow fields.[10]

It is now known that minimal tillage and light plows conserve moisture, reduce soil compaction, and are less erosive than deep plowing. A family did not require large soil-depleting cash crops to reproduce its subsistence. Few were able to hire the wage labor necessary to produce marketable surpluses.[11]

This "extensive system" of land use changed to an "intensive system" of market-oriented management during New England's capitalist ecological revolution. But it was not the "wasteful" practices of colonial farmers that initiated this revolution. Patriarchal land inheritance reduced farm sizes so that all sons could not inherit the farms that reproduced the extensive system. In the 1790s, unusual European meat and grain needs stimulated commercial production. Ecology, production, and reproduction interacted to bring about the transformation. How did the elements of the extensive system operate together ecologically and what was the dynamic that led to its collapse?

Woodlots

Settlers in the inland-upland regions used the forest in conjunction with agriculture and animal husbandry (Figure 5.2). This traditional combination of spatial and sequential uses of the same piece of forest land for both crops and grazing is today being reevaluated in light of the emerging science of agroforestry. As opposed to modern agriculture and forestry which separate tree crops from food crops, agroforestry views trees as an integral part of agricultural ecology. Complementary relationships exist between the protective and productive aspects of trees and the use of space, soil, water, and light in conjunction with crops and animals. Agroforestry is especially significant for small farm families in which labor is scarce and in hilly or marginal areas like those of inland and upland New England. Such systems made efficient use of both human labor and natural resources.[12]

The first element of the extensive system of agriculture was a long-fallow method of land clearing. In areas beyond ready access to markets, where agriculture was oriented toward subsistence, the clearing of woodlots proceeded more slowly than along the coasts and northern logging rivers. For example, settlers who in 1733 went to Petersham, Massachusetts (officially founded in 1754), about twenty-five miles northwest of Worcester and about thirty-five miles east of the Connecticut River (above the fall line), lived primarily by subsistence farming for some sixty years before improvements in its few winding, hilly wagon roads began to make market journeys practicable. Here cash was always in limited supply, and the first bank was not established until 1854. But Petersham, a town that doubled its inhabitants from 707 in 1765 to 1,560 in 1790 (see Appendixes C-1 and C-2), had cleared only about 10 percent of its forest by 1771 and only 15 percent by 1791. A 1771 sample of fifteen similar inland Massachusetts towns, founded between 1684 and 1765, shows between 2.6 and 30.0 percent of their forested lands "improved" for farming (see Appendix C-3).[13]

How much wood was required for household subsistence each year? Eighteenth-century accounts show that the average household burned about thirty cords (piles of logs 4 feet by 4 feet by 8 feet) a year for cooking and heating and that an acre of forest yielded about twenty-five cords. An acre or two a year would thus result in sufficient annual fuel. After the farm became established, a reserve of forty acres would ensure a continual supply of wood.[14]

In 1771, a 100-acre farm in Petersham had 70 to 80 percent of its

Figure 5.2

A Primeval Forest of Central New England, Petersham, Massachusetts, 1700.
The central New England mixed forest consisted predominantly of the conifers, white pine and hemlock, and the deciduous species, red and white oak,
white ash, red maple, American chestnut, and hickory.
Source: From the Harvard Forest Models. Photograph by M. H. Zimmerman.
Reproduced courtesy of the Fischer Museum of Forestry, Harvard Forest, Harvard University.

acreage in woodland and pasture, the two often being synonymous
because pigs and cows grazed in the woods. Only 3 or 4 acres at any
one time were used for crops and fallow (see Appendix C-4). Although some woods were cleared specifically for pasture, as much as
85 percent of Petersham land was never even plowed. After two or
three years of planting, depleted fields were given over to pasture, to
lie fallow for seven to fifteen years, fertilized by animal droppings and
reverting to woods (Figure 5.3). On fallow pastures ecological succession to woods began. As New Hampshire historian Jeremy Belknap
noted in 1812, "when seeding with grass is neglected, the ground
becomes mossy and hard.... Besides, this neglected land is generally overspread with cherry-trees, raspberry bushes, and other wild
growth." This long-fallow system of agriculture was ecologically similar to Indian subsistence (although differing fundamentally in its dependence on livestock and settled agriculture, and in its concept of
private property).[15]

Because the fields were relatively small and because trees slowly

Figure 5.3

An Early Settler Clears a Homestead, Petersham, Massachusetts, 1740. Settlers in inland-upland New England cleared about three to five acres at a time and allowed cattle and pigs to graze in the woods. After two or three years, the land was seeded or abandoned to pasture and a new tillage plot was cleared. *Source*: From the Harvard Forest Models. Photograph by M. H. Zimmerman. Reproduced courtesy of the Fischer Museum of Forestry, Harvard Forest, Harvard University.

returned on fields abandoned for pasture, these inland farms exemplified many of the advantages of traditional agroforestry. Leaf litter and dung helped to restore soils depleted by crops. The surrounding forests and fields harbored birds and the natural enemies of insect pests on crops in the tilled areas. The deep root systems of trees in the pasture-woodlands reached into minerals in the parent rocks, retrieving nutrients leached from the topsoil and recycled them in the form of leaf litter. When this organic matter was added to the soil humus, its nitrogen, phosphorus, and sulfur helped to moderate the tendency toward acid soils. The surrounding trees also helped to break winds and protected the soil from the impact of raindrops. And because of their large canopies and deep root systems, trees created humid microclimates while moderating temperature ranges.[16]

Eighteenth-century settlers used two labor-efficient technologies to clear enough of the "almost universal forest" for initial farming—fire and ax. Their method was either girdling or cutting and burning. Both had survival value in that they employed the least labor to obtain the highest possible yields. Grubbing up trees by the roots expended more time and energy than could be afforded and was used only when root-free land was needed for houses, orchards, or roads. Because New Englanders introduced settled agriculture dependent on livestock and European grains (wheat, rye, oats, and barley), colonial farmers had different land-clearing requirements than did the Indian system of shifting agriculture. Nevertheless, Benjamin Vaughan, who settled in Maine in 1796, advised colonists to learn clearing methods from the Indians. "The presence of a few native Americans ... with their tools, should be obtained; and from such persons ... their art of felling and burning woods ... may be learned with advantage." Each method of clearing, however, had its own labor and ecological rationale.[17]

The native American method of girdling took the least effort, but had some undesirable effects. During the summer, farmers stripped a cylinder of bark from each tree and left it to die standing. In August, they sowed the ground below with winter rye for harvest the following spring. In the eighteenth century, New Englanders adopted the Indian method of planting corn among the girdled trees the first year. In the second year, the trees did not produce leaves, allowing the land to be used as pasture. But the danger to cattle from falling trees and the difficulty of subsequent plowing among the strewn trunks were disadvantages for colonial farmers, as opposed to Indians who lacked livestock and used hoes rather than plows.[18]

Therefore, the second method of cutting followed by burning was preferred although it required more human labor. Tall men with long arms could clear up to an acre in one day, but for most farmers one-third of an acre was a good day's work. Prepared with strategically placed cuts, several trees in a row stood ready to fall like dominoes when the head tree crashed against them, creating a "drive."

As in traditional long-fallow agricultural systems that depend on clearing forest land, a good burn was essential to a good yield. Cutting up trunks and tops, so all the limbs would lie close to the ground, produced a more complete burn than when trees were simply left as they fell. In Maine and New Hampshire, trees were commonly cut in June when the leaves had grown but would remain dead on the branches, helping to spread the fire the following spring. July was too late for cutting, as too many stump shoots would appear the next year, while waiting until winter, when free time increased, shortened the drying period too much.

Timing the burn, the following spring, was also essential to a good yield. An early fire, when the ground was too wet, produced an incomplete burn and a small yield. If the ground was too dry, the burn would be too deep, injuring the soil. When the day was clear and the winds were westerly, a fire near the edge of the cut area was set toward the wind. Then the windward side was lit in several places, burning until it reached the standing forest on the other side. If all but the trunks succumbed, the burn was a success; if not, the unburned branches and limbs were heaped together and burned again. Until then nothing was planted because any stump shoots, sumac, raspberries, and ferns that sprouted the second year on poorly cleared land would have to be cut by hand with a stump scythe, a time-consuming and arduous task. Crops could be sown as early as two days after the burn, but an intervening rain improved the soil. The field was ignited again the second year after the remaining trunks had been cut into logs and drawn into piles with oxen.[19]

The ashes from the burned land enriched the soil with potassium, improving yields even on fresh land. According to Vaughan, "the ashes where large piles of wood have been burned, are in general dispersed, as nothing grows on the ash-heaps; and this fertilizes the land. These ashes are commonly too dirty to sell readily to the makers of pot-ash, who find them apt to foul their kettles, which are of cast-iron."[20]

Burning was not indiscriminate, but controlled over small acreages. Since all the trees in the area to be burned would be converted to ashes, entire woodlots were left intact to provide lumber for farm buildings and firewood. Any timber sold on the market had to be removed in advance. Since uncontrolled fires were a hazard to settlements, most towns soon after settlement enacted legislation regulating burning. Setting fire to the woods was usually restricted to early spring and farmers had to warn their neighbors in advance. Fines were imposed on those who allowed fires on their own property to escape or who set fires on other people's land. Firing the woods on the commons was prohibited because it destroyed food for cattle.[21]

The stumps, cut at waist height to save labor and provide leverage to oxen when later uprooted, left ragged-looking fields that symbolized healthy success to colonists, but were disparaged by travelers sensitive to the beauty of the American landscape. Isaac Weld, who began his travels through the northern states in 1795, was appalled by this unsightly blemish on the picturesque countryside. "The stumps of the trees . . . on land newly cleared, are most disagreeable objects, wherewith the eye is continually assailed." Americans "have an unconquerable aversion to trees; and whenever a settlement is made, they cut away all before them without mercy; not one is spared; all share the same fate, and are involved in the same general havoc. . . . To them the sight of a wheat field or a cabbage garden would convey pleasure far greater than that of the most romantic woodland views."[22]

The cut-and-burn method of clearing sometimes kept farmers out of the timber market. Vaughan chastised farmers for their lack of market consciousness. "The fault does not lie with the system of the Kennebecker, but in his manner of applying it. He would be justified in clearing some of his land in the manner described, but he clears *too much of it at a time*. . . . Did he clear less land, and use the practice of manuring, with other agricultural aids; his timber left on the residue would soon become important even to himself, for fuel, fences, and buildings, and often would it serve him as an object of sale." The family and next generations would all benefit by waiting for the market to overtake them, for wood in the neighborhood of established towns was already as scarce as in many parts of Europe. "These however, are not principles easily relished by Americans."[23]

In the 1790s, when the construction of turnpikes and canals began to give inland-upland villages greater access to markets, forest clearing in inland areas like Petersham accelerated. By 1830, 77 percent of its woodlands had been cleared for the agricultural and lumber markets; by 1850, 90 percent. With markets for crops at hand, yields could be increased by putting more land into production and shortening fallow. Larger, more substantial farmhouses dotted the landscape, none more than a quarter of a mile from a road. Population, however, increased only from 1,560 individuals in 1790 to a peak of 1,775 in 1840 (see Appendixes C-1 and C-2). More woodland was cleared under the stimulus of profit and trade than under subsistence production.[24]

Towns with access to urban centers such as Concord, Massachusetts, about eighteen miles northwest of Boston in Middlesex County, experienced faster depletion of woodlands. In the valuations of 1786 and 1801, the proportion of woodland in the town was constant at 28 percent. But as farmers supplied more wood for expanding Boston, woodlands decreased in each decade thereafter, the total being reduced to 11 percent by 1850 (see Appendix D-1). Between 1749 and

1850 the number of farms remained nearly constant at about 200 with an average of 60 acres each. At 30 cords of wood per household, the town would have needed 6,000 cords of wood or 240 acres (each supplying 25 cords) per year. Concord's 3,600 acres of woods were adequate in 1801. By 1850 there were an additional fifty houses, but improvements in stoves and fireplaces and the use of anthracite coal had reduced the number of cords required by each household to 12–14 or 3,500 cords from 140 acres per year for the town. By then, however, the woodlands had been reduced from 3,600 to 1,500 acres. Any excess wood had probably been carted to Boston where in 1840 a cord sold for six dollars (as opposed to four dollars in Concord).[25]

But woodlands and their conversion to pasture and tillage were only one component of the pattern of nutrient transfers in the agro-ecology of New England farms. Subsistence production integrated long-fallow, cut-and-burn methods with polycultures, three-field rotations, and upland pasturing in an ecological whole.

Subsistence Production

Whereas Indians had shifted communal agricultural sites and obtained their protein from hunting, New England colonists brought with them the Old World system of production based on medieval three-field crop rotations and protein-producing livestock. Colonists were granted free land on the condition that they "improve" it with agriculture and artifact within a certain period such as three to five years. As John Locke put it in 1690, "As much land as a man tills, plants, improves, cultivates, and can use the product of, so much is his property. He by his labor does, as it were, enclose it from the common."[26]

Seventeenth-century farms granted to a town's founding proprietors were typically 200–300 acres, but in subsequent land divisions newcomers might receive only 20 or 30 acres. The division of farms among a proprietor's sons further reduced the holdings of the third and fourth generations. In the early commons system, each farmer cultivated his own plot with crops of his own choice, but livestock were fenced out and tended by town herders. Along the coast and river valleys, where settlers appropriated Indian old fields, 8–12 acres were planted in crops, allowing surpluses to be exported. Alewives, codfish heads from fishing harbors, and seaweed buried in the corn hills or spread on the fields helped to enrich the earth and increase yields. In the inland towns 3–5 acres in tillage were more typical. Cattle, grazing in fields and orchards, supplied most of the manure that replenished the soil.[27]

The second element in the settlers' subsistence system involved the planting of polycultures. Until the European tetrad of wheat, rye, barley, and oats was successfully established, colonists were dependent on the Indians' corn, bean, and squash complex. But in appropriating this form of agriculture, they substituted the ox and plow for the hoe and the male for the female in the field. Rather than planting corn on old hills with stone hoes and corn planters, as had the Indian women, they reduced the labor requirements by plowing, laying out furrows six feet apart to form squares, and planting the corn seed at the intersections. Plows were scarce in new villages but many neighbors shared them, while those without used hoes. Like Indians, colonists planted corn in April after the leaves of the white oak had formed and planted vegetables between the rows. According to John Winthrop, Indians and English both "will plant a kind of beans with the corn ... and in the vacant places and between the hills, they will plant squashes and pumpkins, loading the ground with as much as it will bear; the stalks of the corn serving instead of poles for the beans to climb up. ... Many English also after the last weeding their ground sprinkle turnip-seed between the hills, so have after harvest a good crop of turnips in the same field."[28]

Settlers also appropriated the Indian timetable for weeding in May, when the weeds had grown higher than the new corn shoots, but used the plow to clear weeds from between the rows. Dead weeds left to decay on the ground supplied humus to the soil as they were broken down by bacteria and fungi. Almanacs such as the *New England Almanack* for May 1702 instructed, "Now mind weeding your Indian Corn." Soon the corn was high enough to help smother new weeds. In early July, the settlers cleared the remaining weeds and built up hills around the cornstalks as instructed by the almanac:

> The toilsome labouring working swain
> Now with his hoe doth take great pain
> To finish hilling Indian Grain.

Horace Greeley (b. 1811) reported that as a boy in Vermont his task was "to precede my father as he hoed his corn, dig open the hills, and kill the wire-worms and grubs that were anticipating our dubious harvest." The corn harvest took place in September or October depending on the weather, and ears were husked, threshed, and stored, or sent to the mill to be ground into meal. The stalks left in the field served as fodder for cattle and swine who were let into the tilled fields, their dung manuring the ground.[29]

The same ecological advantages that enhanced the corn, bean, and squash harvest of the New England Indians aided the farmer's subsistence. These included higher yields from polycultures of mixed crops than from monocultures, genetic adaptations of the three crops to each other, nitrogen fixation from beans, the addition of humus from two weedings per season, insect control by microclimates created through companion planting, and the harboring of insect-eating birds and insect enemies on field borders (see Chapter 3).

The third element in the agroecological system was crop rotation. Along with European grains, colonial farmers introduced the three-field rotation system of the Middle Ages, a subsistence system that had successfully sustained life for centuries until markets and population increases encouraged more intensive methods of cropping. In New England, the three fields were planted in a sequence that started in the first field with corn in the first year, rye the second, and weed fallow the third year to recover fertility. This combination produced the common staple bread, made from Indian corn and European rye. The second field often contained oats for fodder or barley for beer, instead of rye, with spring wheat being a primary crop after 1640. Wheat blast (black stem rust), after its advent in about 1660, made the wheat crop problematical, however, for the next two centuries. By the early eighteenth century, its host, the barberry bush, had been recognized; although legislation was passed for its removal, compelling neighbors to do so was difficult. The third field was sometimes sown with buckwheat which cleaned it of weeds and provided flowers for honey bees. Other crops included peas, which, like beans, were a nitrogen-restoring legume, and were used in the staple meals pease porridge and pork and peas; flax for linen; and tobacco for home use.[30]

The fourth element was the pasturing of livestock. The introduced livestock complex consisted of oxen (neat cattle) and horses for draft; cows and goats for milk, butter, and cheese; sheep for mutton and wool; and pigs and beef cattle for salt meat stores. But raising them on American grasses—wild rye (*Elymus* sp.) and broom straw (*Andropogon* sp.)—proved difficult, owing to the large ratio of bulk to food value. Carex, the native meadow grass, provided good hay until live-stock herds increased too much. Consequently, English hay—blue-grass and white clover introduced in the seventeenth century, and red clover and timothy (Herd's grass) in the eighteenth—was seeded in upland pastures. After 1750 English hay was planted more widely, helping to restore soil nutrients. Cornstalks and husks, along with wheat and rye straw, supplied additional fodder during the winter. In late summer pigs and beef cattle were fattened on grain for slaughter.[31]

During the seventeenth century herds ranged on common pas-tures—woods, uncleared hills, and uplands—with milk cows, horses, and oxen on the nearer fields and pigs and dry cows on those more remote. Elaborate rules governed the opening of the commons to livestock after the fall harvest. Each farmer who had tilled the area had a certain number of "cow rights" or equivalents in goats, horses, and oxen. During the eighteenth century, however, pastures began to come into private ownership.[32]

Between 1750 and 1790, upland villages devoted to grazing were founded in central and western New England on hillsides too steep or stony for tillage. Either immediately after the removal of the forest cover, or after one or two years of planting corn or rye among girdled trees, lands were seeded with English grasses and turned to pasture. Drovers gathered up cattle and pigs from local farms and herded them to market towns on hoof. Because the grass was seeded before the soil was exhausted, its natural fertility was retained far longer than in crop-producing areas. The English grasses were efficient conservers, extending the soil's natural fertility in these areas until well into the nineteenth century.

After 1790, pasture expansion resulted primarily from converted worn-out croplands in older market settlements. In the Connecticut Valley and coastal areas such pastures were used principally to raise livestock for manure in order to fertilize grainfields. These pastures showed more rapid deterioration than upland pastures because the lack of manure gradually depleted the soil. Livestock then had to be reduced, in turn lowering crop yields.[33]

In the life cycle of a piece of soil under the four elements of the extensive system, several uses might follow in succession. "Unim-proved" woodland would be cut for fuel and placed in tillage. For a few years the "fresh" acreage would produce crops, be rotated through fallow, and perhaps be manured as yields began to fall. Soil, "worn out" for tillage, could then be seeded to hay for a few more years until yields fell below about half a ton per acre, when it might be abandoned to pasture. As pasture in turn wore down, the plot would begin to "keep" fewer and fewer animals. Brush and woods would begin to creep in, and the land would revert back to the category "unimproved" or "unimprovable."

Gender and Production

Like Indian subsistence, colonial agriculture depended on the division of labor by gender. Women and men each had separate tasks and separate genderized production spaces. Male and female were equals in subsistence production, each sex being essential to the family's economic survival. The reproduction of social roles took place in these separate spaces. Girls participated in their mothers' space-time zones, boys in those of their fathers.

Men's space extended outward from the barn and had a wider circumference than women's. Heavy square-timbered beams with notched ends, laid out in squares and raised by practiced neighbors who knew the rules, produced the farmer's first barn, center of his world and symbol of his husbandhood. Wood house, smokehouse, corncrib, wagon shed, and springhouse followed, intersecting with women's domain and circumscribing the farmyard. The field layout reflected walking time, with crops nearby, meadows and hayfields beyond, and woodlots and uplands on the periphery. From the farmstead's eye, radii of varying lengths led down dusty roads to the nearby village and the distant town.[34]

Women's domain radiated outward from the farmhouse kitchen. Farmhouses were divided into sleeping rooms, parlor, and kitchen, all expandable as the family grew larger, with a root cellar below. Kitchens could be enlarged by adding ells or sheds with lean-to roofs. Just outside the kitchen door was the essential herb garden and beyond it, as time and labor allowed, the vegetable garden. Outbuildings provided space for butter, cheese making, poultry, and privy; at the orchard's edge, overlapping men's space, trees offered their branches for clothes drying. Beyond lay a friendly neighbor's kitchen, the village store, and the meetinghouse.[35] A flowery adage in the *New England Farmer* described the farmwife and husband's organic interdependence:

Man is the rugged lofty pine,
That frowns on many a wave-beat shore;
Woman's the slender graceful vine,
Whose curling tendrils round it twine,
And deck its rough bark sweetly o'er.[36]

But although women and men were equal partners in production, colonial relations of reproduction were patriarchal. Lineage and property rights that reproduced family power passed through the male. Almanacs repeated the Bible's anatomical justification for woman's productive and reproductive roles in patriarchal society. Eve was made of a rib from Adam's side, not from his head to be his superior, nor from his feet to trample on her, "but out of his side, to be equal with him; under his arm, to be protected; and near his heart to be beloved." Man was the head of creation and, although man was made of refined dust, woman was of double-refined dust, one step farther from the earth than he. Although a partner in subsistence, under colonial patriarchy a good wife must be submissive, humble, modest, silent, and revere her husband.[37]

Woman's role in production and reproduction was far harsher than the almanacs' homilies revealed, and woman's labor was intensely demanding. From tending and slaughtering chickens, cutting and cooking meat, carrying wood, milking cows and goats, to making cheese, butter, candles, and bread, growing and weeding vegetables, spinning and carding wool, often while pregnant or tending young children, she worked hard even into old age, when the farm and its management may have passed entirely into her hands. Like her husband, she engaged in trade and transactions with neighbors and townspeople (both male and female), kept notes (sometimes on the kitchen wall), and sometimes recorded her work life in her diary.[38]

Widowed women and spinsters who inherited farms managed them with the help of hired hands and might assume tasks traditionally assigned to men. At age forty-one, Samantha Barrett, her older sister, their mother Zeloda, and their eighty-one-year-old grandmother, Susanna, ran a farm in New Hartford, Connecticut. In her diary for 1828, she entered various activities: "Abijah plowed our garden." "Loda planted peas and beans." "Sold Mr. Munson one of our calves for three dollars." "Rode to the carding machine." "I began to cross plow." "Cooked a woodchuck." "Loda and myself rode to Canton—sold my flannel for two and nine pence per yard—sold thirteen pair of socks, one and nine pence per pair." "Read about the Greeks." Anna Howell, who inherited a farm and fisheries from her husband at the age of fifty, recorded in her almanac diaries tasks she herself either carried out or managed: "I killed my red cow some time this month." "I killed 11 hogs." "Began to mow the upper meadow." "This day finished threshing my rye of last year. 27 bushels."[39]

Women's traditional production activities interacted directly with the environment and included care of the herb and vegetable gardens, dairying and cheese making, and poultry raising. They planted herb and vegetable gardens just outside the kitchen door with medicinal herbs that treated ailments and acted as purgatives and with culinary herbs that added flavor to routine daily meals: tansy, peppermint, spearmint, wormwood, rue, spikenard, lovage, elecampane, pennyroyal, boneset, thyme, and sage. They weeded and manured the soil, while their free-ranging poultry kept down insect pests and added dung. During the summer as the herbs came into bloom, they gathered them into bundles to be hung in the kitchen or attic to dry. Women also planted vegetables for "green sauce" to add to stews and later as side dishes for the main meal. From the seventeenth century on gardens included roots such as turnips, parsnips, carrots, onions, garlic, leeks, and radishes, and greens such as cabbage, spinach, lettuce, and collards. Used in season during spring and summer, by the mid-eighteenth century they were increasingly stored in root cellars for winter use. Potatoes, introduced to New Englanders by Scotch-Irish immigrants in the 1720s, were added to gardens and field crops by mid-century.[40]

Cheese and butter making were also important contributions to family subsistence and added protein in the diet. The techniques had been handed down from woman to woman since ancient times. Nineteenth-century farm journals codified ancient lore and recommended improvements. The prime cheese season was May to September. About a gallon of milk was needed to produce a pound of cheese for the family each week, two for a pound of butter. The thin cows of the period produced two to four gallons of milk a week. Almost all rural families had at least one milk cow for milk and cheese, with additional cows adding butter to the diet. Those without dairy equipment probably shared or traded products with neighbors. To produce cheese, women used rennet produced from the cleaned, salted, and dried stomach bags, or maws, of milk cows. After the maw had been steeped in brine for twenty-four hours, a teacupful would turn the milk of ten cows into cheese. Sufficient salt was important or the rennet would become rancid and the cheese rank. The milk was warmed and curdled on the fire, the curds broken, shaped into cheese, and pressed in the cheese press. They were then placed on cheese ladders to be rubbed and turned until ready for consumption.[41]

Sarah Anna Emery, who grew up in Newburyport, Massachusetts, in the 1790s, recalled, as a nonagenarian, making cheese with her mother and grandmother. "During breakfast the milk for the cheese was warming over the fire, in the large brass kettle. The milk being from the ten cows, my mother made cheese four days, Aunt Sarah having the milk the remainder of the week. In this way good-sized cheeses were obtained. The curd having been broken into the basket, the dishes were washed, and unless there was washing or other extra work, the house was righted. By the time this was done the curd was ready for the press. ... After dinner the cheeses were turned and rubbed; then mother put me on a clean frock, and dressed herself for the afternoon."[42]

Butter making required great care and cleanliness. According to the *New England Farmer*, for best quality, the dairy house was to be as close to the springhouse or icehouse as possible since carrying the milk agitated it too much. The tin pails had to be scalded and then sun or fire dried. The cows were to be milked at night, the last drawn milk being the richest and creamiest. It was kept cool overnight to prevent souring and the morning milk added. The cream was then skimmed off, the first to rise being of the highest quality. When the mixture began to change, it was ready to churn. In the cooler months the change might not begin until the next day and warm water might be necessary to bring it to the proper churning temperature. After the butter was "well come," the buttermilk was released through a plug in the bottom of the churn, cold water was poured in, and the milk was separated out by additional churning. With a wooden ladle, the woman lifted out the butter and worked it with salt three times at one-hour intervals until it was ready to be molded in stone pots or oak kegs.[43]

Farm women also raised bees for their honey. Anna Howell recorded the dates when her bees swarmed in May and June, and copied into her diary Crèvecoeur's advice on recovering bees that had strayed into the woods. She exuded warmth and sympathy for her bees: "I took a bee hive today that I think swarmed in June. The hive was in two boxes. They had filled them both completely. The upper with delicious honey the lower one with comb principally. I robbed the poor little things of their honey, and returned them the box with the empty comb. Its a common place to destroy them with fire and brimstone. They say that if you take their honey, they will starve. I will give mine a chance ... and feel in hopes they will make provisions enough for the winter. If they do not I will assist them." But she began her new diary for 1825 with the note, "My poor bees that were deprived of their honey died for want of food." Her other bees met an even sadder fate. In September, their entire summer work was destroyed by miller moth larvae. "I never saw them before nor had an idea that they could have caused such total ruin," she lamented.[44]

By the early nineteenth century, almanac articles and farm journals aided farm women in keeping up with developments through special columns on "domestic economy." To female readers of the *New England Farmer*, Cousin Tabatha and Aunt Betty offered advice on the care of young chickens and turkeys to prevent the "gapes." The chicks would eagerly devour a mixture of two cut-up hard-boiled eggs, mustard, ground pepper, and a little Indian meal. Mustard planting could be timed so it would be young and tender when the chicks hatched. By following their advice, they claimed, a woman could raise eighty to one hundred turkeys from eight females and one male.[45]

The *New England Farmer* also offered women advice on food preservation. After harvest, apples could be kept sweet and juicy, even into July, by placing them in glazed jars with pebbles on the bottom to draw out the dampness and a wood slab covered with mortar on the top to absorb the air. Grapes could be preserved until winter if enclosed in white muslin or crepe bags tied with string (to keep out insects) and hung in a warm, dry room. Dipping eggs for a second or two in boiling water or oiling the shells would prevent spoilage; or they could be packed in lime water or wood ashes in a keg. Delicious pickled beets could be prepared with vinegar, horseradish, onions, ginger, mace, cloves, allspice, and salt.[46]

In its "Hints to Housekeepers" column, the journal advised "Mother Pug" to turn her cheeses every day and to keep her girls spinning and away from the mirror, lest the boys "shiver for want of clothes next fall." A mother should not degrade her boys' opinions, and they should not fish or hunt foxes after harvest for more than a day.[47]

When the *New England Farmer* published articles on cheese and butter making, it was helping to codify female empiricism and farm

lore into scientific dairy farming useful to male farmers. With nineteenth-century specialization, men began to take over women's traditional areas of dairying, poultry raising, and vegetable production.
The traditional dairy areas of western Massachusetts expanded as
more farmers took up dairy farming and poultry raising (see Chapter
7). Agricultural specialization and farm management became significant components of the capitalist ecological revolution.

Subsistence Economy

In addition to having intellectual roots in the traditions of Renaissance Europe, subsistence-oriented households were tied economi-
cally to the production of use values (objects used for subsistence)
as described by Aristotle. In elaborating the politics of householding
economies, Aristotle had distinguished between two uses of a shoe—
one for wear, the other for exchange. The first was its natural or
proper use—that for which the shoe was made. The second use, as an
exchange item for money, was not its "natural" use, for a shoe was not
made primarily for the sake of exchange.[48]

Twenty-three centuries later, writing about the politics of capitalist
economies, Karl Marx elaborated on Aristotle's distinction between
use value and exchange value. Things of nature such as air, soil, or
natural meadows could be of use to human beings when mixed with
human labor. "Whoever directly satisfies his wants with the produce
of his own labor creates indeed use values, but not commodities." A
thing became a commodity when it was not needed for immediate
use and was instead brought to the market for exchange.[49]

Almanacs not only embodied the shared belief system of the subsistence farmer, but, when used as diaries, they became a record of the
use value economy within which most farmers operated. No household produced all its own food, clothing, and fuel or supplied all its
own labor. The New England village was not a sum of self-sufficient
families, but a cooperative community in which food, labor, tools, and
services were exchanged through the recording medium of the account book.

Farmers kept records, often in interleaved almanacs, of the time
they spent working for their neighbors, the amount and value of
home produce and food exchanged, and the value of books, shoes,

linen, or wool obtained from neighbors who practiced a craft. Money, especially in pounds sterling or specie, changed hands far less frequently than the money values recorded in account books seemed to indicate. Almanac diaries were used to record credits and debits pertaining to labor time and crop values often over long periods of time and when no money may actually have changed hands. As Marx said of such an economy, "Instinctively they conform to the laws imposed by the nature of commodities. They cannot bring their commodities into relation as values and therefore as commodities except by comparing them with ... [a] universal equivalent." This equivalent was money value.[50]

An anonymous New England farmer used an interleaved Ames' almanac for 1746 as an account book. He bartered labor, food, and goods and recorded them all in money values. In January, he obtained flax from Henry Plimpton at values of 15, 23, and 30 shillings, and from Jedediah Morse for 2½ shillings and recorded the amount for combing the flax at 3 pounds, 5 shillings, and 9 pence. On Ephraim Cheney's account, he recorded Indian corn at 6 shillings per bushel totaling 3 pounds, 6 shillings; rye at 2 shillings, 4 pence; oats at 1 pound, 8 shillings; digging stones at 8 shillings; a half basket of huckleberries at 13 shillings, 4 pence; and spinning at 28 shillings, 6 pence. He paid to John Allen 4 Spanish dollars for a shingle and a side of sole leather, and borrowed 46½ shillings from Thomas Baxter.[51]

Joseph Andrews, a farmer in Scituate, Massachusetts, kept line-a-day diaries between 1752 and 1787, recording the weather and planting dates, as well as work done for others, such as carting rock for his uncle and Gideon Smith's help in planting corn.[52]

A Wakefield, New Hampshire, farmer, Mr. Clark, kept records between 1817 and 1829 in interleaved *Farmer's Almanacs*, recording the weather, planting dates, and labor performed for neighbors. In early February 1817, he hauled logs for nine days for S. Went and in April for J. Brown and H. Cook. In April he also built a wall for William Allen, and dug and hauled rocks for Samuel Fellow; at the end of the month John Clark helped him break ground in the upper field. In June he plowed for Spence Wentworth.[53]

Family members, relatives, and neighbors helped each other physically, emotionally, and intellectually. Estate inventories show that families were not self-sufficient, but differed in the range of tools and utensils they owned. Women regularly borrowed iron pots, tin basins, eggs, and sugar from their neighbors. Some did not return the borrowed equipment; others resorted to stealing, but most women knew that they might soon need a return favor.[54]

Sometimes neighborliness could become oppressive, as a spoof by Barbara Catnip on Hester Peepinthedrawer and her children revealed. Barbara, a young unmarried woman of modest means, purchased a small house in a "good neighborhood." No sooner had she moved in than a stream of neighborhood children poured through asking on behalf of their mother to "borrow" two dozen eggs, a wash basin, towel, ax, tub, thread box, clothesline, lace cap, and "cinnamon-colored calash to make calls in." Her patience exhausted, Barbara advertised her house for auction the following Monday.[55]

Men also used almanac diaries, account books, and daybooks to record trips made to markets in nearby and distant towns, transportation costs, and prices received for goods. Massachusetts farmers made market journeys ranging from 5 to 20 miles for trips to country stores. Occasionally long trips up to 175 miles were taken to cities, to visit relatives, or to establish new land claims, products for sale or barter being included. The 20-mile journey was the most frequent, with trips over 25 miles made far less often. Farmers used oxcarts, wagons, sleds, and sleighs drawn by oxen or horses. Despite the greater ease of travel in the winter, Massachusetts farmers made fewer market trips on the average during the snowy months than during the remainder of the year. Most trips were made at harvest time in the fall, with the lowest number in December and January.[56]

This network of face-to-face obligations and exchanges was essential to family survival. Despite the fact that every town reflected a spectrum of wealth differences with a few gentlemen farmers who traded on the market at the top, the focus of the lives of most eighteenth-century New Englanders was the local community. Here the family produced its subsistence over time and traded its surpluses with neighbors, local storekeepers, or urban markets. Production and exchange represented the human side of local ecology. Soil exhaustion, nutrient cycling, and forest succession were manifestations of nature's side of the interaction. Human activity and nature's activity existed in dynamic reciprocity with each other. At a structural level once removed from this immediate interaction of production with the environment, and exerting pressure on the system of production, were the relations of human reproduction. In the subsistence system, production was oriented toward reproduction.

Reproduction

Reproduction in its broadest definition is the key to the history of life. Each generation must biologically reproduce a new generation and in addition maintain its own life by interacting with the natural environment. The active adults must produce enough food on a daily basis to sustain the lives of their children, the future producers, and their elders, the past producers. In Euro-American history these goals were accomplished by (1) the biological reproduction of individuals, (2) the daily reproduction of the energy of these individuals, (3) the social reproduction that transmitted the gender roles that maintained each interdependent community over time, and (4) the legal and political reproduction that transmitted property within and between generations and maintained the larger social order (see Figure 1.1).

The first aspect of reproduction was the generation of individuals. Because of the scarcity of labor in colonial America, the family supplied and had to biologically reproduce its own labor force. For population to increase, more children than adults must live until they, in turn, can reproduce the succeeding generation. Because the American soil was productive and nutrition good, people survived and population grew. In contrast to comparable rural English and French villages, which experienced zero population growth during the late seventeenth and early eighteenth centuries, colonial mortality rates were low. Because of the need for labor and the ready availability of land in America, marriage ages for women were lower (about twenty to twenty-one) than in comparable European rural villages (about twenty-eight to twenty-nine). Good soil and successful farming averted the subsistence crises induced by crop failures and famines that kept rural European populations stable. In general, New Englanders had an adequate diet, comfortable subsistence, and an expanding population throughout the colonial period. A system of partible inheritance oriented to providing land for the family's sons, combined with the lower death rate, subdivided and filled town boundaries with family farms.[57]

The second aspect of reproduction was the maintenance of food, clothing, and shelter over time. To maintain bodily energy for labor, subsistence had to be reproduced on a daily basis. Food grown on family farms, town house lots, and the commons was either consumed by the household or bartered with neighbors or the town storekeeper. In addition people fished in local lakes and streams, hunted, and gathered berries in nearby woods. In assessing the extent to which families were able to reproduce their own subsistence, the amount of food needed to sustain a typical three-generational household consisting of three adults (including a married couple and a grandparent or grown child) and two-to-five young children must be estimated.[58]

What were the basic requirements for daily subsistence? In colonial America they included protein from cattle, sheep, pigs, poultry and fowl, eggs, game, fish, and vegetables; dairy products from cows or goats; apples for cider and/or barley for beer; oxen or horses for plowing and hauling; pastures and woodlands for summer forage; meadows to provide hay for winter fodder; and wood for fuel. Because agriculture was based on a productive season followed by a nonproductive period during which the harvested grains and salted meats were consumed, supplements from the commons and the dairy were particularly important in spring and early summer.

No documents or inventories provide all the information necessary to determine the minimum requirements for family subsistence or whether families were able to meet them in various places and periods of New England's history. Typical farm sizes; grain, meat, vegetable, fruit, and dairy yields; and caloric and protein requirements are needed. Tax valuation lists, probate inventories, census data, yield surveys, and laws are some of the most useful sources for reconstructing the requirements of daily life. But because all are based on assumptions and are subject to interpretation, they are inconclusive even when taken as a whole.

A major problem with exclusive dependence on these documents is that their basis in property inheritance precludes information on food sources from the commons. Even when court and tax valuation records indicate that a town or region as a whole may not have produced enough farm products for subsistence, supplements from the commons may have tipped the balance except in urban areas. Such foods included saltwater and freshwater fish and shellfish, fowl (such as wild turkeys, quail, pigeons, ducks, and geese), game animals (such as rabbit, woodchuck, and deer), fruits and berries (such as strawberries, blueberries, blackberries, and cranberries), and maple sugar. In Boston, John Winthrop acknowledged the plenitude of fish and fowl as supplements to beef and mutton in the 1630s, and Samuel Sewell at the turn of the century reported eating salmon, pickerel, salted fish, venison, and wild fowl. In frontier communities, the fare included deer, bear, squirrels, rabbit, partridge, and fish. Horace Greeley, who was born in Vermont in 1811, believed that, down to 1800, people ate "many more pounds of fish than of beef and mutton together—perhaps of all meats save those obtained by the chase." Thoreau celebrated berry picking by women and children as an ancient connection to nature. "The very sides of the road are a fruit garden. The earth there teems with blackberries, huckleberries, thimbleberries, fresh and abundant.... Women and children ... are seen making haste thither ... with half their domestic utensils in their hands."[59]

Amelia Simmons's *First American Cookbook*, published in 1796 in Hartford, Connecticut, taught women how to cook fish and game in addition to domestic "dunghill fowl" and livestock. It contained saltwater fish recipes for salmon, shad, hanahills, blackfish, lobsters, oysters, flounder, bass, cod, haddock, and eels, while recipes for freshwater fish included trout, perch, and roach. The author discussed food preparation and cooking methods for wild fowl (turkeys, wild ducks, woodcocks, snipes, partridge, and pigeons), game (hare, leverets, and rabbit), and turtles. To some farmers there was "no better eating than a good fat woodchuck" stuffed and baked with herbs.[60]

Farm production, however, was the primary method of maintaining food stores. Estate inventories for Middlesex County, Massachusetts, for 1653–74 list the following farm foods: Indian corn, rye, wheat, salt pork, salted beef, salted fish, butter, cheese, peas, vegetables, malt, barley, hops, cider, beer, fruit, and condiments. Until the advent of wheat blast in the 1660s, Indian corn and wheat were the major bread grains; thereafter rye replaced wheat as a secondary grain. Barley for beer was the primary additional grain, but in the 1700s cider production from apple orchards increased, releasing additional tillage to bread grains and representing an intensification of land use. Most house lots had at least one cow for dairy products and a pig, with additional cattle and swine dependent on the amount of pasture available from uplands and commons. The primary vegetables were legumes: peas, the traditional English cold-weather staple from which pease porridge was made, and beans. After 1760, the cultivation of root crops—potatoes and turnips—represented a further intensification of land use.[61]

How much grain and livestock were needed per year for the subsistence of a typical household? Historians have calculated consumption needs from the quantities of farm produce allocated to a widow to sustain her remaining years (the widow's allotment or widow's thirds). In the estimation of household requirements from the widow's portion, women are assumed to consume two-thirds of the food of a man and children one-half. But reliance on the widow's allotment to determine family subsistence requirements has been questioned. If a "middle-class" widow baked a typical allotment of ten to twelve bushels of grain per year into bread, she would be consuming 2,300 calories a day in bread alone. Clearly some of her grain was meant for trading for other essentials, for feeding poultry, and for fattening swine.[62]

Another approach to determining the minimum requirements for subsistence comes from the law. In the early nineteenth century, states began passing laws that exempted certain quantities of food, livestock, and farm equipment from collection for the payment of debts. These exemptions from attachment allowed the debtor, his wife, and his children to retain the items necessary for sustaining life. Besides food and livestock, the exemptions included clothing, bedding, and household items; the stove; tools of trade; the arms and uniforms of militiamen; Bibles and schoolbooks; and the family pew and cemetery plot. From early nationhood to the present, the New England states passed, tested, and amended laws that were similar in content but adapted to the special conditions of livelihood in each state. The quantities that the law considered necessary for subsistence are an important clue to the reproduction of human life through farming.

The six New England states agreed on certain basic levels of subsistence: one cow (and sometimes a heifer under three years), one to two swine, six to ten sheep and the wool shorn from them, a pair of oxen or a horse for hauling, the hay necessary to sustain the livestock through one winter, all standing crops, about twenty to thirty bushels of corn and grain including the meal ground from them, and ten to twelve cords of firewood.

Quantities of these subsistence items were refined over time by each state. Maine allowed thirty bushels of corn and grain, Connecticut ten bushels of each plus the meal, Vermont five bushels of grain. Vermont law added twenty bushels of potatoes and all growing crops in 1840, but held to its five-bushel grain limit. In 1835 Connecticut allowed up to two hundred pounds of beef and pork, up to two hundred pounds of fish, five bushels each of potatoes and turnips, and ten bushels each of corn and rye; by 1849 it had added two hundred pounds of wheat flour and allowed an additional two hundred pounds of meat. Massachusetts allowed debtors to keep "provisions necessary, procured, and intended for the use of the family," but not those intended for sale. These included "corn, potatoes, and cabbages planted and raised by the debtor for the use of his family, and ripe for harvest though not yet severed from the soil." New Hampshire's limit in 1843 and 1854 was twenty dollars worth of provisions and fuel, while Rhode Island's provision included the pork of a pig and a hog when slaughtered and the wages due a debtor, his wife, and children up to specified amounts.

Winter fodder needed to maintain the livestock was also spelled out. Maine in 1840 exempted two tons of hay for ten sheep and thirty hundred (3,000 pounds) of hay for one cow. New Hampshire in 1843 exempted less total hay than Maine—one and one-half tons were specified for the cow—but it also had a lower limit of six sheep. Connecticut law in 1835 allowed a total of two tons of hay for ten sheep and a cow. Massachusetts specified two tons for a cow and six sheep; Rhode Island allowed one and one-half tons of hay for a cow and did not include sheep. Vermont law simply exempted, but did not specify, the forage necessary for keeping ten sheep and one cow through one winter.[63]

Using these quantities as rough guidelines to the minimum requirements for a family's subsistence, probate and tax valuation data can be used to estimate the minimum acreages of tillage, pasture, meadow, and woodland needed for a family farm. The results can then be compared with farm acreages actually available in a sample of inland-upland towns in 1771 in Massachusetts, casting light on the adequacy of subsistence production and whether marketable surpluses were produced.

How much grain did a family need for bread and for fattening its livestock before slaughter? The New England staple bread was a coarse dark bread with a heavy crust baked from rye and Indian (corn) meal. (Flour meal from wheat was not commonly used since wheat was not harvested in large quantities after the onset of black stem rust.) Lydia Child's *American Frugal Housewife*, written in 1827, stated: "Six quarts of meal will make two good sized loaves of *Brown Bread*. Some like to have it half Indian meal and half rye meal; others prefer it one third Indian, and two thirds rye." A "modern" loaf of "rye 'n' Injun" made with two pounds of meal divided equally between rye flour and cornmeal produces two 1.4-pound loaves of bread each containing about 1,600 calories, 52 grams of protein, and 328 grams of carbohydrates.[64]

A soldier's ration was 1 pound of bread a day. (A 1-pound loaf of the above rye 'n' Injun would supply 1,163 calories per day.) If this were an indication of the bread consumption of an adult male, then a family of five consisting of a man, wife, grown son, and two smaller children would require 1,338 pounds of bread a year. This converts to 28 bushels of grain a year for bread made of half cornmeal and half rye flour. These figures are consistent with Connecticut and Maine's debt exemption allowances of 20 and 30 bushels of corn and rye and with Ezra Stiles's observation in 1777 that the average New England family consumed 30 bushels of grain a year for the people and cattle.[65]

How many acres of tillage were required to produce these grain levels for bread and livestock? The acreage needed varied with yield. Tax valuation lists report total grain yields only and do not usually differentiate between corn and rye. The 1771 valuation list for Reading, Massachusetts (north of Boston), however, lists separate totals for a small sample of seventy-seven farms. Corn yields were 19.8 bushels per acre; rye yields, 12.2 bushels per acre. Total grain yields were about 18.4 bushels per acre on an average of 2.2 acres of tillage per farm. This would provide about 40 bushels of grain a year to feed the family, to fatten cattle and poultry, and to trade with neighbors. Two to 3 acres planted in grain would therefore be adequate with yields like those of Reading, whereas 5 acres or more would be needed if grain yields fell to 10 or fewer bushels per acre. If 1 or 2 acres of tillage were left in fallow, then 3 to 7 acres would be needed. A sample of fifteen inland Massachusetts towns on the tax valuation list of 1771 corroborated this finding, showing a range of 2.5 to 8.6 acres per farm in tillage (see Appendix C-4).[66]

How many acres of pasture would support the cattle, sheep, and horses needed for minimum subsistence? Tax assessors were required to ask farmers the number of cows their pasture would keep (an index of grass fertility) along with their yields of salt marsh hay, meadow hay, and upland and English mowing hay. The sample of fifteen inland farming towns shows a range of 1.2 to 3.4 acres of pasture needed to keep 1 cow (an adult cow, steer, or ox), with an average of 1.9 acres per cow (see Appendix C-5). For grazers other than cattle, 7 sheep or 0.75 horses are each equivalent to 1 cow. The livestock exempted in the debt laws—1 cow (or a steer and a calf), 10 sheep, and 2 oxen (or an ox and a horse)—would be 4.43 cow (or animal) units. If the pastures were fertile, 5.4 acres would be sufficient to keep the exempted livestock, while 15 acres would be needed if the pastures were worn out and close to abandonment. Since cattle often grazed in the woods, along roadsides, and on public lands, the necessary pasture size might be smaller, but young cattle, sheep, and horses (not counted in the tax valuations) would increase the requirements. Actual pasture sizes in the sample towns corroborated these requirements, ranging from 4.0 to 14.5 acres (see Appendix C-4).

How much meadow hay for winter fodder was required to support the animals exempted from debt? Meadow hay was harvested from salt marshes along the coast, whereas in inland towns it derived from river meadows, beaver meadows, and drained marshes. Upland pastures seeded with English hay supplemented the natural meadow hay. If, as specified by the debt laws, a cow required one and one-half tons of winter fodder, two oxen would need three tons and ten sheep two tons. The total winter fodder necessary to support the animals exempted by law would be six and one-half tons. Hay yields on the 1771 sample of farms in fifteen Massachusetts towns ranged from one-half to one ton per acre, with fresh meadow hay yields generally somewhat higher than English (see Appendix C-5). A range of 6.5 to 13.0 acres of mowing land would therefore be required to produce winter fodder. Combined mowing and fresh meadow acreages on the sample farms were consistent with these requirements, ranging from 7.0 to 14.5 (see Appendix C-4).

How many animals did families in the inland-upland towns keep on their pastures? The debt laws exempted 1 cow for milk (or a steer and a calf). The sample of fifteen inland towns showed a range of 1.8 to 4.7 cattle with an average of 2.9 per household (see Appendix C-6). Most families therefore had at least a milk cow and a steer for beef with a small surplus for home use or market exchange. The debt laws allowed 6 to 10 sheep for wool and mutton. Sheep and goats listed together ranged from 4.8 to 11.2 with an average of 6.4 per household (see Appendix C-6). Also exempted from debt were 2 oxen (or an ox and a horse) for hauling. Combined totals for oxen and horses showed a range of 1.7 to 5.8 with an average of 2.5 per house (see Appendix C-6). These figures indicate that inland families had enough livestock for their own home consumption, with a small subsistence surplus to trade within the town or to offer to cattle or sheep drovers who annually collected herds and drove them to urban markets. While wealth strata clearly existed, the average family was not engaged in livestock management for profit.[67]

If the family relied on 2 swine per winter (as exempted by the debt laws) rather than beef cattle, the required acreage to support them could be reduced. Pigs could roam in the woods and orchards (if cornfields and gardens were well fenced), eating acorn mast, apples, and other foods unfit for the table. Two or 3 swine could easily be raised on the home lot even if the family did not own a farm. The number of swine averaged between 1.2 and 3.3 per household in the sample towns (see Appendix C-6).

A vegetable garden and an orchard together required one additional acre. Gardens supplied radishes, carrots, garden peas, garlic, onions, leeks, melons, artichokes, skirret, and herbs. Yields of vegetables and the mix of crops varied greatly. While data for vegetable production do not appear in the 1771 valuation, probate inventories in Middlesex County (extending northwest of Boston to the New Hampshire border) in the 1770s showed beans and potatoes predominating, followed by garden peas, carrots, turnips, and onions. The proportion of vegetables increased steadily from 13.2 percent in the early eighteenth century to 63.0 percent in the 1830s. Cider replaced beer in the eighteenth century as the most prevalent drink, representing an intensification of land use, but many farms did not produce cider themselves. In the sample of fifteen inland Massachusetts towns in 1771, farms that produced cider averaged about nine barrels a year (see Appendix C-7). Cider production increased during the nineteenth century. Recalling his younger years in the 1820s and 1830s, Horace Greeley noted that "in many a family of six or eight persons, a barrel tapped on Saturday barely lasted a full week."[68]

The figure of ten to twelve cords per year of firewood allowed to debtors probably reflected nineteenth-century improvements in fireplace efficiency. Using an eighteenth-century estimate of thirty cords per house per year and a yield of about twenty-five cords to an acre, then 1.2 acres of woodland would be needed for cutting each year. Over thirty years, a 30- to 40-acre permanent woodlot would provide sufficient firewood for the farm.[69]

How large a farm therefore was required for basic subsistence under the "extensive system" of farming in the eighteenth century? With good yields on fertile or fresh soils, a subsistence-oriented farm

would require 15 acres of improved farmland (3 acres of tillage and
fallow, and 12 acres of pasture and meadow). On poor or worn soils,
35 acres of improved land (with 7 acres in tillage and fallow, and 28 in
pasture and meadow) would be needed. Improved acreages in the
sample towns were again consistent with these requirements, ranging from 16.5 to 33.7 acres (see Appendix C-4). An additional 1-acre
home lot for vegetables and fruits and a 30-acre woodlot would mean
that a farm complete in all components would require a total of 45 to
65 acres.

But with greater reliance on fish, berries, and game from the
ocean, lakes, and forests, summer vegetables, poultry, dairy products,
and apples from the homestead, salt pork in the winter, and bread
grains from tillage, the need for beef cattle and pasture was reduced.
When combined with bartering of foods, wood, and services, smaller
farms than the above could produce an adequate subsistence. For
households in the inland towns, consuming food from the commons
in lieu of farm products was unlikely to yield great profits because of
the lack of ready access to urban trading centers, ports, and navigable
rivers.

The use of widows' dowers to estimate minimum subsistence requirements has led historians to assert the existence of subsistence
crises from increases in "man/land" ratios. Overpopulation in relation to tillage and pasture, they argue, propelled people westward as
older towns filled up and farms were subdivided. Reliance on the
middle-class widow's food allotment results in inflated figures when
used to estimate the improved acreage necessary for subsistence.[70]

Moreover, the use of widows' dowers is based on a theory of labor
that assigns power in food production to the male farmer in the field
and uses improved acreage to calculate subsistence needs. It masks
food sources from the commons and women's contribution to food
production and trade. Lower acreages can support a household if
more recognition is given to female food sources and to fish, game,
and berries. Eggs (the purest form of protein known), milk, cheese,
poultry, vegetables, nuts, and berries all supply necessary protein
and calories and constitute farm women's traditional contributions to
the diet. Amelia Simmons's cookbook mentions the "frequent use" of
dunghill fowl (turkeys, chickens, capons, geese, and ducks). Women's
increasing skills in the preservation of root crops in sand in cellars
and the drying or pickling of fruits and vegetables by using salt,

spiced vinegar, and sugar compotes extended their use beyond summer into winter and spring.[71] Of her food in upstate Richmond, Vermont, in the 1830s, Ellen Brodt wrote:

> Our table was what would now be considered poor, but we all thrived on this simple fare of potatoes, pork, beans, bread, butter, a little fresh meat, simple puddings, and occasionally a pie. . . . We used to make corn meal mush . . . which we ate swimming in maple syrup. . . . How I loved to gather a bowl of strawberries, over which I poured thick cream, and with a slice of Mother's good bread and butter, go out and eat it under the apple trees. . . . Mother had an old crockery crate, in the yard, in which she had an old hen turkey with a large brood of little ones. (She had great success raising turkeys). . . . [She] used to make her own cheeses, and every time she made one, she let me have enough curd to fill my little cheese frame, which held about a quart. When Mother turned her cheeses, I oiled and turned mine. . . . No one kept vegetables for sale. All that we had, we raised in our garden, which was usually prolific. I remember we raised some pumpkins, where the pig sty had formerly been. One pumpkin weighed 300 . . . pounds.[72]

The consistency between the subsistence requirements specified by the debt laws and the actual yields and acreages in the inland-upland towns supports the existence of a subsistence-oriented sector of the economy in the areas beyond ready access to urban markets. Yet the ranges in yields also indicate that in some years some farms produced subsistence surpluses. Although poor roads prevented transportation over long distances by cart, livestock could be driven to market on the hoof. Differences in social status indicate that a few market-oriented individuals existed in most inland towns. In coastal towns or those near an urban area, subsistence surpluses could be more easily sold on the market, but food from the commons may not have been as readily available to supplement marketed food.

Eighteenth-century New England was thus a region of dual economies. For subsistence-oriented farmers, production existed for the sake of family reproduction, while market farmers planned and planted for profit. Although clear differences existed in wealth and diet, no food, clothing, and shelter crises plagued New England towns as was the case for rural Europe. By the end of the century, however, New England was poised for radical transformation. Yet the crisis that led to its capitalist ecological revolution was not a subsistence crisis. It was a crisis generated by tensions between the requirements of production and reproduction in the extensive system of farming.[73]

Production and Reproduction in Tension

Inherent in "extensive" farming in America was a fundamental contradiction between the requirements of production and those of reproduction. Production depended on a family labor force. Biological reproduction generated the laborers; food, clothing, and shelter reproduced and conserved their daily energy. But for the New England extensive system to reproduce itself generationally, the sons had to inherit farms. Property ownership and family inheritance were essential components of legal-political reproduction. Initially, large farms could be subdivided, but after two or three generations the original family farm was too small for further division. Sons who did not inherit land on the family homestead could often acquire fresh lands in new communities in the western and northern portions of New England, allowing the extensive system to reproduce itself. But increasing populations and shrinking farm sizes put continual pressure on the extensive method of production.[74]

The effects of the contradiction were felt first in the oldest communities. In Connecticut, as populations expanded, the average family farm shrank from 486 acres in 1680 to 166 acres in 1750 and to 81 in 1790. In Concord, Massachusetts, by the 1720s land was no longer being divided among sons, the farm being passed down intact, usually to the eldest, with the younger sons migrating out. The number of farms remained constant at about two hundred and the average farm size stayed at about 60 acres down to the Civil War. By contrast, in Chebacco, Massachusetts (near Ipswich), 90 percent of the farms between 1730 and 1749 were inherited by two or more sons. Alternatively, some fathers concentrated their land on one son, but endowed the others with a few acres that in combination with a trade would keep them in the village. About 10 percent of the fathers were able to provide their sons with land in central Massachusetts or southern New Hampshire. In general, parents wanted their sons in close proximity for subsistence, security, and comfort in old age.[75]

Inheritance practices also affected farmers' abilities to provide for their daughters and wives. Instead of land, daughters received dow-ries at marriage and household goods or money after the parents' death. A widow received dower rights—one-third of the real estate for use during her remaining life and one-third of the household goods forever. Some widows' dowers spelled out exact amounts of provisions, space, and passage rights within the homestead. Exact specifications helped to reduce tensions among the widow, her children, in-laws, or other occupants of the farm after her husband's death. When Joanna Wakefield, a Vermont widow, sold her late husband's ninety-acre farm to John White, she reserved for herself the use of "the southwest room, the west entry and closepress [sic], and the front yard, reserving also a right or privilege of putting into the barn a horse when I wish for myself and company. Reserving also the use of the bedroom in the chamber, also a privilege in the cellar, also a right to use from the orchard and garden all the fruit which I want for my own private use, also a right in the woodshed to cord 3 cords of wood, also the right to put into the barn half a ton of hay.... Said White to have no right or use of that part which I have reserved until after my decease."[76]

The father's obligation to give his daughters household goods or money, his wife an adequate subsistence in old age, and his sons a start in life either through land, money, or an education meant that in older areas, where farms were too small for further subdivision or there were too many children, a farm had to produce more than a bare subsistence if possible. This aspect of legal-political reproduction was determined by inheritance laws and customs and by the amount of taxes extracted by a town. In order to meet social obligations, ordinary farmers were under pressure to expand their production over and above daily subsistence by buying and selling land, livestock, grain, and wood. Even without a money-making entrepreneurial spirit, production for the sake of reproduction gave rise to a second inherent conflict within "extensive" farming.

This second contradiction occurred between human production and ecology. The extensive system required fresh lands for new production and the demotion of worn lands as yields declined. At the top of the ecological cycle, fertile woodlands with humus-covered soil were taken into production, and at the bottom worn-out pastures were abandoned to return to woods. The activity of humans as they used the land for production thus existed in tension with nature's active response to change.

In older towns, soil and pasture fertility continually declined during the eighteenth century. In Concord, for example, in 1749 it took 1.4 acres of pasture to support a cow for a year; in 1771, 2.2 acres; in 1781, 2.5 acres; and in 1791, 4.1 acres. Between 1749 and 1771, grain yields declined from 13.2 bushels per acre of tillage to 12.2 bushels, meadow hay yields from 0.82 to 0.71 tons per acre.[77]

The extensive system was in trouble. Between 1749 and 1771, the number of cattle grazing on Concord pastures had increased by 20 percent and, even though the number of sheep had declined by 40 percent, farmers were hard put to supply the herds with hay. Owing to declining yields farmers had to increase their pastures by 84 percent. Eighty percent of Concord's improved land was by now in pasture and meadow. Farmers who could afford it began to graze their cattle on fresh lands outside of town.[78]

This process repeated itself in most towns. As long as fresh land was available on the family farm and within New England as a whole, the requirements of human production and reproduction mutually supported each other. Eventually, however, the need for continual inheritance of farms to reproduce the system came into tension with the continual creation of worn soil. Patriarchy had come into conflict with ecology.

The inherent tensions between the requirements of production and reproduction and between production and ecology, which increased as towns grew older, were balanced during the seventeenth and eighteenth centuries by outward migration to fresh lands in western New England. But the settled Hudson River Valley and the Iroquois lands of New York blocked further westward migration into the better soils of the Mohawk and Genesee valleys. From the 1760s onward, New Englanders were forced to create new communities in the more marginal stony uplands in central and western Massachusetts and the hills of New Hampshire, Maine, and Vermont. By 1790, New Hampshire boasted 198 towns. Ninety-four Maine towns were founded between 1759 and 1776. Vermont was settled largely between 1760 and 1800.[79]

But in the 1790s, two events relieved the crisis and set the stage for the capitalist ecological revolution. The first was the settlement of Iroquois and British claims to New York which opened up the possibility of migration to better farmlands. New York ceded the eastern part of the state to Massachusetts. In 1787 the Iroquois lost title to two million acres in upstate New York, and in 1796 the British evacuated Fort Oswego near the Pennsylvania border. Pent-up farm families could now burst the dams that had confined them to marginal soils and small farms.[80]

The second circumstance was the commercial boom of the 1790s that created opportunities for market expansion. The American Revolution had required increased production of surpluses for the troops during the 1770s. After the postrevolutionary depression, easier credit became available in the 1790s, and Europe, which entered the era of the Napoleonic Wars, began importing large quantities of grain and salted meat. The cash and profits helped to encourage further production of marketable surpluses. Turnpikes and canals constructed in the late eighteenth and early nineteenth centuries facilitated market journeys. The large numbers of "strolling poor," who wandered from town to town receiving continual "warnings out," along with landless sons who wished to remain in their hometowns and the surfeit of single women constituted a ready market in labor.[81]

At this point two broad choices became available to New Englanders that relieved the mounting tensions: westward migration to the fruitful soils of New York or a change to intensive farming or nonagricultural production. When families moved west, they could retain the older extensive system by taking up fresh lands and maintaining a lower labor output per person than required by the intensive system. The availability of free lands was thus integral to the retention of extensive farming. Many families opted to migrate when the first children were sufficiently grown to provide labor, the parents were still relatively young and healthy, and the new farmlands were large enough to be divided among the sons at the parents' death. A "great migration" out of New England surged westward. "The immigrations," marveled James Wadsworth of Durham, Connecticut, in 1790, "are almost beyond belief." One winter day in 1795, an inhabitant of Albany, New York, counted five hundred sleighs loaded with household goods. The following summer twenty boats a day made their way west along the Mohawk River.[82]

Many families who stayed behind began to adopt an agricultural system oriented toward production for the market. For some, this option was an unparalleled economic opportunity. Yet the availability of a market for crops and cattle did not necessarily represent the unleashing of a latent entrepreneurial impulse in all New Englanders. The need for land and money to give children a start in life, to provide for them after the parents' death, and to ensure security in old age remained an important incentive to enter the marketplace for profit. Nevertheless, a turning point in American consciousness had been reached.[83]

The choice of increasing production for the market sometimes entailed labor-intensive fertilizing, or plowing and harvesting additional tillage. Or, it could involve expansion of the extensive system through addition of pasture and meadow so that larger herds could be driven to urban markets. Sometimes it meant specialization into woman's domain of dairying, poultry, or vegetable production. In most cases, it involved risk taking, experimentation, and possibly mortgaging the family farm to obtain the capital for fertilizers, experimental seed, additional livestock, and hired hands.

In Concord, in the late eighteenth century, the number of farms remained constant as landless taxpayers increased (see Appendix D-1). These men became artisans or wage laborers in lumbering and farming. As lumbering expanded, woodlands shrank dramatically (see Appendix D-2). The average size of oxen holdings increased as woods were cut for fuel for the town and nearby Boston (see Appendix D-3). Increasing amounts of English hay (clover, timothy, and herd's-grass) were planted on the plowed converted woodlands to supply fodder for cattle (see Appendix D-4). The average number of cows per landowner increased as the dairying and meat markets claimed the energies of more farmers (see Appendix D-3). The total amount of town land in tillage fell from 20.0 percent in 1771 to about 10.8 percent in 1781 and then declined slowly to 7.3 percent in 1850. By 1801 grain yields were up from 12.2 bushels per acre in 1771 to 15.1, while English hay yields rose from 0.69 to 0.87 tons per acre.[84]

On the more intensively farmed tillage, gentlemen farmers increased manure on their crops and began to experiment with fertilizers, legumes, five- and six-field rotation systems, deep plowing, and new crops in order to increase yields. Travelers and elites criticized ordinary farmers for careless habits and contrasted them with English farmers who had increased yields through intensive methods. Agricultural improvers such as the anonymous author of *American Husbandry*, who traveled through New England in 1775, asserted that farmers mismanaged their lands, wasted their soil, neglected their orchards, ignored the advice of agricultural improvers, and consequently underproduced. Americans, like James Warren of Massachusetts, in 1786, and Timothy Dwight, president of Yale University who traveled in New England during the 1790s, were also sharply critical of farming methods. Their criticisms appeared at the time of the important transition in land use from extensive to intensive farming. From a market-oriented perspective, most New Englanders were not producing the crop and timber yields to achieve economic success. Suggestions for improvement focused on quantities and money— bushels per acre, cost per bushel, fertilizer weights, transport costs, profits, and mortgages.[85]

Market opportunities declined with the English embargo during the War of 1812; but after the war's cessation in 1815 and the opening up of lands to the Mississippi, a second wave of tremendous expansion began to turn coastal mercantilism into an internal national market economy. During the period between 1815 and 1860, although punctuated by panics and booms, the American economy and consciousness were transformed. With the takeoff, ecology and production came into new types of tensions.

Market Production and Ecology

A farm is an ecological whole. Changes in its woods, meadows, and pastures over time affect its nutrient balance. If nutrients move from one part of the farm to another in the form of wood, potash, cattle, and manure, or if they leave the farm altogether for a distant market, the ecology changes. If tillage or pasture or woodlot is used intensively to produce a cash crop without nutrient compensation from another part, the whole is slowly degraded. The quality of the farm's soils and climate, the extent to which a farm is used for subsistence or commerce, and the system by which the land is cropped and fertilized determines the speed of degradation.

Access to easier transportation allowed farmers to intersect with the market economy in several ways that depleted the land more rapidly than did subsistence alone and had important ecological consequences. For some products, such as potash, money made a long, tiring journey worth the inconvenience, and potash was frequently a new settler's first cash crop. Planks and staves could be bartered at the local country store for kettles, gunpowder, rum, salt, molasses, or occasionally cash, but because of the availability of wood local demand was not high. To sell them meant hauling them long distances by oxcart. Until the 1790s when roads and turnpikes began to connect them to larger commercial centers, and credit and trade increased, most of the interior and upland villages used the forest primarily for subsistence.

The most widespread method for marketing the forest was to convert wood ashes to potash or pearlash (potassium carbonate), which in liquid form produced lye, much needed in colonial America to make soap, glass, dyes, and gunpowder. Even on the frontier, the price obtained for potash usually made its production worth the effort. By the early nineteenth century potash sold for $160–$200 per ton. About 550 bushels of field ashes from oak or maple (elm, hickory, and beech yielded somewhat less) produced a ton of potash. In return, farmers obtained money or credit to buy axes, spades, plows, and clothing. Or, alternatively, they hired plowing and planting help, allowing them to clear more land the second year and make more potash. Those with larger amounts of capital could afford additional laborers to clear the land quickly and completely. The profits paid the expenses and the land was ready to farm in the second year. By the 1840s, Vermont and then Maine had become major producers of potash and pearlash in New England.[86]

Mill owners and shopkeepers frequently installed potash works and bought ashes directly from local farmers for conversion. During the summer, the farmer or miller mixed the ashes with water until damp, drew off the liquor, and then slowly boiled them to evaporation in large cast-iron kettles to produce a dirty-brown lump potash. Careful calcination at low temperature in a furnace removed the organic impurities. To make white, 95 percent pure pearlash, the potash was again dissolved, concentrated, evaporated, and dried. Eventually potash manufacture became a major industry, encouraged by governments and regulated by laws.[87]

But potash making had important consequences, for it withdrew nutrients from the ecosystem. Tench Coxe, in the 1790s, wondered whether

farmers in the long cleared counties of New England, New York, and New Jersey, do not injure themselves very much by making pot-ash and pearl-ash, considering how necessary the wood ashes are to manure their farms, many of which are impoverished, and many naturally light. . . . It is doubtful whether he does not injure the soil, by burning the half rotten leaves and light mould, or earth, which have been made from the rotten leaves of

many years.... There is an opinion, that the ashes left from
burning the trees greatly enrich the land.... The soil of all new
countries appears to have for its upper part, a layer or stratum
of half rotten vegetable materials, which are capable of being
burned, but which it would be a great benefit to plough into the
earth. Potatoes, the best food for new settlements, grow abundantly in that rotten vegetable soil.[88]

That potash left the farm ecosystem for the city, depleting the soil of
nutrients, was lamented in an 1850 Patent Office report: "Down to
this day, great cities have ever been the worst desolators of the
earth.... Their inhabitants violated the laws of nature, which govern
the health of man and secure the enduring productiveness of the
soil.... Why should the precious atoms of potash, which organized
the starch in all the flour, meal, and potatoes consumed in the cities
of the United States in the year 1850, be lost forever to the world? Can
man create a new atom of potash or of phosphorus when the supply
fails in the soil, as fail it must, under our present system of farm
economy?"[89]

Selling cordwood for fuel was another lucrative venture for farmers
near large towns, especially along the coast, where wood soon became scarce. Large stockpiles of wood stood on the banks of rivers
ready for transport. By the 1840s, Maine farmers were each cutting
about five cords a year, farmers in Massachusetts eight cords, Rhode
Island nine, Connecticut seven, and Vermont four. A cord that brought
the farmer in Maine $1.50 sold for $7.00 in Boston in 1829.[90]

In addition to selling their wood and potash, farmers participated in
the timber economy by making shingles and barrel staves at home.
According to the chronicler of the town of Union, Maine, writing in
1851: "The husband and the wife, in the winter season, would go into
the woods, and, one at each handle of a long saw, work hard through
the day, cutting trees into blocks. It may be doubted which of the two
was the most expert in splitting and finishing them. And often has the
wife come to the Common—eight miles—on horseback with a child
in her arms, and a heavy bunch of shingles on each side of her horse,
balanced by means of ropes and withes across the beast's back." On
rainy days in the summer, the farmer went into his cooper shop to
make barrel staves and casks, exchanging them at the village store
for flour, groceries, or money with which to pay taxes.[91]

Cattle and sheep were the mainstays of market farming in New

England, and because they could be driven to urban markets on the hoof became even more important during the commercial boom of the 1790s and the market revolution of the nineteenth century. The increased production of livestock, however, had even more subtle implications for farm ecology than did lumbering. To support the additional livestock, pastures had to be expanded. Much of the woodland, after being burned for potash or cut for timber, was turned to tillage, then hay, and finally pasture. The additional manure produced during the winter by the increased livestock was spread on tillage, thereby increasing grain yields. During the first half of the nineteenth century grain and hay production increased in many New England towns.

The ecological problem, however, lay in the failure to adequately fertilize the hay fields. Nutrients were being transferred from the hay field to the crop field via the manure of cattle. The crops then left the farm for the market carrying the nutrients with them. Although farmers seeded clover in their hay fields, which would potentially build up nitrogen, they did not apply lime to the clover in sufficient quantities to counteract the high acidity of New England soils. Thus, while tillage was being intensively managed, the older extensive system was still being used in the transition of hay fields to pastures and finally back to woods.[92]

Individual farmers, pressed by needs and incentives to produce for the market, were thus locked into an "extensive system" of shrinking farms, woods, and soil fertility. Attempting to produce greater surpluses with traditional techniques, they were unable to make worn soils yield greater fruits. Ultimately, those farmers who remained in New England resolved these systemic problems by individual decisions to change farming techniques, to specialize production, to hire wage laborers, to keep quantitative records, and consequently to become capitalist farmers (see Chapters 6 and 7).

During the first quarter of the nineteenth century, New England experienced the effects of market competition. Roads, turnpikes, and canals integrated older towns like Concord and upland towns like Petersham into a national market system. On the Connecticut River canals at Enfield Falls, Hadley Falls, Turners Falls, Bellows Falls, Quechee Falls, and White River Junction by 1810 extended navigability into New Hampshire and Vermont. The Middlesex Canal linked the Merrimac River to Boston in 1803, while the Wicasee, Cromwell's, Union, Amoskeag Falls, Hooksett, Bow, and Sewell's canals led to increased use of the Merrimac. The Blackstone Canal (1828) on the

Map 5.3
Canals of Nineteenth-Century New England

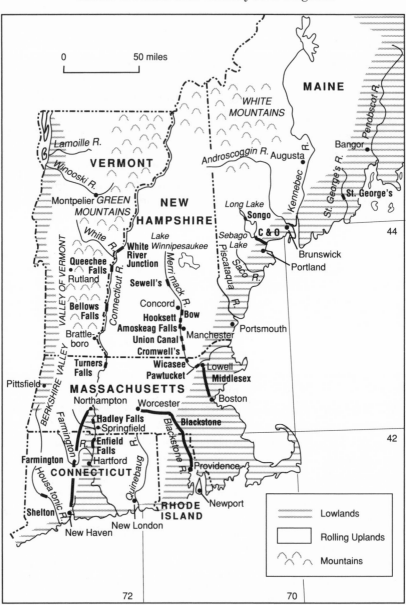

Source: William F. Robinson. *Abandoned New England: Its Hidden Ruins and Where to Find Them* (Boston: New York Graphic Society), p. 21.

Figure 5.4

Height of Cultivation for Farm Crops, Petersham, Massachusetts, 1830. Population, forest clearing, lumbering, and intensive agriculture all peaked in the mid-nineteenth century. Seventy-seven percent of Petersham's land had been cleared by 1830, 90 percent by 1850. A network of roads linked Petersham with neighboring towns.
Source: From the Harvard Forest Models. Photograph by M. H. Zimmerman. Reproduced courtesy of the Fischer Museum of Forestry, Harvard Forest, Harvard University.

Blackstone River brought Worcester into closer communication with Providence and Newport, Rhode Island (Map 5.3).

In Petersham, the height of cultivation occurred by 1830 with 77 percent of the land cleared for agriculture (Figure 5.4). Logging for the lumber market, begun in the 1830s, resulted in additional clearing, with 90 percent of the forests cut by 1850. Between 1845 and 1855 sawed timber increased from about 200,000 to over 1 million board feet. But in 1825, the opening of the Erie Canal began to make the farmlands of New York and Ohio competitive with those of New England. Then the Fitchburg railroad, completed in 1847, brought lower-priced midwestern grain and livestock into the region. Linking Boston and Concord with western New England, it bypassed Petersham in favor of Athol to the north which grew exponentially with the takeoff of manufacturing.

In Petersham farms were abandoned as farmers or their sons and daughters moved west. Population in Petersham, which had peaked at 1,795 in 1840, began a slow but steady decline back to 757 by 1910.

Figure 5.5

Farm Abandonment, Petersham, Massachusetts, 1850. In the 1850s railroads brought midwestern grain and flour to New England. The Fitchburg railroad bypassed Petersham in favor of Athol to the north. Petersham's population declined and farms were abandoned, while Athol turned to manufacturing.
Source: From the Harvard Forest Models. Photograph by M. H. Zimmerman. Reproduced courtesy of the Fischer Museum of Forestry, Harvard Forest, Harvard University.

By 1870 half of Petersham's farmland lay idle, ready for the cedars and pines that would take over the old fields and the summer people who would begin to buy up New England farmhouses (Figure 5.5). Other inland towns such as Ashfield, Chesterfield, and Pelham showed similar patterns of population decline and farm abandonment. But some, such as Worcester, Athol, Templeton, and Dracut, displayed "exponential growth" as transportation networks and manufacturing linked them to the national market economy (see Appendix C-2).[93]

Conclusion

New England's capitalist ecological revolution was initiated by tensions between the requirements of producing and reproducing the "extensive system" of family farming. Felt first in older towns surrounding expanding urban areas, subsistence production changed its orientation increasingly toward planning and planting for the market.

But as farmers used the techniques of the older extensive system to take advantage of new economic opportunities, ecological impacts intensified. Production for family reproduction, while continually requiring fresh lands, had cultivated small plots and pastures within forests, paying its dues by returning worn land to woods. The transition to a capitalist economy in the nineteenth century, however, had ecological repercussions beyond those tied to coastal mercantilism. Markets increased both the scope and rapidity of clearing and siphoned off nutrients from local communities to distant cities. As more land was put into production it had to be managed more intensively to ward off collapse. Tillage had to be manured, pastures expanded or improved to handle more stock, and forests conserved or replanted.

Faced with declining yields, farmers took up more calculating, systematic methods of management. Simultaneously, the older fusion of folk and Puritan worldviews that had guided eighteenth-century farming was losing its efficacy as a legitimating framework. Ordinary farmers increasingly opened themselves up to the mechanistic worldview articulated by gentlemen farmers, improvers, and scientists. As the market extended its tentacles into New England's lands and hinterlands in the nineteenth century, it was also transforming the consciousness of its people.

6

. . . .

The Mechanization of Nature: Managing Farms and Forests

New England's capitalist ecological revolution began in the late eighteenth century and was structurally complete by the 1860s. The colonial revolution had appropriated Nature's matter by transforming subjects into objects and living organisms into commodities for exchange on the market. The capitalist revolution gave back to nature "her" nutrients, but appropriated "her" labor. By transferring Nature's regenerative powers to society, the land was rendered passive and manageable. No longer was it necessary to let fields lie fallow to be restored as the Sabbath restored humans. No longer must forests be left to the activity of plant succession, but species needed for human use could be planned, planted, and harvested by foresters and agronomists. The colonial mercantile exchange of commodities was transformed into a system of production units that employed wage labor on farms, in forests, and in factories. The capitalist ecological revolution was characterized by the efficient organization of land, labor, and capital, competition in the marketplace, and the emergence of large-scale control over resources.

Capitalist agriculture broke the largely closed circuits of subsistence-oriented farming communities. Farming changed from an extractive industry to a manufacturing industry that could be operated like a factory. Fertilizers were imported; farm produce was exported. Places of production separated from places of consumption. Horses began to be replaced by tractors, human labor by mowers, reapers, and threshers. The farm was managed not for the reproduction of daily life, but for long-term profit. Although farmers continued to adopt ever more sophisticated technologies and accounting methods into the twentieth century, the elements of capitalist agriculture in New England were in place by the 1860s.[1]

Mechanism and the Domination of Nature

The mechanistic philosophy developed by the natural philosophers of seventeenth-century Europe legitimated the capitalist revolution and its domination of nature. Mingled with the rhetoric of the Great Chain of Being, Mother Earth, and the Garden of Eden that focused New England thought in the eighteenth century had been an undercurrent of instrumental concepts that would structure the management of nature in the nineteenth century. Mechanical metaphors and the rhetoric of manifest destiny became core concepts of a modern philosophy that saw the world as a vast machine that could be mathematically described, predicted, and controlled. A new chemical paradigm would quantify associations and dissociations of elements in soils and plants so that yields and profits could be predicted and increased. Mother Nature was delivered to the laboratory to undergo scientific experimentation.

In the seventeenth century, Descartes had characterized the human body as a machine and compared it to a clock that operated according to mechanical laws, while English political theorist Thomas Hobbes (1588–1679) had described the body politic in terms of springs, strings, and wheels. Newton's *Mathematical Principles of Natural Philosophy* had integrated celestial and terrestrial mechanics into a cosmology founded on the certainty of mathematical law and the divisibility of matter into inert atoms moved by external forces. Mechanism thus offered a unified theory of the human body, society, and the cosmos.[2]

The mechanistic construction of nature is based on a set of ontological, epistemological, methodological, and ethical assumptions about "reality." First, nature is made up of discrete particles (atoms or later subatomic particles). Second, sense data (information bits) are discrete. Third, the universe is a natural order, maintaining identity through change, and can be described and predicted by mathematics. Fourth, problems can be broken down into parts, solved, and reassembled without changing their character. And fifth, science is context-free, value-free knowledge of the external world. As constructed by the seventeenth-century "fathers" of modern science, the mechanistic model served to legitimate the human prediction, control, and manipulation of nature.[3]

During the eighteenth century, Enlightenment elites appropriated from the scientific idiom metaphors that described human society in terms of instruments, machines, gears, pulleys, and balances. The homes of gentlemen exhibited pendulum clocks, cannonball escapements, orreries (working models of the solar system), music boxes with moving figurines, telescopes, microscopes, meteorologic instruments, pulley systems for raising food or opening doors, mechanically driven fountains, hydraulic devices whose sudden commencement surprised and startled garden visitors, and a host of other machines and playthings. Thomas Jefferson's home at Monticello was filled with copies of European models as well as with inventions of his own. In the 1800s New England clockmakers produced large numbers of shelf clocks, wall clocks, and grandfather clocks with second hands and rocking manikins or ships that indicated whether the clock was operating.[4]

Mechanical language derived from European philosophers permeated the writings of the nation's founding fathers and their fundamental documents—the Declaration of Independence and the Constitution. Scottish philosopher Adam Smith (1759) had explained how "all the several wheels of the machine of government [might be] made to move with more harmony and smoothness, without grating upon one another, or mutually retarding one another's motions." Referring to his role in the adoption of the Declaration of Independence, John Adams hoped that he had been "instrumental in touching some springs and turning some small wheels" of historical development. The language of the Declaration itself was Newtonian in emphasizing the necessity for action based on observation of a sequence of events. James Madison's "Federalist 10" (1788) treated society as a balance among atomized factions. The Constitution of the United States (1789) was constructed as a system of balances among the powers allocated to the three separate elements of government.[5]

Mechanical metaphors also began to infuse the popular literature of eighteenth-century America. Since their inception, almanacs had taught Copernican astronomy and Newtonian science to their readers. But a mechanical philosophy going beyond instruction on scientific laws extended the description of nature as machine. Nathaniel Ames informed the readers of his *Almanac* in 1754 that the Divine Artificer initially had made the body of man "a machine capable of endless duration"; but after Eve's ingestion of the forbidden apple, the living principle within had fallen into disharmony with the body, disrupting the smooth functioning of the parts.[6]

Similarly, Ames's son and successor, Nathaniel, described the human body a decade later as "an infinitely more curious machine or piece of clockwork than anything contrived by man." Just as a clock-maker should know the make and machinery of the clock before attempting to repair it, a doctor should know the "make and machinery of the body." The physician must set his reason to work to "find out which of the pipes, springs, or strainers is out of order . . . whether they want stiffening or loosening, oiling or cleaning."[7]

The mechanical paradigm of association and dissociation of atoms provided the rationale for agricultural and social improvement, while males moving in free association became the entrepreneurial pattern. The westward movement encouraged spatial mobility; emerging capitalism promoted social mobility. Manufacturers produced machines made of interchangeable parts, while managers hired wage laborers as replaceable cogs in the machinery of production. Men organized businesses for the specific purpose of profit making, and each male was free to associate with or to dissociate from them as opportunities arose. Efficiency dictated that each remain a part of a company or operation only as long as it was profitable and then be ready to move onward or upward to a new venture. Productivity and profit were the deciding factors rather than emotive bonds between individuals.[8]

The rhetoric of manifest destiny sanctioned the spatial motion that encouraged control over natural resources as Europeans swept westward bearing the torch of "civilization." The elder Ames foresaw the day when art and science would change the "face of nature" west of the Appalachians as far as the Pacific Ocean. As civilization moves across the western deserts, he wrote in 1754, "the residence of wild beasts will be broken up, and their obscene howl cease for ever." Instead, rocks and trees would dance to the music of Orpheus, and gold and silver treasures would be discovered in barren rocks long hidden from "ignorant aboriginal natives." Iron ore already dug in the East would be set to practical use in creating plowshares and swords. All this would be sanctioned by God and the Gospel as the heathens were dispelled by light.

In extolling the present superiority of Christianized European civilization, Ames sent forth the ripples of manifest destiny that would legitimate the nineteenth century's westward movement: "the progress of human literature (like the sun) is from the east to the west; thus has it traveled thro' Asia and Europe, and now is arrived at the eastern shore of America." He concluded with a prophetic message to

those of us who live today: "Ye unborn inhabitants of America!...
when your eyes behold the sun after he has rolled the seasons round
for two or three centuries more, you will know that in anno domini
1758 we dream'd of your times."[9]

Ames had anticipated by almost one hundred years Missouri's Thomas Hart Benton, whose famous 1846 address to the Twenty-ninth Congress justified American expansion to the Pacific. Using the Bible as
legitimation for manifest destiny, he proclaimed that the white race
had "alone received the divine command to subdue and replenish the
earth: for it is the only race that ... hunts out new and distant lands,
and even a New World to subdue and replenish." By then (as Ames
had predicted), the red race had almost disappeared from the Atlantic. "The van of the Caucasian race," Benton gloried, "now top the
Rocky Mountains, and spread down on the shores of the Pacific." In-
evitably, white influence on the 400 million people comprising the
yellow race of Asia would be felt, "a race once the foremost of the
human family in the arts of civilization" but now grown degenerate.
Under the influence of white trade and marriage, the sun of civilization would once again shine on them.[10]

And Massachusetts' own John Quincy Adams, that same year, in
promoting American expansion into the rich farmlands of Oregon,
quoted from Genesis 1, urging the young nation to "make the wilderness blossom as the rose, to establish laws, to increase, multiply, and
subdue the earth, which we are commanded to do by the first behest
of God Almighty."[11]

Upward mobility was to be achieved through extraction of natural
resources from the earth by the most efficient and profitable method.
In 1844, Yale's Whig essayist Calvin Colton characterized America as
a "country of self-made men" and the American environment as a
source of unlimited natural resources. "Providence has [given] us a
rich, productive, and glorious heritage.... The wealth of the country
is inexhaustible, and the enterprise of the people is unsubdued....
Give them a good government, and they can not help going ahead,
and outstripping every nation on the globe."[12]

Echoing the rhetoric of upward mobility, agricultural improvers exhorted farmers to become rich, like the self-made men of other
classes, by calling upon the resources of the earth mother. "When he
would add to his earthly treasure," advised Reverend H. M. Eaton in
his speech to the farmers of Kennebec County, Maine, "he draws from
the boundless resources of wealth concealed in the bosom of *mother*

earth. She has a treasure for the farmer of such a nature, and so vast in extent, that giving does not impoverish her, and by withholding she is not enriched."[13]

Subduing the Earth

To the biblical mandate for dominion over nature that had guided the Puritan transformation of the environment, nineteenth-century science added mechanical and chemical methods for altering it. A harmonious fusion between the Bible and Baconian instrumentalism established science as the method to be used in subduing the earth to improve the human condition. Francis Bacon's *New Atlantis* (1627) had been dedicated to the alteration of nature through scientific instruments and experiments. Fully compatible with the mechanistic view of nature, his scientific research program sought to command nature by obeying its laws. Grounded in the mechanical and chemical paradigm and augmented with an array of new mechanical technologies, Baconian utilitarianism became the ethic of agricultural improvement.[14]

Improver Henry Colman began his address to the Hampshire, Franklin, and Hampden Agricultural Society of Massachusetts by quoting Bacon's principle: "The effort to extend the dominion of man over nature, is the most healthy and most noble of all ambitions." Just as "the great master of philosophy" had linked control over a female earth to the recovery of the garden that Eve had lost for humankind, Colman characterized the earth as a female whose productivity would help advance the progress of the race. Agricultural improvement, he believed, was the most salient example of how human power and creativity could help in controlling nature. "Here man exercises dominion over nature; ... commands the earth on which he treads to waken her mysterious energies ... compels the inanimate earth to teem with life; and to impart sustenance and power, health and happiness to the countless multitudes who hang on her breast and are dependent on her bounty."[15]

Speeches made to farmers at local societies for promoting agriculture routinely drew on female earth rhetoric. M. B. Bartlett in his address to the farmers of West Oxford County, Maine, eulogized the pioneer struggles "with mother earth" that had created "sinewy arms and brawney chests" in the transformation of the cold, granite bedrock of New England into a habitable climate. Until only recently the wolf had prowled on the outskirts of town and bear were encountered in the forests; older farmers recalled Indian attacks and scalpings. Those who had gone west, Bartlett admonished, should have stayed to complete New England's transformation into a garden. He exhorted those who remained behind to finish the struggle: "Force the earth to yield to you her hidden wealth, act out your destiny with all the force and goodness that is in you."[16]

As God's agent, echoed Ezekial Holmes, the farmer had submitted nature to "repeated and successive blows of the axe, hewing out, as it were, a farm and a homestead from Nature herself ... making the wilderness blossom as the rose, and ... converting the lair of the wild beast into smiling farms and thriving villages."[17]

The transformation of the "howling wilderness" into "fruitful fields" and "smiling farms" was pushed with such frequency in journal articles, speeches, and commentaries as to become commonplace. John Goldsbury, writing for the *New England Farmer* in 1855, queried whether the descendants of Adam and Eve could have obeyed God's command to "be fruitful and multiply and replenish the earth and subdue it" without cultivating the land, even if they had retained their abode in the Garden of Eden. Human labor coupled with the progress made in agriculture, mechanics, science, and art had changed New England to prosperous towns of happy, enterprising people. "Agriculture is the mother of some and the nurse of all the mechanic arts," John Bullard told the Western Society of Middlesex Husbandmen in 1803. By cutting down the trees and clearing the land of rubbish, the earth could be made "an agreeable ... abode to the children of men." Once the fields had been tilled and planted the farmer could delight in the valleys of corn, the pastures filled with sheep, and the perfume of the fields.[18]

Like Bacon, Sidney Perham reminded Maine's Oxford County Agricultural Society that "knowledge is power." He advocated that the farmer follow and learn from nature's laws rather than subjugating it; but in true Baconian spirit, he also advised that this be done through scientific experiment. "We must enter her laboratory, and learn her various modes of distributing and combining her elements for the production of given results; and then we shall find her a co-worker with us."[19]

While the ethic of the animate cosmos had urged farmers to imitate nature and hasten its own processes, the mechanical paradigm offered new techniques and powerful machines to fundamentally transform it. Dr. N. T. True, addressing Maine's Cumberland County Agricultural Society, urged farmers to appropriate nature's own processes wherein "instead of suffering the land to go fallow ... she makes use of a rotation in crops." In planting pines on worn-out lands, nature provided deep roots that brought up potash and other nutrients. Deciduous trees used the potash in their leaves, returning it to the soil when they fell. "You will find nature slowly, but surely at work, forming a suitable soil for some other crop, which in the lapse of ages she may see fit to introduce."

But in rotating crops and improving the land, True advised the farmer to use machines. He should hoe and shell corn, mow and rake hay, reap, thresh, and winnow grain, pull stumps, saw wood, pare apples, and churn butter with the new agricultural machinery. He should plow deeper, manure more heavily, and cultivate better than had his father and grandfather. With crop rotation, he need no longer blame his "good mother, earth" for failed harvests. "Be kind to your mother," pleaded True, "and she will always be kind to you in return. . . . The more carefully we study her in her works, the more probable will be our success in our attempts at imitation."[20]

Nature was the best teacher when it came to managing her woodlots for shipbuilding timber. Even if the back forty had been improvidently hacked for firewood or exterminated in conflagrations, "Kind Nature, man's best friend, attempts to repair these breaches in her sylvan shades." She planted seedlings of oak, pine, ash, maple, and many other useful trees important for a "commercial people." But if thwarted by turning out cattle and sheep to graze, she would retaliate with thistles, burdocks, and brambles.[21] Yet even as elites offered their allegiance to the earth as mother and teacher, their mechanical, instrumental view of nature was subtly legitimating and advocating its management and manipulation.

The Chemical Paradigm in Agriculture

As improvers were mechanizing the animate cosmos, New England's agricultural chemists were participating in a crucial debate over the nature of crops, soils, the earth, and indeed life itself. Was there a vital organic principle involved in the transmission of chemicals from soil to plant? Or were the observed changes merely a manifestation of mechanical associations and dissociations of simple elements into new chemical compounds? Was the cosmos fundamentally animate and alive, or was life a transitory grouping of atoms? As mechanists gained victory over vitalists, they were simultaneously transforming grains and fertilizers into scientific objects, farms and fields into laboratories, and farmers into chemists.

Vitalists such as chemist and geologist Samuel L. Dana, of Lowell, Massachusetts, who wrote the enormously popular *Muck Manual for Farmers* (1842), asserted that the growth of plants resulted from a fundamental life principle—humus. He called humus "geine" after the Greek earth goddess, Gaia, who had also given her name to the earth sciences geology and geography. Dana followed European vitalists such as England's Sir Humphrey Davy whose *Elements of Agricultural Chemistry* (1813) had been published in New York in 1815 and Philadelphia in 1821.

According to Davy, plants obtained their food solely from the organic matter of the soil—humus, dung, urine, and animal and vegetable matter. But animal and vegetable manures were unusable as plant food unless they had first been rendered soluble by fermentation in the compost heap or by oxidation in the atmosphere. When fresh manure and green crops were plowed into the ground, they fermented in the warm soil and were absorbed by plant roots. Dry straws of wheat, oats, barley, beans, and peas first had to be composted before they could be applied. Minerals, Davy asserted, could not be absorbed by the plant's roots. Any minerals found in plant tissues came from the soil itself rather than from mineral fertilizers. The function of minerals was to render the soil's vegetable matter soluble.[22]

The humus theory had also been supported by German physician and chemist Albrecht Thaer (1752–1828), who published his *Principles of Agriculture* between 1809 and 1812. To Thaer, humus was the condition of life itself. An organic force that could not be derived solely from the inorganic elements of "dead nature," it fed the living plant and was therefore the source of the life of all higher animals and plants. Even in the ashes of burned plants was a vestige of life invisible to the senses. Dead plants, animals, and their ashes were essential for the production of new life. The more life, the more humus could accumulate to support men and animals. In the history of humus lay the history of the world.[23]

The vitalistic theory of fertilizers attracted a large following during the early nineteenth century. But in 1840, German chemist Justus Liebig boldly attacked the humus theory with the question, "where did the humus that supported the first plant life come from?" In its place he asserted his own theory of mineral manures. His *Organic Chemistry in its Applications to Agriculture and Physiology* (1840) was published in several editions in Cambridge, Massachusetts, and New York beginning in 1841.

Liebig's mechanistic approach to inorganic mineral fertilizers limited the role of humus in plant growth to supplying the plant's roots with carbon dioxide. Instead, the primary function of the roots was to absorb minerals such as phosphoric acid and the bases potash, soda, lime, and magnesia. These had to be spread on the soil to keep it productive. The amount of minerals needed by the soil could be detected by burning the plant and analyzing the ash. "It is the greatest possible mistake to suppose that the temporary diminution of fertility in a soil is owing to the loss of humus," he asserted; "it is the mere consequence of the exhaustion of the alkalies."[24]

To Liebig, animal and vegetable manures did not supply some nebulous "organic force," but provided essential inorganic materials (silicate of potash and the phosphates of lime and magnesia). When crops were harvested and sent to market in the city, phosphates went with them. They could be replaced by seeding the fields to hay fertilized with dung. Fields could be kept fertile by replacing the minerals removed by harvesting grain and vegetables. If more minerals were added than taken away, production would be increased. To achieve this, artificial phosphates could be produced in chemical factories by combining sulfuric acid with bones.

Liebig downplayed the role of nitrogen in relation to the more important contribution of the inorganic minerals. Rather than deriving nitrogen from animal manures, he argued, plants obtained nitrogen from the ammonia in the atmosphere. While wild plants received sufficient nitrogen, cultivated plants did not.[25]

Liebig's primary objective was to establish the laws of chemistry and physics as explanations for biological processes. Numbers were the key to his method of analysis and his polemic against the vitalists. Through careful laboratory analysis, the weight of each element in a plant, animal, or soil sample could be determined. The quantities of each element withdrawn from the field by crops or from the farm by driving animals to market could then be compared with the elements restored to the land through the addition of fertilizers. His arguments almost always relied on mathematical calculations (although he did not always divulge the sources for his numbers). Crop yields could be predicted and the amount of food necessary to support a given population calculated. The mechanical approach of combining and recombining elements in the laboratory should be applied to nature itself.

In Lowell, Dana violently disagreed with Liebig's rejection of humus. He attacked the mineral theory in a series of notes and appendixes to the first American edition of Liebig's book in 1841 and in his own *Muck Manual* the following year. Using Swedish chemist J. J. Berzelius's theory of geine and the vitalistic theories of Dutch chemist Johann Mulder (1802–80) of Utrecht (a vituperative enemy of Liebig), Dana argued that geine was essential for renewing fertility. Geine was the vital principle that rendered inorganic salts soluble for absorption by plant roots. "The vital principle ... merely by its presence, gives to the elements power to enter into new combinations. ... So too, the presence of a growing plant ... impresses, on the soil, both on the organic and inorganic elements, power to enter into new arrangements."[26]

Animal and vegetable manures, according to Dana, were compounds of salts with geine. They contained both inorganic salts and the organic matter needed by living things. To maintain soil fertility, salts of the first class, the carbonates (such as lime, shells, and marl), nitrates (such as ammonia and niter), and phosphates (such as bones and hoofs) were needed. The second class of salts contained poisons, such as sulphates and chlorides, beneficial only in small quantities.

In addition to Dana, followers of the organic theory of fertilizers included John Pitkin Norton (1822–52), professor of agricultural chemistry at Yale, who established a laboratory there in 1847. Norton had studied in the Edinburgh laboratory of chemist James F. W. Johnston, a supporter of Mulder. In 1846 he returned to Europe to work with Mulder and arranged for the publication of an American edition of Mulder's 1845 text, *The Chemistry of Vegetable and Animal Physiology*. He also wrote an introduction to Johnston's practical *Catechism of Agricultural Chemistry and Geology*, published in Albany in 1846. Liebig's inorganic mineral theory, on the other hand, had a contingent of disciples at Harvard in a laboratory that opened in 1848 headed by one of his students, Eben Norton Horsford (1818–93).

Yet Norton, like Horsford, adopted many of Liebig's techniques of analyzing soils for their mineral content and advocated correcting their deficiencies with mineral fertilizers as well as with barnyard manures. In a series of monthly letters to the *Cultivator* and the *American Agriculturalist* between 1844 and 1852, Norton and Horsford helped arouse a nation of farmers to the importance of soil chemistry. Both laboratories taught soil and ash analysis and produced an active group of students, some of whom went on to publish papers and do advanced work in Europe. At his laboratory at Yale, Norton and his students analyzed farmers' soils free of charge, and Norton journeyed to the meetings of local agricultural societies to lecture on the importance of using appropriate fertilizers.[27]

With the work of these New England chemists, vitalistic approaches gave way to mechanical ones. Corn and potatoes changed from simple commodities to scientific compounds. Bird droppings, swamp muck, and barnyard manure were transformed from squishy, smelly substances spread on fields into objects to be studied in the laboratory. No longer an analogy to the secretions of animate Mother Nature, as for the eighteenth-century author of *Curiosities of Nature and Art*, manures were reconstructed by nineteenth-century chemists as scientific-technical objects comprising atoms of nitrogen and phosphorus in precise quantities.

From the vantage point of his Yale Analytical Laboratory, John Pitkin Norton described the simultaneous transformation of commodities into scientific objects and the "worthy farmer" into a junior chemist-physiologist:

He has left the region of facts and substantials, and has penetrated into a land where all is unknown, now half stifled by ammonia, with an occasional whiff of other highly nitrogenous bodies. . . . [He] is overwhelmed by a cloud of ashes in the form of inorganic manures. . . . His hair stands on end as he peruses even the names, of the awful substances which are described as constituting what he has heretofore looked upon as simple turnips and potatoes, and his own respiration becomes impeded as he thinks of the combustion that is going on in the lungs, and the transformations in the stomachs of his friends and neighbors.

But slowly and persistently, Norton continued, these scientific "enemies with hard names" were "brought under the farmer's power," and soon he had "a full commission to torture nature, and compel her answers to every question." Instead of toasting apples and cracking nuts at the end of a day of toil, he would "cook his own soils over his own fire, and separate all of their parts just as easily as cut a turnip into slices." In the evenings he would meet with other farmers to "compare the properties of their acids and alkalies, to speculate upon some new theories of vegetable physiology, and to wax warm in discussing the relative merits of phosphoric and sulphuric acids."[28]

Moreover, as farmers became chemists and commodities chemical compounds, fields were transformed into laboratories. For the quantitative methods and predictions of the chemist to be replicated, the farm itself had to be reconstructed as a laboratory. By extending the laboratory's walls to embrace the farmer's fields, precise proportions of the new scientific objects could be applied to the soil. The laboratory prescribed the farmer's methods and circulated its "facts" to the field. As sociologist of science Bruno Latour put it: "Scientific facts are like trains, they do not circulate outside their rails. You can extend the rails and connect them, but you cannot drive an engine through a field." Science's facts could become the farm's facts when the field had been reconstructed as a laboratory.[29]

New England improvers had duly noted this new unity of laboratory and field. "The earth is a great laboratory, and the farmer is the chemist," Dr. Ezekiel Holmes told the Lewiston Cattle Show and Fair. Wheat, corn, turnips, fruits, and flowers were simply chemical compounds—fixed determinate proportions of elements acting in accordance with nature's laws. God kept the proportions balanced, just as he kept the planets in their orbits. The farmer was God's earthly agent "carrying out his designs and executing his laws." Let the farmer omit one necessary chemical from the fields when the crop was sowed and the harvest would not be profitable. Let the housewife neglect to add the water, alkali, or grease and the soap would not form.[30]

Closely related to the interest in soil analysis was the analysis of fertilizers. Ambitious farmers in the 1840s began experimenting with mineral manures such as gypsum, marl, lime, ashes, and bones and with organic fertilizers such as guano, muck, and night soil. Produced in many parts of the eastern United States, they were advertised and distributed as cures for "worn-out" soil. A Rhode Island manufacturer produced fish manure from menhaden from the Providence River, and the Philadelphia Guano Company began selling guano from islands off the coast of Venezuela. The manufacture and distribution of superphosphates by treating natural rock phosphates with sulfuric acid was begun in Baltimore, Maryland, Richmond, Vir-

ginia, and Charleston, South Carolina, while "Professor" John Mapes
of New Jersey advertised his "Mapes' Superphosphates" and "Mapes'
Nitrogenized" in his journal, *The Working Farmer*. Samuel W. Johnson (1830–1909), a student of Liebig, who along with Norton became
a professor at Yale, and his students analyzed the chemical contents
of each fertilizer and compared their costs for the benefit of farmers
overwhelmed by the immense number of products and advertising
claims.[31]

As turnpikes, canals, and rails circulated the market's commodities,
farm journals and scientific texts inscribed and circulated the newly
constructed scientific facts. The vitalist-mechanist debate in agriculture was a contest for power over the terms of scientific discourse.
The new texts pouring off the steam printing presses linked ordinary
farmers and their home landscapes with laboratory scientists in a
new infrastructure of production. The market farm was not an economic context outside the laboratory, but a transformation of it. The
new scientific-technical objects were wrenched from their ecological
contexts, quantitatively analyzed in the laboratory, reconstituted as
chemical compounds, and recirculated as objects outside the laboratory walls. In the process of reconstruction, muck, geine, Gaia, and
vital forces—the animate world's terms of discourse—fell as the laboratory rose. "Give me a laboratory," wrote Latour, paraphrasing Ar-
chimedes on the lever, "and I will raise the world. . . . If this means
transforming society into a vast laboratory, then do it."[32]

The ideological power struggle over vitalistic and mechanistic discourse in soil chemistry continued until Louis Pasteur (1822–95) asserted that fermentation was caused by microorganisms (ca. 1857)
and twentieth-century science described humus as the product of
microbes acting on plant and animal residues. The controversy was
one more step in the breakup of the animate, vitalistic cosmos of the
agrarian age and its replacement by the mechanistic, instrumental
universe of the industrial era.

Mechanism and Farming

Agricultural improvement had begun as an elite movement among
eighteenth-century gentlemen farmers. Americans read the texts of
European agricultural improvers, traveled and studied abroad, and
listened to the advice of travelers and visitors who compared Ameri-

can and European systems. But in the early nineteenth century, steam printing presses began to supplement the almanacs and other printed sources available to ordinary farmers. Almanacs, farm journals, state and county societies for promoting agriculture, and agricultural fairs meant that New England farmers no longer needed to rely solely on local know-how for guidelines. The improvers and their spokespersons—almanac makers, doctors, clergy, newspaper editors, and scientists—trumpeted science, management, and numbers.

By the late eighteenth century the advice columns of almanacs were already encouraging farmers to become rich and prosperous through good management of lands wrested from "the state of nature." In 1765, Nathaniel Ames urged his readers to apply manure and to use good techniques of husbandry. Dig marl from bogs and marshes, plant clover seed in gardens and fields, manure both heavy and light soils, he urged. Heavy soils should be plowed early in the spring to expose the muck to the nitrous particles in the air. Sea sand mixed with sea ooze and sheep's dung would render it mellow and crumbly for fall wheat planting. Sowing wheat seed soaked in strong brine crusted with lime would yield a prodigious harvest. Every fourth year, clover seed soaked in soot and urine should be planted and covered with several loads of manure.[33]

Nathanael Low's *Astronomical Diary* taught early nineteenth-century farmers to be both "instructor and physician to the vegetable creation." Upgrade the quality of the manure laid on fields by feeding animals more grass, green food, and turnips, Low advised. His 1815 almanac offered a short course on soils and their constituents. All soils were different combinations of two or more of the four primitive earths: calcareous (chalk and limestones), magnesia (Epsom salts), argil (clay which produced alum), and siliceous (flint, quartz, and sand). In the two succeeding years, Low continued his lessons on analyzing soils and manures and followed them with a discussion of the food of plants. He also offered his readers advice on a wide variety of other matters, such as methods of propagating fruit trees, pruning and manuring orchards, healing wounds in trees, washing the wool of merino sheep, feeding horses, and curing sheep diseases.[34]

Robert Bailey Thomas's (1766–1847) *Old Farmer's Almanac*, published in 1793 in Boston, Massachusetts, took the bold step of omitting the Man of the Signs and included practical hints for farm and household in the "Farmer's Calendar" section each month. He gave tips on the application of manures, planting buckwheat and potatoes, and transplanting and cultivating fruit trees, and debated the advantages of deep versus shallow plowing.[35]

Agricultural societies and farm journals soon followed suit. In 1799, the Massachusetts Society for Promoting Agriculture began publishing its transactions. Monthly journals especially for farmers sprang up all over New England during the first half of the nineteenth century. In Connecticut the *Rural Magazine and Farmer's Monthly Museum* appeared in 1819, and in Massachusetts Thomas G. Fessenden's journal, *New England Farmer*, started its presses rolling in 1823. And as the middle decades advanced, a host of local farmers' journals began broadcasting the gospel of improvement. The *Yankee Farmer* of Portland, Maine (1832), *Maine Farmer* (1832), *Boston Cultivator* (1838), *Cheshire Farmer* of Keene, New Hampshire (1838), *Cultivator's Almanac and Cabinet of Agricultural Knowledge* of Boston (1840), *Farmer's Monthly Visitor* of Concord, New Hampshire (1839), *Connecticut Farmer's Gazette and Horticultural Repository* of New Haven (1839), and *Farmer and Artizan* of Portland, Maine (1853) were among the many new publications.

Through the new societies and journals the gentlemanly classes transmitted entrepreneurial values to ordinary farmers and brought them under the hegemony of the market. To support a burgeoning urban civilization, farmers and mechanics needed to be convinced of their economic importance lest they migrate west and be lost as an essential support system. "Farmers and mechanics form the great body of our population," reformer and editor Jesse Buel told the Agricultural Institute of New London and Windham counties in Connecticut. "Their labors constitute the principal source of our wealth. They are to the community what the body is to the animal system—the seat of nourishment, of vigor, and of life. . . . We might better spare a limb than to suffer the body, upon which all the limbs are dependent for life, to sicken and die." The farmer's productive labor was not only a source of wealth; it also brought moral health to the body politic. It should be respected and honored by an enlightened society.[36]

Farmers and mechanics were urged to unite. Journals addressed themselves to the interests of both, while local fairs displayed their products. "I congratulate the farmers and mechanics of this county," announced reformer Sidney Perham to Maine farmers. "Let the farmers and mechanics of Oxford county arise and . . . go forward . . . determined to be . . . men, in the highest, noblest, and most exalted sense of that term."[37]

Progress and improvement go hand in hand, hammered the improvers: "How to do a thing in the best way at the least expense, and consuming the least time." A farm was too large if any portion was left uncultivated, pronounced Massachusetts improver Henry Colman. One well-manured acre was worth more than two that were poorly cultivated. But better still were two well-cultivated acres; and when a farmer could produce a profit on two acres, he should plant ten, and then twenty, carrying his profit to the utmost.[38]

To become good managers, farmers had to keep accounts. "Nor should the practice of using the barn door for a day book and ledger be perpetuated because it was so done by our forefathers. . . . These antiquated practices should be given up," complained clergyman H. M. Eaton at the annual exhibition of Maine's Kennebec society.[39] To teach farmers the value of profits, the *Maine Farmer* printed an article on "Farm Accounts" in 1834 with examples of expenses and proceeds. "There could not, perhaps, be a more effectual method fallen upon to break up old habits, and bad courses of farming, and to lead to new and improved methods of cultivation, than to have the Dr. [debit] and Cr. [credit] of plantation operations, presented to the eye in the form of a balance sheet."[40]

Well-kept account books by nineteenth-century market-oriented farmers are commoner in New England's historical archives than those of their subsistence-oriented counterparts. Exemplifying the new approach was a Hampstead, New Hampshire, farmer writing in 1817. His account book listed the tasks performed, followed by columns for the number of hands, yoke of oxen, horses, hours, and days of labor. Most of his field tasks employed two hands, one yoke of oxen, and occasionally an additional horse; the hours varied from one to ten. Referring to his fields by number, he recorded the quantities of plaster, ashes, and manure added and the labor involved in breaking up and plowing fields, sowing and harrowing seed, furrowing, weeding, and hoeing crops. He detailed the labor time expended in grafting and pruning fruit trees, burning brush, hauling stones, mending brush fences, planing fence boards, hewing fence posts, repairing the kitchen hearth, shearing sheep, killing calves, shaving a wagon tongue, repairing the horse barn floor, making a beehive and hiving bees, carrying grain to the mill, and transporting bean poles.[41]

Not only should they keep account books, farmers were told, but they should also balance their accounts with nature. Every crop withdrew chemicals from the soil for which "the earth demands an equivalent, . . . if . . . not repaid she soon closes her doors and suspends payment." If sufficient manure were returned to the land and a fallow crop planted, the accounts could be kept current, rendering "naked" fallows a thing of the past. Since land and stock were capital, double-entry records like those of the merchant should be kept of everything invested in the land and raised on it.[42]

To balance nature's accounts "every farmer must . . . replenish the earth with the proper nutriments of plants." Manures of all kinds should be put on the soil, weeds subdued, fences built, and timber preserved. Each farmer must learn and experiment with the best methods for farming his particular soil to obtain the greatest quantity of produce for the least labor. "The more productive the earth is rendered by cultivation," lexicographer Noah Webster taught Massachusetts farmers, "the more inhabitants and domestic animals may be subsisted on a given extent of territory; and the greater is the wealth and strength of a nation."[43]

Intensive labor was a prerequisite for intensive agriculture. "The laboring man . . . is the truly happy man," John Goldsbury wrote to the *New England Farmer*. God, who labored six days to create the world, had not meant labor to be degrading or derogatory, but uplifting. Through industry and perseverance the farmer could show himself to be "Nature's true nobleman."[44]

State and county societies for promoting agriculture offered annual prizes for the highest yields on carefully measured acreages. To qualify, farmers recorded their costs to plow, manure, hoe, harrow, and harvest the plots. They listed the soil type, number of seeds planted, and the kinds and quantities of manures used. The reports, verified by witnesses, were published in the societies' transactions in order to educate other readers.

Joseph Frost of the York County (Maine) society planted one acre of land with the traditional corn, bean, and pumpkin polyculture. He added 15 loads of compost manure (50 bushels to the load) and 8 bushels of ashes. He planted five grains of corn, three bean seeds, and one pumpkin seed per hill; cultivated each row twice; and added 4 bushels of plaster. His yield for the acre was 71 bushels of shelled corn (143 in the ear), 2 bushels of beans, and 1 load of pumpkins for a profit of $69.16. Daniel Craig of Maine's Kennebec society, using similar methods, did even better. He harvested 142 bushels of corn ears, 3½ bushels of beans, and 3 cartloads of pumpkins for a profit of $91.50.[45]

Mr. Day of York County, Maine, planted only corn. He covered two and one-half acres of land with forty cartloads of compost manure for a yield of seventy-four bushels of shelled corn per acre. Oliver Foster, of Kennebec, who used twelve cords of manure, four bushels of plaster, and twelve bushels of ashes, harvested ninety-one bushels of shelled corn per acre. Vegetable garden polycultures planted on one acre also showed increased yields of potatoes, corn, beans, beets, cabbages, and turnips for home consumption, with the surplus sent to market for profit. These yields exemplified to readers that lower acreages farmed with increased labor could not only produce adequate food, but a surplus and profit as well.

Preoccupation with good management extended to women thrust into market farming through inheritance. Few women farmers kept diaries, but a set in the American Antiquarian Society in Worcester, Massachusetts, by Anna Blackwood Howell (1769–1855) of Gloucester County, New Jersey, covering twenty years indicates the problems faced by female farmers. At age fifty, on the death of her husband Joshua in 1818, Howell took over the family farm and fisheries. Her diaries, interleaved in agricultural almanacs put out under the auspices of the Philadelphia Society for Promoting Agriculture, record her attempts to improve her farming; her observations on nature, the weather, and her bees; and the anguish and loneliness with which she pursued farm management. Anna Howell (who lived to be eighty-six) kept her almanac diaries until the age of seventy, "to profit by the experience of the past year."[46] She recorded the names of numerous hired hands who helped her with plowing, planting, and harvesting, acknowledging "we are never sensible of our dependence upon the working classes till we are deprived of their services." She entered the dates on which she planted watermelons, sweet potatoes, cucumbers, pumpkins, beans, squash, and corn and the dates and quantities of the products she sent to market.[47]

In July 1824, she lamented that her early potatoes, cucumbers, and squash were the only crops that had not been "injured by neglect or injudicious killing. . . . My water melons and sweet potatoes will not pay for the manure." But she resolved to improve her farming by sowing lime on her early corn and cucumbers to try to prevent grub infestation. In August, she chastised herself for "some shamefully neglected potatoes. They were grown over as inexcusable." On December 8, a day when she "killed 11 hogs, weight 2.01g," she summed up her progress in management for the year: "My farming of the present year has been miserably conducted. William Thursts professed himself manager and as he was the greater part of his time under the influence of stimulants, . . . indolence and bad management in every sense of the word attended my business." She resolved in January that the coming year would be better: "Another year has come round. My last year's farming was unproductive. I must endeavour if I am spared my life and health to have it managed better."[48]

In January 1833, at age sixty-four, as she sat before her fire, Anna Howell saw the present state of her affairs as bleak indeed. "I feel too much alone tonight even to enjoy reading. It is truly dreary to be separated from every being in whom I feel an interest. My children— where are they? All removed to such a distance that I am deprived of their society almost entirely. If I read, it is a solitary gratification—I have no one to enjoy it with me to whom I can impart a passage or exchange an idea."

Howell's anguish over better management was symptomatic of the psychological pressure and isolation that the doctrine of agricultural improvement imposed on individuals in an increasingly atomistic society. A new generation of farmers was expected to assimilate the techniques of good management and to advance themselves for the good of society. S. E. Todd's *Young Farmer's Manual* in 1867 set the tone for the future: "Success will depend on a man's general management. It is the management—management first, management last, as well as the best of management, intermediately and collaterally—that crowns a farmer's labors with success. This will involve everything when taken in one harmonious combination—the management of crops and the management of manures; the management in the field and the management within doors." It is not surprising that some farmers opted to resist the competitive values of the market and to retain the satisfactions of the small farm and the neighborliness of the domestic community.[49]

Resisters

While gentlemen farmers were busy trying out and promoting the new techniques, many ordinary farmers seemed noteworthy for their "backwardness" and intransigence, stubbornly clinging to "outmoded" methods and habits. Improvement required too much time, risk, and capital for those contented with the older ways. "Improvements in agriculture ... travel slow, are received with distrust, and adopted with reluctance," complained improver Jesse Buel. Farmers "seem to think that their fathers knew all that is to be known, and a departure from the beaten track in which they trod would be viewed with as much horror as breaking all the ten commandments."[50]

To break out of the animate cosmos, farmers would have to give up their old superstitions about planting by the moon and the signs. "There is not a man in middle life," lamented N. T. True in 1853, "who cannot recall some neighbor that would not sow his grain at any other time than on the increase of the moon; who would not kill his pork on the wane of the moon, as it would certainly shrink in boiling. . . . Nor could he be induced to wean his young animals till he had consulted the signs in Robert B. Thomas' almanac."[51]

The influence of the moon on crops and animals was debated in farm journals and put to experiment by the more progressive farmers. The 1823 *New England Farmer* reprinted an article by German astronomer Heinrich Olbers (1758–1840) on "The Influence of the Moon Upon the Seasons," arguing that scientific experimentation had failed to establish any connection between the moon's phases and the weather, human health, the weight of animals, the germination of seeds, or the evaporation of fluids. J. Harrison Howard (1801–61), a farmer and nurseryman of North Bridgewater, Massachusetts, tested the theory of the moon in 1830 by killing hogs in its decrease ("notions unfavorable thereto have prevailed") to see if they weighed less. The hogs, purchased a year and two months earlier, seemed not to have suffered. The larger had gained a total of 275 pounds and the smaller 210 pounds. He also defied the old proverb, "grafting during an east wind will not succeed," by setting ten grafts on pear trees on a day when the wind was from the east. Yet many farmers, accustomed to planting, harvesting, and reading weather by the moon, were not convinced by the new "scientific" tests.[52]

Many of the new technologies advocated by improvers and scientists made little sense within the use-value orientation of the ordinary farmer. The English improver Jethro Tull had advocated extensive use of horses and drill plows in his book *Horse-hoeing Husbandry* (1731). His theory held that deep plowing with teams of horses would loosen the subsoil and allow roots to spread, while several additional plowings each season would keep the soil pulverized and remove weeds, increasing yields. For this extra work the faster horse was more efficient than the slow-moving ox. But premarket farmers had depended on easily trained, quickly maturing oxen because horses were more expensive, easily injured, and of no food value when their shorter working lives ended. Speed in plowing was of little significance to the farmer whose criteria for technological selection were based on survival and family well-being rather than on quantities, costs, budgets, profits, and accumulation.[53]

A farmers' committee of the Worcester Agricultural Society reaffirmed its faith in the ox in 1826. While the glamorous horse had been starring in shows and parades, the patient ox had been subduing the rocky soils of New England. The farmers doubted that any labor-saving machines would ever replace the ox's strength and docility. Especially impressive was the "great Sutton Team" of sixty-nine yoke of stately oxen that had conquered many stony Massachusetts fields. Even the improver Henry Colman affirmed that the ox increased his own capital, whereas the more expensive horse deteriorated in value.[54]

The "new horse-hoeing husbandry" was inappropriate for most American farmers, taught Samuel Deane in his *New England Farmer, or Georgical Dictionary* (1790). More labor was required for the new techniques to be successful than most could afford. The extra hoeing of wheat and rye caused grain to ripen later, making it prone to blasting. Moreover, New England frosts raised and mellowed the soil every year to a greater depth than could horse hoeing. The new drill plows recommended by Tull required care and attention and could not be given over to hired hands, especially in turning New England's rocks, roots, and stumps. The "new husbandry" worked best, Deane believed, on winter wheat that would ripen early and was planted on warm soil in a field absolutely clear of obstructions.[55]

New England farm journals presented mixed reviews of deep plowing. While acknowledging it to be currently in fashion, Thomas G. Fessenden's *New England Farmer* warned that it was not appropriate for all soils. Deep plowing was most successful on wet or poor soils where neither top nor bottom were particularly good. In most soils, however, an exchange of layers would only bury the topsoil that had been enriched for centuries and raise infertile subsoil that had been deprived of atmospheric influence. Using fertilizers was a less costly way to improve shallow soils.[56]

Samuel Deane likewise clung to the old theory of the absorption of nitrous particles from the atmosphere. Mineral, vegetable, and animal steams continually rose from the soil and mixed with the air, providing much of the food needed by living things. When plowed and fallowed, "the fertilizing particles in the air ... enter the soil, when it is loose and open, and much exposed to the air."[57]

The value of planted, fertilized fallows over "naked" or summer fallows was also debated. Too much fertilizer seemed to overstimulate the land and cause crops to decay, making naked fallows essential at regular intervals. As God had commanded the children of Israel, "six years thou shalt sow thy field and six years thou shalt prune thy vineyard, but the seventh year shall be a Sabbath of rest unto the land." Because of the "prolific principle" in the air, niter, ammonia, and other agents released into it by manure descended to fertilize the soil during its "Sabbath."[58]

Between the poles of improvers and resisters lay farmers who might try a new technique if a neighbor initiated it first and foot-draggers who might slowly introduce a change or two periodically. Some farmers became innovators who tried out every fad; others became experimenters or gentlemen scientists, poring over the new scientific books and treatises. Yet gradually the older values and technologies of the resisters lost ground to those of the scientific agriculturalists. By the 1860s, agriculture had adopted the patterns of large-scale machine production. Through the scientific management of agricultural production, human control over nature was increased. But this appropriation of nature's labor entailed harder human work, increased efficiency, and carefully kept accounts of crop yields, fertilizer weights, field sizes, labor time, and profit margins.

The new mechanical and chemical paradigm that legitimated this control reconstructed nature as the circulation of atoms, molecules, and physical forces. Algebraic science converted the colonial domain of the geometrically fenced landscape into numbered, measured fields. Within them, grains and vegetables once grown primarily for subsistence became marketable yields inscribed into the sum and difference columns of account books. Animate nature, whose forces and retributive powers had been accepted fatalistically by eighteenth-century farmers, was delivered to the laboratory for reduction to the ashes and atoms that would permit calculation of the soil nutrients needed to feed urban populations. Chemical laboratories inserted into the landscape allowed resources to be cycled through them for analysis. Resource objects became scientifically constructed objects; knowing became numbering. With the emergence of the new ontology and epistemology, agriculture came of age as an analytic, algebraic science.

Forest Capital and Logging Labor

Farm expansion in nineteenth-century New England occurred in tandem with forest clearing. The lumber industry expanded throughout the century as canals and railroads linked previously isolated areas to urban markets. By 1840 Maine was grossing $1,808,683 in lumber products. Massachusetts led the New England states in stove fuel with 278,069 cords of wood sold in 1840, followed by Maine with 205,011 cords. Maine boasted a total of 1,381 sawmills, Massachusetts 1,252, and Vermont 1,081, while Vermont was out in front in potash production showing 718 tons (see Appendix E).[59]

As in agricultural improvement, utilitarian, instrumental thinking began to permeate the ideology of nineteenth-century forestry. Cutting and planting decisions by timber merchants and foremen simplified habitats; labor and trees became interchangeable parts. Loggers moved from one camp to another according to the availability of work.

Within the logging industry a distinct social class of wage laborers evolved which owed its livelihood to timber merchants and landed proprietors. Like the resources they helped to extract, these property-less loggers were an integral part of an emerging system of resource management. While some of the loggers were farmers who worked during the winter to supplement family income, most were unmarried men. Jeremy Belknap, in his *History of New Hampshire* (1784–92), recognized the class differences that had emerged within the industry. "The contractors and agents made large fortunes by this traffic; but the laborers who spent their time in the woods ... anticipated their earnings, and were generally kept in a state of poverty and dependence."[60]

Logging spawned an array of semiskilled jobs that attracted those looking for a start in life or needing to augment subsistence. Work began in the winter, the most propitious time for felling timber since oxen could pull the trees over the snow. Before downing a large, potentially breakable mast pine, the "cutters" determined a favorable direction and then prepared a bedding of smaller trees whose branches would catch the falling pine like a safety net, breaking its fall. "Barkers" stripped the bark from the bottom surface to ease its journey over the snow. "Swampers" cleared straight paths from the tree to a nearby river. Then "teamsters" hitched their oxen to a sled at one end of the log and the cattle, with much straining, set it in motion. Additional oxen, attached to the rear of the log, slowed its forward motion on steep slopes. On hilltops these rearguard oxen could be suspended and perhaps killed unless the teamsters took great care.

In the spring the log drive downstream to the sawmills and shipping ports began. There the logs were sorted according to brands and chained together in a boom until cut. The work of the "drivers" was wet, cold, and dangerous; and with logjams frequent, agility was essential. "Raftsmen" chained the logs together and propelled them to the mill, where "scalers" measured them for volume and number of board feet. "Sawyers" worked from sunrise to sunset in the mills of village entrepreneurs to cut five hundred planks a day using straight saws powered by undershot waterwheels. After 1820 steam power eased their labor, and in the 1850s circular saws increased their output.[61]

While some lumberjacks availed themselves of opportunities to work themselves upward in the hierarchy to superintendents and mill owners, the plight of most loggers seemed to some observers to be a blemish on American life. Yale College president Timothy Dwight, who traveled extensively in New England at the turn of the eighteenth century, contrasted the lumbermen, fur traders, and fishermen who had been Maine's primary inhabitants until after the American Revolution with the farmers who settled there later. "Very many of [the former] are in a great measure destitute of property through life.... Those who are lumbermen are almost necessarily poor. Their course of life seduces them to prodigality, thoughtlessness of future wants, profaneness, irreligion, immoderate drinking, and other ruinous habits. The farmers of New England have never willingly resided among people of such a character."[62]

Edward Kendall, whose travel diaries in the northern United States were published in 1809, also contrasted this wage-earning class of loggers with the farmers whose thrift and hard work had made America strong. Somewhat like Crèvecoeur, who had likened frontier settlers to forest animals, Kendall wrote that the habits taken on by work in the forest were antithetical to "the system of preserving industry" because they alternated "toil and indolence." Unlike the farmer who worked today for fruits to be reaped tomorrow, the lumberer, too poor to possess land, preyed on the future. "Maine is covered with wood; wood, in all its forms, is marketable; and to the settlers is therefore equivalent to furs or fish; and the settlers have consequent-

ly degenerated, not into hunters nor fishermen, but into lumberers.
... As the hunter and the fisherman neglect the tillage of the earth to
pursue their game; as the wild herdsman moves from place to place,
content to pasture his cattle on the herb that he has been at no toil to
raise; so the lumberer wanders through the forest, making spoil in
his turn of the wealth of nature. . . . What nature has planted he en-
joys, but he plants nothing for himself."[63]

Kendall's economic analysis of resource use extended beyond a
simple environmental determinism. Because the lumberers freely
appropriated products from nature, without giving back anything in
return, they lost both time and money. Time was capital leading to
future advancement; money was gained from the market. "The wood
contained in his logs or shingles has cost him nothing; and he is but
too apt to value his time as nothing." With no capital of his own, the
lumberer sold his logs immediately at low prices in a saturated market, obtaining not cash but commodities for subsistence. Without the
rewards of accumulation and advancement, his life degenerated to
one of hardship and debauchery, his soul fed by "spiritous liquors"
that in turn weakened his body.[64]

Karl Marx, writing about fifty years later, would have agreed with
Kendall's insight about the free appropriation of nature's products.
But rather than advocating more time, capital, and accumulation as
the solution to the logger's dilemma, Marx stressed the structural
problem created by the division between merchant capital and (logging) labor. The laborer was an integral part of the appropriation
process, adding value to the free timber that nature had produced
and passing it on to the merchant to sell at a profit. As opposed to
using the wood for subsistence, the logger was alienated from his
own production, taking from nature something that did not improve
his own life. Or as Engels put it: "To make earth an object of huckstering—the earth which is our one and all, the first condition of
our existence—was the last step toward making oneself an object of
huckstering. It was and is to this very day an immorality surpassed
only by the immorality of self-alienation."[65]

Ecological Repercussions

The entrepreneurial interests, which had built the lumber business
from mercantile trade in the seventeenth century to a capitalist ven-

ture with distinct classes by the nineteenth, found by then that enthusiasm for exploitation had depleted the very resource base on which their fortunes depended. As lumber diminished near the coast by the 1790s, the mills gnashed their way upstream. Near Waldoborough, Maine, plank lumber was gone by 1790 and cordwood was nearly depleted. Elsewhere, a cord took two days by oxcart to reach the markets. Near Windham, a thriving timber village, which had built a sawmill in 1740 on Maine's Presumscot River, "where a magnificent forest of pine, hemlock, oak, and ash timber grew in profusion," closed its shops and houses in the 1820s and moved upstream to the new cotton mill. "As the land became denuded of trees suitable for milling purposes," lamented its chronicler, "this once flourishing village began to show signs of decay and dissolution ... until but two or three of the original dwellings were left, and aside from these nothing remained ... but ruined cellars and moss-grown foundation stones."[66]

Sawmills also disrupted the ecology of rivers. In Bedford, New Hampshire, the apple blossoms once signaled the opening of the fishing season; and before the waters were blocked by milldams and canals, people caught hundreds of fish with scoop nets set across falls and seines drawn across rivers. On the Presumscot River, near Falmouth, Maine, salmon, alewives, and shad could no longer swim upstream to spawn. Obstructions on the Merrimac and other rivers interfered with the salmon catch and particularly affected the poor. Soon legislation required that channels be provided for fish to swim around the milldams, and fishing privileges were temporarily restricted to allow fish to spawn and rebuild their numbers.[67]

Inland, forests along unnavigable rivers with tortuous currents required new techniques. To deal with the new problems, cooperative ventures, such as lumbering associations, river driving associations, and boom associations, formed to transport logs to the mill. New cargo carriers with small drafts and clamps to prevent sidewise current swings were developed, to be followed in the 1840s by sluices and canals to circumvent falls and oxbows, and finally by steamboats and railroads. In older areas paper mills began using young pulp timber, installed vats, and started employing young women at twelve cents a day plus room and board. Shingle-making machines, producing thirty-three shingles a minute, took over much of the work of the backwoods shingle industry.[68]

The nineteenth-century heyday of logging all over New England

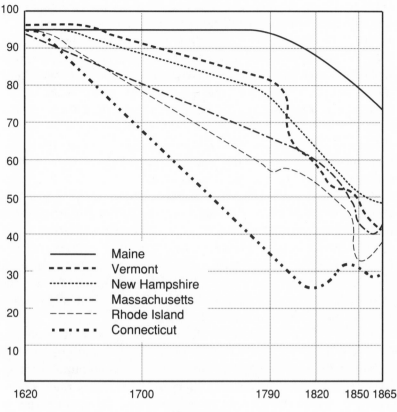

Figure 6.1

Estimated Percentage of Forest Area in Each New England State, 1620–1865.
Source: Ronald M. Harper, "Changes in the Forest Area of New England in
Three Centuries," *Journal of Forestry* 16, no. 4 (April 1918): 447.

transformed the land. Facilitated by the market and transportation
revolutions, forest cover disappeared at an alarming rate. From a
uniform high of 95 percent at the time of European settlement, Connecticut's forests had been reduced to 30 percent by 1850, Rhode
Island's to 32 percent, Massachusetts' to 40 percent, Vermont's to 45
percent, New Hampshire's to 50 percent, and Maine's to 74 percent
(Figure 6.1).

The resulting environment was very different from that encountered by Pilgrims and Puritans. Thousands of acres of woodlands had
disappeared, swamps had been drained, beaver ponds had vanished,
streams and rivers had been dammed. Indians had been virtually

annihilated by European diseases and warfare, and the forests of their ancestors were nearly depleted of the resources needed for subsistence. The oaks and hickories had been replaced by cattle and sheep grazing in pastures planted with English grasses. Springtime carpets of native forest flowers had yielded to fields of dandelions, English daisies, buttercups, clover, hawkweed, and chicory. Wolves and cougars, deer and moose had all but vanished from wooded lands.

In New England, observed George Perkins Marsh in 1864, "the great commercial value of the pine and the oak have caused the destruction of all the best . . . specimens of both. . . . The thinning of the woods by the axe of the lumberman has allowed the access of light and heat and air to trees of humbler worth." Eventually as the forest disappears, he warned, "all is changed. . . . The climate becomes excessive, and the soil is alternately parched by the fervors of summer, and seared by the rigors of winter. . . . The face of the earth is no longer a sponge, but a dust heap. . . . The earth stripped of its vegetable glebe, grows less and less productive." Eventually it is "no longer fit for the habitation of man."[69]

To many Americans, however, the new landscape that resembled Old England was far healthier than the pristine wilderness that had confronted their forebears. The moist vegetation and humidity of the forest caused colds, coughs, and catarrhs, its frequent rains were a nuisance, and the stagnant air of swampy lowlands was a perpetual ferment for noxious vapors. Now winters were warmer, summers less humid. The climate had been significantly altered by human intervention. Many scientists, doctors, and learned gentlemen of the late eighteenth century such as Dr. Hugh Williamson of the American Philosophical Society reveled in the improvements. "While the face of this country was clad with woods and every valley afforded a swamp or stagnant marsh, . . . the air was constantly charged with a gross putrescent fluid. . . . Fevers . . . are now evidently on the decline. . . . Pleuretic and other inflammatory fevers, with the several diseases of cold seasons, are also observed to remit their violence, as our winters grow more temperate."[70]

Conservation Consciousness

Even as these accolades to human progress were being pronounced, a conservation consciousness among elite easterners was
emerging. Gentlemen farmers, agricultural improvers, gardeners,
nurserymen, naturalists, scientists, presidents, governors, and army
and navy officers were calling for an end to thoughtless denudation of
woodlands and for managed reforestation. Wood shortages were becoming acute in eastern cities and the price of firewood was rising.
The American navy, like the English, was becoming concerned about
supplies of masts. James Madison (1818) thought that one of the
country's most serious problems was the "injudicious and excessive
destruction of timber and firewood." Noah Webster (1817) feared that
"our country cannot sustain the present consumption of wood for a
century to come." New York's Governor De Witt Clinton held out little
hope for change in people's habits until they had been seriously deprived by lack of wood.[71]

The Marquis de Chastellux, who traveled in America in 1780–82,
reported a conversation he had with Thomas Jefferson calling for
moderation in clearing future lands: "It appears equally dangerous
either to cut down or to preserve a great quantity of wood; so that the
best manner of proceeding to clear the country, would be to disperse
the settlements as much as possible, and to leave some groves of trees
standing between them." Dr. Benjamin Rush, in a paper presented to
the American Philosophical Society in 1785, suggested planting trees
around millponds and marshes, instead of draining them, to convert
unhealthy vapors to oxygen.[72]

Farsighted individuals, such as the revolutionary war general Benjamin Lincoln, whose notes on the cultivation of oaks were published
posthumously in 1814, were concerned that little timber could be
found within twenty miles of coastal towns and that builders had to
transport lumber thirty or forty miles. He recommended acorn planting for the sake of future generations who would need a strong navy
and lucrative commerce. But, he sighed, "there is little hope these
things will change for the better, since the tenure of our land cannot
secure them in the family for any distant period. Thus is destroyed
one great motive which would lead the grandsire to plant the acorn
... we cannot expect the pleasure of seeing the old man tottering in
the field, though aided by his staff, therewith piercing the ground for
the reception of the seed." In 1820, the Massachusetts Society for

Promoting Agriculture offered a prize, to be awarded seven years later, for the best plantation of white oaks of not less than one thousand trees per acre raised from acorns.[73]

The *New England Farmer*, edited by Thomas G. Fessenden, which began publication in the 1820s, carried numerous articles on tree planting, woodlot conservation, and forest uses. "Every farm ought to have a piece of wood-land, or forest, sufficient for fuel and other purposes," it recommended in 1828. When clearing land for farming, woodlands should be preserved on the least tillable sections for future fuel, tools, buildings, and carriages. Cattle should be kept out at all times. Thinly forested sections should be reseeded and a sufficient canopy maintained to allow young trees to survive. Trees planted along roads, insisted another writer, should be selected for usefulness as well as beauty, since in some future emergency they might be needed for fuel. Instructions on how to prepare and plant the seeds of forest trees were furnished by the editor so that all land capable of improvement could be seeded for the sake of future generations.[74]

In 1846, naturalist George B. Emerson presented to the Massachusetts legislature his *Report on the Trees and Shrubs Growing Naturally in the Forests of Massachusetts* in response to concern about the destruction of forests. Near the coast, building materials had to be brought from other states. The woodcraft industry of the Berkshires was in dire straits because of the lack of ash, beech, and linden. Materials for tanning, dying, baskets, carriages, and furniture had to be imported from Maine, New York, and the South. "Those old woods are every where falling. The axe has made ... wanton and terrible havoc." "The new settler clears in a year more acres than he can cultivate in ten, and destroys at a single burning many a winter's fuel, which would better be kept in reserve for his grandchildren."

As a solution, Emerson offered a rationale for careful management and information on the propagation of Massachusetts' native trees. Written for "the common, unlearned citizens, who live on farms, in the country, and have few books and little leisure," his proposal detailed the benefits of forests. Trees held back erosion and improved the soil by releasing air through their roots. Their decaying leaves produced mold that fertilized other plants. Forests kept the earth warmer in winter, protected it from too much heat in summer, and cut down the violence of winds, especially near the coast. To humans they afforded "an inexhaustible store-house of colors" and furnished building materials, transportation, and fuel. To farm animals they provided protection from heat and increased survival. He recommended that trees be planted near every farmhouse, pasture, and pond; that waste be curtailed; and that forests be reserved for future generations.[75]

By the 1850s, those who owned land and sawmills were beginning to look westward for speculation to the forests of Michigan, Wisconsin, and Minnesota, and southward to Pennsylvania and Louisiana. As capital flowed west, so followed labor. Local Maine newspapers carried advertisements from Wisconsin offering "a rare chance ... to enterprising practical lumbermen, where they may easily accumulate a fortune." Louisiana papers tried to shock southerners out of lounging in "listless indolence," while "eastern lumbermen" bought up their forests. Some who had worked their way upward from cutters or rafters to foremen or superintendents were able to invest in the new midwestern forest lands. With them the Maine lumberers took their skills, technology, and entrepreneurial vision. Behind them they left a forest depleted of its towering pines and spruces, its enormous spreading oaks and resilient hickories. In the late 1800s, those who remained behind to reap the dregs began to learn forest management and conservation, pulp and paper milling, and industrial consolidation. Outside capital poured into the state to build larger dams and waterpower works. Portable steam mills invaded the backcountry. A new phase of Maine forest history had begun.[76]

As lumberers moved west and farmers abandoned their lands, old-field succession set in. Henry David Thoreau, in 1860, formulated a theory about "The Succession of Forest Trees" to explain the environmental changes. Nature's alchemists, who effected transformation on the cutover lands, were the squirrels and birds. When a pine or hardwood forest was cut, a forest of the opposite type seemed mysteriously to spring up. Yet all over the forest floor were the tiny, barely noticeable seedlings of outlying trees. How did they get there? Each pine seed was encased in a sack with a wing to transport it on the wind. But the heavier acorn just fell to the ground beneath its parent. The planter of acorns was the squirrel, the pines their protectors. If the squirrel did not return to dig up its dinner, the acorn would sprout. Then when the pines were cut, the sunlight reached the oak seedlings allowing them to grow. "While the wind is conveying the seeds of pines into hard woods and open lands, the squirrels and other animals are conveying the seeds of oaks and walnuts into the pine woods, and thus a rotation of crops is kept up.... It has long been known to observers that squirrels bury nuts in the ground, but I am not aware that any one has thus accounted for the regular succession of forests."[77]

Alleviation of the eastern fuel crisis was afforded by new technology and a new source of fuel—coal. Large, drafty fireplaces, built in the days when log-cutting labor was at a premium, lost about 80 percent of their heat up the chimney. Replaced gradually by cast-iron Franklin stoves, fireplaces eventually became outmoded. After 1815 hundreds of patents on wood-burning stoves were issued, and in the 1830s anthracite-burning grates and stoves began to be used widely in New England and the Middle Atlantic states. Throughout the remainder of the nineteenth century, demand for wood as a fuel decreased as anthracite coal came into greater use in industries, railroads, and homes. The forests began to recuperate.[78]

Conclusion

The merger of mechanistic science with technology and capitalism during the first half of the nineteenth century sculpted an American instrumental mentality. Nature was engineered with machines to maximize production, while aesthetics was assigned to the realm of the private. Replanting forests and fertilizing soils returned nature's materials, not because it was a living partner, but because commercial farming and forestry required efficient management for market competition. Conservation consciousness was a utilitarian, homocentric ethic subservient to pragmatic means, not an ecocentric ethic that allowed a forest, lake, or swamp simply to exist. Instrumentalism depended on the separation of ends and means, values and facts, ethics and science.

The colonial ecological revolution had transformed Indian mimetic consciousness from an epistemology that gave equal value to all the senses to one dominated by the visual. Puritan and Jesuit religion worshiped a transcendent God through spiritual vision, replacing an animism inherent in nature. In the eighteenth century, Newtonian science was fused with Lockean empiricism and Cartesian rationalism into a framework of experiment and analysis. Empiricism was dominated by the physical eye, rationalism by the mind's eye.

During the market revolution of the nineteenth century, triggered by internal economic and geographic expansion after the War of 1812, a capitalist consciousness transformed American culture. Mechanistic science, on the cutting edge of elite intellectual development, became the legitimating framework for economic transformation. Transportation and industrial technology, the mechanical arts, agricultural chemistry, accounting, and printing came together with capitalist development to form an instrumental mentality.

The capitalist revolution separated private from public life. The public sphere of marketplace and politics was dominated by men, the private sphere of home and family by women. Nature was also severed: science and technology became the instrument for economic development, spirit and emotion a counterpoint to competition. From the first perspective, land was a "virgin" to be conquered and controlled; from the second, a mother who embodied moral law.

7

. . . .

Nature, Mother, and Industry

During the capitalist ecological revolution of the nineteenth century, nature—teacher, mother, and bringer of natural disasters
in the animate cosmos—was split into an abstract order of mechanical forces and a romanticized moral mother. The market economy
that dominated nature by extracting its wealth and secrets was offset
by the personal engagement of the romantic. Both nature and woman
became the locus of moral law and emotive expression. The new
forms of mechanical and moral consciousness legitimated capitalist
modes of production, reproduction, and ecology.

As production goals shifted toward the creation of capitalist profits,
new relationships between production and ecology emerged. Colonial mercantile capitalism had used European capital to extract colonial resources, shipping them to England for processing, while, in
subsistence-oriented communities, farm production had existed for
the sake of the reproduction of daily life. Now American private enterprise used American resources and labor to promote internal economic growth. Production shifted away from the circulation of nutrients and useful products within the local farm or community toward
the importation of raw materials and the exportation of finished commodities. In the early putting-out systems, a storekeeper imported
materials and exported finished goods. But in the industrial system,
textile mills converted entire rural communities into exporting factories.

Ecological side effects appeared as externalities hidden from economic calculation. To increase yields on commercial farms, fertilizers were imported from abroad or produced in chemical factories.
To increase efficiency, wool and cotton were produced on northern
farms or southern plantations and transported to New England textile mills for processing. But these commercial gains had ecological
costs. Topsoil fertility and water quality were not part of the cost of
raw materials. Air pollution, water pollution, and soil deterioration

were not included in the calculation of profits. Runoffs, sewage, and chemical dyes were flushed away in streams. Steam engines discharged soot into the air. Milldams blocked the progress of migrating fish. The costs of pollution and depletion were paid by the poor and by later generations.

The capitalist ecological revolution split production and reproduction into two separate spheres. As male farmers began to specialize in women's traditional dairy, poultry, and vegetable production, and as textile mills took over their clothing production, woman's primary domain was redefined as reproduction. Woman's sphere still included her biological and social roles of childbearing and child rearing (although nineteenth-century family sizes dropped dramatically), but her traditional farmyard and garden production was constricted to the reproduction of daily life within the household walls. Her role as equal producer in subsistence agriculture changed to reproducer as her outdoor labor turned to indoor domesticity. With these changes the quantity of her labor did not decrease, and probably even increased. Within the home she may also have done putting-out work such as braiding palm leaf hats, weaving rag carpets, or making silk twist buttons or taken in boarders to help support her family, especially if single or widowed. Her role as moral mother, however, emphasized the daily care of the family and the socialization of children.

The structural split between productive and reproductive spheres was necessary for the maintenance of the market economy. Within the household, as within the larger social whole, male and female, head and heart, calculation and emotion expressed the dualities of industrial capitalism. The outward motive sphere of the male was balanced by the inward emotive sphere of the female. Conjugal and motherly love bound the husband, wife, and children together in a family unit. Man's role was to compete in the marketplace or provide labor for a male entrepreneur. Woman's role was to express superior moral virtue in setting standards of purity, piety, and nurture for her family. Woman could work for wages while single, but as wife and mother she focused her energies on the home. For middle-class women, capitalist production severed woman the reproducer and homemaker from man the producer and money-maker.[1]

Capitalist Production

Agricultural specialization and industrialization worked together to displace nineteenth-century men and women from their traditional roles in farm production. Male farmers began specializing in women's traditional domain of dairying, vegetable gardening, and poultry raising, as well as in sheep raising for the new textile factories. In colonial New England, dairy farming had been an important enterprise. Before the American Revolution, New England exported an average of 165,513 pounds of butter and cheese annually, compared with net imports for the middle and southern colonies. But these exportable surpluses were in reality quite small. Rhode Island's exports of close to 200,000 pounds of cheese were offset by Boston's need to import butter and cheese. The Connecticut Valley, a primary producer of cattle, flax, and grains, was not a major exporter of dairy products, and New Hampshire sent butter only in small lots to north-coast towns.[2]

In the nineteenth century, however, dairying became a major farm industry as a rising urban, manufacturing populace required perishable foods. Although many farmers continued to make their own cheese, Berkshire County, Massachusetts, and Litchfield County, Connecticut, increased their production of butter and cheese for the New York, Boston, and southern markets, while Rhode Island specialized in butter and milk for seaport towns. By the 1850s, Vermont and New Hampshire were turning from sheep raising to dairying. New England's total production of cheese in 1850 was about 27 million pounds or an average of 11 pounds per capita. Butter production was about 43 million pounds or an average of about 18 pounds per capita.[3]

Journals, such as the *New England Farmer*, published numerous articles on good dairying techniques by men who had learned them from their wives, along with a few communications from women. The articles advised would-be dairymen to maintain fertile pastures and clean dairies, and suggested putting older daughters in charge of butter and cheese making. Dairy farms should have plenty of sunshine and south-facing pastures near rushing streams, not lowland marshes. Cows needed air and sweet feed supplemented with meal until spring grasses grew high. Yields could be increased by plowing, composting, and manuring pastures, and rotating them with mowing lands and tillage. A well-ventilated, clean dairy house was needed for processing superior milk, sweet cream, and buttermilk. Quality butter was to be lightly salted and packed tightly in spruce or white ash tubs for shipping.[4]

Vegetable gardening for the Boston and overseas markets transformed many farms in Essex and Middlesex counties in eastern Massachusetts in the 1820s, 1830s, and 1840s. Wage labor and heavy use of manures from farms and cities increased yields as well as the value of farmlands.[5]

Poultry and egg farming also became a major business. Augmenting the stocks of Plymouth Rock hens and Rhode Island Reds were Italian Leghorns, Scotch Grays, and English Dorkings. Rhode Island became a leader in the production of poultry, with Washington County specializing almost entirely in the business. In 1849 a New England Society for the Improvement of Domestic Poultry, consisting of farmers, poulterers, doctors, and lawyers, was organized. A poultry show in 1850 in Boston displayed over 12,000 birds to 20,000 people. In an article in the *New England Farmer*, poultry farmer Allen Dodge promoted the advantages of poultry as a business. The objectives of poultry husbandry, he pointed out, were, first, to raise and fatten chickens and, second, to obtain eggs for the market. Both fowl and eggs sold quickly and brought good prices. The skeptical farmer need only stand outside a grocery store and watch the rate at which the piles of eggs disappeared, examine the account balance at the end of the year, and note the number of eggs used by urbanites, hotels, and bakeries. "With such a demand, increasing every season," Dodge advised, "will it not pay well for our farmers to keep more fowls ... and to make the rearing of poultry an object of equal importance with that of raising swine or fattening calves?"[6]

Poultry farmer W. Bacon agreed that no stock paid so high a return on investment as poultry. Formerly ridiculed as small-time egg money, made only by farmers' wives willing to collect and sell what they could carry, a dozen eggs would now bring in eighteen cents compared to sixty-five cents for an entire bushel of corn. Howard Coffin bragged about pullets weighing up to nine pounds apiece and a cock that tipped the scales at eleven and one-half. In Lynn, Massachusetts, two poulterers killed three hundred to five hundred chickens a week, employing men full-time to buy up local chickens.[7]

While poorer or more isolated farm women continued to rely on home-produced butter, eggs, and cheese, many middle-class rural wives found purchasing cheaper than production. The direction of these changes in dairying, vegetable, and poultry farming to commercial agriculture was to decrease women's direct interaction with the natural environment in the sphere of production.

Another displacement took place within women's traditional roles in household textile production. In 1810, when Albert Gallatin submitted his report on American manufactures to Congress, textiles and clothing were produced primarily in the home. Woolen, cotton, linen, leather, and buckskin clothing varied according to the availability of sheep, cattle, deer, cotton, flax, and hemp. Men herded the sheep and cattle, hunted the deer, planted and harvested the flax, and cut the wild hemp from which women produced clothing. To make woolen cloth, women and girls tore and washed the sheep fleeces, and carded, rolled, combed, greased, and spun them into yarn. After weaving the yarn into cloth, they softened it at a local fulling mill; dyed it with bark, berries, indigo, madder, or cochineal; and sewed it into garments. They also combed, spun, bleached, and wove cotton, flax, and silk into softer, finer fabrics. From the coarser textiles, they made shirts, dresses, trousers, towels, tablecloths, bedticks, sheets, and pillowcases; from finer materials, aprons, gowns, handkerchiefs, ribbons, lace, and buttons.[8]

By the late colonial period, however, women in some areas could take their fleeces, yarn, or cloth to local spinning, carding, and fulling mills where machines could be substituted for one or two of the home operations. In 1790, Samuel Slater, who had been an apprentice in the Arkwright and Strutt textile mill in England, copied from memory the Arkwright design for a water frame for spinning yarn. In collaboration with William Almy and Moses Brown, he set up a spinning mill in Pawtucket, Rhode Island. Using waterpower from a dam built on the Blackstone River, it employed nine children as a permanent labor force. Three years later the partners enlarged the dam and built a new mill with three carding machines and two spinning frames. Their putting-out system imported raw cotton and sold the factory-produced yarn to women who wove it into cloth. By 1800 they were employing families of over one hundred workers, and production expanded again during the embargo on English goods during the War of 1812.[9]

In 1815, with the introduction of the power loom, developed from memory by merchant Francis Cabot Lowell with the aid of mechanic Paul Moody at Waltham, Massachusetts, weaving also became cheap and efficient. The Boston Manufacturing Company in Waltham integrated all the steps in a single location on a scale far larger than the

Rhode Island putting-out system. Two hundred power looms in a 45-by-150-foot room with an elevated desk for an overseer and additional rooms for carding, spinning, drawing, and repairing constituted the factory. Waltham systems powered by water mills were introduced on even larger scales at Lowell in 1820; Dover and Nashua, New Hampshire, and Chicopee, Massachusetts, in the 1820s; Manchester, New Hampshire, in 1831; and Saco-Biddeford, Maine, in 1840. The number of mills operated by stationary steam engines reached 117 by 1838, with larger mills being erected in subsequent years in the seaport towns of Newburyport and Salem, Massachusetts, and in Portsmouth, New Hampshire.[10]

In addition to men and whole families, the textile mills recruited young single women as labor by offering wages high enough to attract them from family farms, but below those of men. In these factories, boys and girls, men and women were all employed in a series of semiskilled to skilled and supervisory jobs. Boys worked as lapboys, carrying the full cans of carded laps from the breakers to the finishers and from the finishers to the drawing frames. Bobbin girls and boys removed full bobbins of spun yarn and replaced them with empty ones. Men operated the picking and carding machines since they required strength, worked in the mill yards and repair shops, and assumed supervisory roles as second hands and overseers. Women operated the machines in all intervening steps. Lowest paid were those who fixed broken threads and restarted the spinning throstles and drawing frames. Weavers who repaired threads and replaced shuttle bobbins on two looms simultaneously needed greater skill and received higher wages. Dressers worked in larger, airy rooms maintaining the temperature and level of the sizing, repairing threads, and determining when the yarn was dry enough to be wound. The most skilled and efficient women worked at drawing in the threads of the warp through the harness and reed, preparing the beams for the weavers (see Figure 7.1).[11]

By the 1830s, textile production had moved out of the home. Prices for finished cloth fell sixfold between 1815 and 1830, leaving women with little reason to produce their own cloth. Farm girls found employment during maidenhood in the spinning mills, but as wives and mothers they were relieved of time-consuming textile production. Instead, they could purchase the finished cloth from which to sew their families' clothing.[12]

To supply the mills with wool, New England farmers increased

Figure 7.1
"Woman Drawing in Warp Ends." The most highly skilled occupation for women in the New England textile mills was that of drawing in the warp threads through the harness and reed. Reproduced from *A History of Wonderful Inventions* (1855), courtesy of the Museum of American Textile History, North Andover, Massachusetts.

their commercial production of sheep. Sheep were especially adapted to the rocky hills of Vermont and New Hampshire, and these states began specializing in sheep production to the exclusion of other staples and marketable commodities. By 1836, towns bordering the Connecticut Valley in the two states had become huge sheep runs grazing

5,000 to 10,000 sheep apiece. By 1840, the number of sheep in New Hampshire reached 617,000 or 2¼ sheep per person, while those in Vermont totaled 1,681,000 or 5¾ per person. But as western markets began to produce wool more cheaply by the late 1840s, New England hill farmers were forced to turn to the more labor-intensive business of dairying, many building up their herds to between twenty and forty head. Butter and cheese in the Boston market now brought in two to four times the profits per animal than could be obtained from sheep.[13]

Capitalist Ecological Relations

The textile mills altered older conceptions of water rights as well as stream ecology. Colonial common law assumed that the flow of streams was part of the natural order. People could use or otherwise enjoy the water that flowed past their land, but could not alter the rights of other users on the same stream. Any obstruction such as a milldam had to be for a necessary purpose and needed the consent of those whose interests were at stake.

Grain mills, iron mills, sawmills, and textile mills all obtained waterpower by damming streams. Massachusetts had passed its first Mill Act regulating mill development in 1713 and Rhode Island followed in 1734. Mill owners could build dams and flood upstream farmlands if they paid a damage rent to the owners. The early grain and fulling mills were considered essential to farmers' welfare, not a development for profit. Mill owners worked seasonally when grain was available to be ground or lumber to be sawed.

The mills had a significant ecological impact in obstructing the routes of spawning fish. Alewives, shad, and Atlantic salmon migrated up the rivers each spring to spawn. The early milldams could be opened during fish runs and fishways were built along their sides. Furthermore, Fish Acts regulated mill construction, protecting the public's right to catch fish for subsistence during the spring "starving time" when grain supplies were low. Rhode Island's Fish Acts of 1719 preserved and improved river fishing by preventing obstructions that would hinder fish migration. No dams could be built without a town's permission and those that hindered fishing could be removed. The 1735 Fish Act further stipulated that mill owners had to provide fishways during the spring runs.[14]

By the late eighteenth century, however, farmers and mill owners increasingly conflicted over the right to fish versus the right to use streams for capitalist development. When Rhode Island iron millers in 1769 petitioned for a water-powered blast furnace on the Pawtuxet River, they were exempted from the Fish Act of 1735. But in 1773, farmers retaliated by pushing through legislation that allowed them to blast away rocks at dams on the Blackstone River so that fish could pass upstream. In 1792 Slater and Brown met resistance from long-established grain mill owners when they tried to build their cotton mill above the falls on the Blackstone. But the more intensely capitalistic cotton mill ultimately triumphed over both the grain mills' common-law rights and the farmers' traditional fishing rights. Commercial fishermen then seized the opportunity to repeal a law that had prohibited them from using nets below the falls, spelling the end of the fish migrations. Capitalist enterprise was the ultimate victor over both fish and farmer.[15]

In these victories of textile mills and commercial fishermen, both the fish and the streams became natural resources in the private enterprise system. Neither the rights of fish to spawn nor those of streams to maintain their own natural flow were considered in the legal battles. These traditional "ecological rights" became externalities in the capitalist system.

Vermont's fish commissioner, George Perkins Marsh, commented on the ecological connections between mill expansion and fish depletion in 1857. In a report to the Vermont legislature, entitled "The Artificial Propagation of Fish," he warned that dams and reservoirs contributed to soil erosion, industrial wastes polluted the streams in which fish spawned, and the lumbering of forests changed stream flows, altering the supply of insect larvae needed by the young fish. "Almost all the processes of agriculture, and of mechanical and chemical industry," he wrote, "are fatally destructive to aquatic animals within reach of their influence. Industrial operations are not less destructive to fish which live or spawn in fresh water. Mill dams impede their migrations, if they do not absolutely prevent them, the sawdust from lumber mills clogs their gills, and the thousand deleterious mineral substances, discharged into rivers from metallurgical, chemical, and manufacturing establishments, poison them by shoals."[16]

In *Man and Nature* (1864), Marsh argued that the earth had been given to humans for "usefruct alone, not for consumption." In New England, as all over the globe, humans were disturbing influences, disrupting long-evolved harmonies on the heels of which followed unanticipated consequences. Humans introduced new species of plants and animals, hunted large mammals to extinction, cut down forests, and poured industrial wastes into streams. "Of all organic beings, man alone is to be regarded as essentially a destructive power ... though living in physical nature, he is not of her, ... he is of more exalted parentage, and belongs to a higher order of existences than those born of her womb and submissive to her dictates." Instead of destroying their environment, he advised, humans should use their talents to restore nature. They should "become coworkers with nature in the reconstruction of the damaged fabric," reforest the land, return runoffs to their natural watercourses, cut new canals to open up stagnant streams, and create reservoirs to equalize atmospheric humidity so that vegetable and animal life could thrive.[17]

The introduction of steam power made it possible for textile mills to move into cities. This technological innovation brought additional ecological costs in the form of air pollution from the burning of coal, wood being in short supply. The first steam engine in New England was built for the Middletown Woollen Manufacturing Company of Connecticut in 1811. It drove the machinery for all textile operations as well as heating the mill in winter. A second was built in Rhode Island for the Providence Woollen Company in 1812. Slater's adoption of steam power in 1827 lent credibility to the new engines despite the ready availability of waterpower throughout New England. By 1838 Providence had 23 engines, and in Boston 114 engines were operating sawmills, woodworking shops, machine shops, cordage factories, ironworks, tanneries, distilleries, breweries, chemical laboratories, laundries, and bone mills. In New England as a whole, 317 stationary steam engines, 46 steam boats, and 51 locomotives were burning coal. By the 1840s anthracite from Pennsylvania was supplementing bituminous coal in seaboard cities such as Providence, New Haven, New Bedford, Newburyport, and Salem. To operate its engines in 1841, Boston was importing 90,000 cords of wood, 124,041 bushels of bituminous coal from Richmond, Virginia, 12,754 tons of foreign coal, and 110,432 tons of anthracite from eastern Pennsylvania. Coal was being delivered by canal and rail to Hartford, Springfield, Lawrence, and Lowell.[18]

From the vantage point of Walden Pond, Henry David Thoreau commented on the environmental effects of the commercial use of steam power in New England. "The whistle of the locomotive penetrates my woods summer and winter ... informing me that many restless city merchants are arriving within the circle of the town.... They shout their warning to get off the tracks ... timber like long battering-rams going twenty miles an hour.... All the Indian huckleberry hills are stripped, all the cranberry meadows are raked into the city. Up comes the cotton, down goes the woven cloth; up comes the silk, down goes the woollen.... I meet the engine ... with its steam cloud like a banner streaming ... I hear the iron horse make the hills echo with his snort like thunder, shaking the earth with his feet, and breathing fire and smoke from his nostrils."

The steam engine, along with steam-driven lumber and textile mills, made possible the export of timber, wool, and fish and the import of cotton and fertilizers beyond the local community to the wider economy of the United States. "Here goes the lumber from the Maine woods," Thoreau continued, "... pine spruce, cedar,—first, second, third, and fourth qualities, so lately all of one quality, to wave over the bear, and moose, and caribou. Next rolls Thomaston lime, a prime lot, which will get far among the hills before it gets slaked.... This closed car smells of salt fish, the strong New England and commercial scent, reminding me of the Grand Banks and the fisheries." Such were the commercial advantages, but also the ecological costs of capitalist development (see Figure 7.2).[19]

Reproduction

The changes in water law, with their concomitant ecological effects, were part of a wider transformation in legal-political reproduction. While the common-law framework of the colonial era had supported the reproduction of daily life and the public good, the nineteenth-century instrumentalist conception legitimated competitive economic development. The legal-political system was dominated by males who held positions of power in state and national governments and the legal profession. Business interests lay at the core of national power during the administrations of the Federalists and mid-century Whigs, punctuated by the more liberal administrations of Jefferson and Jackson during which democratic reforms and the interests of ordinary people found expression.

Albert Gallatin's vision of a program of internal improvements stimulated development of the transportation infrastructure neces-

Figure 7.2
Steam Locomotive Arriving at Walden, painted by an unknown artist of the
late nineteenth century. In *Walden* (1854), Thoreau lamented the whistle of
the train and rattle of the cars that interrupted the solitude of Walden Pond
and the environmental disruption that the railroad system facilitated. Reproduced courtesy of the Concord Free Public Library, Concord, Massachusetts.

sary for continued market expansion. Throughout the nineteenth
century, canals, bridges, roads, and railroads received political and
financial support. The first national bank and a series of protective
tariffs promoted the interests of business, while new laws and policies encouraged settlement of western lands acquired during the War
of 1812.

The emerging legal framework sanctioned a national policy of improving and cultivating land, through a revision of the common-law
doctrine concerning "waste." In England, where land had been highly
developed since the Renaissance, the common law held that, if a ten-
ant cleared land, he was wasting it and was liable for damages. But,
ruled a New York judge in 1810, "the doctrine of waste, as understood
in England, is inapplicable to a new unsettled country."[20]

The new interpretation of waste favored male heirs whose fathers
had left them undeveloped land. Although women had never had
power in the legal-political sphere, the instrumentalist conception of
law removed some of their common-law rights to develop property

inherited from their husbands or fathers. A Massachusetts judge in 1818 ruled that a widow's "estate would be forfeited if she were to cut down any of the trees valuable as timber. . . . The mere change of the property from wilderness to arable or pasture land . . . might be considered waste . . . the heir having a right to the inheritance, in the same character as it was left by the ancestor." Thus the right to improve property and to benefit from its increased value lay with men.[21]

Not only were women's legal-political rights curtailed, but their traditional roles as biological reproducers were also constricting. New England was leading a dramatic century-and-a-half-long decline in childbearing. Nationwide, women who married in 1800 bore an average of 6.4 children, those who married between 1800 and 1849 had about 4.9 children, while those who married between 1870 and 1879 had 2.8 children. A study of the decline in Sturbridge, Massachusetts (representative of rural central New England), shows a drop-off from 8.83 children for women marrying in the period 1730–59 to 5.30 for those marrying between 1820 and 1839. Between 1730 and 1840, the age of first-time brides rose from about nineteen to about twenty-five years, while the age for men at first marriage rose from twenty-five to twenty-nine years. The number of pregnant brides decreased from a fourth of all women in the 1730 cohort to less than 3 percent of those in the 1820 cohort. Additionally, the age of women when their last child was born declined from thirty-eight for those married in the 1730s to thirty-five for those married in the 1820s.[22]

This demographic transition was achieved both through economic changes that favored later marriage ages and through conscious family limitation. First, with fewer farms that could be subdivided and increasing costs of land, men and women had to wait until they were older to obtain the economic resources necessary to start a family. Capitalist farming, factories, and putting-out systems provided the means to accumulate financial resources.

Second, a new consciousness about biological reproduction supported the economic transition to capitalism. A flood of manuals, articles, and lectures on abortion and sexuality helped to deal with undesired pregnancies and repress sexual expression. In the early 1800s manuals described herbs, exercises, and other abortion techniques that could be used before quickening, and by the 1850s newspapers and magazines advertised chemicals, condoms, diaphragms, and sponges for preventing conception. John Todd, William Alcott, and Sylvester Graham (all New Englanders) lectured young men, particularly those who had left home to work in cities and factories, about the evils of masturbation and premarital sex. Their recommended social controls over the body included limitations on sex, food, and alcohol consumption, as well as increased exercise and cleanliness. The sublimation of sexual energy into harder work and moral virtue fueled the expansion of capitalism.[23]

The constriction of female roles in the arenas of biological and legal-political reproduction was compensated by an expansion of duties in the other two areas of reproduction—the reproduction of daily life within the home and the socialization of children and husbands. As the amorality of the marketplace created its moral antithesis in domesticity, high ideals were attached to women's functions within the home.

The invention of housework for the middle-class wife was a product of the capitalist revolution. Although home spinning and weaving declined, the increased availability of cotton, linen, and woolen cloth meant that families expected more clothing. With the increase in clothing came an increase in sewing and washing, including the physical work of heating and carrying water, and scrubbing, wringing, and carrying the garments; and a concomitant increase in ironing, mending, folding, and putting the clothes away. Work in the kitchen also increased. As more white flour from western mills found its way to local stores and as eggs and butter could be readily purchased, more fancy baked goods were produced. The new coal-burning stoves had to be stoked, tended, and cleaned. Under colonial production men had worked in the kitchen in the evenings husking and shelling corn, peeling apples for cider, whittling bowls and spoons, making cradles, and assisting in weaving. Agricultural specialization and industrialization relieved many men of these and other tasks, such as butchering hogs, chopping and splitting wood, building fireplaces, and making shoes. The home became a place of refuge and leisure for men, a place of increased labor for women.[24]

The second domain into which women's roles under capitalism expanded was the socialization of children. The trilogy of mother, wife, and home focused the ideology of social reproduction. As mother and wife, woman embodied the moral law. Her home was the space in which she instilled morals in her husband and children. Both a morally uprighteous mother and a healthy natural environment were necessary to produce a healthy child.[25]

Farm journals especially focused on the role of nature in creating moral values. No spot on earth was freer from vice and immorality than a farm home. Shielded from urban contamination, the fresh breezes offered strength for body and soul. At the day's end, the industrious farmer could seat "himself around the hearthstone, with his affectionate wife and smiling children." Protected from the tempests of nature, the financial risks and speculations that beset the merchant, and the commotion of the politician, the farmer in his homestead remained stable and secure. "His corn ripens, his garden flourishes, and mother earth bountifully rewards him for all his toil." "Here, in the return of every season, and the opening of every flower, [children] are continually beholding the ever varying works of nature, the wisdom and goodness of its author, and learning to love and adore nature's God."[26] Female values, in combination with agricultural management, would tame and improve wild nature while simultaneously "civilizing" and elevating husbands and children. Under woman's influence on the farm, weedy pastures and fields would give way to abundant harvests and dilapidated cottages would be replaced by neatly painted farmhouses.[27]

In 1848, under the editorship of S. W. Cole, the *New England Farmer* added a "Ladies" or "Domestic Department" which instilled society's expectations in female readers. Woman reproduced the social whole, not with scepter, but with moral suasion, the column argued. To her "the church and the State must come for their origin and support," and children should come to feel their mother was holy. A mother's look, a father's nod of approval should be followed by lessons from nature. Walking in green, daisy-filled meadows, admiring birds' nests, humming bees, and creeping ants directed the child's thoughts "to nature, . . . virtue, and . . . to God himself."[28]

To preserve republican institutions, continued the Domestic Department, it was important to produce mothers with high moral character. If mothers were idle, vain, or addicted to fashion, their neglected children would grow like weeds in uncultivated fields; but if their influence fell silently, subtly, and constantly like the dew, it would have a lasting effect through their sons' brilliant deeds. Because mothers molded the family's morals, shaping boys to the age of ten or twelve and girls far longer, they should be well educated. "Wherever there is a well educated intelligent mother, there is also an intelligent family of children." Moreover, educated women were essential to the well-ordered farm. "Much of the success, prosperity, and comfort of every farmer depends upon the management of his indoor concerns by his wife."[29]

As wife, a woman must also keep her husband from falling into vice. She was the Deity's most powerful means of instilling him with virtue. A good farmwife, proclaimed Maine's N. D. True, could civilize and uplift both wild nature and rough-hewn men. A wife was a man's model, helping him to obey nature's moral law. No farmer or entrepreneur could expect to prosper if his animal passions continually occupied and debased his life. Dr. James Bates struck fear in the hearts of men guilty of masturbation and untamed sexuality with his stern warning about nature's retribution. "Nature is a strict accountant, an inexorable judge and executioner; no one violates her laws physically, sensually, mentally or morally, and escapes retribution. She needs no witnesses, but has an intuitive perception of offences committed against her laws, whether in the secret chambers or on the house top." Men must control their sexual passions according to the example set by their mothers so that those "shameful outbreaks, which disgrace our natures, would rarely occur." When passion was "permitted to take the reins ... licentiousness, and destruction of body, mind, and character" resulted.[30]

Thus, as women's outdoor farm and indoor textile production declined, their reproductive roles were elevated. Until marriage a young farm woman might work outside the home in textile production or supervise her father's dairy, but her obligation to society was the biological reproduction that created the next generation of producers and the social reproduction that prepared her offspring to take their places in society. She must be educated in order to consciously and responsibly carry out her duties. No longer was it sufficient to learn social roles mimetically through observing the hard work, frugality, and piety of elders. A mother must actively engage herself in passing down to her children a complex of moral virtues that would redeem the amorality of the marketplace and provide a refuge from the stress of competition. Men still reproduced patriarchal society through politics, property, and production, but these were now balanced by the elevation of womanhood, motherhood, and domesticity.

Production and Reproduction in Utopia:
Mother Ann and the Shakers

Shakerism offered New Englanders an alternative to the gender inequalities of market production, property ownership, and patriarchical religion. Through cooperation the Shakers were able to support larger groups of people on their communal farms than could market farm families. They eschewed biological reproduction, recruiting members through conversion. Their religious consciousness celebrated nature and their art and song appreciated the natural world as a representation of the heavenly world. The Shaker utopian model represented a viable ecological alternative to the environmental depletions caused by commercial expansion.

The Shakers derived their egalitarian religious mores from Mother Ann Lee (d. 1784), an illiterate hat cutter and textile worker from Manchester, England, who came to America and founded the first Shaker community in 1774 in Watervliet, New York. Mother Ann and her community of Shaker elders migrated through New England on an evangelical tour from 1781 to 1784, converting hundreds of new members and creating Shaker communities in Enfield, Stonington, Preston, Windham, and Cheshire, Connecticut; and Grafton, Upton, Petersham, Ashfield, Rehoboth, Norton, and Harvard, Massachusetts. Her followers continued the residential method of conversion in Vermont, New Hampshire, and Maine. Smaller "outfamilies" were created at Cheshire and Savoy, Massachusetts; Guilford and Pittsford, Vermont; Tuftonboro, New Hampshire; Saybrook, Connecticut; and Gorham, Maine.[31]

Mother Ann believed in a dualistic male-female God who created men and women in its image, according to Gen. 1:27: "In the image of God created he him; male and female created he them." Instead of a masculine triune God, Shakers worshiped a quaternity: Father, Holy Mother wisdom, son (Jesus), daughter (Mother Ann). The masculine God was power and truth, the feminine God wisdom and love. All complete human beings, born of God, partook of the original fatherhood and motherhood. Shakers expected equal leadership from men and women: male and female ministers, deacons and deaconesses, sisters and brothers. Forbidding sexual relations, they lived and worked in separate spaces, but faced each other for worship, conversation, singing, and dancing.[32]

Shaker communism represented an alternative to private enterprise farming. Against patriarchal ownership of property, all shared
equally in the community farm. Because land did not have to be subdivided and passed down to sons, higher populations could be supported than on single-owner farms. The goal of Shaker communities
was self-sufficiency, and they developed a high level of husbandry.
Intensive farming used and replenished the soil, while innovative
techniques such as the round barn made dairy and manure production efficient. The famous three-story barn, built in 1826 in Hancock,
Massachusetts, had a diameter of 55 feet and a circumference of 270
feet. A 35-foot-high circular haymow held 400 tons of hay loaded
directly from the driveway. On the floor below, fifty-two cows, with
heads pointed inward toward a central feeding trough, were milked
from moveable stanchions. Their manure fell into the basement floor
whence it could be loaded onto carts for spreading on fields. With
their efficient gravity-flow barn-to-field manure system, the Shakers
harvested high yields of corn, rye, oats, barley, wheat, and flax and
bred high-quality cows, horses, oxen, sheep, and swine. They also
marketed products such as apples, garden seeds, and herbs.[33]

A simple life-style avoided the fetishizing of commodities, yet craft
production allowed the acquisition of necessary items not produced
by the community. They converted broom corn into quality brooms
and brushes, and wove the wool of carefully bred sheep into cloaks
and cloths. Shaker sisters produced shirts, bonnets, capes, canned
goods, herbs, and medicines as well as invented the cut nail, circular
saw, and revolving oven. Shaker brothers invented an apple corer, a
washing machine, and "a summer covering for a flat-iron stove" that
cooled the room as the stove heated. Others of unknown sex invented
a clothespin, butter worker, and cheese press. Rejecting capitalism
and refusing to patent their inventions, Shakers made them available
for the rest of the world to use.[34]

Shaker religious consciousness idealized nature and celebrated it
in ritual and art. In 1837, Mother Ann's second coming opened a new
era of divine inspiration manifested in songs, dances, and drawings.
Several young Shaker girls in Watervliet, New York, began dancing,
shaking, and dreaming that they were wandering in lovely fields,
picking delicious fruits in bountiful gardens, gathering beautiful
flowers, and laughing and singing. The mysticism spread and other
Shaker communities were also awakened. Each community cleared a

nearby mountaintop and the members sang and danced their way up the hillsides to feast and sow spiritual seeds in an intense outpouring of emotion.[35]

In the 1840s, heaven-inspired visions of nature were received by community members, mostly sisters, from Mother Ann and other departed souls. Trees, baskets of fruit, flowers, hearts, roses, and doves symbolized the New Jerusalem with its streets of gold, fountains, and singing birds. Clocks with hands pointing to different hours in each painting announced the advent of the apocalypse.[36]

Trees were especially celebrated. The Tree of Life in Revelation was seen to "yield her fruit" that the earth's nations might be healed. Orchards bore nourishing fruits of all kinds. Each fruit symbolized a virtue: apples represented love (rather than the traditional temptation), cherries hope, grapes strength. The Tree of Blazing Light, which was seen as distinctly as a "natural tree," was depicted with silver streaming from each leaf.[37] In one of her paintings, Shaker artist Hannah Cohoon celebrated Mother Ann's relationship to trees and their fruits: "Blessed Mother Ann came into meeting. . . . I saw the small trees bearing the fruit of Paradise very plainly, there was much ripe fruit on them . . . each berry appeared to grow separately close to the limbs." In another message she saw Judith Collins bringing a "little basket of beautiful apples."[38]

Although Shakers gave expression to the body in ritual dance, song, and art, they rejected sexual expression, reproduction, childbirth, and actual motherhood. In celebrating Mother Ann and the transcendent forms of trees, flowers, and birds, however, they shared with nineteenth-century culture a religious idealization of nature and mother.

Romantic Consciousness:
Female Responses to Nature

The instrumental consciousness that manipulated nature for commercial gain found its antithesis in the romantic consciousness of personal involvement with nature. The same forests and mountains that were being exploited for lumber for the market economy were being visited, painted, and eulogized as sources of personal peace and serenity. The same middle-class couples who benefited from the capitalist use of nature as resource also needed the antidote of weekend excursions to New England's lakes and mountains. The same men who were subjected to the stresses of competition needed the balance of nature's psychic comfort. These dualities within nature and culture were integral to the capitalist ecological revolution.

The romantic movement in America cast a golden light on wild nature. Mountains, forests, meadows, and rivers inspired emotional outpourings from poets, artists, novelists, explorers, and scientists. The tranquility of landscape was savored as the picturesque, the majesty of rocky cliffs as awe of the sublime. Artists such as Thomas Cole painted precipitous peaks shrouded in dense clouds against a foreground of pastoral calm. His painting of the White Mountains in 1828 captured the dark mysteries and sublime splendor of wild nature. His 1836 painting of the Connecticut River from Mount Holyoke, "The Oxbow," contrasted the dark clouds, rugged cliffs, and tree trunks of the wilderness with the rural utopia of homes below bathed in filtered sunshine. Authors like John James Audubon described the tumultuous force of waters bursting forth from the release of a Maine logjam. The melodious serenades of orchard birds and the delicate fringes of bog flowers delighted genteel culture on weekend outings. Here nature was hidden from the deleterious effects of production and pollution.[39]

Middle-class women, whose direct impact on nature through production had decreased, found opportunities to influence consciousness about nature by educating themselves in the natural sciences, by writing children's books, and later by preserving nature through women's clubs. Leisure time was often used for getting in touch with the beauties of the natural world and its creator. The study of natural history became popular during the 1820s and 1830s. Women along with their husbands attended local lyceum lectures on science and religion. They deepened their appreciation of nature through the study of botany, geology, and mineralogy. Stimulated by European books such as Jean-Jacques Rousseau's *Letters on the Elements of Botany Addressed to a Lady* (London, 1785) and Priscilla Bell Wakefield's *Introduction to Botany, in a Series of Familiar Letters* (1786), plant collecting and identification gained acceptance in New England society and its burgeoning female academies as appropriate expressions of female piety. Painting flowers, describing them in travel diaries, and collecting herbarium specimens induced love of God. A growing consciousness of the value of plants, animals, rural scenery, and wilderness, coupled with the need to improve urban environments, propelled middle-class women into active work in the conservation movement toward the end of the century.[40]

In his 1824 *Manual of Botany*, Amos Eaton, professor of science at Albany's Rensselaer School, observed that "more than half the botanists in New England and New York are ladies." His student Almira Hart Lincoln Phelps, who learned her science from lyceum lectures in Brattleboro, Vermont, and from open lectures at Rensselaer, wrote a textbook, *Familiar Lectures on Botany*, in 1829. Enormously popular, it went through seventeen editions by 1842 and sold 275,000 copies by 1872, helping to secure her election as one of the first female members of the American Association for the Advancement of Science. By studying nature, she believed, women could develop and discipline their minds, strengthen their religious faith, and become better mothers.[41]

As reproducers of social values, women found expression for their ideas by teaching children about the natural world. Jane Kilby Welsh's *Familiar Lessons in Mineralogy* was published in Hollowell, Maine, in 1832, while Mary Swift's *First Lessons on Natural Philosophy for Children* appeared in Hartford, Connecticut, in 1859. In her textbook on elementary physics, Swift used the question-and-answer format to discuss motion, force, gravitation, light, sound, the five simple machines (the lever, wheel and axle, wedge, screw, and pulley), clocks, steam power, pumps, barometers, and the causes of natural phenomena such as lakes, springs, and winds. As examples of increased labor through the use of machines, she used cotton factories where "they have machines to card, and spin, and weave; so that a very few persons can make hundreds or thousands of yards of cloth in a day, from cotton that is brought in the same morning" and the steam engine which can "draw many heavily loaded cars thirty miles in one hour." "Who teaches man how to save his labor by contriving these machines?" she asked her readers. "Our Creator."[42]

Mary Lyon, founder of Massachusetts' Mount Holyoke Seminary in 1837, learned chemistry from Amos Eaton when he visited and lectured at Amherst College in 1824. Her enthusiasm for chemistry infused her lectures at Mount Holyoke where, despite the heavy burden of administration, she continued to teach the subject, believing it a marvelous way to appreciate the works of God in the natural world.[43]

Underlying the appreciation of nature was the assumption that an intimate connection between science and morals stemmed from the

Deity. Hannah Gale (1818–51) of Northborough, Massachusetts, attended the Greene Street School in Providence, Rhode Island, in 1837–38 while preparing to become a teacher. One of her instructors was transcendentalist philosopher Margaret Fuller. Gale wrote in her diary that, in teaching her pupils "moral science," Fuller argued that ideas about duty and religion could not have arisen from the "light of nature" alone, but required revelation. According to Gale, Fuller greatly admired Socrates and "thought that no one ever had or ever could exceed the views which he formed." She emphasized a transcendent reality grasped by the mind and revealed through nature. She lectured on the transcendentalist account of the "music of nature" heard by the spiritual ear, similar to the ancients' "music of the spheres." To her pupil Hannah Gale, nature's music resembled the poetry of mathematics discovered by Isaac Newton "as he sat under the apple tree and discovered by the fall of the apple, the laws by which the world was governed." Of all the senses, sight was to her the most precious for it allowed her to "see the grand and beautiful scenes which Nature presents to us." Her greatest ambition was to be able to draw them as a constant reminder of the beauty revealed by the Deity.[44]

Also influenced by a transcendent "religion of nature" was teacher Caroline Barrett White, who recorded her responses in her diaries from 1849 when she was twenty-one until her death at eighty-seven. Born in Ashburnham, Massachusetts, she taught school there as well as in Shirley and Worcester from 1849 until her marriage in 1851. She saw an intimate connection between a scientific understanding of nature and human morality. Despairing of her own capacity to avoid the sins that beset humanity, she participated in moral efforts to ameliorate social ills through the Ladies' Olive Leaf Association. Attending evening lyceum lectures and agricultural fairs educated her about the application of science to the improvement of the human condition. At the first agricultural fair held in Claremont, New Hampshire, in 1849 she was struck by the quality of the improvements in domestic animals and vegetables, and was impressed by Professor Brewster of Hanover's appeal to New Hampshire farmers to "make their profession an object of scientific investigation."

Extraordinarily sensitive to the effects of nature on her feelings, White observed nature's signs and activities as evidence of a transcendent reality created by an all-powerful Deity. The changing seasons dramatized the existential meaning of the life cycle and the transitoriness between the worlds of life and death. "This is the final day of Autumn—quickly has the summer flown, like a dream." How swiftly, she lamented, are we all hurrying on toward the land "whence no traveller returns" beyond the "vale of tears." Winter wind provoked awe and reverence for God's power. Sunsets symbolized both the separation and the connection between human and heaven, while eyes, ears, and tongue transmitted nature's emblems to the human heart.

On excursions to nearby mountains and lakes, she described nature in deeply personal terms pervaded by religious feelings and experiences of the sublime. Sunset inspired a "tumult of feeling" that subsides into a calm, making the heart swell with love of God and creation. "When I contemplate nature my heart expands with an intensity and feeling of love, of admiration, of reverence for that Being who has spread out before us the sublime works of creation and opened the boundless treadmill of knowledge for our research."[45]

To these middle-class women, science offered a way to understand and express feelings about nature that were acceptable within the nineteenth-century ideology of motherhood and morality. For other romantics of the period, however, nature itself was experienced as mother in intimate personal terms.

Romantic Consciousness: Nature as Mother

An emotive response to nature as mother was articulated by a small number of elite males who appreciated wild nature and the values associated with Renaissance naturalism and the animate cosmos. For these men, Nature was a human being writ large, an individual with whom one could develop a personal relationship. A vestige of personal animism—the "I-thou" relationship to the land so critical to American Indians—was one ingredient of their consciousness.

New England romantics such as Henry David Thoreau and Ralph Waldo Emerson described nature in deeply personal terms. Participants in the transcendentalist movement in New England, they not only looked deep into wild nature for intimate experience, but back to the period when nature had been elevated as a mother, nurse, and teacher. Thoreau frequently quoted the seventeenth-century alchemists and Cambridge Platonists in articulating some cherished idea about the inner vigor of nature's processes. Emerson looked to Neoplatonism for validation of nature as an emblem of higher universal truths.

The writings of the ancient Platonists, Stoics, Gnostics, and Hermetics as well as Renaissance Neoplatonists and naturalists were nostalgic ties to an era before nature had been mechanized. To Emerson the New World held indications that Mother Earth was still alive: "There in that great sloven continent still sleeps and murmurs and hides the great mother, long since driven away from the trim hedgerows and over-cultivated gardens of England."[46]

For Thoreau, writing in the 1840s but immersed in the vision of an earlier era, the earth was "not a fossil earth, but a living earth; compared with whose great central life all animal and vegetable life is merely parasitic." "The earth I tread on," he asserted, "is not a dead inert mass; it is a body, has a spirit, is organic and fluid to the influence of its spirit." In the midst of Concord's commercialization of agriculture, Thoreau looked back for his vision of the earth to the traditions of a Renaissance past that had been transplanted to the American colonies. Deriving from Plato's *Timaeus*, which had described the world soul as the source of motion in the spherical cosmos, medieval philosophers had personified nature as the lower portion of the anima mundi—God's vice-regent in the mundane world. *Endelechia*, the upper portion, translated God's reason into ideas, while *Natura* fashioned the individuals of the created world as copies of these pure forms. Revered as a teacher superior to humans, Natura guided them in discovering the pathway to God's hidden patterns in the lower world. Thoreau drew on this ancient tradition when he wrote, "Nature is a greater and more perfect art, the art of God, though referred to herself she is genius."[47]

Thoreau's relationship to nature was not only one of pupil to teacher, but also of son to mother. "Sometimes," he wrote longingly, "a mortal feels in himself Nature—not his Father but his Mother stirs within him, and he becomes immortal with her immortality." At other times he felt "a certain tender relation to Nature," one that for every man "must come very near to a personal one; he must be conscious of a friendliness in her." As had the Hermetic philosophers and Cambridge Platonists two centuries before him, he found nature to be a "constant nurse and friend, as do plants and quadrupeds."[48]

Like the ancient and Renaissance philosophers, Thoreau personified Nature as a female—all parts of her anatomy were used to paint a
verbal picture of her body and its functions. Nature had physiological
systems that were projections of human functions. The "warm driz-
zling rain" was Mother Earth's sweat. "After this long dripping and
oozing from every pore, she began to respire again more healthily
than ever." The late afternoon "haze over the woods was like the
inaudible panting, or rather the gentle perspiration of resting nature
rising from a myriad of pores into the attenuated atmosphere." In
addition to her elimination and respiratory functions, she had circulatory and nervous systems as well. "Globule[s] from her veins steal
. . . up into our own."[49]

Thoreau described Nature's brain, breasts, and buttocks in intimate
detail. A woodland lake in summer was "the earth's liquid eye, a mirror in the breast of nature." Tasting beer as "strong and stringent as
the cedar sap" was "as if we had sucked at the very teats of Nature's
pine-clad bosom." Too early, he complained, were we "weaned from
her breast to society." Her face bore expressions recognizable to any
poet who took the trouble to gaze on her countenance. She who was
"superior to all styles and ages, is now, with pensive face, composing
her poem Autumn with which no work of man will bear to be compared." Her head was adorned "with a profusion of fringes and curls,"
although, sadly enough, the lumberer was capable of "shearing off
those woods, and making earth bald before her time."[50]

A third view of Thoreau's relationship to nature was as a lover.
Sometimes, he warned, as seductive as a mistress, "by one bait or
another, Nature allures inhabitants into all her recesses." Pressed to
the limit nature's laws held their dangers for human beings, but for-
tunately "she is very kind and liberal to all men of vicious habits."
Emerson, too, found nature seductive and alluring when he observed
that "the solitude of wilderness is a sublime mistress, but an intoler-
able wife."[51]

Writing in the mid-nineteenth century when the market revolution
had begun to take its toll on older farming values, Thoreau was an
articulate champion of the preservation of the values of subsistence
farming. His work can be viewed as a wide-ranging radical critique of
the market revolution. As a Harvard senior in 1837, he denounced the
acquisitive work ethic of capitalism that made people slaves to producing wealth, recommending, instead, one day of work a week and
six of rest.[52]

Thoreau's preservationist message was unequivocal: tread lightly on the land, manage nature as little as possible, and immerse oneself in the tonic of wildness. *Walden*, the result of an experiment in living that took place between 1845 and 1848 south of Concord, Massachusetts, was an inquiry into the question: How can a human being obtain the physical and spiritual necessities for survival with as little impact on nature as possible? To begin living at Walden Pond, one did not need to drain a marsh or clear-cut the land. In the communal spirit of the subsistence culture, Thoreau borrowed a few tools, cut down only those pines essential for timbers, recycled the siding and windows of an old shanty, and reused bricks, shingles, and windows to construct a dwelling oriented toward the sun. Rather than a property owner, he considered himself a visitor passing through nature, availing himself of squatter's rights.[53]

Thoreau's garden was planted, not for cash crops, but to raise enough to feed himself and repay his debts. Two and one-half acres planted in corn, beans, peas, potatoes, and turnips sufficed. His predecessor who had exhausted the sandy soil claimed it was "good for nothing but to raise cheeping squirrels on." Because he owned no oxen or horses, Thoreau added no manure, but instead relied on the "virgin mold" and the "vital spirits" that the living earth extracted from the air. As John Evelyn and Kenelm Digby had recommended, he turned over the mold with a spade and relied on the dew and rain to restore its fertility. It was easier and less costly to the human spirit to rotate the garden to a fresh spot periodically than to keep horses and oxen, for the farmer does not hitch the ox, the ox hitches him.[54]

He managed his bean field only enough to harvest a few bushels, taking as little away from the "cinquefoil, blackberries, johnswort, sweet wild fruits, and pleasant flowers" as possible. "What right had I to oust the johnswort and the rest and break up their ancient herb garden?" he queried. Even so, he had to combat a few worms, woodchucks, and weeds with hand and hoe. His bean field represented the "connecting link between wild and cultivated fields," his beans, like him, "cheerfully returning to their wild and primitive state."[55]

For their part, the market farmers of Concord had nothing but contempt for Thoreau's methods and values. How could anyone farm without livestock, manure, wood ashes, or gypsum? "Beans so late? Peas so late?" "Corn, my boy, for fodder." Thoreau did not find his bean field listed in Henry Colman's report on the yields of Concord's gentlemen farmers. Nor was he awed by the works of famous agricultural improvers such as Arthur Young, the eighteenth-century English farming expert, learning instead from his own experience of the year before.[56]

What was it that Thoreau believed market farming did to the souls of men and women? From unfettered, free individuals, they became slaves to their profits and property. Young farmers who had inherited farmland, houses, barns, cattle, and tools were only to be pitied because they remained forever in debt to their mortgage. Property was much harder to get rid of than to acquire. Although husbandry had been a sacred art in ancient poetry and mythology, "It is [now] pursued with irreverent haste and heedlessness, our object being to have large farms and large crops merely." The Concord farmers "sacrificed not to Ceres but to the infernal Pluto. By avarice and selfishness and a grovelling habit ... of degrading the soil as property ... the landscape is deformed, husbandry is degraded and the farmer leads the meanest of lives. He knows nature but as a robber."[57]

By the mid-nineteenth century, American social and economic values had been transformed. While many farmers still resisted the market's commodities and status, most had at least been touched by its demands for efficiency and profit. Mainstream culture had moved beyond the values of the animate cosmos with which the resisters still identified. Nature had been deeply divided into two separate realms, one subservient to economic progress, the other to the human soul. Male and female values had likewise been split into utilitarianism and romanticism. At bottom, however, they were two sides of the coin of capitalist culture.

Conclusion

In his 1862 essay, "Wild Apples," Thoreau mourned the demise of the subsistence culture that had imbibed apples as both food and drink and the "struggling cider-orchards," planted "by every wallside." He identified with the escaped apple trees, which could never be confined within walls or reduced to geometric patterns in fields. These wild apples "belong to children as wild as themselves ... to the wild-eyed woman of the fields ... who gleans after all the world, and moreover, to us walkers." With production for the market, farmers have "grafted trees, and pay a price for them, they collect them into a plat by their houses, and fence them in."[58]

Thoreau's wild apples embodied the full depth of participatory consciousness endemic to the older animate cosmos. Wild apples restored the lost oneness between mind and body, senses and intellect, humans and nature. Their qualities permeated the body, reviving it with their inner wisdom and zest for life. Their smells were sweeter, their taste was more tart, and their touch was more piercing than the tame, watery, cultivated apples. The native North American crab apple, aboriginal like the Indians, with its glorious rose-colored flowers, was even wilder, with a stronger pucker to the taste. Of all the wild apples, these native crabs were the most beautiful, had the most delicious odor, and made the tangiest cider. They symbolized the fullest range of sensations experienced by native Americans.

The Indians' mimetic consciousness was once the primary process through which humans were linked to nature. Indian hunters mimicked the sounds, smells, and behavior of the animals they captured for food. Indian women's forest clearings planted with corn, beans, squash, and pumpkins mimicked nature's polycultural patterns. The Indian's oral-aural culture of myths, songs, and poems by which tribal values were transmitted generationally was grounded in the mimetic oral mode of knowing. In peasant agriculture, dancing in the fields awakened the generative powers of nature. Spreading cider, cake, or corn on the ground was a way of actively influencing the seasonal cycles through bodily participation in them. Food and herbs healed the body because their inner knowledge (*scientia*) became one with the body's own knowledge.

But Platonism in ancient Greece and mechanistic science in early modern Europe undermined the mimetic tradition by elevating analysis to a position of reverence. To Plato, mimesis was simply a catalog of responses learned by rote. Not recalling and participation, but problem solving and analysis mattered. The song and narrative were replaced by logic, arithmetic, and science. The knower was separated from the known, the subject from the object.

The first model of the earth, constructed in 1492, was called an earth apple. But modeling the earth as an object to be held in the hand and studied was itself a step in the process of separating humans from nature. The globe was being mapped and its organisms were being cataloged as commodities. The closed earth-centered cosmos was expanding with Copernicus's revolution in stellar distances and his heliocentric perspective. The God of the English settlers was not in nature, but above and beyond it in transcendent space.

The infinite homogeneous space of the Newtonian universe began to permeate the thinking of American elites by the late eighteenth century. To the disciples of Newton, the analysis of nature proceeded by dividing it into atomic parts and changing it through external forces. To the followers of Francis Bacon, imitation meant obeying nature in order to command it. Nature was to be dominated, not by following, but by prodding and searching out its secrets. The animate cosmos, in which nature acted and developed from within, was giving way to a worldview that sanctioned external manipulation and control. By the 1850s, the geometric outlines of landscaped fields cleared of forests and connected by the straight tracks of railroads dominated the visual world of most New Englanders. The distancing and separation provided by this perspective facilitated perception of the New England homeland as object and commodity.

Over the 260 years between 1600 and 1860, modes of knowing nature had dramatically changed. The epistemological equality of all the senses had given way to the domination of the visual and then to the analytic reasoning of a disembodied intellect. New England's landscape had also been fundamentally altered. The fences, fields, houses, roads, canals, and railroads that mapped the surface of the soil constrained it within grids imprinted by human minds that were guided by the goals of capitalist production. Human reason had become one with the instruments of change. A calculating people had taken up mechanistic science as their supreme instrument. Mimesis had been replaced by mathematics, animism by atomism. Perceiving the consequences of this capitalist ecological revolution, Thoreau called for a return to an animistic consciousness and the ways of subsistence farmers. Treading lightly on the land would restore a nature that was active, vital, and deeply sensual.

8

. . . .

Epilogue:
The Global Ecological Revolution

Twentieth-century New England is a product of the colonial and capitalist ecological revolutions. Its native Americans have been reduced to small but resilient communities that have adapted to mainstream culture while retaining many tribal traditions. The region is deeply embedded in an interconnected modern world structured by capitalist forms of production, reproduction, and consciousness. As a member of a global ecological network, it is affected by the availability and scarcity of natural resources. It is an integral part of the Western capitalist core economies that depend on peripheral Third World economies for resources and cheap labor.

Most of the energy, food, and clothing needed to sustain the lives of New Englanders comes from external markets. Roughly 80 percent of its meat, vegetables, and fruit are imported from outside the region. The availability and the cost of food are affected by transportation strikes and midwestern droughts. Energy comes from imported oil and gas, augmented by wood-burning stoves and some locally generated nuclear energy. Energy availability is subject to global shortages and price variations. Clothing is largely imported from southern and foreign textile mills, where wage labor is cheaper and supplemented by local and cottage clothing industries. As in the country as a whole, fast food is often prepared from imported beef raised in Central and South America at the expense of tropical rainforests and served in styrofoam containers at the expense of the global ozone layer.

This dependence on outside markets has moved some types of environmental degradation beyond New England's boundaries, allowing portions of its own environment to recover. The twentieth-century decline in farming and the changeover to oil have resulted in the regrowth of the New England forest. Eighty percent of the land is once again forested, close enough to the 95 percent on the eve of colonization to provide a sense of how the original forest (minus its largest giants) might have looked. Maine, New Hampshire, and Vermont are among the four most heavily forested states in the nation. Sixty-two percent of New England's forested acreage, however, is held in small parcels by individuals, most of whom own less than fifty acres, and many of whom are urbanites with country retreats who are conscious of environmental preservation. The lumber industry owns only 32 percent of this acreage; the remaining 6 percent is public land. Major public policy issues are involved in deciding how the forests should best be used.[1]

Yet this regenerated forest is itself the victim of industrial capitalism. Acid precipitation from the smokestacks of the East and Midwest has attacked New England's crops, trees, and shrubs. Acid rain leaches nutrients from leaves, makes plants more vulnerable to fungal and bacterial infections, and reduces tree seedlings and plant productivity. Between 700 and 1,400 wild species are thought to suffer from sulfur dioxide and ozone emissions. The effects are most visible in higher-elevation coniferous forests, but the damage is universal. Acid rain has raised the acidity of thousands of lakes all over New England and introduced mercury, cadmium, and lead into their ecosystems. With the reduction of zooplankton, phytoplankton, and mollusks, fish populations have declined, along with waterfowl such as herons, ducks, loons, and ospreys.[2]

The growth of high technology and computer-based industries further connects New England to the rest of the planet, altering human perceptions of the earth. The Computer Age has mapped the earth's surface as a grid of Cartesian coordinates bounded by and enclosed within a communications network. Today, the "whole earth" image from a satellite's eye view is no longer an earth apple, but a two-dimensional photograph. Viewed from afar by the spectator, it has become a flat object detached from human participation. Computer advertisements and popular media depict the earth variously as electronically wired; encircled by floating cars, calculators, and computers; enclosed within laboratory flasks; squeezed by human hands and lemon juicers; and dominated by oversized white males standing on its surface. The symbols of nature that permeate and structure modern consciousness present a mechanized, artificial, instrumental nature. It has become completely mechanical, having lost any semblance of organic life.[3]

The adoption of the mechanistic paradigm throughout the Western world has implications that extend far beyond New England's borders. Based on the mechanistic model, capitalist agriculture over the whole globe has moved increasingly in the direction of artificial ecosystems, built on simplified monocultures that are vulnerable to pest outbreaks and catastrophic collapse. Identical rectangular and circular fields precisely laid out for efficient cultivation, irrigation, and harvesting replicate atomic and latticelike patterns, replacing the diversity of small, haphazard patchworks of fields within forests. Stimulated by urbanization and industrialization, agriculture has developed more efficient machines, genetically "improved" strains of crops and animals, artificial fertilizers, and chemical pesticides. The external energy needed to produce the chemicals, operate the farm machinery, and process, store, and transport the products often surpasses the calories the foods themselves supply. Most of this external energy comes from fossil fuels by way of industrial systems rather than from the sun by way of photosynthesis.[4]

Ecological thinking, however, offers the possibility of a new relationship between humans and nonhuman nature that could lead to the sustainability of the biosphere in the future. The assumptions of the ecological paradigm contrast with those of the mechanistic, resting on a different set of assumptions about nature: (1) everything is connected to everything else in an integrated web; (2) the whole is greater than the sum of the parts; (3) nonhuman nature is active, dynamic, and responsive to human actions; (4) process, not parts, is primary; and (5) people and nature are a unified whole.

Ecology also offers a new ethic for grounding human relations with nature. Mechanism is consistent with a homocentric ethic of "natural rights" in which each individual uses nonhuman nature to maximize his or her self-interest. An ecocentric ethic, however, is based on a network of mutual obligations rather than natural rights, and on values that are based on the ecosystem rather than on human interests. The land ethic of ecologist Aldo Leopold (1949) enlarges the boundaries of the community to include "soils, waters, plants, and animals, or collectively, the land." "A thing is right," according to Leopold, "when it tends to preserve the integrity, beauty, and stability of the biotic community. It is wrong when it tends otherwise."[5]

Although much of scientific ecology has appropriated the reductionist approach of the mechanistic model, human ecology includes human beings as part of the natural world and recognizes their ability both to destroy as well as to live within the limits of local ecosystems. But for an ecological model to replace mechanism as the dominant paradigm for decision making would require not merely an intellectual, but a global social and economic revolution. The capitalist relations of production and the patriarchal relations of reproduction that support mechanistic consciousness would have to give way to new socioeconomic forms, new gender relationships, and an ecological ethic.[6]

Nevertheless, the possibility exists that such a global ecological revolution may be occurring. A global ecological crisis that transcends national boundaries could trigger a transition to a sustainable earth. Global resource depletion and pollution have appeared at the intersection of capitalist (as well as Soviet) economic production and ecology. Nuclear war and nuclear power plant accidents threaten the earth with radioactive, cancer-causing emissions. The burning of fossil fuels for industrial production increases carbon dioxide in the atmosphere, while the cutting of tropical rainforests for grazing and crops reduces its conversion to oxygen, resulting in global warming and melting ice caps. This "greenhouse effect" alters weather patterns that affect agriculture, fishing, and the ecology of local habitats. Nondegradable industrial plastics pollute soils and oceans. As chlorofluorocarbons are produced for refrigerants and styrofoam packaging, the earth's protective ozone layer is threatened. Toxic wastes from chemical industries enter groundwater supplies, threatening human health. Acid rain from coal-burning "smokestack" industries crosses national boundaries, increasing the acidity of lakes and damaging forests. Habitat destruction from industrial expansion endangers hundreds of indigenous species around the whole globe.

Other disjunctions are occurring at the intersection of production and reproduction. Global population continues to grow exponentially despite declining reproductive rates in developed nations. Increased populations in developing countries put pressure on local economies and consequently on the land. Such pressures challenge traditional sex-gender roles and create new patterns in both production and biological reproduction. The emergence of worldwide "green" political parties is in part a response to the failure of the legal-political frameworks that reproduce capitalist society to regulate pollution and depletion. These tensions within production and reproduction are experienced as threats to the health and survival of both human and nonhuman nature.

The outcome of this global ecological crisis in production and reproduction could be negative or positive. A pessimistic scenario would be the crisis and collapse predicted by the "limits to growth" models of the 1970s and the Malthusian dilemma of exponential population growth outrunning the food supply. A positive outcome, however, could be the crisis and reorganization implied by the "order out of chaos" approaches of Ilya Prigogine and Erich Jantsch, moving the entire globe toward ecological and economic sustainability in the twenty-first century.[7] New forms of production, reproduction, and consciousness could structure the world differently for twenty-first century citizens (Table 8.1).

The transition to a sustainable world would entail changes in production and reproduction that emphasize ecodevelopment in both developed and developing countries. Colonial and capitalist forms of exploitation of nature and Third World peoples would give way to priorities that fulfill subsistence and quality-of-life needs. These would be enhanced by global efforts to conserve energy and renewable natural resources, recycle nonrenewable resources, and adopt appropriate technologies. Ecological and economic development, if sensitively structured by the developing countries themselves, could pave the way to the demographic transition that has lowered reproductive rates in developed countries. Changes in production would thus support changes in reproduction and both together would alleviate human pressures on the global ecosystem. This transition would be legitimated by changes in values and in ways that people perceive, know, and structure reality.

Supporting the emergence of a transformation of consciousness are calls by physicists, ecologists, feminists, poets, and philosophers for philosophical changes that would reintegrate culture with nature, mind with body, and male with female modes of experiencing and representing "reality." They suggest that nature as actor may now be breaking out of the mechanistic straitjacket in which human representations have confined it for the past three hundred years. Through the social construction of a new reality, future generations may learn a worldview that is nonmechanistic. When philosopher Max Horkheimer, writing in 1947, called for the revolt of nature, he invited it to speak in a language other than instrumentalism. "Once it was the endeavor of art, literature, and philosophy to express the meaning of things and of life, to be the voice of all that is dumb, to endow nature with an organ for making known her sufferings, or we might say, to call reality by its rightful name. Today nature's tongue is taken away.

Table 8.1
The Global Ecological Revolution

	Postindustrial Society
Nonhuman Nature	Nature as active partner
	Integrated, whole subjects
	Space as oikos, bioregionalism
Human Production (economy)	Sustainable agriculture Decentralized, egalitarian economy
Human Reproduction —Biological —Social —Political	Steady state: no-growth society Postpatriarchal egalitarian homes, reintegration of home and work life. Green politics
Forms of Consciousness Symbols of Nature Knowledge	Participatory consciousness: all senses, visceral, erotic Partnership, reciprocity with nature, land ethic Integrated thinking: "Mind in Nature," tacit knowledge

Once it was thought that each utterance, word, cry, or gesture had an intrinsic meaning; today it is merely an occurrence." The voice with which nature speaks and is heard by humans is tactile, sensual, auditory, odoriferous, and visual—not disembodied reason, but visceral understanding.

"In the present crisis," Horkheimer continued, "the problem of mimesis is particularly urgent. Civilization starts with, but must eventually transcend and transvaluate, man's native mimetic impulses.... Conscious adaptation and eventually domination replace the various forms of mimesis.... the formula supplants the image, the calculat-

ing machine the ritual dances." To survive we must once again recover the meaning of mimesis, actively making ourselves "like" the
environment, not as object, but in the deepest sense of visceral re-
merging with the earth.[8]

Emerging from concerns over the earth's future is a spectrum of
new sciences infused with an ecological perspective. At their root is
mimesis in a new form—integrative thinking. Imitation, synthesis,
and a creative reciprocity between humans and nonhuman nature
constitute a form of consciousness in which tacit knowing through
the body and information networks ("mind") in nature links humans
to the nonhuman world. The new theoretical frameworks challenge
positivist epistemology through participatory forms of consciousness.
Gregory Bateson's "ecology of mind" sees nature as a network of information moving from brain to hand to stick to rock to earth to eye to
brain. "Mind" in nature integrates human subject and active object
into a larger network of energy and information exchange. Nature
is a changing whole consisting of interactions and processes interpreted by humans. The body's tacit knowledge is one with the mind.[9]

Philosophers have proposed alternatives to the mechanistic framework based on nature's inherent activity, self-organization, perme-
able boundaries, and resilience. Deep ecologists argue that reform
environmentalism is insufficient to deal with the magnitude of global
environmental problems. They call for a fundamental transformation
in Western epistemology, ontology, and ethics. Deep ecology represents a change from a mechanistic to an ecological consciousness
rooted in biospecies equality, appropriate technologies, recycling,
and bioregions as ecological homes. The new philosophy is infused
with an environmental ethic oriented toward establishing sustainable
relations with nature.[10]

Structural changes within science itself may also be indicative of
the emergence of a new paradigm. The new physics of David Bohm
contrasts the older world picture of atomic fragmentation with a new
philosophy of wholeness expressed in the unfolding and enfolding of
moments within a "holomovement." His cosmology is one of the primacy of process rather than the domination of parts. The Gaia hypothesis of British chemist James Lovelock proposes that the earth's
biota as a whole maintain an optimal chemical composition within
the atmosphere and oceans that support its life. Gaia, the name of the
Greek earth goddess, is a metaphor for a self-regulating (cybernetic)
system that controls the functioning of the earth's chemical cycles.

Chaos theory in mathematics offers tools for describing complexity and turbulence consistent with the idea that nature as actor offers surprises and catastrophes that cannot be predicted by linear equations and mechanistic descriptions.[11]

Coupled with these changes in science, epistemology, and ethics are new applied sciences oriented toward effecting a transition to ecological sustainability. Restoration is the active reconstruction of pristine ecosystems (such as prairies, grasslands, rivers, and lakes). By studying and mimicking natural patterns, the wisdom inherent in evolution can be re-created. Rather than taking nature apart and simplifying ecosystems, as the past three centuries of mechanistic science have taught us to do supremely well, restorationists are actively putting it back together. Rather than analyzing nature for the sake of dominating and controlling it, restorationists are synthesizing it for the sake of living symbiotically within the whole.[12]

Agroecology looks back to traditional agriculture and mimics its polycultural patterns. Traditional farming—developed over generations of trial and error through deep local knowledge and the transmission of successful adaptations from fathers and mothers to sons and daughters—is joined with an understanding of local ecology. The polycultures of traditional farmers often are more productive, are more resistant to pests, and use better-adapted varieties of crops than are monocultures of imported seed supported with herbicides and artificial fertilizers. In designing agroecosystems, the spatial arrangements and seasonal development of wild plant species are used as models. Arrangements of local species of grasses, vines, shrubs, and trees are simulated in designing integrated cereal, vegetable, fruit, and tree crop systems. Similarly, agroforestry restores the complementary arrangements of trees, crops, and animals in combination with ecological principles in order to maintain productivity without environmental degradation. Orchards planted with ground covers of legumes or berries and foraged by poultry, pigs, and bees keep down pests and produce well-mulched and manured soil.[13]

The biological control of insects also uses natural ecosystems as models. Uncultivated land surrounding fields harbors birds and insect enemies as well as pests. Flowers along roadsides and fences are especially attractive to beneficial insects. Diversity in crops and surroundings and arrangements of beneficial plants mimic natural conditions, making crops less visible to insect enemies and acting as barriers to pest dispersal. By imitating nature, agricultural systems can be designed that both suppress pests and maximize total yield.[14]

A global ecological revolution would also reconstruct gender relations between women and men and between humans and nature. The domination of women and nature inherent in the market economy's use of both as resources would be restructured. Both radical and socialist feminist theories present alternatives to patriarchal and capitalist ecological relations. But while radical feminism has delved more deeply into the woman-nature connection, socialist feminism is more consistent with the concept of the social construction of ecological revolutions.

For radical feminists and ecofeminists, human nature is grounded in human biology. Humans are biologically sexed and socially gendered. Sex-gender relations give men and women different power bases; hence the personal is political. The ontology and epistemology of the mechanistic worldview are deeply masculinist and exploitative of nature, which has historically been characterized in the female gender. Male-designed and produced technologies neglect the effects of nuclear radiation, pesticides, hazardous wastes, and household chemicals on women's reproductive organs and on the ecosystem. Often stemming from an antiscience, antitechnology standpoint, radical feminism celebrates the relationship between women and nature through the revival of ancient rituals centered on goddess worship, the moon, animals, and the female reproductive system. Its philosophy embraces intuition, an ethic of caring, and weblike human-nature relationships. Yet in emphasizing the female, body, and nature components of the dualities male/female, mind/body, and culture/nature, radical feminism runs the risk of perpetuating the very value hierarchies it seeks to overthrow.[15]

Socialist feminism and socialist ecofeminism incorporate many of the insights of radical feminism, but view both knowledge and reality as historically and socially constructed. What counts as human nature is the product of historically changing interactions between humans and nature, men and women, social classes, races, ages, and national origins. Like Marxist feminists, socialist feminists see nonhuman nature as the material basis of human life, supplying the necessities of food, clothing, shelter, and energy. Nature is transformed by human science and technology for use by all humans for survival. Any meaningful analysis must be grounded in an understanding of power in both the personal and political spheres. Like radical feminism, social-ist feminism is critical of mechanistic science's treatment of nature as passive and its male-dominated power structures. It deplores the omission of women's reproductive roles and gender analysis in his-tory and would give reproduction a central place in theory construc-tion. Socialist feminism views change as dynamic, interactive, and dialectical, rather than linear or incremental. Although as yet social-ist feminism has had little to say about ecology, it is compatible with a view of nonhuman nature as a historical actor, with the ecological goal of developing sustainable, nondominating relations with nature, and with female equality in production and reproduction.[16]

An ecological transformation in the deepest sense entails changes in ecology, production, reproduction, and forms of consciousness. Ecology as a new worldview could help resolve environmental prob-lems rooted in the industrial-mechanistic mode of representing na-ture. In opposition to the subject/object, mind/body, and culture/nature dichotomies of mechanistic science, ecological consciousness sees complexity and process as including both culture and nature. In the ecological model, humans are neither helpless victims nor arro-gant dominators of nature, but active participants in the destiny of the webs of which they are a part.

Although many changes leading to a healthier, sustainable bio-sphere seem to be occurring, the forces that encourage the current patterns of global resource depletion and pollution are very strong. Patriarchy, capitalism, and the domination of nature are deeply en-trenched and function to maintain the present direction of develop-ment. Yet one may hope that a sustainable global environment, so-ciety, and ethic will emerge in the twenty-first century.

Appendixes

Appendix A
Foods of Southeastern New England Indians, 1600–1675:
Food Resources, Gender Roles, Availability, Extractive Technology

Animal Products (men and women)

1. Animal and bird carcasses: primarily men, although women and children went along on nearby hunts.
    Animals: especially fall, winter, spring; bow and arrow, deadfall trap, v-shaped hedge drive, snare, spear.
       Deer, beaver, bear, moose, otter, raccoon, wildcat, muskrat, wolf, fox, squirrel, rabbit, woodchuck, probably skunk and porcupine.
    Birds: fall, winter, spring; net, bow and arrow.
       Blackbird, turkey, partridge, heath cock, pigeon, owl, crane, swan, goose, brant, duck, cormorant.
2. Eggs: spring nesting season only; probably women.
3. Fish and shellfish: all year, but especially spring and summer; bone hook and line, hemp net, weir, spear and arrow; both sexes.
    Crustaceans and shellfish:
       Lobster, crab, soft-shelled long clam, hard-shelled quahog, mussel, oyster.
    Sea fish or fish running from salt to fresh water:
       Cod, mackerel, turbot, halibut, plaice, flounder, skate, haddock, bream, striped bass, sturgeon, Atlantic salmon, shad, menhaden, alewife, herring, frostfish, eel, lamprey.
    Freshwater fish:
       Trout, roach, dace, pike, perch, catfish.

Vegetable Products (primarily women)

4. Grains: August to May.
    Corn (yellow, red, blue, white).
5. Grain alternatives: winter to spring.
    Ground nut (tubers of *Apios tuberosa*).
    Jerusalem artichoke, water lily root.
6. Nuts and leguminous seeds: fall.
    Acorn, walnut, chestnut, hazelnut.
    Bean (cultivated).
7. Vegetables and fruits: summer to fall.
    Vegetables:
    Squash, pumpkin, watermelon (cultivated).
    Wild leek, possibly onion (cheboll) and garlic.
    Purslane, pennyroyal, winter savory, sorrel, brooklime, liverwort,
    carvel, watercress, yarrow.
    Fruits:
    Strawberry, raspberry, blackberry (mulberry), blueberry, huckle-
    berry (hurtleberry), currant, gooseberry, treacle berry (from
    Solomon's seal), plum, haw (from whitethorn), grape, cranberry.
8. Vegetable fats: fall.
    Walnut oil, acorn oil.

Source: M. K. Bennett, "The Food Economy of the New England Indians, 1606–75," *Journal of Political Economy* 73, no. 5 (October 1955): 369–97. Data based on Daniel Gookin, "Historical Collections of the Indians in New England (1674)," in *Collections of the Massachusetts Historical Society*, 1st ser., 10 vols. (Boston: Massachusetts Historical Society, 1792); Thomas Morton, "New English Canaan (1632)," in *Tracts and Other Papers Relating Principally to the Origin, Settlement, and Progress of the Colonies in North America, From the Discovery of the Country to the Year 1776*, 2 vols., ed. Peter Force (Washington, D.C.: Peter Force, 1838); Roger Williams, *A Key into the Language of America: Or, An Help to the Language of the Natives in that Part of America, called New England* (London, 1643; reprint, Providence, R.I.: Narragansett Club, 1866); John Smith, *A Description of New England* (London: Humphrey Lownes, 1616); John Josselyn, *An Account of Two Voyages to New England Made During the Years 1638, 1663*, 2d ed. (1675; reprint, Boston: William Veazie, 1865); Mary Rowlandson, "The Captivity of Mrs. Mary Rowlandson (1682)," in *Narratives of the Indian Wars, 1675–1699*, ed. Charles H. Lincoln (New York: Charles Scribner's Sons, 1913).

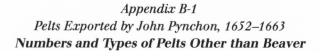

Appendix B-1
Pelts Exported by John Pynchon, 1652–1663
Numbers and Types of Pelts Other than Beaver

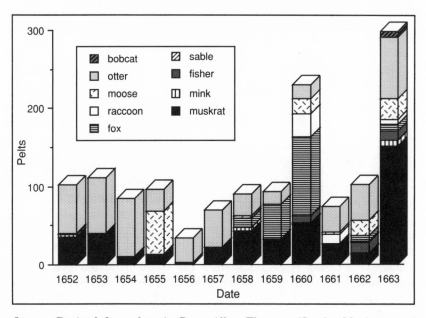

Source: Derived from data in Peter Allen Thomas, "In the Maelstrom of Change: The Indian Trade and Cultural Process in the Middle Connecticut River Valley: 1635–1665" (Ph.D. dissertation, University of Massachusetts, 1979), p. 474.

Appendix B-2
Pelts Exported by John Pynchon, 1652–1663
Number of Beaver Pelts versus Other Pelts

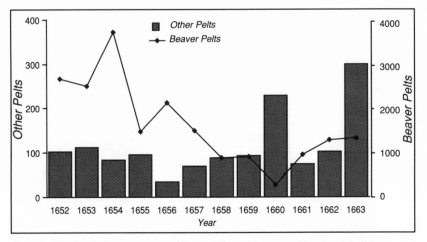

Source: Derived from data in Peter Allen Thomas, "In the Maelstrom of Change: The Indian Trade and Cultural Process in the Middle Connecticut River Valley: 1635–1665" (Ph.D. dissertation, University of Massachusetts, 1979), pp. 473–74 using conversion factor on p. 287.

Appendix C-1

Profile of Fifteen Inland Massachusetts Towns

Statistical View of Population, 1771–1850

Town	Founding Date[a]	1771[b]	1790[c]	1800[c]	1810[c]	1820[c]	1830[c]	1840[c]	1850[d]
Ashburnham	1765	505	951	994	1,036	1,230	1,402	1,652	1,875
Ashfield	1765	530	1,459	1,741	1,809	1,748	1,732	1,610	1,394
Athol	1762	765	848	993	1,041	1,211	1,325	1,591	2,034
Blandford	1741	665	1,416	1,778	1,613	1,515	1,590	1,427	1,418
Brimfield	1731	1,205	1,211	1,384	1,325	1,612	1,599	1,219	1,420
Charlmont	1765	380	665	875	987	1,081	1,065	1,127	1,173
Chesterfield	1762	795	1,183	1,323	1,408	1,447	1,416	1,132	1,014
Dracut	1702	1,045	1,217	1,274	1,301	1,407	1,615	2,188	3,503
Littleton	1715	1,060	854	904	773	955	947	927	987
Pelham	1743	325	1,040	1,144	1,185	1,278	904	956	814
Petersham	1754	770	1,560	1,794	1,490	1,623	1,696	1,775	1,527
Shutesbury	1761	540	674	930	939	1,029	986	987	912
Stockbridge	1739	1,005	1,336	1,261	1,372	1,377	1,580	1,992	1,941
Templeton	1762	900	950	1,068	1,205	1,331	1,552	1,776	2,173
Worcester	1684	2,145	2,095	2,411	2,577	2,962	4,173	7,497	8,574

a. Massachusetts, Office of the Secretary of State, *Historical Data Relating to Counties, Cities, and Towns in Massachusetts*, prepared by Paul Guzzi, 4th ed. (Boston: Commonwealth of Massachusetts, 1975).

b. Bettye Hobbs Pruitt, ed., *The Massachusetts Tax Valuation List of 1771* (Boston: G. K. Hall, 1978). Polls have been multiplied by a factor of five as per Thomas Hutchinson's suggestion (1773): "it is thought by many not too large a computation when the number of males and females of all ages are made to be five times the number of polls in these estimates." Quoted from Evarts B. Greene and Virginia D. Harrington, *American Population before the Federal Census of 1790* (Gloucester, Mass.: Peter Smith, 1966), p. 16, n. 11.

c. Jesse Chickering, *Statistical View of the Population of Massachusetts, From 1765 to 1840* (Boston: Charles C. Little and Majes Brown, 1846).

d. *U.S. Census, 1850: Statistical View of the United States . . . Compendium of the Seventh Census* by J. D. B. DeBow (Washington, D.C.: A. O. P. Nicholson, Public Printer, 1854).

Appendix C-2
Profile of Fifteen Inland Massachusetts Towns
Graphic View of Population, 1771–1850

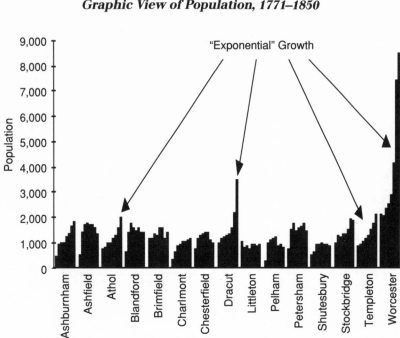

Population Figures for years: 1771, 1790, 1800, 1820, 1830, 1840, and 1850

Source: Derived from data in Appendix C-1.

Appendix C-3

Profile of Fifteen Inland Massachusetts Towns

Town Land Use, 1771

Town	Founding Date[a]	Total Acres in Town[b]	Acres of Tillage	Acres of Pasture	Acres of English & Upland Mowing Land	Acres of Fresh Meadow	Acres of Improved Land	% Improved Land
Ashburnham	1765	32,000	155	347	246	95	843	2.6
Ashfield	1765	26,000	332	201	402	—	935	3.6
Athol	1762	23,000	518	461	601	186	1,566	6.8
Blandford	1741	34,000	224	328	500	42	1,094	3.2
Brimfield	1731	23,000	852	1,277	1,253	533	3,915	17.0
Charlmont	1765	17,000	385	219	348	—	952	5.6
Chesterfield	1762	24,000	263	293	568	38	1,162	4.8
Dracut	1702	16,000	742	978	466	576	2,762	17.3
Littleton	1715	13,000	646	1,700	604	942	3,892	29.9
Pelham	1743	21,000	500	616	584	397	2,097	10.0
Petersham	1754	23,000	436	852	918	258	2,444	10.6
Shutesbury	1761	20,000	237	216	436	67	956	4.8
Stockbridge	1739	27,000	887	808	637	54	2,386	8.8
Templeton	1762	35,000	277	1,221	778	182	2,458	7.0
Worcester	1684	27,000	1,244	1,888	1,280	1,168	5,580	20.7

Source: Bettye Hobbs Pruitt, ed., *The Massachusetts Tax Valuation List of 1771* (Boston: G. K. Hall, 1978). Calculated data.

a. Massachusetts, Office of the Secretary of State, *Historical Data Relating to Counties, Cities, and Towns in Massachusetts*, prepared by Paul Guzzi, 4th ed. (Boston: Commonwealth of Massachusetts, 1975).

b. Edward Cook, Jr., *The Fathers of the Towns* (Baltimore: Johns Hopkins University Press, 1976). Acreages as of 1765.

Appendix C-4
Profile of Fifteen Inland Massachusetts Towns
Land Use per Farm, 1771

Town	Number of Houses	Number of Farms[a]	Average Tillage in Acres	Number of Farms with Pasture	Average Size of Pasture in Acres	Number of Farms with Upland Mowing Land	Average Acreage of Mowing Land	Number of Farms with Fresh Meadow	Average Acreage of Fresh Meadow	Combined Mowing and Meadow Acreage	Combined Average Improved Acreage
Ashburnham	63	57	2.7	59	5.9	53	4.6	21	4.5	9.1	17.7
Ashfield	62	63	5.3	48	4.2	57	7.0	—	—	7.0	16.5
Athol	96	93	3.4	78	4.2	89	6.8	42	4.4	11.2	18.8
Blandford	85	66	3.4	65	5.0	66	7.6	7	6.0	13.6	22.0
Brimfield	147	131	6.5	127	10.0	130	9.6	70	7.6	17.2	33.7
Charlmont	40	45	8.6	32	6.8	44	7.9	—	—	7.9	23.3
Chesterfield	95	75	3.5	54	5.4	76	7.5	6	6.3	13.8	22.7
Dracut	124	116	6.4	108	9.0	100	4.7	102	5.6	10.3	25.7
Littleton	121	112	5.8	117	14.5	110	5.5	105	9.0	14.5	34.8
Pelham	94	97	5.2	84	7.3	100	5.8	67	5.9	11.7	24.2
Petersham	117	122	3.6	103	8.1	111	8.3	42	6.1	14.4	26.1
Shutesbury	66	67	3.5	54	4.0	64	6.8	10	6.7	13.5	21.0
Stockbridge	60	114	7.8	79	10.2	91	7.0	10	5.4	12.4	30.4
Templeton	123	112	2.5	116	10.5	111	7.0	44	4.1	11.1	24.1
Worcester	234	189	6.6	180	10.5	180	7.1	166	7.0	14.1	31.2

Source: Bettye Hobbs Pruitt, ed., The Massachusetts Tax Valuation List of 1771 (Boston: G. K. Hall, 1978). Calculated data.

a. A farm is defined as land owned by a male taxpayer reporting crops and livestock on the tax valuation list. The number of farms listed in column 2 is equal to the number of taxpayers with tillage. Taxpayers owning houses sometimes owned livestock without tillage or pasture. Some farms consisted of pasture without tillage (column 4) or upland mowing land without tillage (column 6) owned by taxpayers living in other towns.

Appendix C-5

Profile of Fifteen Inland Massachusetts Towns
Crop Yields, 1771

Town	Bushels of Grain per Year	Bushels of Grain per Acre	Bushels of Grain per House	Tons of English Hay per Year	Tons of English Hay per Acre	Tons of Fresh Meadow Hay per Year	Tons of Fresh Meadow Hay per Acre	Pasture Fertility: Acres of Pasture Needed for One Cow
Ashburnham	2,106	13.6	33.4	208	0.84	92	0.97	1.48
Ashfield	3,064	9.2	49.5	373	0.93	—	—	1.59
Athol	3,618	11.4	57.7	472	0.78	169	0.91	1.25
Blandford	1,172	5.2	13.8	313	0.62	35	0.83	1.53
Brimfield	8,326	9.8	56.6	823	0.66	467	0.88	1.93
Charlmont	3,731	9.7	93.3	335	0.96	—	—	1.66
Chesterfield	2,874	10.9	30.3	492	0.87	39	1.02	2.02
Dracut	9,056	12.2	73.0	306	0.65	570	0.99	2.02
Littleton	8,704	13.4	71.9	574	0.62	559	0.59	3.38
Pelham	4,105	8.2	43.6	349	0.60	267	0.67	1.50
Petersham	6,094	14.0	52.1	637	0.69	220	0.85	1.68
Shutesbury	1,995	8.4	30.2	242	0.56	42	0.63	1.31
Stockbridge	8,340	9.4	139.0	487	0.76	52	0.58	2.01
Templeton	3,498	12.6	28.4	516	0.66	154	0.85	2.29
Worcester	17,606	14.2	75.2	1,028	0.80	1,047	0.90	1.56

Source: Bettye Hobbs Pruitt, ed., The Massachusetts Tax Valuation List of 1771 (Boston: G. K. Hall, 1978). Calculated data.

Appendix C-6
Profile of Fifteen Inland Massachusetts Towns
Livestock, 1771

Town	Horses	Horses per House	Oxen	Oxen per House	Cattle	Cattle per House	Goats and Sheep	Goats and Sheep per House	Swine	Swine per House	Livestock per House
Ashburnham	51	0.5	80	1.3	155	2.5	307	4.9	106	1.7	10.8
Ashfield	36	0.6	69	1.1	112	1.8	295	4.8	78	1.2	9.5
Athol	62	0.6	142	1.5	236	2.4	674	7.0	157	1.4	15.0
Blandford	85	1.0	94	1.1	220	2.6	559	6.6	173	2.0	13.3
Brimfield	142	1.0	256	1.7	487	3.3	1,645	11.2	353	2.4	19.6
Charlmont	57	0.9	60	1.5	91	2.3	221	5.5	67	1.7	11.9
Chesterfield	58	0.6	120	1.3	198	2.1	662	7.0	140	1.5	12.4
Dracut	73	0.6	256	2.1	421	3.4	695	5.6	282	2.3	13.9
Littleton	119	1.0	200	1.6	436	3.6	721	6.0	229	1.9	14.1
Pelham	102	1.1	178	1.9	282	3.0	754	8.0	245	2.6	16.6
Petersham	140	1.2	204	1.7	484	4.1	1,122	9.6	210	1.8	18.5
Shutesbury	47	0.7	68	1.0	128	1.9	393	6.0	95	1.4	11.1
Stockbridge	160	2.7	185	3.1	284	4.7	670	11.2	199	3.3	25.0
Templeton	75	0.6	151	1.2	317	2.6	751	6.1	160	1.3	11.8
Worcester	270	1.2	367	1.6	864	3.7	1,540	6.6	432	1.8	14.8

Source: Bettye Hobbs Pruitt, ed., *The Massachusetts Tax Valuation List of 1771* (Boston: G. K. Hall, 1978). Calculated data.

Appendix C-7
Profile of Fifteen Inland Massachusetts Towns
Cider Production, 1771

Town	Number of Farms Producing Cider	Barrels of Cider Produced per Year	Average Number of Barrels Produced per Farm	Average Number of Barrels Produced per House	Average Number of Barrels of Cider per Person
Ashburnham	—	—	—	—	—
Ashfield	2	14	0.20	7.0	0.05
Athol	15	111	1.10	8.5	0.14
Blandford	35	158	1.80	4.5	0.24
Brimfield	74	862	5.80	11.6	0.72
Charlmont	4	38	0.90	9.5	0.10
Chesterfield	—	—	—	—	—
Dracut	74	781	6.20	10.5	0.75
Littleton	98	1,620	15.30	16.5	1.53
Pelham	67	695	7.30	10.3	2.14
Petersham	45	301	2.50	6.6	0.39
Shutesbury	22	132	2.00	6.0	0.24
Stockbridge	12	106	1.70	8.8	0.10
Templeton	2	5	0.04	2.5	0.01
Worcester	149	2,235	9.50	15.0	1.04

Source: Bettye Hobbs Pruitt, ed., *The Massachusetts Tax Valuation List of 1771* (Boston: G. K. Hall, 1978). Calculated data.

Appendix D-1
Land Use in Concord, Massachusetts
Landowning and Landless Taxpayers, 1749–1850

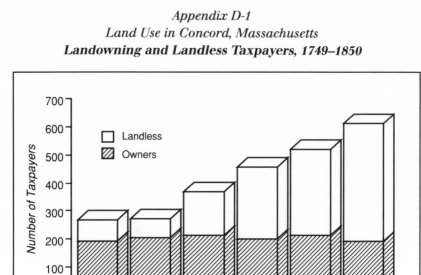

Number of Taxpayers

Source: Derived from data in Robert A. Gross, "Culture and Cultivation: Agriculture and Society in Thoreau's Concord," *Journal of American History* 69, no. 1 (June 1982): 57.

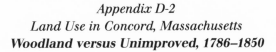

Appendix D-2
Land Use in Concord, Massachusetts
Woodland versus Unimproved, 1786–1850

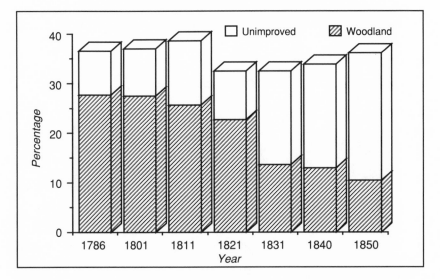

Source: Derived from data in Robert A. Gross, "Culture and Cultivation: Agriculture and Society in Thoreau's Concord," *Journal of American History* 69, no. 1 (June 1982): 58.

Appendix D-3
Land Use in Concord, Massachusetts
Average Size of Livestock Holdings, 1749–1850

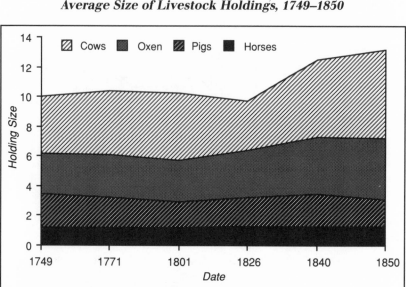

Source: Derived from data in Robert A. Gross, "Culture and Cultivation: Agriculture and Society in Thoreau's Concord," *Journal of American History* 69, no. 1 (June 1982): 57.

Appendix D-4
Land Use in Concord, Massachusetts
Fresh Meadow versus English Meadow, 1781–1850

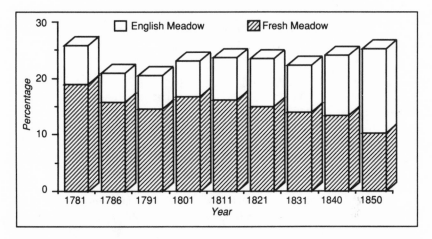

Source: Derived from data in Robert A. Gross, "Culture and Cultivation: Agriculture and Society in Thoreau's Concord," *Journal of American History* 69, no. 1 (June 1982): 57.

Appendix E
Products of the New England Forest, 1840

State	Fuelwood (cords sold)	Potash (tons)	Skins and Furs ($)	Sawmills (number)	Lumber Products ($)
Connecticut	159,062	—	19,760	673	147,841
Maine	205,011	261	8,027	1,381	1,808,683
Massachusetts	278,069	6	60	1,252	344,845
New Hampshire	116,266	114	2,230	959	433,217
Rhode Island	48,666	—	—	123	44,455
Vermont	98,924	718	1,750	1,081	346,939

Source: Michael Williams, "Products of the Forest: Mapping the Census of 1840," Journal of Forest History 24, no. 1 (January 1980), p. 7.

Notes

Chapter 1

1. Marsh, *Man and Nature*, epigraph on p. 36, quotations on p. xviii. On Marsh's distress over the environmental transformation of Vermont, see Lowenthal, *George Perkins Marsh*, pp. 246–76, esp. p. 251. Portions of this chapter appeared as Carolyn Merchant, "The Theoretical Structure of Ecological Revolutions."

2. Cronon's *Changes in the Land* also discusses the ecological history of New England. My *Ecological Revolutions* by contrast emphasizes not only the colonial period, but also the market and industrial revolutions to 1860. I make a distinction between mercantile capitalists and subsistence farmers in the colonial period, whereas Cronon tends to view the colonists primarily as market-oriented entrepreneurs. I also emphasize intellectual frameworks, worldviews, science, and epistemologies, while Cronon is mainly concerned with changes brought about by colonial production. I integrate an analysis of gender and reproduction and include quantitative data, tables, and graphs. Finally, I present a theory of environmental history as ecological and social transformations that helps to account for the magnitude and direction of change, rather than seeing New England's environmental history as simply "changes in the land."

3. Kuhn, *Structure of Scientific Revolutions*.

4. Karl Marx, "Preface to *A Contribution to the Critique of Political Economy*," pp. 182–83:

> ... the guiding thread of my studies, can be briefly formulated as follows: In the social production of their life, men enter into definite relations that are indispensable and independent of their will, relations of production which correspond to a definite stage of development of their material productive forces. The sum total of these relations of production constitutes the economic structure of society, the real foundation, on which rises a legal and political superstructure and to which correspond definite forms of social consciousness. The mode of production of material life conditions the social, political and intellectual life process in general. It is not the consciousness of men that determines their being, but on the contrary, their social being that determines their consciousness. At a certain stage of their development, the material productive forces of society come in conflict with the existing relations of production, or—what is but

a legal expression for the same thing—with the property relations within which they have been at work hitherto. From forms of development of the productive forces these relations turn into their fetters. Then begins an epoch of social revolution. With the change of the economic foundation the entire immense superstructure is more or less rapidly transformed.

For a view of society as a tripartite structure, see Harris, *Cultural Materialism*, pp. 51–75.

5. For accounts of basic ecological concepts, see G. Tyler Miller, Jr., *Living in the Environment*, pp. 43–73; Nebel, *Environmental Science*, pp. 11–70, 86–92, 114–16; Ricklefs, *Economy of Nature*, pp. 110–27. "Gross production refers to the total energy assimilated by photosynthesis. Net production refers to the accumulation of energy in plant biomass, or plant growth and reproduction. The difference between the two represents respiration by the plant" (Ricklefs, *Economy of Nature*, p. 112).

6. On ecology as a social construction, see Bird, "Social Construction of Nature"; Knorr-Cetina, *Manufacture of Knowledge*; Knorr-Cetina and Mulkay, *Science Observed*. On the bioeconomic language of ecology, see Worster, *Nature's Economy*, pp. 312–13.

7. Heraclitus, *Selections from Early Greek Philosophy*, pp. 84–97. Quotations on p. 91, fragments 41–42; p. 92, fragment 69; p. 91, fragment 46.

8. Merchant, *Death of Nature*, pp. 19–20, 111–17, 275–89.

9. Parsons, *Marx and Engels on Ecology*, pp. 136, 129. Marx's realist philosophy looks for the underlying causes of historical and natural change. Marx saw real, active human beings interacting with real, active nature. "To say that man is a corporeal, living, real, sensuous, objective being full of natural vigor," wrote Marx, "is to say that he has real, sensuous, objects as the objects of his life, or that he can only express his life in real, sensuous objects" (ibid., p. 134). These real objects are the material beings that form the basis of Marx's philosophy of nature.

10. Parsons, *Marx and Engels on Ecology*, p. 133. On the mode of production and the domination of nature, see Baudrillard, *Mirror of Production*; Leiss, *Domination of Nature*.

11. Engels, *Dialectics of Nature*, quotations on pp. 289–90.

12. *Compact Oxford English Dictionary*, 2:2512: Denham, *Cato Major, Of Old Age*, quotation on p. 107; Yeats, *Natural History of Commerce*, quotation on p. 2. On the meaning of resource as gifts of the earth, see Meeker, "Resourceful Resurrection" and "Footnote about That Awful Word."

13. *Compact Oxford English Dictionary*, 2:2315: d'Acosta, *Natural and Moral History of the Indies*, bk. 4, chap. i, quotation on p. 203; McCulloch, *The Principles of Political Economy*, bk. 2, chap. i, quotation on p. 61. On the productions of nature, see Samuel Williams, *Natural and Civil History of Vermont*, 1:81, 97–98; Belknap, *History of New Hampshire*, 3:73.

14. G. Tyler Miller, Jr., *Living in the Environment*, pp. 75–87; Nebel, *Environmental Science*, pp. 71–92; Odum, *Fundamentals of Ecology*.

15. Prigogine, *From Being to Becoming*; Prigogine and Stengers, *Order out*

of Chaos; Jantsch, *Self-Organizing Universe*. On the implications of Prigogine's approach for the study of history, see Toffler's forward to Prigogine and Stengers, *Order out of Chaos*, pp. xi–xxvi, esp. pp. xv–xvi.

16. On reproduction, see Nebel, *Environmental Science*, pp. 73–78.

17. On generation, see *Compact Oxford English Dictionary*, 1:1128; on reproduction, see ibid., 2:2501. Until the eighteenth century, biological reproduction, following Aristotle, was called generation, or the production of plants, animals, and other substances by natural means. The process of generation was contrary to that of corruption and the two processes together described all changes in the cosmos. Buffon, in *Natural History* (1781), 2:16, used the term "reproduction" to mean the general phenomenon of generation in all species. In 1776, Adam Smith wrote that "the demand for men regulates the production of men," thus tying production to reproduction (*Wealth of Nations*, 1:84). Engels in his *Origin of the Family, Private Property, and the State* linked the production and reproduction of immediate life with the production of food, clothing, and shelter, on the one hand, and the production of the human species, on the other. (See Marx and Engels, *Selected Works*, p. 455.) I am grateful to Barbara Duden for pointing out these changes in the use of the terms "generation" and "reproduction." On reproduction as an organizing category, see Peterson, "Gender-Sex Dimension in Swedish Politics." On the application of the concept of reproduction to capitalist cultures, see Women's Work Study Group, "Loom, Broom, and Womb"; Beechey, "On Patriarchy"; Young, "Socialist Feminism." For an argument that reproduction should be reduced to production, see Jaggar and McBride, " 'Reproduction' as Male Ideology."

18. Marvin Harris, *Cultural Materialism*, pp. 52, 66–70, 79–92.

19. Meillassoux, *Maidens, Meal, and Money*. Critiques of Meillassoux include O'Laughlin, "Production and Reproduction"; Mackintosh, "Reproduction and Patriarchy."

20. Meillassoux, *Maidens, Meal, and Money*, pp. 14–19. The concept of human energy, argues Meillassoux, is an advance over Marx's concept of labor. "It covers all the energy produced by the metabolic effects of foodstuffs on the human organism. . . . Labor-power is only that fraction of human energy with exchange-value" (p. 50).

21. Ibid., pp. 38–42. "The social organisation of the domestic agricultural community is built both upon the relations of production . . . and upon the relations of reproduction necessary to perpetuate the productive cell. . . . It is evident that reproduction is the dominant preoccupation of these societies. All their institutions are organized to this purpose" (p. 38).

22. Ibid., pp. 50–57.

23. Ibid., pp. 36, 39. "The process of reproduction in the domestic community is achieved by means of very-long-term commitments (vows, engagement, marriage, dowry, etc.)" (p. 39). These juridical rules result from the requirements of production and serve to perpetuate them.

24. Ibid., pp. 75–78. "The agriculturalist," argues Meillassoux, "is condemned to marry. . . . Young men cannot fulfill themselves socially unless they

have a wife" (p. 78). "Women, despite their crucial role in reproduction, never appear as vectors of the social organization. They are hidden behind men, behind fathers, brothers, and/or husbands" (p. 75).

25. Peterson, "Gender-Sex Dimension in Swedish Politics," quotation on p. 6. Peterson's fourfold taxonomy of political interests included (1) issues related to the interests of intergenerational reproduction, (2) issues related to the interests of intragenerational reproduction in the family, (3) issues related to the interests of intragenerational reproduction in the public sector, and (4) issues related to the interests of reproduction workers (women), that is, so-called women's liberation issues. Peterson also applied her taxonomy to the politics of reproduction in the Swedish environmental movement. (See Peterson and Merchant, " 'Peace with the Earth,' " pp. 472–74.)

26. Engels, *Origin of the Family, Private Property, and the State*, p. 455. On population in relation to the mode of production, see Meek, *Marx and Engels on the Population Bomb*; Harvey, "Population, Resources, and the Ideology of Science."

27. Bridenthal, "Dialectics of Production and Reproduction in History."

28. Geertz, "Religion as a Cultural System," pp. 87–125; Charles Taylor, "Neutrality in Political Science," pp. 144–46, 154–55.

29. On mimetic, participatory consciousness, see Berman, *Reenchantment of the World*; Merriam, "Disenchantment of the World." On the gaze, see *Compact Oxford English Dictionary*, 1:1123: "said of a deer, also of persons, especially in wonder, expectancy, bewilderment." "The hart, stag, buck, or hind when borne in coat-armour, looking affrontée or full faced is said to be at gaze . . . but all other beasts in this attitude are called guardant" (quoted from William Berry, *Encyclopedia Heraldica*, 1:s.v. "gaze"). On ordained killing, see Speck, "Penobscot Tales and Religious Beliefs," p. 25; on imitative magic and the hunter's relationship to the hunted, see Calvin Martin, *Keepers of the Game*, pp. 113–49, esp. pp. 116, 124. On Koyukon Indian versus white methods of hunting deer, see Nelson, "The Gifts," esp. pp. 122–23. On imitation of animals by humans in hunting, see Randall L. Eaton, "Hunting and the Great Mystery of Nature." Daniel Boone described a method of using the gaze to hunt deer by tricking it with a panful of blazing pine knots: "The deer, reposing quietly in his thicket, is awakened by the approaching cavalcade, and instead of flying from the portentous brilliance, remains stupidly gazing upon it, as if charmed to the spot. The animal is betrayed to its doom by the gleaming of its fixed and innocent eyes. This cruel mode of securing a fatal shot, is called in hunter's phrase, *shining the eyes*" (quoted from Kolodny, *Land before Her*, p. 86). On Indian senses and consciousness, see Highwater, *The Primal Mind*.

30. Axtell, "Power of Print in the Eastern Woodlands" and *Invasion Within*.

31. Havelock, *Preface to Plato*. See also Keller and Grontkowski, "The Mind's Eye"; Berman, *Reenchantment of the World*.

32. Latour, "Visualization and Cognition," quotations on pp. 22, 29.

33. Haraway, "The Contest for Primate Nature"; Foucault, "Questions on Geography," pp. 63–67; Bentham, *Panopticon*; Associated Press, "Satellites Serve as Eyes on Wildlife."

34. Bird, "Social Construction of Nature." In the agricultural sciences, insects resist pesticides by mutating to new strains. In the health sciences, human social practices help to create environments for the mutation of disease-causing viruses.

Chapter 2

1. U.S. Department of Agriculture, *Atlas of American Agriculture*, pp. 7, 31, 35, 39.

2. Jorgensen, *Guide to New England's Landscape*, pp. 1–76; Thomson, *Changing Face of New England*, pp. 1–18; U.S. Department of Agriculture, *Changing Fertility of New England Soils*; Wright, "Regions and Landscapes of New England."

3. [Stuart], "My Friend, the Soil," quotation on p. 158.

4. U.S. Department of Agriculture, *Changing Fertility of New England Soils*, pp. 2–5, 15–18, 23–26.

5. Thomson, *Changing Face of New England*, pp. 55–67, 82–100, 116–40.

6. The following discussion is based on Davis, "Phytogeography and Palynology of Northeastern United States"; Westveld et al., "Natural Forest Vegetation Zones"; Bromley, "Original Forest Types"; Peattie, *Natural History of Trees*; Dame and Brooks, *Handbook of the Trees of New England*; Raup, "Recent Changes of Climate and Vegetation"; Harper, "Changes in the Forest Area"; Hawes, "New England Forests in Retrospect"; Nichols, "Vegetation of Connecticut"; Thomson, *Changing Face of New England*; Belknap, *History of New Hampshire*, 3:73–96; Hepting, "Death of the American Chestnut."

7. Thoreau, "Succession of Forest Trees," *Natural History Essays*.

8. Thomson, *Changing Face of New England*, pp. 26–32; Bromley, "Original Forest Types," pp. 71, 74, 76; Korstian and Stickel, "Natural Replacement of Blight-killed Chestnut."

9. Bromley, "Original Forest Types," p. 67; Audubon, "The Passenger Pigeon," quotations on pp. 169, 171.

10. Calvin Martin, *Keepers of the Game*, pp. 62, 117; Dugmore, *Romance of the Beaver*, pp. 40, 66–67; Mills, *In Beaver World*, pp. 139–49, 213–21, quotation on pp. 219–20.

11. Mills, *In Beaver World*, pp. 65, 74; Rupp, "Beaver-Trout Relationship," p. 76; Hair et al., "Beaver Pond Ecosystems."

12. Peirce, "Letter," in Belknap, *History of New Hampshire*, 3:118–19, quotation on pp. 118–19; Kendall, *Travels*, 3:176.

13. Babcock, "Beaver as a Factor," p. 185; Wyllys, "Letter ... to George Wyllys"; "Foote, Nathaniel (Wethersfield) Inventory," November 20, 1644, in Manwaring, *Digest of the Early Connecticut Probate Records*, 1:4; "Williams, Thomas, Sen. (Wethersfield) Inventory," February 28, 1692–93, in Manwaring, *Digest*, 2:139; "Smith, Joseph (Haddam) Inventory," September 15, 1732, in Manwaring, *Digest*, 3:112.

14. Wilbur, *New England Indians*; Snow, *Archeology of New England*; Haviland and Power, *Original Vermonters*, pp. 22–89; Davis, Spear, and Shane,

"Holocene Climate of New England"; Rosier, "True Relation of the Voyage of Captain George Waymouth," p. 385; [Davies], "Relation of a Voyage to Sagadahoc," p. 412; Day, "Indian as an Ecological Factor"; William Wood, *New England's Prospect*, quotation on p. 16; Thomas Morton, "New English Canaan," quotation on p. 37; Dwight, *Travels*, vol. 1 (letter, vol. 8); Bromley, "Original Forest Types," p. 65.

15. Cook, *Indian Population of New England*, pp. 1–12, 84, gives estimates for the population of the southern New England tribes. I have omitted Long Island and included the Eastern Abenaki as calculated by Snow, *Archeology of New England*, pp. 31–42. Snow estimates the density of the Eastern Abenaki at 20 persons per 100 square kilometers. His estimates for southern New England are higher than Cook's. Salisbury, *Manitou and Providence*, pp. 30, 251, n. 37, suggests a population range of 126,000 to 144,000 for New England as a whole and calculates a population density for southern New England as ten times that of the Eastern Abenaki. Haviland and Power, *Original Vermonters*, pp. 155–64, estimate a density six times greater in southern than northern New England and suggest that the northern gatherer-hunter populations were relatively stable at about 25 percent of carrying capacity, while the southern horticulturists may have been close to carrying capacity.

16. Hayden White, "Forms of Wildness." For biblical references, see Holy Bible, Gen. 1:28, 2:18–20; Lev. 18:23.

17. On the symbolism of Caliban in Shakespeare's *Tempest*, see Leo Marx, *Machine in the Garden*, pp. 46–54. On witchcraft and animal lust, see Merchant, *Death of Nature*, pp. 132–43. On animal symbols, see Machiavelli, *The Prince*, chap. 13, p. 64; Meeker, *Comedy of Survival*, pp. 92–97; Alden T. Vaughan, "English Policy and the Massacre of 1622."

18. Baldwin, *Sumptuary Legislation*, p. 47; Elias, *The Civilizing Process*, pp. 117–19.

19. Elias, *The Civilizing Process*, pp. 117–22, quotations on p. 85.

20. Baldwin, *Sumptuary Legislation*, pp. 9, 12, 23, 33, 47–50.

21. Murray Grant Lawson, *Fur*, pp. 1–3.

22. Stubbes, *Anatomie of Abuses*, quoted from Fairholt, *Costume in England*, p. 261; Repton, "Observations on the Various Fashions of Hats," p. 178; Brooke and Laver, *English Costume*, pp. 154, 184, 200, 208. Charles I quoted from Murray Grant Lawson, *Fur*, p. 4.

23. Murray Grant Lawson, *Fur*, pp. 5–6.

24. Speck, *Penobscot Man*, pp. 17–18, 23, 26, 218–21, and "Penobscot Tales and Religious Beliefs," pp. 1, 24, 27–29, 38–43; Fisher, "Mythology of the Northern and Northeastern Algonkians," pp. 228–29, 238; Haviland and Power, *Original Vermonters*, pp. 148–55.

25. Barfield, *Saving the Appearances*, pp. 28–35; Berman, *Reenchantment of the World*, pp. 135–42.

26. Speck, "Penobscot Tales and Religious Beliefs," quotations from myths on pp. 39–40.

27. Ibid., pp. 25–27.

28. On the imitation of the animal by the hunter, see Calvin Martin, *Keepers*

of the Game, pp. 113–49, esp. pp. 116, 124. See also Ortega y Gasset, *Meditations on Hunting*:

> To hunt is to experience extreme oneness with Nature. The hunter is not on the earth but in it: He listens with the ears of the deer, sees with the eyes of the crow. The hunter expands outward into nature and is absorbed by it. Submerged wholly in nature with an attention best described as a kind of universal concentration, the hunter imitates his prey to the point of identity.... When they are in the field the axis of the whole situation is that mystical union with the animal, a sensing and presentiment of it that automatically leads the hunter to perceive all his surroundings from the point of view of the animal, with the animal's particular attention to detail ... wind, light, temperature, ground contour, minerals, vegetation, all play a part.... Only the hunter, imitating the perpetual alertness of the wild animal, for whom everything is danger, sees everything and sees each thing functioning as a facility of difficulty, as risk or protection (quoted from Randall L. Eaton "Hunting and the Great Mystery of Nature," pp. 47–48).

Anthropologist Richard K. Nelson, who has studied the hunting habits of the Koyukon Indians of Alaska, describes the moment of locking eyes while hunting a deer:

> This is a very large buck. It comes so quickly that I have no chance to shoot, and then it is so close that I haven't the heart to do it. Fifty feet away, the deer lowers his head.... In the middle of a step he raises his head all the way up, and he sees me standing there—a stain against the pure white of the forest. A sudden spasm runs through his entire body, his front legs jerk apart, and he freezes all akimbo, head high, nostrils flared, coiled, and hard. I can only look at him and wait, my mind snarled with irreconcilable emotions. Here is a perfect buck deer. In the Koyukon way, he has come to me; but in my own he has come too close. I am as congealed and transfixed as he is, as devoid of conscious thought. It is as if my mind has ceased to function and I only have eyes (Nelson, "The Gifts," p. 122).

29. On the primal gaze of locking eyes and the change from oral to visual culture, see Keller and Grontkowski, "The Mind's Eye." On exchanges of looks between humans and animals, see Berger, *About Looking*, pp. 1–26. On mimicking, see Snow, "Wabanaki 'Family Hunting Territories,'" p. 1149; Speck, *Penobscot Man*, pp. 34–36, 38–44, 46, 207; Champlain, *Voyages*, p. 55; Haviland and Power, *Original Vermonters*, pp. 161–62.

30. Speck, "Penobscot Tales and Religious Beliefs," pp. 1, 24, 28–29, and *Penobscot Man*, pp. 218–21.

31. Speck, "Penobscot Shamanism," pp. 244–46, 250, 252–53, 258, 260; Snow, "Solon Petroglyphs and Eastern Abnaki Shamanism"; Alvin Hamblen Morrison, "Wabanaki Women Extraordinaire," pp. 125–36.

32. Moore, "Divination—A New Perspective."

33. Speck, *Penobscot Man*, p. 53.

34. Snow, "Wabanaki 'Family Hunting Territories'": "There is considerable evidence against strict or even preferred patrilocal residence among Algonquian groups having family territories. Speck found at least as many and perhaps more examples of matrilocal than patrilocal residence within one generation in the Mistassini 'band.' Similar residence practices can be seen among the Wabanaki. Leacock sums up the case for a strong matrilocal tendency among the various groups of the Labrador Peninsula, and points out that in many cases, the local band form is best termed 'composite'" (p. 1144). See also Leacock, "Matrilocality," pp. 31–47.

35. Speck, *Penobscot Man*, pp. 17–18, 23, 26. On the personal, historical, and spiritual meaning of landscapes for the northern hunters, see Nelson, *Make Prayers to the Raven*, pp. 244–45.

36. Foucault, "Questions on Geography," pp. 63–77.

37. Wilford, *Mapmakers*, pp. 60–61, 75–77, 81–86.

38. Dexter, *Maps of Early Massachusetts*, pp. 54–55, 58–61, 74–75. On the use of animals on maps, see George, *Animals and Maps*.

39. Salisbury, *Manitou and Providence*, pp. 50–56, quotation on p. 52.

40. Pring, "Voyage Set Out from the Citie of Bristol," p. 350; Champlain, *Works*, 1:295–96; Salisbury, *Manitou and Providence*, p. 61; John Smith, *Description of New England*, pp. 1, 12, and "New England's Trials," p. B3; Snow, "Keepers of the Game"; Bishop, "Northeastern Indian Concepts of Conservation."

41. Rosier, "True Relation of the Voyage of Captain George Waymouth," pp. 368–71, 373–79, 385, quotation on p. 371.

42. [Davies], "Relation of a Voyage to Sagadahoc," pp. 403, 416, 419.

43. Snow, "Abenaki Fur Trade" and "Wabanaki 'Family Hunting Territories'"; Purchas, "Description of the Country of Mawooshen," 19:400–405; Cook, "Significance of Disease," pp. 489–90, quotation on p. 489; Crosby, "God . . . Would Destroy Them."

44. Snow, "Abenaki Fur Trade," pp. 8–9.

45. Maloney, *Fur Trade in New England*, pp. 25–31; Anonymous, "Edward Ashley."

46. Maloney, *Fur Trade in New England*, pp. 34–36; Preston, "Laconia Company of 1629"; Buffinton, "New England and the Western Fur Trade," pp. 163–65.

47. Leger, *Catholic Indian Missions in Maine*, quotation on pp. 69–70.

48. Charles F. Carroll, *Timber Economy of Puritan New England*, pp. 71–72, 112; Sargent, *York Deeds*, bk. 5, pt. 1, fols. 16, 31, 36, 39; Willis, *History of Portland*, pp. 249–55; Eckstrom, "Lumbering in Maine," 3:689–95.

49. Anonymous, "Of the Mission of the Assumption," 31:185, 189–93, quotation on p. 193; Leger, *Catholic Indian Missions in Maine*, pp. 38–49; Duffy, "Smallpox and the Indians," p. 329; Roberts, "Fur Trade of New England," pp. 170–215.

50. Anonymous, "Of the Mission of the Assumption," 31:202–3.

51. Ibid., 31:195, 197.

52. Rasles, "Letter . . . to Monsieur his Brother," 67:211. On the fetishism of commodities, see Taussig, "Genesis of Capitalism."

53. Rasles, "Letter . . . to Monsieur his Brother," 67:213.

54. Chadwick, "Account of a Journey," quotations on p. 143; Babcock, "Beaver as a Factor," p. 195.

55. Quotation from Kendall, *Travels*, 3:73. In modern times, a retribution of sorts was paid to the Abenaki. In 1980, as a result of legal suits (based on the Nonintercourse Act of 1790 requiring federal approval of any transaction between Indians and states or individuals), the descendants of the Penobscot, Passamaquoddy, and Malisset Indians of Maine won an $81.5 million settlement (Brodeur, *Restitution*).

56. St. George, " 'Set Thine House in Order,' " pp. 162–70.

57. Oaks, "Things Fearful to Name," pp. 274–78. According to Oaks, the fact that 40–50 percent of all farm boys had sexual contact of some kind with animals (reported by Kinsey in 1948) may indicate similar tendencies in the farming culture of the seventeenth century. He also notes that explorers' accounts suggesting that human intercourse with apes had produced many black Africans may have helped to legitimate an emerging racism. On bestiality in Europe, see Monter, "Sodomy and Heresy in Early Modern Switzerland." I thank Jonas Liljeqvist for these citations.

58. Rowlandson, "Captivity," quotations on pp. 132, 137. On the first war between the Abenaki and the English colonists, see Siebert, "First Maine Indian War," p. 151: "The majority of the English regarded the Indians with ill-concealed contempt as inferior beings who were to be tolerated until such time as they could be either acculturated or driven away."

59. Rowlandson, "Captivity," p. 159.

60. Rasles, "Letter . . . to Monsieur his Nephew," 67:141, 93.

61. Crèvecoeur, *Letters from an American Farmer*, pp. 40–42; Thomas, *Old Farmer's Almanac*, quoted from Kittredge, *Old Farmer and His Almanack*, p. 85.

62. Parker, "Origin, Organization, and Influence of the Towns of New England," p. 37.

63. Edward Johnson, *Wonder Working Providence*, p. 71.

64. Murray Grant Lawson, *Fur*, pp. 32–38.

65. Benjamin Smith Barton, *Notes on the Animals of North America*, p. 1.

66. Hodgdon and Hunt, "Beaver Management in Maine," pp. 55–59.

67. Seton, *Lives of Game Animals*, quotations from 3:247; Goodwin, "Big Game Animals."

68. Ralph S. Palmer, "Late Records of Caribou in Maine," quotation on p. 37; Seton, *Lives of Game Animals*, 3:59, 176.

69. Goodwin, "Big Game Animals," pp. 48–50.

70. DeForest, *History of the Indians of Connecticut*, pp. 43–44.

Chapter 3

1. On the relationships between cosmology, mythology, ethics, and rituals, see Geertz, "Ethos, Worldview, and the Analysis of Sacred Symbols," p. 127. On the history of corn cultivation among the Indians of southern New England, see M. K. Bennett, "Food Economy of the New England Indians"; Eva L. Butler, "Algonkian Culture."

2. Roger Williams, *Key*, pp. 24–25, 148, 269–70, 56—n. 50, 158, quotation on p. 23.

3. Ibid., pp. 24–25, 114; Thomas Morton, "New English Canaan," p. 168.

4. Speck, "Penobscot Tales and Religious Beliefs," p. 75.

5. Speck, *Penobscot Man*, pp. 194–95; Mechling, *Malecite Tales*, pp. 87–88; Witthoft, *Green Corn Ceremonialism*, pp. 81, 77–79.

6. Geertz, "Religion as a Cultural System," pp. 2–11, 81–85; Eva L. Butler, "Algonkian Culture," pp. 24–25; William Simmons, *Spirit of the New England Tribes*, p. 13.

7. Roger Williams, *Key*, p. 197; quotations in Witthoft, *Green Corn Ceremonialism*, pp. 6–9.

8. Geertz, *Agricultural Involution*, pp. 16–24; Russell, *Indian New England*, pp. 165–70; Roger Williams, *Key*, p. 123.

9. Aupaumut, *First Annual Report*, p. 42, quoted from Eva L. Butler, "Algonkian Culture," p. 13.

10. Wood, *New England's Prospect*, p. 13; Geertz, *Agricultural Involution*, pp. 16–24.

11. Josselyn, *Account of Two Voyages to New England*, p. 99; Willoughby, "Houses and Gardens of the New England Indians."

12. M. K. Bennett, "Food Economy of the New England Indians," p. 392; Russell, *Indian New England*, pp. 147–52.

13. Fowler, "Agricultural Tools and Techniques."

14. Van Wassenaer, "Historisch Verhael," quoted from Jameson, *Narratives of New Netherland*, pp. 61–96, see pp. 72, 69; Ceci, "Watchers of the Pleiades."

15. Letter of Isaack de Rasieres to Samuel Blommaert, in Jameson, *Narratives of New Netherland*, pp. 97–115, quotation on p. 107; Geertz, *Agricultural Involution*, pp. 24–25.

16. Those who question the use of fish fertilizers by New England Indians include Rostlund, "Evidence for the Use of Fish as Fertilizer," p. 225; Ceci, "Fish Fertilizer"; Goode, "Use of Agricultural Fertilizers." The same authors attribute the use of fish to seventeenth-century New England colonists.

The three sources attributing the use of fish to Indians were as follows: William Bradford's *Of Plymouth Plantation*, ed. Wish, is the source of the famous description of Squanto's demonstration on how to plant corn. He showed the colonists "both the manner how to set it, and after how to dress and tend it. Also he told them except they got fish and set with it (in these old grounds) it would come to nothing, and he showed them that in the middle of April they should have store enough come up the brook" (p. 76).

Second, Edward Winslow, in a letter of 1621 describing the planting of Indian corn "according to the manner of the Indians," related that "we manured our ground with herrings, or rather shads, which we have in great abundance and take with great ease" (Winslow, "Letter," p. 488). But it is unlikely that Winslow observed any Indians using fish as fertilizer, inasmuch as the original inhabitants of the Plymouth area had been virtually annihilated in the epidemic of 1616. His informant therefore could also have been Squanto. (See Ceci, "Fish Fertilizer.")

The third source is John Winthrop, Jr.'s essay on "Indian Corne," published posthumously in London in 1678: "Where the ground is not very good, or hath been long planted and worn out, the Indians used to put two or three of those forementioned fishes under each place upon which they planted their corn, or if they had not time before planting, then they would put them afterwards into the earth by the sides of those corn hills, and by these means had far greater crops then that ground would otherwise produce, many times more then double" ([John Winthrop, Jr.], "Description, Culture, and Use of Maize"; see also Mood, "John Winthrop, Jr. on Indian Corn").

17. Ceci, "Fish Fertilizer," p. 27; William Wood, *New England's Prospect*, quotation on p. 13.

18. Ceci, "Fish Fertilizer," pp. 28–30.

19. Gliessman and Altieri, "Polyculture Cropping Has Advantages"; Risch and Hanson, "Population Dynamics of Insect Pests"; Risch, "Insect Herbivore Abundance."

20. Russell, *Indian New England*, pp. 165–70.

21. William Wood, *New England's Prospect*, quotation on p. 100; Winthrop, "Indian Corne," p. 127; Champlain, *Voyages*, p. 62.

22. Altieri, "Crop-Weed-Insect Interactions."

23. Kaplan, "Archeology and Domestication," p. 359. On the use of maize and beans with other foods, see Gookin, "Historical Collections," p. 150.

24. Roger Williams, *Key*, quotation on p. 124; Gookin, "Historical Collections," pp. 190–91; M. K. Bennett, "Food Economy of the New England Indians," pp. 391–94. Bennett writes:

Two heaps of 12 bushels each would yield 1,344 pounds per year for a family of five (Gookin's figure for estimating population....); which equals something over 1,150 calories per person per day. Three heaps of 20 bushels each would yield more than 2,900 calories per person for a family of five. If we take the middle of Williams' range and reckon on an average family of six rather than five, the calculation results in a little over 1,700 calories per person per day which would be 68 per cent of the assumed total daily ingestion of 2,500 calories.... Corn may have provided some 65 per cent or a little less of total food calories, much more than the animal and bird carcasses at 10 per cent or a little more (p. 394).

(According to U.S. government standards, one bushel of corn equals 56 pounds.) Bennett also notes: "Fletcher, historian of agriculture in Pennsylvania, thinks that an Indian family there ordinarily 'cultivated one to one and a half acres of corn and harvested forty to sixty bushels'" (p. 391).

25. Hart, "A Bean, Corn, and Manioc Polyculture Cropping System," p. 380; Gliessman and Amador, "Ecological Aspects of Production."

26. William Wood, *New England's Prospect*, p. 100.

27. Josselyn, *Account of Two Voyages to New England*, p. 64; Roger Williams, *Key*, quotation on p. 43.

28. Thomas Morton, "New English Canaan," pp. 44–45; Roger Williams, *Key*, pp. 120–22; William Wood, *New England's Prospect*, p. 70; Merriam, "The Acorn," pp. 129, 133; Salwen, "Indians of Southern New England and Long Island," p. 162; M. K. Bennett, "Food Economy of the New England Indians," p. 392; Rasles, "Letter . . . to . . . Monsieur his Nephew," 67:93–95; Schuette and Schuette, "Maple Sugar," p. 215; Henshaw, "Indian Origin of Maple Sugar." On feminist anthropology, see Slocum, "Woman the Gatherer."

29. Roger Williams, *Key*, pp. 188–899; Champlain, *Voyages*, p. 55; William Wood, *New England's Prospect*, pp. 92–94, 101.

30. Burtt, "Methods of Fishing"; William Wood, *New England's Prospect*, pp. 100–101; Frederick Johnson, *The Boylston Street Fishweir*; M. K. Bennett, "Food Economy of the New England Indians," p. 393.

31. M. K. Bennett, "Food Economy of the New England Indians," pp. 378–83.

32. Grumet, "Sunksquaws, Shamans, and Tradeswomen," pp. 46–53.

33. Gookin, "Historical Collections," quotation on p. 154; Roger Williams, *Key*, p. 149; Grumet, "Sunksquaws, Shamans, and Tradeswomen," pp. 53–54.

34. For an analysis of complementary dualism in subsistence cultures, see Marburg, "Man's Role, Woman's Place" and "Women and Environment."

35. Crosby, "Ecological Imperialism" and *Ecological Imperialism*; Bidwell and Falconer, *History of Agriculture*, pp. 19–20. Crosby argues that a fourfold complex of white populations, associated animals, pathogens, and weeds established themselves over most of the northern and southern temperate zones of the world, establishing "Neo-Europes." He calls these "the lands of the Demographic Takeover."

36. Josselyn, "New England's Rarities," 4:220–24.

37. Ibid., 4:216–19.

38. Cook, "Significance of Disease"; Duffy, "Smallpox and the Indians"; Crosby, "God . . . Would Destroy Them" and "Virgin Soil Epidemics."

39. Peter Allen Thomas, "Contrastive Subsistence Strategies," pp. 13–14. I have drawn on Thomas's method of comparison between Indian and colonial land needs, but have revised his numbers for colonial towns.

40. Ibid.; Maloney, *Fur Trade in New England*, pp. 46–49; Roberts, "Fur Trade of New England," pp. 145–68; Buffinton, "New England and the Western Fur Trade," pp. 165–76.

41. Innes, *Labor in a New Land*, pp. 3–16 (quotation on p. 6), 31–33; McIntyre, *William Pynchon*, pp. 9–11, 25–26; Green, *Springfield*, p. 12; Judd, "Fur Trade on the Connecticut River," pp. 217–19; Maloney, *Fur Trade in New England*, pp. 52–54; Peter Allen Thomas, "In the Maelstrom of Change," pp. 287, 473–74.

42. Gardner, "His Relation of the Pequot Warres," p. 154.

43. Cook, *Indian Population of New England*, pp. 2–3, 84.

44. Bradford, *Of Plymouth Plantation*, quotations on p. 176; Duffy, "Smallpox and the Indians," p. 328; Cook, "Significance of Disease"; Crosby, "Virgin Soil Epidemics."

45. Cook, *Indian Population of New England*, p. 84, and "Interracial Warfare," pp. 6, 9, 12, 21; Jennings, *Invasion of America*, p. 29; Gookin, "Historical Collections," pp. 147–49. Jennings added to Gookin's data an estimate for the Wampanoag equal to the population of the Massachuset Indians.

46. Shurtleff, *Records of the Governor and Company of the Massachusetts Bay*, 4, pt. 1:102–3. On the use of land improvement as a rationale for dispossessing native Americans, see Washburn, "Moral and Legal Justification."

47. Shurtleff, *Records of the Colony of New Plymouth*, 4:31; Rogers and Field, *Early Records of the Town of Providence*, 17:18.

48. Farmington Indians, "Farmington Indians to the General Assembly."

49. On the conflicting land interests of whites in Connecticut, see Bushman, *From Puritan to Yankee*, pp. 83–103. On the land disputes and population of the Connecticut Indians, see DeForest, *History of the Indians of Connecticut*, pp. 274–345, 301.

50. Pequot Indians, "Petition," quotation on 4:320. See also DeForest, *History of the Indians of Connecticut*, pp. 427–30.

51. Avery, "Letter . . . to Governor Talcott."

52. Mahomet, "Petition . . . to the King"; DeForest, *History of the Indians of Connecticut*, p. 346.

53. DeForest, *History of the Indians of Connecticut*, pp. 291–92, 296, 311.

54. Mason and Mason, "Petition," 5:139–59. Samuel Mason (b. 1707) and his brother John (b. 1702) were the sons of Captain John Mason of Stonington, Connecticut, and the grandsons of Major John Mason (d. 1672). Samuel Mason, his father John, and Mahomet went to London in 1736 to assert their claims on behalf of the Mohegan. Mahomet was the son of Oweneco Uncas and the grandson of Uncas. Mahomet and John Mason both died in London in 1736 shortly after their arrival and Samuel Mason remained there to prosecute the case. On the background of the land grants, see also DeForest, *History of the Indians of Connecticut*, pp. 291–93.

55. Mason and Mason, "Petition," 5:142–43. See also DeForest, *History of the Indians of Connecticut*, pp. 323, 305–8, 315.

56. DeForest, *History of the Indians of Connecticut*, pp. 310–11, 304, 333.

57. Mason and Mason, "Petition," 5:151–53. See also DeForest, *History of the Indians of Connecticut*, pp. 327–28, 330, 332, 334.

58. Talcott, "Governor Talcott to Francis Wilks (Hartford, Sept. 17, 1736)"; Wilks, "Francis Wilks to Governor Talcott," 4:374. See also Sharpe, "John Sharpe to Francis Wilks," 5:113.

59. Mohegan Indians, "Humble Petition of the . . . Mohegan Indians," 5:159; Talcott, "Governor Talcott to Francis Wilks (January 11, 1739/40)," 5:196.

60. Talcott, "Governor Talcott to Francis Wilks (January 11, 1739/40)," 5:207.

61. DeForest, *History of the Indians of Connecticut*, pp. 328, 335, 340–42.

62. Thomas Morton, "New English Canaan," pp. 33–34.

63. On the awe of Indians over writing and the Bible, see Axtell, "Power of Print in the Eastern Woodlands."

64. On Christianizing the Indians of Massachusetts, see Salisbury, "Red Puritans," pp. 27–54; William Simmons, "Conversion from Indian to Puritan."

65. DeForest, *History of the Indians of Connecticut,* pp. 343–46; William Simmons, "Red Yankees," pp. 253–71; Salisbury, "The Great Awakening," pp. 25–36. On the maintenance of Indian tribal culture, see William Simmons, *Spirit of the New England Tribes,* pp. 37–64 and passim.

66. Bailyn, *New England Merchants,* pp. 20–21, quotation on p. 21. For an example of the use of the term "commodity" to mean products of nature, see Gorges, *A Brief Narration,* p. 52. The grant to Gorges included "all the woods, waters, rivers, soils, havens, harbors, island, and other commodities." See also *Compact Oxford English Dictionary,* 1:482: Higden, tr. (1432), "Flandres is replete with many commodities as with pastures, bestes, marchandise, waters, hauenes."

67. Bailyn, *New England Merchants,* p. 61, quotations on pp. 99, 187; Rutman, *Husbandmen of Plymouth,* pp. 13–21, 66–72. While Plymouth farmers may have traded some items with Massachusetts Bay colonists, representative inventories of Plymouth farmers showed only modest numbers of marketable livestock and little harvested grain. That of a well-off farmer showed two steers, one heifer, five calves, six cows, and four young pigs. A less well-to-do farmer owned six cows, two calves, and five pigs. The estate of an average farmer listed one steer, three cattle, and six swine. After family subsistence needs had been met, the surplus steers, calves, and swine would have been potential market animals. On the timber trade with Spain, the Canaries, Barbados, and Newfoundland, see Charles F. Carroll, *Timber Economy of Puritan New England,* pp. 77–87, 93–94, 106–13. On John Pynchon's production for the West Indies markets, see Innes, *Labor in a New Land,* pp. 33, 44–71. On the change in meaning of commodity to include money, see *Compact Oxford English Dictionary,* 1:482: John Locke, "Some Considerations of the Lowering of Interest and Raising the Value of Money in a Letter of 1691" (1692), wrote that "commodities are moveables valuable by money," and McCulloch, *Principles of Political Economy* (1825), bk. 3, chap. iv, p. 294, stated, "Money is itself a commodity, whose value depends on the same circumstances that determine the value of other commodities." Cronon, *Changes in the Land,* has an excellent discussion of commodities as isolated, extractable components of ecosystems and of the changing meaning of the term over time; see pp. 20–22, 76.

68. Lockridge, *A New England Town,* pp. 69–75, 148–58.

69. Strachey, "Extract"; Thomas Morton, "New English Canaan," quotation on p. 10; Kolodny, *Lay of the Land,* p. 12.

70. Chamberlin and Feldman, *Dartmouth Bible,* "Exodus," 15–17, pp. 96–97; "Numbers," p. 130. "In the Wilderness" is the Hebrew title of the book of Numbers and describes the Hebrews' additional thirty-eight years of wandering in the desert after their escape from Egypt.

71. Bradford, *Of Plymouth Plantation,* pp. 60–61; Thomas Morton, "New English Caanan," 2:1–132; Peter N. Carroll, *Puritanism and the Wilderness,* p. 50.

72. Peter N. Carroll, *Puritanism and the Wilderness,* quotations on pp. 13–14.

73. Bulkeley, *The Gospel Covenant;* quotations of Bulkeley and Hooker from Peter N. Carroll, *Puritanism and the Wilderness,* pp. 69 and 68, respectively.

74. Fritzell, "The Wilderness and the Garden," pp. 21–22; Heimert, "Puritanism, the Wilderness and the Frontier."

75. On the beliefs of southern New England Indians in shamans, witches, ghosts, devils, and giants, see William Simmons, *Spirit of the New England Tribes.*

76. On the decline of piety and church membership in seventeenth-century New England, see Jon Butler, "Magic, Astrology, and the Early American Religious Heritage," p. 317; Rutman, *Winthrop's Boston,* pp. 141–63; Lockridge, *A New England Town,* pp. 87–90.

77. Stilgoe, *Common Landscape of America,* pp. 17–21. On wilderness concepts in the Old World and colonial America, see also Nash, *Wilderness and the American Mind.*

78. Keith Thomas, *Religion and the Decline of Magic,* pp. 68–70; Botkin, *Treasury of New England Folklore,* pp. 423, 332; Crow, *Occult Properties of Herbs and Plants,* pp. 20–22; Charles Francis Adams, *Three Episodes of Massachusetts History,* 1:180–81; Bradford, *History of Plymouth Plantation,* quotation on 1:245, see also n. 1, p. 245:

The observation of Christmas Day in England was appointed by Statute 5 and 6 Edward VI c. 3, but the Puritans regarded it as abused by superstition and profaneness, and as one of other pagan or popish festivals. Ainsworth says in his Arrow Against Idolatrie: "Our purple Queen hath made many moe holy dayes then ther be monethes (that I say not weeks) of the yere, in honour of her Ladie and all her Saincts, and these some of them correspondent to the paynim festivities, as Christmas, Candlemas, Fasgon or Shrovetide, according to the times and customes of the gentiles Saturnal, Februal and Bacchus feasts." (Ed. 1640, p. 156).... New England held days of fasts and thanksgiving, and not until the latter part of the seventeenth century were Christmas and other holidays observed.

79. Bradford, *History of Plymouth Plantation,* quotations from 2:48–51, see also n. 2, p. 48:

Mayday and its festivities have been traced to the Roman feast of Flora, which began on April 28, and lasted some days. Stow, in his Survey of London (1603), thus summarizes the festivities of the day: "I find also that, in the moneth of May, the citizens of London ... had their seuerall mayings, and did fetch in Maypoles, with diuerse warlike shewes, with good Archers, Morice dauncers, and other deuices, for pastime all the day long, and towards the Euening they had stage playes, and Bonefiers in the streetes." To the Puritan the festival was obnoxious for its pagan origin and its worldly practices.... In April, 1644, Parliament ordered all Maypoles to be taken down and removed, and the sports and merriments went with the poles. Under Charles II Mayday festivities were renewed and encouraged. Morton's Maypole was not the first erected in New England.

Charles Francis Adams, *Three Episodes of Massachusetts History*, 1:174–82; Drinnon, "Maypole of Merry Mount," pp. 382–410; Zuckerman, "Pilgrims in the Wilderness"; Hawthorne, "Maypole of Merry Mount."

80. Botkin, *Treasury of New England Folklore*, pp. 176–212; Dorson, *American Folklore*, pp. 16–38; Mather, *Remarkable Providences*, pp. 70–73, quotation on p. 71, see also p. 124.

81. Bord and Bord, *Earth Rites*; Andersen, *The Witch on the Wall*, p. 19 and passim.

82. Institor and Sprenger, *The Malleus Maleficarum*, pp. 47–48; Booth, *Witches of Early America*, pp. 1–51.

83. Mather, *On Witchcraft*, pp. 44–47, 110–11, 116–17, 16, quotations on pp. 45–46, 16. On witches' power to transform farm animals and their intimate contact with animal familiars, see Demos, *Entertaining Satan*, pp. 140–41, tree quotation on p. 352.

84. Karlsen, "The Devil in the Shape of a Woman." Data on accusations and executions were consolidated from Karlsen's tables 1 and 2, pp. 64–65, age structure data on p. 82ff, and marital status data on p. 93. Other important studies of witches in New England from perspectives other than feminist include Boyer and Nissenbaum, *Salem Possessed*, and Demos, *Entertaining Satan*.

85. Karlsen, "The Devil in the Shape of a Woman," pp. 270–73.

86. Ibid., pp. 137–61, data on pp. 143, 156.

87. Ibid., pp. 267–69, 278–83; Mary Beth Norton, "Evolution of White Women's Experience," pp. 596, 598–99; Bloch, "American Feminine Ideals in Transition," pp. 102–3.

88. Jon Butler, "Magic, Astrology, and the Early American Religious Heritage," pp. 341–42; Kerr and Crow, *Occult in America*.

89. Franklin, "Remarks Concerning the Savages," pp. 89–98, quotation on p. 92.

90. Ibid., p. 91.

91. Havelock, *Preface to Plato*, pp. 20–35.

92. Ibid., pp. 197–213; Jonas, "The Nobility of Sight"; Keller and Grontkowski, "The Mind's Eye," pp. 207–23.

93. Havelock, *Preface to Plato*, pp. 215–33.

Chapter 4

1. On the garment metaphor, see Barfield, *Saving the Appearances*, p. 94; on the theater metaphor, see Toulmin, "Inwardness of Mental Life," pp. 2–3, 6.

2. Schwartz, "Sun and Salt," pp. 26–41.

3. Merchant, *Death of Nature*, pp. 1–41, 99–126; Plato, "Timaeus," pp. 14–21.

4. Merchant, *Death of Nature*, pp. 10–11, 105–11; Bowden, "Scientific Revolution in Astrology"; Keith Thomas, *Religion and the Decline of Magic*.

5. Barfield, *Saving the Appearances*, pp. 84–91, 128–29; Berman, *Reenchantment of the World*, pp. 73–76.

6. Bord and Bord, *Earth Rites,* pp. 115–33; Hole, *British Folk Customs*; Ev-

ans, *Pattern under the Plough*; Briggs, *Folklore of the Cotswolds*, pp. 118–39, 153–62; Leather, *Folk-Lore of Herefordshire*, pp. 1–28, 90–110; Roy Palmer, *Folklore of Warwickshire*, 154–72; Kingsley Palmer, *Folklore of Somerset*, pp. 19–58; Porter, *Cambridgeshire Customs and Folklore*; Rowling, *Folklore of the Lake District*, pp. 95–107; Tongue and Briggs, *Somerset Folklore*, pp. 26–29, 45–59, 218–23; Whitlock, *Folklore of Devon*.

7. Bord and Bord, *Earth Rites*, pp. 93–105, 135–56.

8. Heninger, *Handbook of Renaissance Meteorology*, pp. 217–22. Similar lore persisted in New England. See Botkin, *Treasury of New England Folklore*, pp. 346–51.

9. Kerridge, *Agricultural Revolution*, pp. 240–50, 181–221; Seebohm, *Evolution of the English Farm*, pp. 207–75; Fussell, *Crop Nutrition*, pp. 53–92. The most influential English agricultural writers included Platt, *Jewell House of Art and Nature*; Topsell, *Historie of Foure-Footed Beastes*; Markham, *Cheap and Good Husbandry* and *Country Contentments*; William Lawson, *Country Housewife's Garden* and *New Orchard and Garden*; Plattes, *Discovery of Infinite Treasure*; Blith, *The English Improver Improved*; Hartlib, *Compleat Husbandman*; Speed, *Adam out of Eden*; Yarranton, *Improvement Improved*.

10. The Renaissance theory of the cyclical cosmos drew heavily on ancient Greek and Roman texts. The circuit made by water, water vapor, clouds, and rain through the atmosphere and earth was explained by Aristotle (384–322 B.C.) in his *Meteorologica*. The sun drew up two kinds of exhalations from the earth, moist and dry, the causes of atmospheric and terrestrial meteors. The moist exhalation produced warm vapors that congealed into mist, dew, or frost; condensed into clouds; or further condensed into rain, hail, or snow. The dry exhalation created atmospheric meteors such as thunder, lightning, winds, comets, shooting stars, as well as subterranean earthquakes. Rainbows, solar and lunar halos, and multiple suns were reflections in the atmosphere, while eclipses, springs, tides, and volcanoes were combinations of meteors. All had important effects on crops and the life cycle (Aristotle, "Meteorologica," 3, bk. 1, chap. 4, line 341b, and bk. 3, chap. 6, line 348a). On hydrologic theory, see Tuan, *Hydrologic Cycle*; Heninger, *Handbook of Renaissance Meteorology*, pp. 8–10.

11. Pliny, *Natural History*, 3:252–58. The theory of the effects of fertilizing salts on plant growth accepted by most agricultural writers was based on the combined actions of Aristotle's four elements (earth, air, fire, and water) and four qualities (hot, cold, wet, and dry). Soils, plants, and animals were combinations of the four elements. Plants took in preformed mixtures of the elements in the soil through their roots where they were used unaltered by their tissues. Soils were hot, cold, wet, or dry and could be improved by adding fertilizers with the opposite qualities (Browne, *Source Book of Agricultural Chemistry*, pp. 4–5).

12. Paracelsus in Browne, *Source Book of Agricultural Chemistry*, pp. 22–25. For German chemist Johann Rudolph Glauber (1604–68), who worked in Amsterdam, salt was the most important of the three Paracelsean principles. Niter, or salt of the earth, circulated through all living things. As the conserver and destroyer of vegetable life, it caused the "growth, generation and en-

crease of all vegetables, animals and minerals, as also their destruction and regeneration, by a perpetual circulation of the elements." When the earth was depleted of niter, it was dead. Dunging the soil returned the niter removed by growing plants (Glauber from ibid., p. 46).

13. Worlidge, *Systema Agriculturae*, pp. 2–3. *Systema* was reprinted in 1675, 1681, 1687, 1697, and 1716. Worlidge was an agricultural writer from Petersfield in Hampshire, England, who compiled a systematic treatise on agriculture. His book was read by New England farmers. See St. George, "Set Thine House in Order," pp. 174, 188–90.

14. Worlidge, *Systema Agriculturae*, pp. 4–9, 58–71.

15. Digby, *Of the Vegetation of Plants*, pp. 223–25. Thoreau's reference to Digby, when observing that his bean field "as Sir Kenelm Digby thinks likely, attracted 'vital spirits' from the air" (Thoreau, *Walden*, p. 120) seems to be drawn from this essay. Digby writes: "The salt-peter there is like a magnes which attracts a like salt that foecundates the air, and gave cause to the cosmopolite to say, *there is in the air a hidden food of life*. . . . This spirit, then, that is in the air is drawn (as it were by a loadstone) by the saline liquor which is imbibed into the seed which is full of it" (*Of the Vegetation of Plants*, pp. 223–24).

16. Evelyn, *Terra*, pp. 51, 9–10, 58–60, quotations on pp. 64–65, 69, 100. Thoreau cites several passages from Evelyn's *Terra* in his chapter on "The Bean-Field" in *Walden*, p. 120:

> Though I gave them no manure, and did not hoe them all once, I hoed them unusually well as far as I went, and was paid for it in the end, "there being in truth," as Evelyn says, "no compost or laetation whatsoever comparable to this continual repastination, and turning of the mould with the spade." "The earth," he adds elsewhere, "especially if fresh, has a certain magnetism in it, by which it attracts the salt, power, or virtue (call it either) which gives it life, and is the logic of all the labor and stir we keep about it, to sustain us; all dungings and other sordid temperings being but the vicars succedaneous to this improvement." Moreover, this being one of those "worn-out and exhausted lay fields which enjoy their sabbath," had perchance as Sir Kenelm Digby thinks likely, attracted "vital spirits" from the air. I harvested twelve bushels of beans.

17. Evelyn, *Terra*, pp. 64–65, 70, 104–5, 107–8, 100, 110.

18. Kircher, *Mundus Subterraneus*; Godwin, *Athanasius Kircher*, pp. 84–91.

19. Newton, "An Hypothesis Explaining the Properties of Light"; Birch, *History of the Royal Society of London*, 3, quotations on p. 251; Kubrin, "Newton and the Cyclical Cosmos," pp. 334–35; Heiman, " 'Nature Is a Perpetual Worker,' " pp. 8–9.

20. Mayow, "On Sal-nitrum and Nitro-aerial Spirit," quoted in Browne, *Source Book of Agricultural Chemistry*, p. 70; Diana Long Hall, "From Mayow to Haller," pp. 35–59; Guerlac, "John Mayow and the Aerial Nitre," pp. 245–59, and "The Poet's Nitre," pp. 260–74.

21. [Vallemont], *Curiosities of Nature and Art*, quotation on p. 131. *Curiosi-*

ties was reprinted in London in 1767. It went through nine French editions between 1705 and 1753 and three Spanish (1735, 1768, and 1806).

22. Ibid., pp. 3–5, quotations on p. 135.

23. Ibid., pp. 176–77, quotations on p. 176.

24. Ibid., pp. 121–24, quotations on pp. 148, 123.

25. Ibid., pp. 125–27, 133, quotations on p. 125.

26. Ibid., pp. 302–5, quotations on pp. 303, 305.

27. Browne, *Source Book of Agricultural Chemistry*, pp. 36–39; Merchant, *Death of Nature*, pp. 169–72, Bacon quoted on p. 172; Leiss, *Domination of Nature*, pp. 45–71, esp. p. 49.

28. Merchant, *Death of Nature*, pp. 216–35, 275–89.

29. On the change in perceptions of wilderness from satanic to sublime among elites, see Nash, *Wilderness and the American Mind*, pp. 44–66; Perry Miller, "From Edwards to Emerson"; Rogin, "Nature as Politics and Nature as Romance," pp. 5–30.

30. Perry Miller, "From Edwards to Emerson," pp. 184–203, quotations on pp. 194–95.

31. Edwards, *Representative Selections*, quotation on pp. 60–61.

32. On changes in popular religion between the seventeenth and eighteenth centuries, see Jon Butler, "Magic, Astrology, and the Early American Religious Heritage," p. 335.

33. Charles Morton, *Compendium Physicae*, pp. xi, xix, xxiii, xxxi.

34. Charles Morton, *Compendium Physicae*, p. 75. On the influence of alchemic ideas on Morton and other New Englanders, see Wilkinson, "New England's Last Alchemists" and "The Alchemical Library of John Winthrop, Jr."

35. Willard, *Compleat Body of Divinity*, p. 137.

36. Mather, *Christian Philosopher*, p. 292; Ezra Stiles quoted in Morgan, *Gentle Puritan*, p. 69.

37. Mather, *Christian Philosopher*, pp. 87–88.

38. Ibid., pp. 122–23.

39. Greenwood, *Philosophical Discourse*, pp. 15, 18. Greenwood advertised a 1726 lecture course entitled "An Experimental Course of Mechanical Philosophy" on "the wonderful discoveries of Sir Isaac Newton." On astrology in America, see Leventhal, *Shadow of the Enlightenment*, pp. 13–65.

40. Greenwood, *Philosophical Discourse*, pp. 8, 11.

41. Ibid., pp. 16–17.

42. St. George, "'Set Thine House in Order,'" pp. 178–79, 346; Stowell, *Early American Almanacs*, pp. 41, 52.

43. Foster, *Almanack of Coelestial Motions for 1680*, included a description of "The Nature and Operations of the seven planets with the Names and Characters given them by Astronomers." The anonymous *Astronomical Diary or Almanack for . . . 1758* explained on its inside cover the reasons for including the "Man of the Signs," while also expressing skepticism about the moon's influence on the body:

The last column is added to gratify such as still retain the antique notion of the moon's influencing different parts of the human body, as she changes her situation in the ecliptic, to different signs, that they may have the opportunity to perform those bloody operations, which otherways they would esteem extremely hazardous.... Not that I deny the moon and other heavenly bodies to have an influence on the sea, vegetable, and animals; for 'tis too evident to admit of any dispute: But that the moon merely by passing certain constellations (whose names are arbitrary) should affect any one part of the human body more than another, is an affront to common sense; and was introduced to deceive rather than instruct mankind.

44. Stowell, *Early American Almanacs*, pp. 41–50, 62. Foster's *Almanack of Coelestial Motion for 1675* contained on the end cover "A Brief Description of the Celestial Orbs according to the Opinion of that ancient philosopher Pythagoras and of all latter astronomers."

45. Stowell, *Early American Almanacs*, pp. 52–56, 66–72.

46. Tulley, *An Almanack*; Stowell, *Early American Almanacs*, pp. 56, 58–61, 72–76; Lovely, "Notes on New England Almanacs," pp. 264–65, 273–74; Nichols, *Notes on the Almanacs of Massachusetts*, pp. 12–19.

47. Lovely, "Notes on New England Almanacs," p. 274; Sagendorph, *Old Farmer's Almanac Sampler*; Kittredge, *Old Farmer and His Almanack*.

48. Ames, *Astronomical Diary or Almanac*, 1744, endleaf. See also Ames's almanacs for March and April 1760, and the August issues of 1746, 1754, and 1760. For example:

Now Sirius from on high
With pestilential Heat infests the sky,
The Rising Vapours choak the wholesome air
And blasts of noisome Wind corrupt the Year.
Th' Effluvia keen on nervous Moisture feeds,
Ingenders Death and dark Destruction breeds. (August 1746)

49. Ibid., 1753, March. The farmer should follow Nature and learn from her example:

Thus to Man the Voice of Nature spake,
"Go, from the Creatures they Instructions take,
"Learn from the Birds what Food the thickets yield,
"Learn from the Beasts the Physick of the Field,
"Thy arts of building from the Bee receive,
"Learn of the Mole to plow, the Worm to weave. (May 1752)

50. Ibid., 1754, May, September; 1761, December; quotation from 1750, August.

51. Ibid., 1753, June, July; Tulley, *An Almanack*, July 1688; Anonymous, *Almanack*, 1709, quotation from August; Stowell, *Early American Almanacs*, p. 59.

52. Ames, *Astronomical Diary or Almanac*, 1731, July, and 1758, frontis-

piece; Tulley, *An Almanack*, 1693. On the back cover of his 1758 *Almanac*, Ames discussed the strange, wonderful, and prodigious effects of nature during the previous year:

> the production of terrible thunder and lightning, violent storms, tremendous earthquakes, great eclipses of the luminaries, notable configurations of the planets, and strange phaenomena in the heavens: The Aurora Borealis (or Northern Twilight) is very unusual, and never seen in New England (as I can learn) 'till about 11 years ago: Tho' undoubtedly this phaenomenon proceeds from the concatination of causes. For hot and moist vapours, exhaled from the earth, and kindled in the air by agitation according to their motion may cause strange appearances. I do not say that this is the true cause of these Northern Lights but that they are caused some such way must be granted. Nor must they be disregarded or look'd upon as ominous of neither good nor ill, because they are but the products of Nature; for the great god of Nature forewarns a sinful world of approaching calamities, not only by prophets, Apostles, and teachers, but also by the elements and extraordinary signs in the heavens, earth, and water.

53. The basic theory of astrology can be found in Ptolemaeus, *Ptolemy's Tetrabiblos*. John Foster's *Almanack of Coelestial Motions for 1680* contained a discussion of "The Natures and Operations of the seven planets with the Names and Characters given them by Astronomers," which concluded: "These effects of the planets are more apparent when they are near the earth and when in conjunction or opposition with others of the same nature: so likewise being associated with fixt stars of like influence increaseth their operation. And the full moon is conceived cold in summer and temperate in the winter season; the new moon warm in summer, and produceth the coldest nights in winter; and in general the conjunctions of the luminaries bring the fairest weather, and their oppositions the greatest store of rain."

54. Ames, *Astronomical Diary or Almanac*, 1738, endpapers.

55. Ibid., 1740. Astrology and Newtonian science were mixed in Anonymous, *Astronomical Diary or Almanack for... 1758*. The author instructed his readers in the physics of light as small particles, air as an elastic fluid, the nature of Newtonian gravitation, and the magnetic qualities of the lodestone.

56. Leventhal, *Shadow of the Enlightenment*, pp. 14, 34–35, 40–41; Anonymous, "The Moon," p. 266.

57. [Whittemore], *An Almanack*, inside end cover; Staples, "Instructions for Farmers"; Capron, "The Moon's Influence on Vegetation."

58. Low, "Cutting of Bushes," endpapers; Eliot, *Essays Upon Field Husbandry*, pp. 123–24.

59. Eliot, *Essays Upon Field Husbandry*, pp. 35, 113, 90–91. Belief in the idea of the absorption of nitrous salts through sympathetic attractions prevented some farmers from trying out the improvers' recommendations for adding fertilizers. John Binns, an agricultural improver of Maryland (ca. 1761–1813), reported that his neighbors objected to adding gypsum (plaster of Paris) to worn-out fields. The plaster had "a power of attraction from the earth and

[would] in the course of five or six years draw all the nitrous particles out of the earth and render it poor." For similar reasons the older farmers objected to the improvers' idea of deep plowing which, they argued, only turned up the lifeless subsoil that could neither absorb nitrous particles from the atmosphere nor exhale moisture. "The old farmers," Binns observed, "still adhere to shallow ploughing and assert that the yellow clay when turned up is nothing but a dead substance and will totally ruin the land" (Binns, *Treatise on Practical Farming*, pp. 27, 49).

60. Eliot, *Essays Upon Field Husbandry*, pp. 70–71.

61. Leventhal, *Shadow of the Enlightenment*, pp. 223–31; Frank Dawson Adams, *Birth and Development of the Geological Sciences*, chaps. 4, 9.

62. Charles Morton, *Compendium Physicae*, pp. 113, 121, quotation on p. 122.

63. Edward Taylor, "Great Bones Dug up at Claverack," quotation on p. 57; Leventhal, *Shadow of the Enlightenment*, p. 226. On beliefs about the golden tree growing in the center of the earth, see Frank Dawson Adams, *Birth and Development of the Geological Sciences*, pp. 286–89.

64. Leventhal, *Shadow of the Enlightenment*, pp. 226–29; Willard, *Complete Body of Divinity*, p. 117; Benjamin Martin, *Philosophical Grammar*, p. 257; Charles Morton, *Compendium Physicae*, p. 117.

65. Thacher, "Observations Upon the Natural Production of Iron Ores," pp. 254, 256, quotation on p. 257; Leventhal, *Shadow of the Enlightenment*, p. 230.

66. Jefferson, *Notes on the State of Virginia*, quotation on p. 34; Frank Dawson Adams, *Birth and Development of the Geological Sciences*, chaps. 4, 9.

67. On antimonian religion, see Lovejoy, *Religious Enthusiasm in the New World*. On the Shakers in eighteenth-century America, see Edward Deming Andrews, *The People Called Shakers*. On the primacy of vision, see Keller and Grontkowski, "The Mind's Eye." On participatory consciousness, see Berman, *The Reenchantment of the World*.

Chapter 5

1. Bidwell, "Rural Economy in New England," 20:251.

2. Ibid., 20:318, see also pp. 277–93.

3. The extent of a subsistence- versus market-oriented farming culture has been debated in recent literature. Bidwell's "Rural Economy in New England" (1916) was based on a progressive era interpretation that most farmers underproduced because transportation barriers prevented market incentives. Whereas popular literature emphasized the self-sufficient family farm that produced everything it needed for its own subsistence, most historians consider this model too simplistic. Loehr, "Self-Sufficiency on the Farm" (1952), challenged the idea of the self-sufficient farm and viewed the village storekeeper as a liaison to the wider market system. Hofstader, "Myth of the Happy Yeoman" (1956), pointed out the dangers of romanticizing the rural farmer. Grant, "History of Kent" (1957) and *Democracy in . . . Kent* (1961), argued that even remote frontier towns such as Kent on the western Connecticut border

were market oriented. Lemon, "Household Consumption in Eighteenth-Century America" (1967), followed Grant in using widows' dowers for analyzing consumption and argued that farmers were basically entrepreneurs, producing surpluses for the market.

In the 1970s some historians developed a more complex interpretation of self-sufficiency based on subsistence communities and subsistence culture. Mutch, "Yeoman and Merchant in Pre-Industrial America" (1977), contended that most mid-eighteenth-century Americans were "subsistence farmers and not bourgeois entrepreneurs" and that merchants constituted small local elites (p. 279). Merrill, "Cash Is Good to Eat" (1977), discussed a community barter system in which exchanges of goods were recorded as money values in account books. Henretta, "Families and Farms" (1978), grounded subsistence farming in an ethos oriented to family values and family preservation. Kelly, "The Independent Mode of Production" (1979), defined a mode of production in colonial America in which farmers owned their own means of subsistence through fee simple land titles, which differed from capitalism wherein laborers work for a proprietor who owns the capital and tools and from feudalism which entailed in-kind payments to a manor lord for grazing, wood, and water privileges (see esp. pp. 44–46). Clark, "The Household Economy" (1979), discussed the process by which subsistence communities, which are not initially profit oriented, are drawn into production for the market through putting-out systems and a household mode of production.

In the 1980s the subsistence community model was challenged by scholars who used economic data to argue that a market orientation and entrepreneurial values touched almost all American farmers. Rothenberg, "The Market and Massachusetts Farmers" (1981), reviewed the subsistence/market debate and provided data indicating that, although most market journeys in colonial America took place within a ten- to twenty-mile radius of the farming community (p. 290), farmers who made lengthy hundred-mile trips for other purposes (personal communication) also took food and goods to sell. Appleby, "Commercial Farming and the 'Agrarian Myth'" (1982), discussed the importance of a commercial boom in the 1790s when the Napoleonic Wars pushed Europeans to import additional grain (see p. 840). Shammas, "How Self-sufficient Was Early America?" (1982), used a family of nine and Lemon's data for a 125-acre farm in Pennsylvania to question self-sufficiency both on the farm and in the community. She also used probate data from inventories in Massachusetts in 1774 to analyze the extent of women's household spinning and dairying, as well as the household's purchased goods, in arguing for market involvement. Cronon, *Changes in the Land* (1983), assumed a market orientation for all eighteenth-century New England farmers in discussing the ecological degradation caused by New England colonists. Pruitt, "Self-Sufficiency" (1984), challenged Grant's and Lemon's use of widows' dowers to establish consumption requirements and used data from the 1771 Massachusetts tax valuation to show that the median farm size in eighteenth-century Massachusetts was much smaller than that in Lemon's Pennsylvania counties; hence most farms were incomplete in the basic elements necessary for self-sufficiency.

I have drawn on both sides of this debate in offering an ecological interpretation. But I maintain that the subsistence sector of the economy was
strengthened during the eighteenth century and argue for a slower timetable
for market development than does the entrepreneurial school. In supporting
my interpretation, I use ideas from the emerging sciences of agroecology and
agroforestry to provide an ecological rationale for subsistence farming methods. Accepting Pruitt's critique of widows' dowers (see below), I instead use
exemptions from debt, female-directed sources of subsistence production,
and food sources from the commons to help determine minimum subsistence
requirements. I compare them to actual production in a 1771 sample of farms
in inland-upland Massachusetts towns. (Although individual town records
show changes over time, the 1771 tax valuation is the most complete state-
wide record for livestock and grain yields available for the colonial period.)

My interpretation is based on a topographical distinction between coastal
and Connecticut Valley towns and hilly inland-upland towns beyond a trading
radius of about twenty to twenty-five miles of urban centers or easy access to
navigable rivers or ports. I also assume that all towns, wherever they are
located, have both subsistence-oriented and market-oriented individuals, but
that the balance is tipped toward a subsistence orientation in the inland-
upland towns of eighteenth-century New England and that the extent of market participation will vary depending on harvests and weather patterns. While
the quantitative data provided by the entrepreneurial school are extremely
useful, they have inherent limitations. Those who rely on probate inventories
and account books fail to sort the data on the basis of topography. Moreover,
too heavy a reliance on account books skews the overall extent of market
orientation, especially in the eighteenth century, since such farmers were
more likely to keep account records than those producing mainly for family
subsistence. The argument that probate records show households and farms
incomplete in essential foods and equipment necessary for family self-sufficiency can also be an argument for increased community self-sufficiency
based on bartering. My interpretation is inspired by and draws on the work of
Sellers, *The Market Revolution* (forthcoming), who argues for the emergence
of a subsistence culture in the eighteenth century beyond easy access to urban markets with connections to antinomian religion and democratic politics.

4. Bidwell, "Rural Economy in New England," 20:252–57.

5. Kelly, "The Independent Mode of Production," pp. 38–48.

6. Altieri, *Agroecology*, pp. 1–2, 41–42, 21; Spedding, *Biology of Agricultural
Systems*.

7. Harpstead and Hole, *Soil Science Simplified*, pp. 59–71; Kohnke, *Soil Science Simplified*; Bormann and Likens, "Nutrient Cycling," pp. 424–29; G. Tyler
Miller, Jr., *Living in the Environment*, pp. 57–73.

8. Colby, *Pasture Culture in Massachusetts*, pp. 7–9; U.S. Department of Agriculture, *Changing Fertility of New England Soils*, pp. 23–42; Harpstead and
Hole, *Soil Science Simplified*, pp. 26–31.

9. Zirkle, "To Plow or not to Plow," pp. 87–89; Scoville, "Did Colonial Farmers Waste Our Land?," pp. 178–81; Geertz, *Agricultural Involution*, pp. 1–28;
Boserup, *Conditions of Agricultural Growth*.

10. Zirkle, "To Plow or not to Plow," p. 88. Russell, *A Long, Deep Furrow*, p. 66, cites references in seventeenth- and eighteenth-century farmers' diaries to dung carting and manure spreading.

11. Giere, Johnson, and Perkins, "A Closer Look at No-Till Farming," pp. 14–20, 37–41; Phillips et al., "No-Tillage Agriculture," pp. 1108–13; Phillips and Young, *No-Tillage Farming*; Altieri, *Agroecology*, pp. 95–98.

12. Farrell, "Agroforestry Systems," pp. 77–83.

13. Raup, "View from John Sanderson's Farm," pp. 2–11; Raup and Carlson, "History of Land Use in the Harvard Forest," pp. 20–29.

14. Donahue, "Forests and Fields of Concord," p. 30.

15. Belknap, *History of New Hampshire*, 3:100.

16. Farrell, "Agroforestry Systems," pp. 78–80.

17. Benjamin Vaughan, "Account of . . . Preparing Woodlands," pp. 484–85, quotation on p. 488.

18. Belknap, *History of New Hampshire*, 3:97–98.

19. Belknap, *History of New Hampshire*, 3:97–99; Benjamin Vaughan, "Account of . . . Preparing Woodlands," pp. 484–85; Sibley, *History of the Town of Union*, pp. 98–100.

20. Benjamin Vaughan, "Account of . . . Preparing Woodlands," pp. 485–86.

21. On forest fire legislation, see Kinney, "Forest Legislation in America," pp. 363–67; Samuel Trask Dana, *Forest and Range Policy*, p. 6.

22. Weld, *Travels*, 1:232, 41.

23. Benjamin Vaughan, "Account of . . . Preparing Woodlands," p. 487.

24. Raup and Carlson, "History of Land Use in the Harvard Forest," pp. 20–29; Raup, "View from John Sanderson's Farm," pp. 2–11.

25. Gross, "Culture and Cultivation," p. 58, table 4; Donahue, "Forests and Fields of Concord," p. 34, table 2:1, pp. 57–61.

26. Locke, "Essay Concerning . . . Civil Government," 2d treatise, chap. 5, sec. 32; Peter Allen Thomas, "Contrastive Subsistence Strategies," pp. 1–18.

27. Bidwell, "Rural Economy in New England," 20:321–22; Bidwell and Falconer, *History of Agriculture*, pp. 8–12. On land allotments and subsequent divisions of common lands among proprietors and newcomers, see Powell, *Puritan Village*; Lockridge, *A New England Town*; Greven, *Four Generations*; Daniels, *The Connecticut Town*.

28. Winthrop, "Indian Corne," p. 128.

29. *New England Almanac*, 1702, May, June, July, quoted from Walcott, "Husbandry in Colonial New England," pp. 230–31; Greeley, *Recollections*, quotation on p. 38. On farming in Plymouth Village, see Rutman, *Husbandmen of Plymouth*.

30. Bidwell and Falconer, *History of Agriculture*, pp. 12–15; Anonymous, "Barberry Bushes and Wheat."

31. Bidwell and Falconer, *History of Agriculture*, pp. 19–20, 102–5; Piper and Bort, "Early Agricultural History of Timothy."

32. Colby, *Pasture Culture*, pp. 12–13; Bidwell and Falconer, *History of Agriculture*, p. 22.

33. Colby, *Pasture Culture*, pp. 14–16; Belknap, *History of New Hampshire*, 3:97; Donahue, "Forests and Fields of Concord," pp. 35–39, 55.

34. Stilgoe, *Common Landscape of America*, pp. 153–58.

35. Ibid., pp. 159–66. Ulrich, *Good Wives*, pp. 51–54, 65–67.

36. Anonymous, "Man and Woman."

37. Anonymous, *North American Calendar ... for ... 1835*, January. On women in patriarchal society in colonial America, see Mary Beth Norton, "Evolution of White Women's Experience." Scholars have used the idea of the separation of male and female social roles—that is, the doctrine of separate spheres—both as evidence of the structures that subordinated women to men and as a means by which women established support networks and therefore gained autonomy. For a review of this scholarship, see Kerber, "Women's History."

38. On women's accounts and trade with other women, see Ulrich, *Good Wives*, pp. 26–27, 45.

39. Barrett, Diary (1828), May 1, 6, 10, 20, June 11, August 15, 26, October 11; Howell, *Diaries*, November 25, 1824, December 8, 1824, July 28, 1825, March 10, 1820. Although Anna Howell managed a farm in Gloucester County, New Jersey, that she inherited from her husband, I have included an analysis of her diaries here because they are among the few substantive farm diaries written by women that are available for the period and region.

40. McMahon, "A Comfortable Subsistence: History of Diet," pp. 50–61.

41. Ibid., pp. 98–104. On quantities of milk needed for cheese and butter and family consumption estimates, see Lemon, *Best Poor Man's Country*, p. 163; Shammas, "How Self-sufficient Was Early America?," p. 261. On butter and cheese making, see Earle, *Home Life in Colonial Days*, pp. 149–50. For maw preparation, see Anonymous, "Making Cheese"; Macomber, Hayward, and Wood, "Cheese Making."

42. Sarah Anna Emery, *Reminiscences of a Nonagenarian*, quotation on p. 7.

43. *New England Farmer* 2, no. 16 (November 15, 1823): 124–25; 4, no. 44 (May 26, 1826): 350–51; 6, no. 47 (June 13, 1826): 370. Women were advised to grind up rock salt in a gristmill rather than buying it in order to save money (ibid., 3, no. 1 [July 31, 1824]: 1).

44. Howell, *Diaries*, September 13, 1824; 1825, flyleaf. See July 1825 for her description of recovering escaped bees; cf. Crevecoeur, *Letters from an American Farmer*, pp. 26–27; Howell, *Diaries*, September 17, 1824.

45. Aunt Betty, "Best Food for Young Turkies."

46. *New England Farmer* 2, no. 9 (September 27, 1823): 67; 2, no. 38 (April 17, 1824): 297; 3, no. 9 (September 25, 1824): 67.

47. Ibid., 3, no. 1 (July 31, 1824): 2.

48. Aristotle, "Politics," bk. 1. chap. 9, lines 1257b, 7–16; Taussig, "Genesis of Capitalism," pp. 145–47.

49. Karl Marx, *Capital*, 1:35–41, quotation on p. 40.

50. Ibid., 1:86; Merrill, "Cash Is Good to Eat."

51. Anonymous, Diary, interleaved in Ames's *Astronomical Diary or Almanac* for 1746.

52. Joseph Andrews, Diaries, May 1761.

53. Clark, A Farmer of Wakefield, New Hampshire, *Diary*.

54. Ulrich, "'A Friendly Neighbor,'" pp. 392–405, and *Good Wives*, pp. 51–67.

55. Catnip, "Good Neighborhood."

56. Rothenberg, "The Market and Massachusetts Farmers," pp. 287–91, 298.

57. Lockridge, "Population of Dedham," p. 323, and "Land, Population, and the Evolution of New England Society." On the cultural values of subsistence farmers, see Henretta, "Families and Farms." On the colonial diet, see McMahon, "A Comfortable Subsistence: Changing Composition of Diet" and "A Comfortable Subsistence: History of Diet."

58. On family and household sizes, see Greene and Harrington, *American Population before the Federal Census of 1790*, p. xxiii: "The average family size in 1790 was 5.7 to 6. It would hardly have been any smaller in the colonial period, and might have been somewhat larger, but certainly no more than 6 persons to a family. . . . Gov. Bernard estimated 5 or 6 persons to each house, but from the census of 1763–65 in Massachusetts it is apparent that more than one family frequently lived in one house." The 15 inland towns averaged 8.5.

59. For Winthrop and Sewell, see McMahon, "A Comfortable Subsistence: History of Diet," pp. 36–37; Greeley, *Recollections*, p. 115. On fishing in Vermont in the 1820s, Greeley wrote: "Our rivers, unvexed by mill-dams, swarmed in their season with shad, lamphrey-eels, etc., and afforded some salmon, as well as fish of less consideration. . . . Winter brought its sleigh loads of fresh cod, frozen as soon as fairly out of the water. . . . The abundant lakes and lakelets used to abound in perch, bass, and sunfish, while the larger streams afforded, in addition, eels and pike . . . a small, peculiar shad, which with a few pike, bass, mullet, etc., come up from the Lake to spawn . . . are caught with seines drawn by two fishermen" (p. 115). On the importance of hunting and fishing in rural areas, see Hahn, "Hunting, Fishing, and Foraging": "Numerous small landholding and landless farmers . . . depended on common hunting, fishing, and grazing for sustenance" (p. 47). On berrying, see Thoreau, "Huckleberries," quotation on pp. 244–45.

60. Amelia Simmons, *First American Cookbook*, pp. 6–15, 20; Dow, *Old Days at Beverly Farms*, quotation on p. 53, as quoted in McMahon, "A Comfortable Subsistence: History of Diet," p. 216, see also p. 37.

61. McMahon, "A Comfortable Subsistence: History of Diet," pp. 134–64.

62. Use of widows' allotments for estimating household consumption for a typical family of five (a married couple, grown son, and two children) is made in Lemon, "Household Consumption in Eighteenth-Century America," pp. 59–70. In applying the method to New England, Gross, *Minutemen and Their World*, pp. 213–14, n. 35, uses a family of six consisting of a married couple and four children—the functional equivalent of Lemon's model unit. For other applications of the widow's allotment as an index of consumption in New England, see Grant, "History of Kent," pp. 62–69; Richard Holmes, *Communities in Transition*, pp. 24–25. Questions about the accuracy of the widow's portion as an index of consumption have been raised by Pruitt, "Self-Sufficiency," pp. 340–45, and "Agriculture and Society."

63. For the data on exemptions from attachment for debtors in the New England states, see the following sources: Maine, *Laws*, 1821, pp. 332–33, and *Revised Statutes*, 1840, title 10, chap. 114, sec. 38, pp. 486–87; New Hampshire, *Revised Statutes*, 1843, chap. 184, pp. 367–68, and *Compiled Statutes*, 2d ed.,

1854, chap. 185, pp. 468–69; Vermont, *Acts and Laws*, 1811, chap. 22, p. 27, and *Revised Statutes*, 1840, chap. 42, pp. 238–40; Connecticut, *Public Statute Laws*, 1835, title 2, sec. 74, pp. 57–58, and *Revised Statutes*, 1849, title 2, sec. 179, pp. 99–100; Massachusetts, *General Laws Annotated*, 40, chap. 235, sec. 34, pp. 367–74, quotation on p. 371; Rhode Island, *General Laws*, sec. 9–26–4, pp. 725–26. I thank Patricia Gahagan and James Gahagan for suggesting exemptions from attachment for debts as an indicator of subsistence requirements for farmers.

64. Child, *American Frugal Housewife*, pp. 76–77; Carlo, *Trammels, Trenchers, Tartlets*, pp. 68–69. For a discussion of the techniques of bread making, see Ruth Schwartz Cowan, *More Work for Mother*, pp. 48–52. Modern versions of New England bread all add wheat flour. Instead of wheat, I used the eighteenth-century mix of half rye and half cornmeal, weighing out a pound of each and weighing the resulting loaves. I got two loaves weighing a total of 2.75 pounds of baked bread from 1 pound of cornmeal and 1 pound of rye flour. Based on the nutritional information for each pound of rye flour and high lysine (a modern improvement) cornmeal, each of these 1.375-pound loaves contained 1,600 calories, 52 grams of protein, and 328 grams of carbohydrates. The product verified the colonial experience that the "coarse Indian and rye bread . . . was often so stiff and heavy that the crust could be used as a scoop when a spoon was not available" (quoted from McMahon, "A Comfortable Subsistence: History of Diet," p. 31). Those who could afford to use or add wheat flour for company and special occasions did so.

65. Pruitt, "Self-Sufficiency," pp. 344–45 and nn. 27, 31, calculated the bushels of corn needed for an adult male and female based on the militiaman's bread ration of a pound a day. If an adult male ate 1 pound of bread a day for a year, he would consume 365 pounds. An adult woman consuming two-thirds that of a man would require 243.4 pounds and a child consuming one-half that of an adult male would require 182.5 pounds. The typical family of five consisting of a married couple, grown son, and two children would therefore consume 1,338.4 pounds of bread a year. Households were larger than families. A household of eight, consisting of a married couple, two male adults, and four children, typical in the 15 inland towns, would require 2,068.4 pounds of bread or 43.6 bushels of grain per year. Grain per household averaged 55.2 bu/yr (Appendix C-5). More research into raw-to-cooked ratios is needed. Stiles's estimate is from Pruitt, "Self-Sufficiency," p. 345.

I applied Pruitt's method to the above 1,338 pounds of half rye and half cornmeal (she used cornmeal equivalents only), using conversion factors of 50 pounds of cornmeal per bushel of shelled corn and 44.8 pounds of rye flour per bushel of rye, to obtain the 28.22 bushels of grain per year for the family. For the conversion factors, see U.S. Department of Agriculture, *Conversion Factors*, pp. 32, 34. For a discussion of Pruitt's methodology by Daniel Vickers and James Lemon and Pruitt's reply, see Pruitt, "Communication," pp. 553–62. Lemon points out that, for greater precision, the miller's cut should be subtracted from the family's grain to obtain the meal.

Many towns in Middlesex County (extending northwest of Boston to the New Hampshire border) had greater access to Boston markets than did the inland towns. Inventories as a whole show that grain totals (of Indian corn, rye, and wheat) remained stable at about 25 bushels per farm over two centuries. But the inventories also show variations by wealth that indicate a level of about 15 bushels of grain in the lower-wealth quintiles. Thus in the seventeenth century the lowest three quintiles had grain stores of 15 to 19 bushels, the top two 35 and 45. In the early eighteenth century, the bottom three showed 12 to 19 bushels, the top two 28 to 41. At mid-century the bottom three averaged 12 to 19, the top two 30 and 45, while in the decade prior to the American Revolution the poorest quintile fell to 9.3, but the top four ranged from 19 to 53. An important change occurred after the Revolution, however, with inventories in the period 1788–1795 showing that the bottom three quintiles had fallen to 7.2, 14.3, and 20.7, with the top two at 43 and 47; in 1833–35, the bottom three were still low, averaging 9.4, 11.6, and 17.5, the top two 30 and 65. These figures indicate changes in the composition of the diet toward greater diversity in foods (such as potatoes and vegetables) and less reliance on bread. They are also indicative of a major shift to agricultural improvement and an intensive system of land use in the late eighteenth and early nineteenth centuries (McMahon, "A Comfortable Subsistence: History of Diet," pp. 29, 130–74).

66. On yields for Reading, Massachusetts, see Pruitt, *Massachusetts Tax Valuation List of 1771*, pp. 253–54 for acres in tillage and pp. 782–83 for the breakdown between corn and rye harvests for a sample of seventy-seven farms. Of these, forty-five farms planted only Indian corn and reported yields averaging 19.8 bushels per acre on an average of 1.7 acres of tillage or 33.7 bushels per farm. The remaining thirty-two farms planted both corn and rye. From the data, I calculated the average yield for Reading farms planting only Indian corn at 19.8 bushels per acre. I then applied this yield rate to the thirty-two farms planting both corn and rye to obtain the acres planted in Indian corn (61.16); from this and the total grain tillage of 92 acres, I calculated the number of acres planted in rye (30.9). The total quantity of rye harvested from the thirty-two farms was 393 bushels, giving a rye yield of 12.2 bushels per acre. The farms that planted both rye and Indian corn harvested totals of about 50 bushels of grain apiece.

Statistics for two New Hampshire towns showed somewhat lower acreages. New Durham, New Hampshire, a subsistence-oriented town on the New Hampshire–Maine border with a population of 112 rated polls in 1784, had an average of 1.1 acres of tillage per poll. Each taxpayer also had an average of 3.15 acres of mowing hay, 2.25 acres of pasture, and 83.35 acres in unimproved land; each owned an average of 1.15 oxen, 1.57 cows, and 1.33 horses. Langdon, New Hampshire, twenty miles north of the Massachusetts border with a population of 130 polls in 1809, had an average number of 2.15 acres in tillage. Each taxpayer also had an average of 2.5 acres of mowing hay, 7.3 acres of pasture, and 29.6 acres of unimproved land; each owned an average of 0.75 oxen, 1.7 cows, 2.15 cattle, and 0.9 horses. (See Marini, *Radical Sects*, pp. 97–98.)

67. In Middlesex County, Massachusetts, from the mid-seventeenth to the mid-nineteenth century, even the poorest quintile had 1 or 2 swine, 1 milk

cow, and 2 cattle. The poorest thirteen inventories for 1653–74 showed 2.3 swine, 2.5 cattle, 1.7 milk cows, and no sheep; the thirty-two inventories in the wealthiest cohort averaged 8.4 swine, 13.4 cattle, 5.5 milk cows, and 23.3 sheep. At the end of the time period, in 1833–35 the poorest twenty-six inventories showed 1.2 swine, 2.0 cattle, 1.1 milk cows, and 1.3 sheep. Most Middlesex County families were able to maintain barnyard animals such as swine, milk cows, and 1 or 2 cattle (perhaps for hauling).

Almost all families had at least 1 milk cow, with the average for Middlesex County over three centuries fluctuating around 3.4. Milk, butter, and cheese, supplying additional animal protein, would increase with the number of cows. The average number of swine (including hogs, sows, shoats, and pigs) gradually declined from 5.3 in the seventeenth century to 2.6 in the nineteenth. Cattle (including oxen, bulls, cows, steers, heifers, and calves) fluctuated around 7.5 head per farm. Pork in the form of salt pork, bacon, ham, and sausage was the most prominent meat in household larders with salted beef second. Mutton was usually consumed fresh as it did not preserve well. (See McMahon, "A Comfortable Subsistence: History of Diet," pp. 39–50, 130–74.)

68. Ibid., pp. 53, 68; Greeley, *Recollections*, pp. 98–99, as quoted from ibid., p. 68.

69. Donahue, "Forests and Fields of Concord," pp. 30, 57. Data on eighteenth-century firewood consumption from Schumacher, *Northern Farmer and His Markets*. Deane, *The New England Farmer, or Georgical Dictionary*, in 1790 reported that a forty-acre woodlot was required for a sustained wood supply. In the nineteenth century firewood consumption was estimated at twelve to fourteen cords per house (see George B. Emerson, *Report on the Trees and Shrubs . . . of Massachusetts*, p. 19).

70. Richard Holmes, *Communities in Transition*, uses widows' allotments to determine subsistence requirements in Bedford and Lincoln; he argues: "The evidence from Bedford and Lincoln indicates that these communities were gradually approaching the point where a crisis of subsistence was a distinct possibility. . . . Demographic expansion was engendering a crisis" (p. 21; see also pp. 23–24). When widows' allotments are used, higher minimum figures are obtained. See Gross, *Minutemen and Their World*, pp. 213–14, n. 35: "On this basis, two adults and four children required about eight to ten acres of tillage for their grain (rye and corn) and fourteen to sixteen acres of meadow and pasture to obtain their beef and dairy products. Add an additional acre of tillage to fatten hogs for pork and another acre for potatoes and vegetables. Thus a minimum of twenty-four to twenty-eight [improved] acres was needed for a family of six. In 1765 the average household size in Concord was 5.9. To be sure, cattle often browsed along the public ways, so the pasturage requirements may be too high. On the other hand, no provision has been made for horses, sheep, and young cattle in this estimate. In addition, a farmer would also have needed woodland for his fuel." (Holmes and Gross's family of two adults and four children is the functional equivalent of Lemon's married couple, grown son, and two children.)

71. On dunghill fowl, see Amelia Simmons, *First American Cookbook*, p. 7. On food preservation, see McMahon, "A Comfortable Subsistence: History of

Diet," pp. 104–18. The approach of Thomas Malthus and many demographers has been that the pressure of population growth on the land creates crises of subsistence resulting in higher mortality. The exponential rate of reproductive increase is biologically determined by the passion of the sexes, but, because land is finite, food production increases at a slower arithmetical rate, putting pressure on the land. An alternative explanation, put forward by Marx and Engels and other demographers, argues that population growth put pressure, not on the land per se, but on the system of production. Marriage ages, numbers of children, and inheritance patterns, stemming from social and economic considerations, govern reproductive rates, as opposed to biological determinism. Although land acreages may be finite, land productivity is elastic and depends on the mode of production. (See Malthus, *Essay on the Principle of Population*.) On Marx and Engels, see Meek, *Marx and Engels on the Population Bomb*.

72. Brodt, "Autobiography," pp. 2–3, 5, 7, 9. I thank Patricia Gahagan for use of her great-grandmother's autobiography.

73. Pruitt, "Self-Sufficiency," p. 343: "We know that people *were* subsisting somehow: no famine is recorded, and recent scholarship has indicated that people were adequately nourished, even by twentieth-century standards."

74. Older towns in eastern Massachusetts began experiencing the limits of the extensive system before the American Revolution. See Gross's argument on the limits of extensive agriculture in "A World of Scarcity," *Minutemen and Their World*, pp. 68–108, 213–15, and "Culture and Cultivation," pp. 42–61. See also Richard Holmes, *Communities in Transition*, pp. 24–26.

75. Daniels, "Economic Development in . . . Connecticut," p. 432. On Concord, Massachusetts, see Gross, "Culture and Cultivation," pp. 44, 57–58. On Chebacco, Massachusetts, see Jedrey, *World of John Cleaveland*, pp. 80–82. On family values and age stratification, see Henretta, "Families and Farms," pp. 6–10.

76. Joanna Wakefield to John White, "Warrenty Deed." I thank Jane and Weston Cate for pointing out this concept and making this deed available to me. On the custom of reserving the southwest room for the widow, see Walker, *Southwest Corner*. Other widows' dowers specified additional rights of passage:

> We also set off to said Widow the following parts and parcels of the buildings belonging to said estate, the square room in the southeast corner of the house, the bed room that is in the northeast corner of said house and the south half of the buttery in the north west corner of said house, one third part of all the privileges in Kitchen with the privilege of passing through the other rooms in said house to the well, to have one third of the use of the well, all that part of the cellar east of a line northerly and southerly through said cellar . . . thirteen feet in length off the south end of the wood house . . . we also set to the widow the south or new barn, so called, amounting in the whole to the sum of $563.20. Dated at Williamstown, March the 8th, 1826 (Jeffords, "Widow's Dower").

77. Gross, *Minutemen and Their World*, pp. 214–55, nn. 37, 38. Donahue, "Skinning the Land," table 4, "Animal units per acre of pasture." I thank Brian Donahue for allowing me to use his manuscript and for his comments and clarifications on my use of his data.

78. Gross, "Culture and Cultivation," pp. 47–48.

79. [Rosenberry], *Expansion of New England*, pp. 108–14, esp. p. 114; Rutman, "People in Process"; Meeks, "Isochronic Map of Vermont Settlement," p. 96; Wilson, *Hill Country of Northern New England*.

80. [Rosenberry], *Expansion of New England*, pp. 156–58.

81. On economic transformation in the late eighteenth and early nineteenth centuries in New England, see Christopher Clark, "Household, Market, and Capital" and "Household Economy"; Henretta, "Families and Farms," pp. 16–19; Appleby, "Commercial Farming and the 'Agrarian Myth'"; Jones, "Strolling Poor," pp. 28–54. On the market in labor, see Rothenberg, "The Market and Massachusetts Farmers," dissertation. On turnpikes and canals, see Meyer, *History of Transportation*, pp. 52, 64, 69, 131–60.

82. Holbrook, *Yankee Exodus*, p. 17; [Rosenberry], *Expansion of New England*, p. 157 (Wadsworth quotation).

83. Henretta, "Families and Farms," pp. 3–32.

84. Gross, "Culture and Cultivation," pp. 57–58; Donahue, "Forests and Fields of Concord," pp. 31–40.

85. Bidwell, "Rural Economy in New England," 20:319–52, see esp. pp. 319–20; Bidwell and Falconer, *History of Agriculture*, pp. 84–89, 132.

86. Benjamin Vaughan, "Account of . . . Preparing Woodlands," p. 486.

87. Kreps, "Vicissitudes of the American Potash Industry," pp. 630–65; Michael Williams, "Products of the Forest," p. 13.

88. Coxe, *View of the United States*, pp. 450–57, quotation on p. 479.

89. Patent Office Report, "How Cities Exhaust the Fertility of Land."

90. Michael Williams, "Products of the Forest," p. 9; Gates, "Problems of Agricultural History," pp. 34–39.

91. Sibley, *History of the Town of Union*, quotation on p. 100, see also p. 104; Eastman, *History of the Town of Andover*, pp. 273–75.

92. Donahue, "Skinning the Land," pp. 1–22.

93. Raup, "View from John Sanderson's Farm," pp. 4, 6; Raup and Carlson, "History of Land Use in the Harvard Forest," pp. 21, 30–31, 43.

Chapter 6

1. Thompson, "Second Agricultural Revolution," pp. 62–77, esp. pp. 63–65.

2. Merchant, *Death of Nature*, pp. 203–15, 226; Wolin, *Politics and Vision*.

3. For a discussion of the way in which these assumptions emerged historically, see Merchant, *Death of Nature*, pp. 192–215.

4. Wills, *Inventing America*, pp. 99, 108; Drepperd, *American Clocks and Clockmakers*, pp. 64–114.

5. Wills, *Inventing America*, pp. 93–94, quotations on pp. 95, 103; Hamilton, Jay, and Madison, *The Federalist*, pp. 53–62.

6. Ames, "An Essay Upon Regimen," in *Astronomical Diary or Almanac*, 1754, endpapers.

7. Ames, "Essay on Physic," in *Astronomical Diary or Almanac*, 1770, endpapers.

8. Marshall and Ryan, "Ultimate Cause of the Civil War: Mother," pp. 23–24.

9. Ames, *Astronomical Diary or Almanac*, 1758, endpapers.

10. Benton, *Congressional Globe*.

11. John Quincy Adams, *Congressional Globe*.

12. Colton, "Labor and Capital."

13. H. M. Eaton, "Address Delivered Before the Kennebec County Agricultural Society," p. 60.

14. Merchant, *Death of Nature*, pp. 172–90.

15. Colman, "Address Before the Hampshire, Franklin, and Hampden Agricultural Society," pp. 5–6, 15, 27.

16. Bartlett, "Address Delivered Before the West Oxford Agricultural Society," pp. 220–21, 223.

17. Ezekiel Holmes, "Address Before the West Lincoln Agricultural Society," p. 252.

18. Goldsbury, "Design and Usefulness of Labor"; Bullard, *Discourse on Agriculture Delivered Before the Western Society of Middlesex Husbandmen*, pp. 6, 11. Bullard included the following unacknowledged quotations in his text: " 'The earth opens her bosom to the ploughshare, and prepares her treasures to recompense the labor of the husbandman.' 'The earth, like a tender mother, multiplies her gifts, according to the number of her children, if they deserve her favors by their diligence' " (p. 6).

19. Perham, "Address Delivered Before the Oxford County Agricultural Society," pp. 195, 189.

20. True, "Address Delivered Before the Cumberland County Agricultural Society," pp. 8–9, 22–23.

21. Smart, "Wood and Timber Lands."

22. Samuel L. Dana, *Muck Manual for Farmers*; Davy, *Elements of Agricultural Chemistry*, pp. 239–306; Browne, *Source Book of Agricultural Chemistry*, pp. 208–11; Rossiter, *Emergence of Agricultural Science*, pp. 11–19, 31–36.

23. Thaer, *Principles of Agriculture*, 2:107–8, 268, quoted from Browne, *Source Book of Agricultural Chemistry*, p. 181. See also Browne, *Source Book of Agricultural Chemistry*, pp. 183, 256, on the history of the humus theory and the influence of Thaer.

24. Liebig, *Organic Chemistry*, quotations on pp. 149, 182; Browne, *Source Book of Agricultural Chemistry*, pp. 266–69. Liebig's book went through numerous German, English, and American editions and revisions between 1840 and 1907. (See Rossiter, *Emergence of Agricultural Science*, app. 1, pp. 178–83.)

25. Rossiter, *Emergence of Agricultural Science*, pp. 21–23, 42–43.

26. Samuel L. Dana, *Muck Manual for Farmers*, pp. 77–85, 90, 100–101, quotation on pp. 93–94; Rossiter, *Emergence of Agricultural Science*, pp. 31–34; Browne, *Source Book of Agricultural Chemistry*, pp. 252–56.

27. Rossiter, *Emergence of Agricultural Science*, pp. 68–88, 99–124, 127–48.

28. John P. Norton, "Pursuit of Knowledge Under Difficulties," pp. 103–4.

29. Latour, "Give Me a Laboratory," quotation on p. 155.

30. Ezekiel Holmes, "Address Before the West Lincoln Agricultural Society," pp. 255–56.

31. Rossiter, *Emergence of Agricultural Science*, pp. 149–53; Schreiner, "Early Fertilizer Work in the United States," pp. 39–47.

32. Latour, "Give Me a Laboratory," p. 154, quotation on p. 166. On contests for power over the terms of scientific discourse, see Haraway, "The Contest for Primate Nature."

33. Ames, *Astronomical Diary or Almanac*, 1765, endpapers.

34. Low, *Astronomical Diary*, 1807, endpapers. See also ibid. for 1810, 1811, 1815, 1816, 1817.

35. Kittredge, *Old Farmer and His Almanack*, pp. 1–24, 39–70; Forpe, *Best of the Old Farmer's Almanac*, pp. 39–45.

36. Carman, *Jesse Buel*, p. 216, see also pp. 217–18.

37. Perham, "Address Delivered Before the Oxford County Agricultural Society," p. 196.

38. H. M. Eaton, "Address Delivered Before the Kennebec County Agricultural Society," quotation on p. 59; Colman, *Address Before the Hampshire, Franklin, and Hampden Agricultural Society*, pp. 20–21.

39. H. M. Eaton, "Address Delivered Before the Kennebec County Agricultural Society," p. 58.

40. Anonymous, "Farm Accounts."

41. Anonymous, A Farmer of Hampstead, New Hampshire, Diary.

42. Ezekiel Holmes, "Address Before the West Lincoln Agricultural Society," quotation on p. 257; Anonymous, "Farm Accounts."

43. Webster, "Address Delivered Before the Hampshire, Franklin and Hampden Agricultural Society," April 1819 (quotation on p. 83), March 1819 (p. 52, quotation on p. 50).

44. Goldsbury, "Design and Usefulness of Labor," p. 413.

45. Frost, "Statement on Crops Raised," pp. 142–44; see also statements of Day, Chadburn, and Dennett, pp. 144–47, 102–7.

46. Howell, *Diaries*, 1819–39, quotation from 1826, cover.

47. Ibid., April 1833.

48. Ibid., July 8, August 23, December 8, 1824, January 1825.

49. Todd, *Young Farmer's Manual*, 2:76, quoted from Danhof, *Change in Agriculture*, p. 135.

50. Perham, "Address Delivered Before the Oxford County Agricultural Society," p. 188; Carman, *Jesse Buel*, p. 216.

51. True, "Address Delivered Before the Cumberland County Agricultural Society," p. 6.

52. [Olbers], "Influence of the Moon"; Howard, Journal, December 9, 1830, April 4, 1831.

53. Bidwell, "Agricultural Revolution in New England," p. 687; Danhof, *Change in Agriculture*, p. 149.

54. Hastings, "Report on Working Oxen"; Colman, "Address Before the Hampshire, Franklin, and Hampden Agricultural Society," p. 23.

55. Deane, *The New England Farmer*, pp. 222–23.

56. [Fessenden], "On Deep and Frequent Ploughing," p. 60, "The Farmer," p. 278, and "Remarks on Ploughing," pp. 113–14, 121.

57. Deane, *The New England Farmer*, pp. 10–11.

58. Brown, "Fertilizing Influence of the Atmosphere."

59. Michael Williams, "Products of the Forest," p. 7.

60. Belknap, *History of New Hampshire*, 3:77–82, quotation from 1:150; Richard G. Wood, "History of Lumbering in Maine."

61. Richard G. Wood, "History of Lumbering in Maine," pp. 96–103, 128–99, 140, 146, 157, 162–63, 166–67.

62. Dwight, *Travels*, 2:160–61.

63. Kendall, *Travels*, 3:75–76; Richard G. Wood, "History of Lumbering in Maine," pp. 185–87.

64. Kendall, *Travels*, 3:78–80.

65. Karl Marx, *Capital*, 1:206; Engels, "Outlines of a Critique of Political Economy," quotation on p. 210.

66. Dole, "Ancient Naguamqueeg," quotations on pp. 410–11.

67. Baxter, *Documentary History of . . . Maine*, 15:72, 21:235; Anonymous, *History of Bedford, New Hampshire*, pp. 204–5; Hammond, *Documents Relating to Towns in New Hampshire*, 12:547.

68. Eckstrom, "Lumbering in Maine," pp. 690–93; Kendall, *Travels*, 3:217.

69. Marsh, *Man and Nature*, quotations on pp. 237, 186–87.

70. Williamson, "An Attempt to Account for the Change of Climate," quotation on p. 453. On climatic and ecological changes in the seventeenth century, see Charles F. Carroll, *Timber Economy of Puritan New England*, pp. 123–28.

71. Hoglund, "Forest Conservation and Stove Inventors," quotations on p. 3.

72. Jefferson discussed by Chastellux, *Travels in North America*, quotation on p. 454. On Rush, see Chinard, "American Philosophical Society," p. 455.

73. [Benjamin Lincoln], "Cultivation of the Oak," quotation on p. 189; A Farmer, "Premium for Forest Trees."

74. Farmer's Assistant, "Forest," quotation on p. 242; Fiske, "Correspondence"; [Fessenden], "Remarks."

75. George B. Emerson, *Report on the Trees and Shrubs Growing*, pp. 2–11, quotations on pp. 2, 9.

76. Richard G. Wood, "History of Lumbering in Maine," pp. 226–35, quotation on p. 226; Eckstrom, "Lumbering in Maine," p. 695; David C. Smith, "The Logging Frontier." On forestry in Maine after 1860, see David C. Smith, *History of Lumbering in Maine*. On lumber supplies at the turn of the nineteenth century, see Kellog, *Timber Supply of the United States*, pp. 1–16. For a more recent appraisal, see Clawson, "Forests."

77. Thoreau, "Succession of Forest Trees," quotation on p. 78.

78. Hoglund, "Forest Conservation and Stove Inventors," pp. 5–6.

Chapter 7

1. Marshall and Ryan, "Ultimate Cause of the Civil War: Mother," pp. 24–27.

2. Sachs, *Invisible Farmers*, pp. 1–14; Schumacher, *Northern Farmer and His Markets*, pp. 26, 29–30, 36, 130, tables, pp. 170–71; Bidwell and Falconer, *History of Agriculture*, p. 109.

3. Bidwell and Falconer, *History of Agriculture*, pp. 421–22, 425–26.

4. Anonymous, "Successful Application of Labor and Skill"; A Butter Dealer, "Directions for Making and Preserving Butter"; [Proctor], "Dairy Management."

5. Bidwell and Falconer, *History of Agriculture*, p. 242.

6. Ibid., p. 442; Cole, "Agricultural Crazes," pp. 634–65; Dodge, "Poultry."

7. Bacon, "Poultry"; Coffin, "Size of Fowls."

8. Tryon, *Household Manufactures*, pp. 202–16.

9. Dublin, *Women at Work*, pp. 15–17.

10. Ibid., pp. 17–18; Gibb, *Saco-Lowell Shops*, pp. 23–149.

11. Dublin, *Women at Work*, pp. 62–69. On women's work in the textile mills, see also Dublin, *Farm to Factory*; Josephson, *Golden Threads*; Abbott, *Women in Industry*, pp. 87–147; Ware, *The Industrial Worker*, pp. 71–100.

12. Tryon, *Household Manufactures*, pp. 242–53, 268, 271–76, 291–93.

13. Wilson, *Hill Country of Northern New England*, pp. 75–94; Balivet, "The Vermont Sheep Industry"; Cole, "Agricultural Crazes," pp. 624–27; Barron, *Those Who Stayed Behind*, pp. 51–77.

14. Horwitz, *Transformation of American Law*, pp. 32–42; Kulik, "Dams, Fish, and Farmers," pp. 28–33.

15. Kulik, "Dams, Fish, and Farmers," pp. 36–45; Horwitz, *Transformation of American Law*, pp. 47–53.

16. Marsh, *Report on the Artificial Propagation of Fish*; also in Marsh, *Man and Nature*, pp. 102–8, quotations on pp. 107–8.

17. Marsh, *Man and Nature*, pp. 35–37, p. 37, n. 35, quotations on pp. 36–37, 35.

18. Pursell, *Early Stationary Steam Engines*, pp. 83–86, 73; Hunter, *History of Industrial Power*, vol. 2, *Steam Power*, pp. 416–17, 422.

19. Thoreau, *Walden and Civil Disobedience*, pp. 86–87, 89.

20. Horwitz, *Transformation of American Law*, pp. 54–55, quotation on p. 55 from *Jackson v. Brownson*, 7 Johns. 236 (N.Y. 1810).

21. Horwitz, *Transformation of American Law*, pp. 56–58, quotation on p. 57 from 15 Mass. 167 (1818).

22. Wells, "Revolutions in Childbearing"; Osterud and Fulton, "Family Limitation and Age at Marriage"; Vinovskis, *Fertility in Massachusetts*, pp. 41–56.

23. Wells, "Revolutions in Childbearing," pp. 50–52; Mohr, *Abortion in America*; Barker-Benfield, "Spermatic Economy"; Smith-Rosenberg, "Sex as Symbol in Victorian Purity," pp. S212–47; Daniel Scott Smith, "Family Limitation."

24. Ruth Schwartz Cowan, *More Work for Mother*, pp. 40–68.

25. On the background to nineteenth-century domesticity, see Welter, "Cult of True Womanhood"; Cott, *Bonds of Womanhood*; Epstein, *Politics of Domes-*

ticity; Kerber, *Women of the Republic*; Kerber and Mathews, *Women's America*.

26. H. M. Eaton, "Address Delivered Before the Kennebec County Agricultural Society," pp. 60, 63–64, quotations on pp. 66–67; Perham, "Address Delivered Before the Oxford County Agricultural Society," pp. 186–87, 189, quotation on p. 186.

27. True, "Address Delivered Before the Cumberland County Agricultural Society," pp. 29–31.

28. Anonymous, "Home and Woman," quotations on p. 56.

29. Anonymous, "Maternal Influence"; A Farmer, "Education of Farmers' Daughters," quotations on p. 178.

30. True, "Address Delivered Before the Cumberland County Agricultural Society," p. 31; Bates, "Address Delivered Before the York County Agricultural Society," quotations on pp. 128–29. On the repression of male sexuality, see Barker-Benfield, "Spermatic Economy."

31. Marini, *Radical Sects*, pp. 88–96; Kern, *An Ordered Love*, pp. 71–134.

32. Ruether and Keller, *Women and Religion*, 1:63–65; Fryer, "American Eves in American Edens," p. 82 ("The Shakers believed according to their creed: '1. That God is a dual person, male and female; that Adam was a dual person, being created in God's image; and that the distinction of sex is eternal, inheres in the soul itself; and that no angels or spirits exist who are not male and female. 2. That Christ is a Spirit, and one of the highest who appeared first in the person of Jesus, representing the male, and later in the person of Ann Lee, representing the female element in God.'"); Melcher, *Shaker Adventure*; Holloway, *Heavens on Earth*, pp. 53–79; White and Taylor, *Shakerism*, pp. 81–97.

33. Edward Deming Andrews, *The People Called Shakers*, pp. 116–21; Townsend, "Looking for the Simple Life," pp. 90–91.

34. Edward Deming Andrews, *The People Called Shakers*, pp. 121–25; Irvin, "The Machine in Utopia."

35. Edward Deming Andrews, *The People Called Shakers*, pp. 152–59.

36. Andrews and Andrews, *Visions of the Heavenly Sphere*, pp. 68–79.

37. Ibid., pp. 86–96.

38. Ibid., pp. 55, 90.

39. Novak, *American Painting*, pp. 61–79, and *Nature and Culture*; Audubon, "Force of the Waters"; Kolodny, *Lay of the Land*, p. 80; Nash, *Wilderness and the American Mind*, pp. 44–83; Woolley, "Development of the Love of Romantic Scenery."

40. Rossiter, *Women Scientists*, p. 3. On women's role in preserving the environment in the late nineteenth century, see Merchant, "Women of the Progressive Conservation Movement."

41. Amos Eaton, *Manual of Botany*, p. ix. On Eaton and women botanizers, see Keeney, "Women and Popular Botany," p. 2, and "The Botanizers," pp. 56–82; Kohlstedt, "In from the Periphery," pp. 86–88; Rossiter, *Women Scientists*, p. 7.

42. Rossiter, *Women Scientists*, p. 3; Kohlstedt, "In from the Periphery," p. 86, n. 17; Swift, *First Lessons*, quotations on pp. 74–75.

43. Rossiter, *Women Scientists*, pp. 7–8.

44. Gale, Diary, pp. 9–10, 12–14, 17.

45. Caroline Barrett White, *Diary*, October 17, 1849, November 13, 1849, March 14, 1850, September 1, 9, 1850.

46. Ralph Waldo Emerson, *Complete Works*, 5:288. For examples of other elites at the root of American preservationism, see Nash, *Wilderness and the American Mind*, chaps. 4–6; Worster, *Nature's Economy*.

47. Thoreau, "Journal," 1:71, 3:65–67, 7:112–13, *Walden*, p. 229, quoted from Worster, *Nature's Economy*, p. 80; *Portable Thoreau*, p. 196.

48. Thoreau, *Portable Thoreau*, pp. 222, 590, 60.

49. Ibid., pp. 145, 197, 222.

50. Ibid., pp. 67, 100, 621, 221, 149, 633.

51. Ibid., pp. 151, 158. Emerson, quoted from Nash, *Wilderness and the American Mind*, p. 126.

52. Leo Marx, "The Two Thoreaus: Young Man Thoreau by Richard Lebeaux."

53. Thoreau, *Walden*, pp. 3, 10, 16, 30–32.

54. Ibid., pp. 40–42, 115, 120, quotations on p. 40. On Thoreau's use of Digby and Evelyn, see above, Chap. 4, nn. 15, 16.

55. Ibid., quotations on p. 113.

56. Ibid., quotations on p. 117.

57. Ibid., p. 123.

58. Thoreau, "Wild Apples," pp. 187, 192, 209, quotation on p. 196.

Chapter 8

1. Portions of this chapter appeared in Merchant, "Restoration and Reunion with Nature," pp. 68–70. On New England's present-day Indians, see William Simmons, *Spirit of the New England Tribes*. On its energy sources, see Lee, "Energy: The Challenge"; on farming, see Lapping, "Working toward a Rural Landscape," and Kramer, *Three Farms*. On the recuperation of the forest, see Mitchell, "Wither the Yankee Forest," pp. 78–80, 82, 93, 97. By 1970, only 100,000 cords of wood were burned in New England stoves, compared to 8 million cords thirty years earlier.

2. Bormann, "Air Pollution Stress and Energy Policy," esp. pp. 110–23.

3. Garb, "Use and Misuse of the Whole Earth Image."

4. Merchant, "Restoration and Reunion with Nature"; Mollison and Holmgren, *Permaculture One*, p. 3.

5. Leopold, *Sand County Almanac*, quotations on pp. 224–25.

6. On reductionist and community-based ecological approaches, see Worster, *Nature's Economy*, chaps. 14, 15.

7. Meadows, Meadows, Randers, and Behrens, *Limits to Growth*; Malthus, *Essay on the Principle of Population*; Prigogine and Stengers, *Order out of Chaos*; Jantsch, *Self-Organizing Universe*. The thermodynamics of Ilya Prigogine contrasts the equilibrium and near-equilibrium dynamics of closed, isolated physical systems described by the mechanistic model with open biological and social systems in which matter and energy are constantly being

exchanged with their surroundings. When biological systems are confronted with catastrophic changes, a major reorganization can be triggered. Nonlinear relationships and positive feedbacks support a new development.

8. Horkheimer, *Eclipse of Reason*, pp. 92–127, quotations on pp. 101, 115. On mimesis, see also Berman, *Reenchantment of the World*, pp. 177–82, 69ff.

9. Bateson, *Mind and Nature*, pp. 237–64; Berman, ibid.

10. Naess, "The Shallow and the Deep, Long-Range Ecology Movements"; Devall and Sessions, *Deep Ecology*; Bookchin, *Ecology of Freedom*.

11. Bohm, *Wholeness and the Implicate Order*; Briggs and Peat, *Looking Glass Universe*; Lovelock, *Gaia*; Gleick, *Chaos*.

12. Merchant, "Restoration and Reunion with Nature," pp. 68–70; Jordan, "Thoughts on Looking Back" and "On Ecosystem Doctoring."

13. Altieri, *Agroecology*, pp. 21–26; Farrell, "Agroforestry Systems." On permaculture as an additional example of sustainable agriculture, see Mollison and Holmgren, *Permaculture One*, pp. 3–11; Mollison, *Permaculture Two*, pp. 1–5, 46–55.

14. Altieri, *Agroecology*, pp. 101–9.

15. On radical feminism and ecology, see Daly, *Gynecology*; Griffin, *Woman and Nature*; Gray, *Green Paradise Lost*; Cheney, "Eco-Feminism and Deep Ecology."

16. On socialist feminism, see Eisenstein, *Capitalist Patriarchy*; Jaggar, *Feminist Politics*; Warren, "Feminism and Ecology," pp. 3–20; Merchant, "Earthcare" and "Ecofeminism and Feminist Theory."

Bibliography

Abbott, Edith. *Women in Industry: A Study in American Economic History.* New York: D. Appleton and Company, 1910.

A Butter Dealer. "Directions for Making and Preserving Butter." *New England Farmer* 3, no. 9 (April 26, 1851): 145–46.

Adams, Charles Francis. *Three Episodes of Massachusetts History.* 2 vols. 1892. Reprint. New York: Russell & Russell, 1965.

Adams, Frank Dawson. *The Birth and Development of the Geological Sciences.* New York: Dover, 1938.

Adams, James T., et al. *New England's Prospect.* 1933. Reprint. New York: AMS Press, 1970.

Adams, John Quincy. *Congressional Globe* 29, no. 1 (1846): 339–42.

Altieri, Miguel A. *Agroecology: The Scientific Basis of Alternative Agriculture.* Berkeley: Division of Biological Control, University of California, Berkeley, 1983.

―――. "Crop-Weed-Insect Interactions and the Development of Pest-Stable Cropping Systems." In *Pests, Pathogens and Vegetation,* edited by J. M. Thresh, pp. 459–66. London: Pitman, 1981.

Amanda. "Female Education: Amusements." *New England Farmer* 1, no. 13 (June 9, 1849): 204.

Ames, Nathaniel. *An Astronomical Diary or Almanac.* Boston: J. Draper, 1726–86.

Andersen, Joergen. *The Witch on the Wall: Medieval Erotic Sculpture in the British Isles.* Copenhagen: Rosenkilde and Bagger, 1977.

Anderson, David D., ed. *Sunshine and Smoke.* Philadelphia: Lippincott, 1971.

Anderson, James, ed. *Recreations in Agriculture, Natural-History, Arts, and Miscellaneous Literature.* London: T. Bensley, 1800.

Andrews, Edward Deming. *The People Called Shakers: A Search for the Perfect Society.* 1953. Reprint. New York: Dover, 1963.

―――, and Faith Andrews. *Visions of the Heavenly Sphere: A Study in Shaker Religious Art.* Charlottesville: University Press of Virginia, 1969.

Andrews, Joseph. Diaries (1752–87). Massachusetts Historical Society, Boston.

Anonymous, A Farmer of Hampstead, New Hampshire. Diary (April 25–October 31, 1817). Old Sturbridge Village, Mass.

Anonymous. *Almanack.* Boston, 1709.

Anonymous. *An Astronomical Diary or Almanack for . . . 1758.* Portsmouth, N.H.: Daniel Fowle, 1758.

Anonymous. "Barberry Bushes and Wheat." In *Publications of the Colonial Society of Massachusetts,* 11:92–93. Boston: Colonial Society of Massachusetts, 1910.

Anonymous. Diary, interleaved in Nathaniel Ames, *An Astronomical Diary or Almanac* (for 1746). Houghton Library, Harvard University, Cambridge.

Anonymous. "Education of Farmers' Daughters (Excerpted from American Board of Education Report)." *New England Farmer* 1, no. 6 (March 3, 1849): 92.

Anonymous. "Edward Ashley: Trader at Penobscot." *Proceedings of the Massachusetts Historical Society,* 3d ser. 45 (October 1911–June 1912): 493–98.

Anonymous. "Farm Accounts." *Maine Farmer and Journal of Useful Arts Devoted to Agriculture, Mechanics, and General News* 2 (October 31, 1834): 324.

Anonymous. "Female Education." *New England Farmer* 2, no. 23 (November 9, 1850): 370.

Anonymous. *History of Bedford, New Hampshire.* Boston: Alfred Mudge, 1851.

Anonymous. "Home and Woman." *New England Farmer* 3, no. 3 (February 1, 1851): 56.

Anonymous. "The Influence of Women." *New England Farmer* 2, no. 5 (March 2, 1850): 82.

Anonymous. "Making Cheese." *New England Farmer* 2, no. 23 (May 22, 1824): 342.

Anonymous. "Man and Woman." *New England Farmer* 5, no. 33 (March 9, 1827): 264.

Anonymous. "Maternal Influence." *New England Farmer* 1, no. 19 (September 1, 1849): 316.

Anonymous. "The Moon." *New England Farmer* 3, no. 34 (March 18, 1825): 266–67.

Anonymous. *North American Calendar or the Columbian Almanac for . . . 1835.* Wilmington, Del.: P. B. Porter, 1835.

Anonymous. "Of the Mission of the Assumption in the Country of the Abnaquiois." In *The Jesuit Relations and Allied Documents: Travels and Explorations of the Jesuit Missionaries in New France, 1610–1791,* 73 vols., edited by Reuben Gold Thwaites, 31:182–207. Cleveland: Burrows, 1896–1901.

Anonymous. "Successful Application of Labor and Skill." *New England Farmer* 1, no. 16 (July 21, 1849): 244.

Appleby, Joyce. "Commercial Farming and the 'Agrarian Myth' in the Early Republic." *Journal of American History* 68 (March 1982): 831–48.

Aristotle. "Metaphysics." In *The Basic Works of Aristotle,* edited by Richard McKeon. New York: Random House, 1971.

———. "Meteorologica." In *The Works of Aristotle Translated into English,* edited by E. W. Webster and translated by W. D. Ross. Oxford, England: Clarendon Press, 1923.

———. "Physics." In *The Basic Works of Aristotle,* edited by Richard McKeon.

New York: Random House, 1971.

———. "Politics." In *The Basic Works of Aristotle*, edited by Richard McKeon. New York: Random House, 1971.

Associated Press. "Satellites Serve as Eyes on Wildlife." *New York Times*, September 22, 1985.

Audubon, John James. "The Force of the Waters." In *Delineations of American Scenery and Character, 1808–1834*, pp. 130–36. New York: G. A. Baker, 1926.

———. "The Passenger Pigeon." In *Sunshine and Smoke*, edited by David D. Anderson, pp. 168–78. Philadelphia: Lippincott, 1971.

Aunt Betty. "Best Food for Young Turkies." *New England Farmer* 2, no. 8 (June 26, 1824): 378.

Aupaumut, Hendrick. *First Annual Report of the American Society for Promoting Civilization and General Improvement of the Indian Tribes of the United States*. New Haven, Conn.: 1824.

Avery, Captain James. "Letter of Capt. James Avery to Governor Talcott (Groton, October 8, 1735)." In *Collections of the Connecticut Historical Society*, 4:323. Hartford: Connecticut Historical Society, 1892.

Axtell, James. *The Invasion Within: The Contest of Cultures in Colonial North America*. New York: Oxford University Press, 1985.

———. "The Power of Print in the Eastern Woodlands." *William and Mary Quarterly*, 3d ser. 44, no. 2 (April 1987): 300–309.

Babcock, H. L. "The Beaver as a Factor in the Development of New England." *Americana* 11 (1916): 181–96.

Bacon, W. "Poultry." *New England Farmer* 2, no. 5 (March 2, 1850): 76.

Bailyn, Bernard. *The New England Merchants in the Seventeenth Century*. 1955. Reprint. Cambridge: Harvard University Press, 1979.

Baldwin, Frances Elizabeth. *Sumptuary Legislation and Personal Regulation in England*. Baltimore: Johns Hopkins Press, 1926.

Balivet, Robert F. "The Vermont Sheep Industry: 1811–1880." *Vermont History* 33, no. 1 (January 1965): 243–49.

Barfield, Owen. *Saving the Appearances*. London: Faber and Faber, 1957.

Barker-Benfield, Ben. "The Spermatic Economy: A Nineteenth Century View of Sexuality." *Feminist Studies* 1, no. 1 (Summer 1972): 45–74.

Barrett, Samantha. Diary (1828). Old Sturbridge Village. Library Manuscript 356.6/1978, 1978.

Barron, Hal S. *Those Who Stayed Behind: Rural Society in Nineteenth-Century New England*. New York: Cambridge University Press, 1984.

Bartlett, M. B. "An Address Delivered Before the West Oxford Agricultural Society at Lovell, October 20, 1853." In *Transactions of the Agricultural Societies in the State of Maine for 1853*, edited by E. Holmes, pp. 207–33. Augusta, Maine: William T. Johnson, 1854.

Barton, Benjamin Smith. *Notes on the Animals of North America*. Edited by Keir B. Sterling. New York: Arno Press, 1974.

Barton, Hal Seth. "The Impact of Rural Depopulation on the Local Economy: Chelsea, Vermont, 1840–1900." *Agricultural History* 54, no. 2 (April 1980): 318–35.

Bates, Dr. James. "An Address Delivered Before the York County Agricultural Society, at their Cattle Show and Fair, held at Alfred, October 5th and 6th, 1853." In *Transactions of the Agricultural Societies in the State of Maine for 1853*, edited by E. Holmes, pp. 117–35. Augusta, Maine: William T. Johnson, 1854.

Bateson, Gregory. *Mind and Nature: A Necessary Unity*. New York: E. P. Dutton, 1979.

Baudrillard, Jean. *The Mirror of Production*. St. Louis, Mo.: Telos Press, 1975.

Baxter, J. P., ed. *Documentary History of the State of Maine*. 24 vols. Portland: Maine Historical Society, 1869–1916.

Beechey, Veronica. "On Patriarchy." *Feminist Review* 3 (1979): 66–82.

Belknap, Jeremy. *The History of New Hampshire*. 3 vols. Dover, N.H.: J. Mann and J. K. Remich, 1812.

Bennett, John. *The Ecological Transition: Cultural Anthropology and Human Adaptation*. New York: Pergamon, 1976.

Bennett, M. K. "The Food Economy of the New England Indians, 1605–75." *Journal of Political Economy* 63, no. 5 (October 1955): 369–97.

Bentham, Jeremy. *Panopticon*, or *The Inspection House*. 1787. Reprint. London: T. Payne, 1791.

Benton, Thomas Hart. *Congressional Globe* 29, no. 1 (1846): 917–18.

Berger, John. *About Looking*. New York: Pantheon, 1980.

Berman, Morris. *The Reenchantment of the World*. Ithaca: Cornell University Press, 1981.

Berry, William. *Encyclopedia Heraldica*. 4 vols. London: Sherwood, Gilbert, and Piper, 1828–40.

Bidwell, Percy Wells. "The Agricultural Revolution in New England." *American Historical Review* 26, no. 4 (July 1921): 683–702.

———. "Rural Economy in New England at the Beginning of the Nineteenth Century." In *Transactions of the Connecticut Academy of Arts and Sciences*, 42 vols., 20:241–399. New Haven: Connecticut Academy of Arts and Sciences, 1916.

———, and John I. Falconer. *History of Agriculture in the Northern United States, 1620–1860*. 1925. Reprint. New York: Peter Smith, 1941.

Binns, John. *A Treatise on Practical Farming*. Fredericktown, Md.: John B. Colvin, 1803.

Birch, Thomas. *The History of the Royal Society of London*. 4 vols. London, 1756–57.

Bird, Elizabeth Ann R. "The Social Construction of Nature: Theoretical Approaches to the History of Environmental Problems." *Environmental Review* 11, no. 4 (Winter 1987): 255–64.

Bishop, Charles A. "Northeastern Indian Concepts of Conservation and the Fur Trade: A Critique of Calvin Martin's Thesis." In *Indians, Animals, and the Fur Trade*, edited by Shepard Krech III, pp. 39–58. Athens: University of Georgia Press, 1981.

Blith, Walter. *The English Improver Improved*. London: Printed for John Wright, 1652.

Bloch, Ruth H. "American Feminine Ideals in Transition: The Rise of the Moral Mother, 1785–1815." *Feminist Studies* 4, no. 2 (June 1978): 101–26.

Bohm, David. *Wholeness and the Implicate Order*. Boston: Routledge and Kegan Paul, 1980.

Bookchin, Murray. *The Ecology of Freedom: The Emergence and Dissolution of Hierarchy*. Palo Alto, Calif.: Cheshire Books, 1982.

Booth, Sally Smith. *The Witches of Early America*. New York: Hastings House, 1975.

Bord, Janet, and Colin Bord. *Earth Rites: Fertility Practices in Pre-Industrial Britain*. London: Granada, 1983.

Bormann, F. H. "Air Pollution Stress and Energy Policy." In *New England Prospects*, edited by Carl Reidel, pp. 85–140. Hanover, N.H.: University Press of New England, 1982.

———, and G. E. Likens. "Nutrient Cycling." *Science* 155 (January 27, 1967): 424–29.

Boserup, Ester. *The Conditions of Agricultural Growth: The Economics of Agrarian Change under Population Pressure*. Chicago: Aldine, 1965.

Botkin, B. A. *A Treasury of New England Folklore*. New York: Crown, 1965.

Bowden, Mary Ellen. "The Scientific Revolution in Astrology: The English Reformers, 1558–1686." Ph.D. dissertation, Yale University, 1974.

Boyer, Paul, and Stephen Nissenbaum. *Salem Possessed: The Social Origins of Witchcraft*. Cambridge: Harvard University Press, 1974.

Bradford, William. *History of Plymouth Plantation, 1620–1647*. 2 vols. Edited by Worthington C. Ford. Boston: Published for the Massachusetts Historical Society by Houghton Mifflin Co., 1912.

———. *Of Plymouth Plantation*. Edited by Harvey Wish. New York: Paragon, 1962.

Bridenthal, Renaté. "The Dialectics of Production and Reproduction in History." *Radical America* 10, no. 2 (March–April 1976): 3–11.

Briggs, John, and David Peat. *The Looking Glass Universe: The Emerging Science of Wholeness*. New York: Simon and Schuster, 1984.

Briggs, Katharine. *The Folklore of the Cotswolds*. London: B. T. Batsford, 1974.

Brodeur, Paul. *Restitution: The Land Claims of the Mashpee, Passamaquoddy and Penobscot Indians of New England*. Boston: Northeastern University Press, 1985.

Brodt, Ellen Sears. "Autobiography of Mrs. Brodt" (1834–1922). American Antiquarian Society Manuscript Collection, Worcester, Mass.

Bromley, Stanley W. "The Original Forest Types of Southern New England." *Zoological Monographs* 5, no. 1 (January 1935): 63–88.

Brooke, Iris, and James Laver. *English Costume from the Fourteenth through the Nineteenth Century*. New York: Macmillan Company, 1937.

Brown, Silas. "Fertilizing Influence of the Atmosphere." *New England Farmer* 2, no. 2 (January 19, 1850): 28.

Browne, Charles A. *A Source Book of Agricultural Chemistry*. Waltham, Mass.: Chronica Botanica Co., 1944.

Buffinton, Arthur H. "New England and the Western Fur Trade, 1629–1675." *Publications of the Colonial Society of Massachusetts* 18 (1915–16): 160–92.

Buffon, Georges Louis Leclerc. *Natural History, General and Particular,* 8 vols., edited by William Smellie. London: Printed for W. Strahan and T. Cadell, 1781.

Bulkeley, Peter. *The Gospel Covenant: Or the Covenant of Grace Opened.* London, 1646.

Bullard, John, A.M. *Discourse on Agriculture Delivered Before the Western Society of Middlesex Husbandmen . . . at Littleton, October 19, 1803.* Cambridge, Mass.: W. Hillard, 1804.

Burrage, Henry S., ed. *Early English and French Voyages, Chiefly from Hakluyt, 1534–1608.* New York: Charles Scribner's Sons, 1906.

Burtt, J. Frederick. "Methods of Fishing Used by the Indians on the Merrimack River." *New Hampshire Archaeologist* 2 (July 1951): 2–5.

Bushman, Richard. *From Puritan to Yankee: Character and the Social Order in Connecticut, 1690–1765.* New York: W. W. Norton, 1967.

Butler, Eva L. "Algonkian Culture and Use of Maize in Southern New England." *Bulletin of the Archeological Society of Connecticut* (December 1948): 1–39.

Butler, Jon. "Magic, Astrology, and the Early American Religious Heritage, 1600–1760." *American Historical Review* 84, no. 2 (April 1979): 317–46.

Capps, Walter Holden. *Seeing with a Native Eye.* New York: Harper and Row, 1976.

Capron, Joseph W. "The Moon's Influence on Vegetation." *New England Farmer* 2, no. 46 (June 12, 1824): 361.

Carlo, Joyce W. *Trammels, Trenchers, Tartlets.* Old Saybrook, Conn.: Peregrine Press, 1982.

Carman, Harry J., ed. *Jesse Buel, Agricultural Reformer: Selections from His Writings.* New York: Columbia University Press, 1947.

Carroll, Charles F. *The Timber Economy of Puritan New England.* Providence, R.I.: Brown University Press, 1973.

Carroll, Peter N. *Puritanism and the Wilderness, 1629–1700.* New York: Columbia University Press, 1969.

Casteel, Richard. "Two Static Maximum Population Density Models for Hunter-Gatherers: A First Approximation." *World Archeology* 4, no. 1 (1972): 19–40.

Catnip, Barbara. "Good Neighborhood." *New England Farmer* 3, no. 14 (October 22, 1824): 104.

Ceci, Lynn. "Fish Fertilizer: A Native North American Practice?" *Science* 188, no. 4183 (April 4, 1975): 26–30.

———. "Watchers of the Pleiades: Ethnoastronomy among Native Cultivators in Northeastern North America." *Ethnohistory* 25, no. 4 (Fall 1978): 301–17.

Chadwick, Joseph. "An Account of a Journey from Fort Pownal—Now Fort Point—up the Penobscot River to Quebec, in 1764." *Bangor Historical Magazine* 4, no. 8 (February 1889): 141–48.

Chamberlain, A. F. "The Maple amongst the Algonkian Tribes." *American Anthropologist* 4, no. 1 (January 1981): 39–43.

Chamberlin, Roy B., and Herman Feldman, eds. *The Dartmouth Bible: An Abridgment of the King James Version, with Aids to Its Understanding as History and Literature and a Source of Religious Experience*. Boston: Houghton Mifflin, 1950.

Champlain, Samuel de. *Voyages of Samuel de Champlain, 1604–1618*. Edited by W. L. Grandt. New York: Scribner's, 1907.

———. *The Works of Samuel de Champlain*. 6 vols. Edited by H. P. Biggar. Champlain Society, 1922–36. Reprint. Toronto: University of Toronto Press, 1971.

Chastellux, Jean François, Marquis de. *Travels in North America, in the Years 1780–81–82*. New York: White, Gallaher, & White, 1827.

Cheney, Jim. "Eco-Feminism and Deep Ecology." *Environmental Ethics* 9, no. 2 (Summer 1987): 115–45.

Child, [Lydia]. *The American Frugal Housewife*. Boston: Carter, Hendee and Co., 1832.

Childe, V. Gordon. *Man Makes Himself*. New York: Mentor, 1951.

Chinard, Gilbert. "The American Philosophical Society and the Early History of Forestry in America." *Proceedings of the American Philosophical Society* 89, no. 2 (July 18, 1945): 444–88.

Clark, A Farmer of Wakefield, New Hampshire. Diary (1817–29). Worcester, Mass.: American Antiquarian Society.

Clark, Christopher. "The Household Economy: Market Exchange and the Rise of Capitalism in the Connecticut Valley, 1800–1860." *Journal of Social History* 13, no. 2 (Winter 1979): 169–89.

———. "Household, Market, and Capital: The Process of Economic Change in the Connecticut Valley of Massachusetts, 1800–1860." Ph.D. dissertation, Harvard University, 1982.

Clawson, Marion. "Forests in the Long Sweep of American History." *Science* 204 (June 15, 1979): 1168–74.

Coffin, Howard B. "Size of Fowls." *New England Farmer* 2, no. 5 (March 2, 1850): 78.

Cohen, Mark N. *The Food Crisis in Prehistory: Overpopulation and the Origins of Agriculture*. New Haven: Yale University Press, 1977.

Colby, William C. *Pasture Culture in Massachusetts*. Bulletin no. 380, pp. 1–43. Amherst: Massachusetts Agricultural Experiment Station, Massachusetts State College, October 1941.

Cole, Arthur H. "Agricultural Crazes: A Neglected Chapter in American Economic History." *American Economic Review* 16, no. 4 (December 1926): 622–39.

Colman, Henry. *Address Before the Hampshire, Franklin, and Hampden Agricultural Society Delivered in Greenfield, Oct. 23, 1833*. Greenfield, Mass.: Phelps and Ingersoll, 1833.

———. *First Report of the Agriculture of Massachusetts*. Boston: Dutton and Wentworth, 1838.

Colton, Calvin. "Labor and Capital." In *The Junius Tracts*. New York: Greeley & McElrath, 1844.

Connecticut, State of. *The Public Statute Laws of the State of Connecticut,*

Passed May 1835. Hartford: John B. Eldredge, 1835.

————. *The Revised Statutes of the State of Connecticut*. Hartford: Case, Tiffany & Co., 1849.

Cook, Sherburne F. "Demographic Consequences of European Contact with Primitive Peoples." *Annals of the American Academy of Political and Social Science* 237 (January 1945): 107–11.

————. *The Indian Population of New England in the Seventeenth Century*. University of California Publications in Anthropology, vol. 12. Berkeley: University of California Press, 1976.

————. "Interracial Warfare and Population Decline among the New England Indians." *Ethnohistory* 20 (Winter 1973): 1–24.

————. "The Significance of Disease in the Extinction of the New England Indians." *Human Biology* 45, no. 3 (September 1973): 485–508.

Cott, Nancy F. *The Bonds of Womanhood: Woman's Sphere in New England, 1780–1835*. New Haven: Yale University Press, 1977.

Cowan, Ruth Schwartz. *More Work for Mother*. New York: Basic Books, 1983.

Cowan, William, ed. *Papers of the Seventh Algonquian Conference, 1975*. Ottawa: Carleton University, 1976.

Coxe, Tench. "View of the United States of America in a Series of Papers Written . . . 1789–1794" (Philadelphia: Hall, 1794), in Gilbert Chinard, "American Philosophical Society and the Early History of Forestry." *Proceedings of the American Philosophical Society* 89, no. 2 (July 18, 1945): 444–88.

Crèvecoeur, J. Hector St. John de. *Letters from an American Farmer*. 1782. Reprint. New York: E. P. Dutton, 1957.

Cronon, William, Jr. *Changes in the Land: Indians, Colonists, and the Ecology of New England*. New York: Hill and Wang, 1983.

Crosby, Alfred W. *Ecological Imperialism: The Biological Expansion of Europe, 900–1900*. New York: Cambridge University Press, 1986.

————. "Ecological Imperialism: The Overseas Migration of Western Europeans as a Biological Phenomenon." *Texas Quarterly* (Spring 1978): 10–22.

————. "God . . . Would Destroy Them, and Give Their Country to Another People. . . ." *American Heritage* 29, no. 6 (October–November 1978): 38–43.

————. "Virgin Soil Epidemics as a Factor in the Aboriginal Depopulation in America." *William and Mary Quarterly* 33 (April 1976): 289–99.

Crow, W. B. *The Occult Properties of Herbs and Plants*. Wellingborough, Northamptonshire: Aquarian Press, 1980.

Daly, Mary. *Gynecology: The Metaethics of Radical Feminism*. Boston: Beacon, 1978.

Dame, Lorin L., and Henry Brooks. *Handbook of the Trees of New England*. Boston: Ginn & Company, 1901.

Dana, Samuel L. *A Muck Manual for Farmers*. Lowell, Mass.: Daniel Bixby, 1842.

Dana, Samuel Trask. *Forest and Range Policy: Its Development in the United States*. New York: McGraw-Hill, 1956.

Danhof, Clarence. *Change in Agriculture: The Northern United States, 1820–1870*. Cambridge: Harvard University Press, 1969.

Daniels, Bruce C. *The Connecticut Town: Growth and Development, 1635–*

1790. Middletown, Conn.: Wesleyan University Press, 1979.

————. "Economic Development in Colonial and Revolutionary Connecticut: An Overview." *William and Mary Quarterly*, 3d ser. 37, no. 3 (July 1980): 429–50.

[Davies, James]. "A Relation of a Voyage to Sagadahoc, 1607–1608." In *Early English and French Voyages, Chiefly from Hakluyt, 1534–1608*, edited by Henry S. Burrage, pp. 399–419. New York: Charles Scribner's Sons, 1906.

Davis, Margaret B. "Phytogeography and Palynology of Northeastern United States." *The Quaternary of the United States*, edited by H. E. Wright and David Frey. Princeton: Princeton University Press, 1965.

————, Ray W. Spear, and Linda C. K. Shane. "Holocene Climate of New England." *Quaternary Research* 14 (1980): 240–50.

Davy, Sir Humphrey. *Elements of Agricultural Chemistry in a Course of Lectures for the Board of Agriculture*. 1813. Reprint. New York: Eastburn, Kirk, 1815.

Day, Gordon M. "The Indian as an Ecological Factor in the Northeastern Forest." *Ecology* 34, no. 2 (April 1953): 329–46.

Deane, Samuel. *The New England Farmer, or Georgical Dictionary*. Worcester, Mass.: Isiah Thomas, 1790.

DeForest, John. *History of the Indians of Connecticut From the Earliest Known Period to 1850*. Hartford, Conn.: Hamersley, 1853.

Demos, John. *Entertaining Satan: Witchcraft and the Culture of Early New England*. New York: Oxford University Press, 1982.

Devall, William, and George Sessions. *Deep Ecology: Living as if Nature Mattered*. Salt Lake City: Peregrine Smith Books, 1985.

Dexter, Lincoln A., comp. and ed. *Maps of Early Massachusetts*. Springfield, Mass.: New England Blue Print Paper Company, 1979.

Digby, Sir Kenelm. *Of Bodies and Of Mans Soul: To Discover the Immortality of Reasonable Souls: With Two Discourses Of the Powder of Sympathy and Of the Vegetation of Plants* [1660]. London: S. G. and B. G. for J. Williams, 1669.

Dodge, Allen W. "Poultry: A Profitable Part of Farm Production." *New England Farmer* 1, no. 1 (December 9, 1848): 4–5.

Dole, Samuel T. "Ancient Naguamqueeg." In *Collections and Proceedings of the Maine Historical Society*, 2d ser., 7:405–12. Portland: Maine Historical Society, 1896.

Donahue, Brian. "The Forests and Fields of Concord: An Ecological History, 1750–1850." In *Chronos: A Journal of Social History*, pp. 15–63. Waltham, Mass.: Brandeis University History Department, Fall 1983.

————. "Skinning the Land: Economic Growth and the Ecology of Farming in Nineteenth Century New England." History Department, Brandeis University, unpublished manuscript, 1984.

Dorson, Richard. *American Folklore*. Chicago: University of Chicago Press, 1959.

Dow, Mary Larcom. *Old Days at Beverly Farms*. Beverly, Mass.: North Shore Printing Co., 1921.

Drepperd, Carl W. *American Clocks and Clockmakers*. Garden City, N.Y.:

Doubleday, 1947.

Drinnon, Richard. "The Maypole of Merry Mount: Thomas Morton and the Puritan Patriarchs." *Massachusetts Review* 21, no. 2 (1980): 382–410.

Dublin, Thomas. *Women at Work: The Transformation of Work and Community in Lowell, Massachusetts, 1826–1860.* New York: Columbia University Press, 1979.

———, ed. *Farm to Factory: Women's Letters, 1830–1860.* New York: Columbia University Press, 1981.

Dudley, Edward, and Maximillian E. Novak, eds. *The Wild Man Within.* Pittsburgh: University of Pittsburgh Press, 1972.

Duffy, John. "Smallpox and the Indians in the American Colonies." *Bulletin of the History of Medicine* 25, no. 4 (July–August 1951): 324–41.

Dugmore, A. Radclyffe. *The Romance of the Beaver.* London: William Heinemann, 1914.

Dwight, Timothy. *Travels in New England and New York.* 4 vols. Edited by Barbara M. Solomon and Patricia M. King. 1823. Reprint. Cambridge: Harvard University Press, 1969.

Earle, Alice Morse. *Home Life in Colonial Days.* 1898. Reprint. Stockbridge, Mass.: Berkshire Traveller Press, 1974.

Eastman, John R. *History of the Town of Andover, New Hampshire, 1751–1906.* Concord, N.H.: Rumford Printing Co., 1910.

Eaton, Amos. *Manual of Botany for the Northern and Middle States of America.* 4th ed. Albany: Websters and Skinners, 1824.

Eaton, Rev. H. M. "An Address Delivered Before the Kennebec County Agricultural Society, at their Annual Exhibition at Readfield, October 12th and 13th, 1853 and South Kennebec Society at Gardiner, October 20th, 1853." In *Transactions of the Agricultural Societies in the State of Maine for 1853,* edited by E. Holmes, pp. 53–73. Augusta, Maine: William T. Johnson, 1854.

Eaton, Randall L. "Hunting and the Great Mystery of Nature." *Utne Reader,* no. 19 (1987): 42–49.

Eckstrom, Fannie H. "Lumbering in Maine." In *Maine: A History,* 5 vols., edited by Louis Clinton Hatch. New York: American Historical Society, 1919.

Edwards, Jonathan. *Jonathan Edwards: Representative Selections, with Introduction, Bibliography, and Notes.* Edited by Clarence H. Faust and Thomas H. Johnson. New York: American Book Co., 1935.

Eisenstein, Zillah. *Capitalist Patriarchy and the Case for Socialist Feminism.* New York: Monthly Review Press, 1979.

Elias, Norbert. *The Civilizing Process: The History of Manners.* 1939. Reprint. New York: Urizen Books, 1978.

Eliot, Jared. *Essays Upon Field Husbandry in New England and Other Papers, 1748–1762.* Edited by Harry J. Carman. 1760. Reprint. New York: Columbia University Press, 1934.

Emerson, George B. *A Report on the Trees and Shrubs Growing Naturally in the Forests of Massachusetts.* Boston: Dutton and Wentworth, 1846.

Emerson, Ralph Waldo. *The Complete Works of Ralph Waldo Emerson.* 12

vols. Boston: Houghton Mifflin & Co., 1903–4.

Emery, Sarah Anna. *Reminiscences of a Nonagenarian*. Newburyport, Mass.: W. H. Huse, 1879.

Engels, Frederick. *Dialectics of Nature*. Edited by Clemens Dutt. New York: International Publishers, 1940.

―――. "Origin of the Family, Private Property, and the State." In *Selected Works*. New York: International Publishers, 1968.

―――. "Outlines of a Critique of Political Economy (Appendix)." In *Karl Marx's Economic and Philosophical Manuscripts of 1844*, edited by Dirk J. Struik. New York: International Publishers, 1964.

Epstein, Barbara Leslie. *The Politics of Domesticity: Women, Evangelism, and Temperance in Nineteenth Century America*. Middletown, Conn.: Wesleyan University Press, 1981.

Etienne, Mona, and Eleanor Leacock, eds. *Women and Colonization: Anthropological Perspectives*. New York: Praeger, 1980.

Evans, George. *The Pattern under the Plough*. London: Faber and Faber, 1966.

Evelyn, John. *Terra: A Philosophical Discourse of Earth*. London, 1675. Reprint. York, England: A. Ward, 1778.

Fairholt, F. W. *Costume in England: A History of Dress to the End of the Eighteenth Century*. London: George Bell and Sons, 1909.

A Farmer. "The Education of Farmers' Daughters." *New England Farmer* 2, no. 11 (May 25, 1850): 178.

A Farmer. "Premium for Forest Trees." *New England Farmer* 6, no. 15 (November 2, 1827): 115.

Farmer's assistant. "Forest." *New England Farmer* 6, no. 31 (February 22, 1828): 242.

Farmington Indians. "Farmington Indians to the General Assembly (May 9, 1692)." In *Collections of the Connecticut Historical Society*, 21:204. Hartford: Connecticut Historical Society, 1924.

Farrell, John G. "Agroforestry Systems." In *Agroecology: The Scientific Basis of Alternative Agriculture*, edited by Miguel Altieri, pp. 77–83. Berkeley: Division of Biological Control, University of California, Berkeley, 1983.

[Fessenden, Thomas G.]. "On Deep and Frequent Ploughing." *New England Farmer* 1, no. 8 (September 21, 1822): 60.

―――. "The Farmer." *New England Farmer* 1, no. 35 (March 29, 1823): 278.

―――. "Remarks." *New England Farmer* 5, no. 21 (December 15, 1826): 161.

―――. "Remarks on Ploughing." *New England Farmer* 2, nos. 15, 16 (November 8, 15, 1823): 113–14, 121.

Fisher, Margaret W. "The Mythology of the Northern and Northeastern Algonkians in Reference to Algonkian Mythology as a Whole." In *Man in Northeastern North America*, edited by Frederick Johnson, pp. 226–62. Andover, Mass.: Phillips Academy, 1946.

Fiske, O. "Correspondence." *New England Farmer* 2, no. 31 (April 10, 1824): 289.

Force, Peter, ed. *Tracts and Other Papers Relating Principally to the Origin, Settlement, and Progress of the Colonies in North America, From the Discov-*

ery of the Country to the Year 1776. Washington: P. Force, 1838.

Forpe, Will, ed. *The Best of the Old Farmer's Almanac.* New York: Harcourt Brace Jovanovich, 1977.

Foster, John. *Almanack of Coelestial Motions for 1675.* Cambridge, Mass.: Samuel Green, 1675.

———. *Almanack of Coelestial Motions for 1680.* Cambridge, Mass.: Samuel Green, 1680.

Foucault, Michel. "Questions on Geography." In *Power/Knowledge: Selected Interviews and Other Writings, 1972–1977,* edited by Colin Gordon. New York: Pantheon, 1980.

Fowler, William S. "Agricultural Tools and Techniques of the Northeast." *Massachusetts Archeological Society Bulletin* 15, no. 3 (1954): 41–51.

Franklin, Benjamin. "Remarks Concerning the Savages of North America." In *Franklin's Wit and Folly: The Bagatelles,* edited by Richard E. Amacher. New Brunswick, N.J.: Rutgers University Press, 1953.

Fritzell, Peter A. "The Wilderness and the Garden: Metaphors for the American Landscape." *Forest History* 12, no. 1 (April 1968): 16–23.

Frost, Joseph. "Mr. Frost's Statement on Crops Raised on One Acre of Land (November 9, 1853)." In *Transactions of the Agricultural Societies in the State of Maine for 1853,* edited by E. Holmes. Augusta, Maine: William T. Johnson, 1854.

Fryer, Judith. "American Eves in American Edens." *American Scholar* 44, no. 1 (Winter 1974–75): 78–99.

Furtado, J. I., ed. *Tropical Ecology and Development: Proceedings of the Vth International Symposium of Tropical Ecology.* Kuala Lumpur: ISTE, 1980.

Fussell, G. E. *Crop Nutrition: Science and Practice before Liebig.* Lawrence, Kans.: Coronado Press, 1971.

Gale, Hannah. Diary (1837–38). American Antiquarian Society Women's History Sources, vol. 1, collection 7631, NUCMC no. 62–3096.

Garb, Yaakov Jerome. "The Use and Misuse of the Whole Earth Image." *Whole Earth Review,* no. 45 (March 1985): 18–25.

Gardner, Leift Lion. "His Relation of the Pequot Warres." In *Collections of the Massachusetts Historical Society,* 10 vols., 3d ser., 3:154. Boston: Massachusetts Historical Society, 1833.

Gates, Paul. "Problems of Agricultural History, 1790–1840." *Agricultural History* 46 (January 1972): 34–39.

Geertz, Clifford. *Agricultural Involution.* Berkeley: University of California Press, 1963.

———. "Ethos, Worldview, and the Analysis of Sacred Symbols." In *The Interpretation of Cultures.* New York: Basic Books, 1973.

———. "Religion as a Cultural System." In *The Interpretation of Cultures.* New York: Basic Books, 1973.

George, Wilma. *Animals and Maps.* London: Secker and Warburg, 1969.

Gibb, George Sweet. *The Saco-Lowell Shops: Textile Machinery Building in New England, 1813–1949.* Cambridge: Harvard University Press, 1950.

Giere, John P., Keith M. Johnson, and John H. Perkins. "A Closer Look at No-

Till Farming." *Environment* 22, no. 6 (July–August 1980): 14–20, 37–41.

Gimbutas, Marija. *The Goddesses and Gods of Old Europe, 6500–3500 B.C.* 1974. Reprint. Berkeley: University of California Press, 1982.

Gleick, James. *Chaos.* New York: Viking, 1987.

Gliessman, Stephen R., and Miguel A. Altieri. "Polyculture Cropping Has Advantages." *California Agriculture* 36, no. 7 (July 1982): 14–16.

Gliessman, Stephen R., and A. M. Amador. "Ecological Aspects of Production in Traditional Agroecosystems in the Humid Lowland Tropics of Mexico." In *Tropical Ecology and Development: Proceedings of the Vth International Symposium of Tropical Ecology*, edited by J. I. Furtado, pp. 601–8. Kuala Lumpur: ISTE, 1980.

Godwin, Joscelyn. *Athanasius Kircher: A Renaissance Man and the Quest for Lost Knowledge.* New York: Thames and Hudson, 1979.

Goldsbury, John. "Design and Usefulness of Labor." *New England Farmer* 7, no. 9 (September 1855): 413.

Goode, G. Browne. "The Use of Agricultural Fertilizers by the American Indians and the Early English Colonists." *American Naturalist* 14, no. 7 (July 1880): 473–79.

Goodwin, George. "Big Game Animals in the Northeastern United States." *Journal of Mammology* 17, no. 1 (1936): 48–50.

Gookin, Daniel. "Historical Collections of the Indians in New England (1674)." In *Collections of the Massachusetts Historical Society*, 10 vols., 1st ser., 1:144–229. Boston: Massachusetts Historical Society, 1792.

Gorges, Sir Ferdinando. "A Brief Narration . . . of New England." In *Sir Ferdinando Gorges and His Province of Maine*, edited by James Phinney. Boston: Prince Society, 1890.

Gough, Kathleen. "The Origin of the Family." In *Toward an Anthropology of Women*, edited by Rayna R. Reiter, pp. 51–76. New York: Monthly Review Press, 1975.

Grant, Charles S. *Democracy in the Connecticut Frontier Town of Kent.* New York: Columbia University Press, 1961.

———. "A History of Kent, 1738–1796: Democracy on Connecticut's Frontier." Ph.D. dissertation, Columbia University, 1957.

Gray, Elizabeth Dodson. *Green Paradise Lost.* Wellesley, Mass.: Roundtable Press, 1981.

Greeley, Horace. *Recollections of a Busy Life.* New York: J. B. Ford, 1868.

Green, Mason A. *Springfield, 1636–1886.* Springfield, Mass.: C. Nichols, 1888.

Greene, Evarts B., and Virginia D. Harrington. *American Population before the Federal Census of 1790.* Gloucester, Mass.: Peter Smith, 1966.

Greenwood, Isaac. "An Experimental Course of Mechanical Philosophy. Lecture Course." Boston: Harvard College, 1726.

———. *A Philosophical Discourse Concerning the Mutability and Changes of the Material World, Read to the Students of Harvard College, April 7, 1731, Upon the News of the Death of Thomas Hollis of London.* Boston: S. Gerrish, 1731.

Greven, Philip, Jr. *Four Generations: Population, Land, and Family in Colo-*

nial Andover, Massachusetts. Ithaca: Cornell University Press, 1970.

Griffin, Susan. *Woman and Nature: The Roaring Inside Her*. New York: Harper and Row, 1978.

Gross, Robert A. "Culture and Cultivation: Agriculture and Society in Thoreau's Concord." *Journal of American History* 69 (June 1982): 42–61.

———. *The Minutemen and Their World*. New York: Hill and Wang, 1976.

Grumet, Robert Steven. "Sunksquaws, Shamans, and Tradeswomen: Middle Atlantic Coastal Algonkian Women during the 17th and 18th Centuries." In *Women and Colonization: Anthropological Perspectives*, edited by Mona Etienne and Eleanor Leacock, pp. 43–62. New York: Praeger, 1980.

Guerlac, Henry. "John Mayow and the Aerial Nitre: Studies in the Chemistry of John Mayow—I (1953)." In *Essays and Papers in the History of Modern Science*, edited by Henry Guerlac, pp. 245–59. Baltimore: Johns Hopkins University Press, 1977.

———. "The Poet's Nitre: Studies in the Chemistry of John Mayow—II (1954)." In *Essays and Papers in the History of Modern Science*, edited by Henry Guerlac, pp. 260–74. Baltimore: Johns Hopkins University Press, 1977.

Hadlock, Wendell S. "War among the Northeastern Woodland Indians." *American Anthropologist* 49, no. 2 (April–June 1947): 204–21.

Hahn, Steven. "Hunting, Fishing, and Foraging: Common Rights and Class Relations in the Postbellum South." *Radical History Review* 26 (1982): 37–64.

Hair, Jay D., et al. "Beaver Pond Ecosystems and Their Relationships to Multi-Use Natural Resource Management." In *Strategies for Protection and Management of Floodplain Wetlands and Other Riparian Ecosystems*, edited by R. R. Johnson and J. F. McCormick, pp. 80–92. General Technical Report WO-12. Washington, D.C.: Forest Service, U.S. Department of Agriculture, 1978.

Hall, David D. "The World of Print and Collective Mentality in Seventeenth-Century New England." In *New Directions in American Intellectual History*, edited by John Higham and Paul K. Conkin. Baltimore: Johns Hopkins University Press, 1979.

Hall, Diana Long. "From Mayow to Haller: A History of Respiratory Physiology in the Early Eighteenth Century." Ph.D. dissertation, Yale University, 1966.

Hamilton, Alexander, John Jay, and James Madison. *The Federalist*. 1788. Reprint. New York: Modern Library, 1937.

Hammond, Isaac W., ed. *Documents Relating to Towns in New Hampshire*. New Hampshire Provincial and State Papers, vols. 11–13. Concord: Parsons B. Cogwell, 1882–84.

Haraway, Donna. "The Contest for Primate Nature: Daughters of Man-the-Hunter in the Field, 1960–1980." In *The Future of American Democracy*, edited by M. E. Kahn, pp. 175–207. Philadelphia: Temple University Press, 1983.

Harding, Sandra, and Merrill B. Hintikka, eds. *Discovering Reality*. Dordrecht, Holland: D. Reidel, 1983.

Harlan, Jack R. *Crops and Man*. Madison, Wis.: American Society of Agronomy, 1975.

Harper, Roland M. "Changes in the Forest Area of New England in Three Centuries." *Journal of Forestry* 16, no. 4 (April 1918): 442–52.

Harpstead, Milo I., and Francis D. Hole. *Soil Science Simplified*. Ames: Iowa State University Press, 1980.

Harris, Marvin. *Cultural Materialism*. New York: Random House, 1979.

Harris, Thaddeus William. *Insects Injurious to Vegetation*. 1862. Reprint. New York: Orange Judd, 1880.

Hart, Robert D. "A Bean, Corn, and Manioc Polyculture Cropping System: II. A Comparison between the Yield and Economic Return from Monoculture and Polyculture Cropping Systems." *Activities at Turrialba* (Costa Rica) 25, no. 4 (October–December 1975): 377–84.

Hartley, Dorothy. *Lost Country Life*. New York: Pantheon, 1979.

Hartlib, Samuel. *Compleat Husbandman*. London: Edward Brewster, 1659.

Harvey, David. "Population, Resources, and the Ideology of Science." *Economic Geography* 50 (July 1974): 256–77.

Hastings, William S. "Report on Working Oxen (Worcester Agricultural Society)." *New England Farmer* 5, no. 19 (December 1, 1826): 148.

Havelock, Eric. *Preface to Plato*. Cambridge: Harvard University Press, 1963.

Haviland, William A., and Marjory W. Power. *The Original Vermonters: Native Inhabitants Past and Present*. Hanover, N.H.: University Press of New England, 1981.

Hawes, Austin P. "New England Forests in Retrospect." *Journal of Forestry* 21, no. 3 (March 1923): 209–24.

Hawthorne, Nathaniel. "The Maypole of Merry Mount." In *Twice Told Tales*. 1837. Reprint. Boston: Houghton, Mifflin, 1895.

Heiman, P. M. " 'Nature Is a Perpetual Worker': Newton's Aether and Eighteenth-Century Natural Philosophy." *Ambix* 20, no. 1 (March 1973): 1–25.

Heimert, Alan. "Puritanism, the Wilderness and the Frontier." *New England Quarterly* 26, no. 1 (March 1953): 361–82.

Heninger, S. K., Jr. *A Handbook of Renaissance Meteorology*. Durham, N.C.: Duke University Press, 1960.

Henretta, James A. "Families and Farms: Mentalité in Pre-Industrial America." *William and Mary Quarterly*, 3d ser. 25, no. 1 (January 1978): 3–31.

Henshaw, H. W. "Indian Origin of Maple Sugar." *American Anthropologist* 3, no. 4 (October 1890): 341–51.

Hepting, George H. "Death of the American Chestnut." *Forest History* 18 (July 1974): 61–67.

Heraclitus. *Selections from Early Greek Philosophy*, pp. 84–97. Edited by Milton C. Nahm. New York: Appleton-Century-Crofts, 1934.

Higgeson, Francis. "New England's Plantation (3rd ed., 1630)." In *Chronicles of the First Planters of the Colony of Massachusetts Bay, from 1623–1636*, edited by Alexander Young. Boston: Charles C. Little and James Brown, 1846.

Highwater, Jamake. *The Primal Mind: Vision and Reality in Indian America*.

New York: New American Library, 1981.

Hodgdon, Kenneth W., and John H. Hunt. "Beaver Management in Maine." *Final Report on Federal Aid in Wildlife Restoration*, pp. 1–102. Project 9-R. Game Division Bulletin, no. 3. [Augusta]: Maine Department of Inland Fisheries, June 1953.

Hofstader, Richard. "The Myth of the Happy Yeoman." *American Heritage* 7 (April 1956): 43–53.

Hoglund, A. William. "Forest Conservation and Stove Inventors—1789–1850." *Forest History* 5, no. 4 (Winter 1862): 2–8.

Holbrook, Stewart. *The Yankee Exodus: An Account of Migration from New England*. New York: MacMillan, 1950.

Hole, Christina. *British Folk Customs*. London: Hutchinson, 1976.

Holloway, Mark. *Heavens on Earth: Utopian Communities in America, 1680–1880*. New York: Dover, 1966.

Holmes, Dr. Ezekiel. "An Address Before the West Lincoln Agricultural Society, at their Cattle Show and Fair, in Lewiston, October 6, 1853." In *Transactions of the Agricultural Societies in the State of Maine for 1853*, edited by E. Holmes, pp. 251–73. Augusta, Maine: William T. Johnson, 1854.

Holmes, Richard. *Communities in Transition: Bedford and Lincoln, Massachusetts, 1729–1850*. Ann Arbor: University of Michigan Press, 1980.

Holy Bible, King James version.

Horkheimer, Max. *The Eclipse of Reason*. New York: Oxford University Press, 1947.

Horwitz, Morton J. *The Transformation of American Law, 1780–1860*. Cambridge: Harvard University Press, 1977.

Howard, J. Harrison. Journal (1830–31). Baker Library, Harvard Business School, Cambridge.

Howell, Anna Blackwood. *Diaries*. Worcester, Mass.: American Antiquarian Society, 1819–39.

Hunter, Louis C. *A History of Industrial Power in the United States, 1780–1930*. 2 vols. Charlottesville: University Press of Virginia, 1985.

Innes, Stephen. *Labor in a New Land: Economy and Society in Seventeenth Century Springfield*. Princeton: Princeton University Press, 1983.

Institor, Heinrich, and Jacob Sprenger. *The Malleus Maleficarum*. 1486. Reprint. New York: Bloom, 1970.

Irvin, Helen Deiss. "The Machine in Utopia: Shaker Women and Technology." *Women's Studies International Quarterly* 4, no. 3 (1981): 313–19.

Jackson, Wes. *New Roots for Agriculture*. San Francisco: Friends of the Earth, 1980.

Jaggar, Alison M. *Feminist Politics and Human Nature*. Totowa, N.J.: Rowman & Allanheld, 1983.

———, and William L. McBride. " 'Reproduction' as Male Ideology." *Women's Studies International Forum* 8, no. 3 (1985): 185–96.

Jameson, J. Franklin, ed. *Narratives of New Netherland, 1609–1664*. New York: Charles Scribner's Sons, 1909.

Jantsch, Erich. *The Self-Organizing Universe*. New York: Pergamon Press, 1980.

Jedrey, Christopher. *The World of John Cleaveland: Family and Community in Eighteenth Century New England.* New York: W. W. Norton & Co., 1979.

Jefferson, Thomas. *Notes on the State of Virginia.* Edited by William Peden. New York: W. W. Norton, 1954.

Jeffords, Percy J. "Widow's Dower." *Vermont History,* n.s. 25, no. 3 (July 1957): 252–53.

Jennings, Francis. *The Invasion of America: Indians, Colonialism, and the Cant of Conquest.* New York: W. W. Norton, 1975.

Johnson, Edward. *Wonder Working Providence, 1628–1651.* Edited by J. Franklin Jameson. New York: Barnes & Noble, 1910.

Johnson, Frederick. *The Boylston Street Fishweir.* Robert S. Peabody Foundation for Archeology Papers, vol. 2. Andover, Mass.: Phillips Academy, 1942.

Johnson, R. R., and J. F. McCormick. *Strategies for Protection and Management of Floodplain Wetlands and Other Riparian Ecosystems.* General Technical Report WO-12. Washington, D.C.: Forest Service, U.S. Department of Agriculture, 1978.

Jonas, Hans. "The Nobility of Sight." *Philosophy and Phenomenological Research* 14 (1954): 507–19.

Jones, Douglas Lamar. "The Strolling Poor: Transiency in Eighteenth-Century Massachusetts." *Journal of Social History* 8 (Spring 1975): 28–54.

Jordan, William R., III. "On Ecosystem Doctoring." *Restoration and Management Notes* 1, no. 4 (Fall 1983): 2.

———. "Thoughts on Looking Back." *Restoration and Management Notes* 1, no. 3 (Winter 1983): 2.

Jorgensen, Neil. *A Guide to New England's Landscape.* Chester, Conn.: Globe Pequot Press, 1977.

Josephson, Hannah. *The Golden Threads: New England's Mill Girls and Magnates.* New York: Russell & Russell, 1949.

Josselyn, John. *An Account of Two Voyages to New England Made During the Years 1638, 1663.* 1675. Reprint. 2d ed. Boston: William Veazie, 1865.

———. "New England's Rarities Discovered in Birds, Beasts, Fishes, Serpents, and Plants of That Country." In *Transactions and Collections of the American Antiquarian Society,* 4:105–238. Introduction and Notes by Edward Tuckerman. London: G. Widdows, 1672. Reprint. Boston: John Wilson, 1860.

Judd, Sylvester. "The Fur Trade on the Connecticut River in the Seventeenth Century." *New England Historical and Genealogical Register* 11, no. 3 (July 1857): 217–19.

Kaplan, Lawrence. "Archeology and Domestication in American Phaseolus (Beans)." *Economic Botany* 19, no. 4 (October–December 1965): 358–68.

Karlsen, Carol Frances. "The Devil in the Shape of a Woman: The Witch in Seventeenth Century New England." Ph. D. dissertation, Yale University, 1980.

Keeney, Elizabeth. "The Botanizers: Amateur Scientists in Nineteenth Century America." Ph.D. dissertation, University of Wisconsin, Madison, 1985.

———. "Women and Popular Botany: A Study in Nineteenth Century American Social Values." Paper read at the Fifth Berkshire Conference on the

History of Women, Vassar College, 1981.

Keller, Evelyn Fox, and Christine R. Grontkowski. "The Mind's Eye." In *Discovering Reality*, edited by Sandra Harding and Merrill B. Hintikka, pp. 207–24. Dordrecht, Holland: D. Reidel, 1983.

Kellog, R. S. *The Timber Supply of the United States*. Circular 97. Washington, D.C.: Forest Service, U.S. Department of Agriculture, April 24, 1907.

Kelly, Kevin D. "The Independent Mode of Production." *Review of Radical Political Economics* 11 (Spring 1979): 38–48.

Kendall, Edward. *Travels Through the Northern Parts of the United States in the Years 1807 and 1808*. 3 vols. New York: I. Riley, 1809.

Kerber, Linda. *Women of the Republic: Intellect and Ideology in Revolutionary America*. Chapel Hill: University of North Carolina Press, 1980.

_____. "Women's History." *Journal of American History* 75, no. 1 (June 1988): 9–39.

_____, and Jane DeHart-Mathews, eds. *Women's America: Refocusing the Past*. New York: Oxford University Press, 1982.

Kern, Louis J. *An Ordered Love: Sex Roles and Sexuality in Victorian Utopias—the Shakers, the Mormons, and the Oneida Community*. Chapel Hill: University of North Carolina Press, 1981.

Kerr, Howard, and Charles L. Crow. *The Occult in America: New Historical Perspectives*. Urbana and Chicago: University of Illinois Press, 1983.

Kerridge, Eric. *The Agricultural Revolution*. New York: Augustus M. Kelley, 1968.

Kinney, J. P. "Forest Legislation in America prior to March 4, 1789." In *New York Agricultural Experiment Station Bulletin*, no. 370, pp. 358–405. Ithaca: Cornell University, 1916.

Kircher, Athanasius. *Mundus Subterraneus*. Amsterdam: J. Janssonium & E. Weyerstraten, 1678.

Kittredge, George Lyman. *The Old Farmer and His Almanack: Being Some Observations on Life and Manners in New England a Hundred Years Ago*. Boston: William Ware, 1904.

Knorr-Cetina, Karin. *The Manufacture of Knowledge: An Essay on the Constructivist and Contextual Nature of Science*. New York: Pergamon Press, 1981.

_____, and Michael Mulkay, eds. *Science Observed: Perspectives on the Social Study of Science*. Beverly Hills, Calif.: Sage Publications, 1983.

Kohlstedt, Sally Gregory. "In from the Periphery: American Women in Science, 1830–1880." *Signs* 4, no. 1 (Autumn 1978): 81–96.

Kohnke, Helmut. *Soil Science Simplified*. Prospect Heights, Ill.: Waveland Press, 1966.

Kolodny, Annette. *The Land Before Her: Fantasy and Experience of the American Frontiers, 1630–1860*. Chapel Hill: University of North Carolina Press, 1984.

_____. *The Lay of the Land: Metaphor as Experience and History in American Life and Letters*. Chapel Hill: University of North Carolina Press, 1975.

Korstian, C. F., and P. W. Stickel. "The Natural Replacement of Blight-killed Chestnut in the Hardwood Forests of the Northeast." *Journal of Agricul-*

tural Research 34, no. 7 (April 1927): 631–48.

Kramer, Mark. *Three Farms.* Toronto: Bantam, 1981.

Krech, Shepard, III, ed. *Indians, Animals, and the Fur Trade.* Athens: University of Georgia Press, 1981.

Kreps, Theodore J. "Vicissitudes of the American Potash Industry." *Journal of Economic and Business History* 3, no. 4 (August 1931): 630–66.

Kubrin, David. "Newton and the Cyclical Cosmos: Providence and the Mechanical Philosophy." *Journal of the History of Ideas* 28, no. 3 (July–September 1967): 325–46.

Kuhn, Thomas. *The Structure of Scientific Revolutions.* Chicago: University of Chicago Press, 1962.

Kulik, Gary. "Dams, Fish, and Farmers: Defence of Public Rights in Eighteenth-Century Rhode Island." In *The Countryside in the Age of Capitalist Transformation: Essays in the Social History of Rural America,* edited by Steven Hahn and Jonathan Prude, pp. 25–50. Chapel Hill: University of North Carolina Press, 1985.

Lapping, Mark M. "Working toward a Rural Landscape." In *New England Prospects,* edited by Carl Reidel, pp. 59–84. Hanover, N.H.: University Press of New England, 1982.

Latour, Bruno. "Give Me a Laboratory and I Will Raise the World." In *Science Observed: Perspectives on the Social Studies of Science,* edited by Karin Knorr-Cetina and Michael Mulkay, pp. 141–70. Beverly Hills, Calif.: Sage, 1985.

———. "Visualization and Cognition." In *Knowledge and Society: Studies in the Sociology of Culture Past and Present,* pp. 1–40. JAI Press, 1986.

Lawson, Murray Grant. *Fur: A Study in English Mercantilism, 1700–1775.* Toronto: University of Toronto Press, 1943.

Lawson, William. *The Country Housewife's Garden.* 1617. Reprint. London: Cresset Press, 1927.

———. *A New Orchard and Garden.* 1618. Reprint. London: Cresset Press, 1927.

Leacock, Eleanor. "Matrilocality in a Simple Hunting Economy (Montagnais-Naskapi)." *Southwestern Journal of Anthropology* 11, no. 1 (1955): 31–47.

Leather, Ella Mary. *The Folk-Lore of Herefordshire.* 1912. Reprint. Wakefield, England: S. R. Publishers, 1970.

Lee, Henry. "Energy: The Challenge." In *New England Prospects,* edited by Carl Reidel, pp. 141–77. Hanover, N.H.: University Press of New England, 1982.

Lee, Richard, and Irwin DeVore, eds. *Man the Hunter.* Chicago: Aldine, 1968.

Leger, Sister Mary Celeste. *The Catholic Indian Missions in Maine, 1611–1820.* Washington, D.C.: Catholic University of America, 1929.

Leiss, William. *The Domination of Nature.* New York: George Braziller, 1972.

Lemon, James. *The Best Poor Man's Country: A Geographical Study of Early Southeastern Pennsylvania.* New York: W. W. Norton, 1972.

———. "Communication." *William and Mary Quarterly,* 3d ser. 42, no. 4 (October 1985): 555–57.

———. "Household Consumption in Eighteenth-Century America and Its Relationship to Production and Trade: The Situation among Farmers in Southeastern Pennsylvania." *Agricultural History* 41 (1967): 59–70.

Leopold, Aldo. *A Sand County Almanac*. New York: Oxford University Press, 1949.

Leventhal, Herbert. *In the Shadow of the Enlightenment: Occultism and Renaissance Science in Eighteenth-Century America*. New York: New York University Press, 1976.

Liebig, Justus. *Organic Chemistry in its Applications to Agriculture and Physiologie*. Edited by Lyon Playfair. London: Taylor and Walton, 1840.

[Lincoln, General Benjamin]. "Remarks on the Cultivation of the Oak." In *Collections of the Massachusetts Historical Society*, 10 vols., 2d ser., 1:187–94. Boston: John Eliot, 1814.

Lincoln, Charles H., ed. *Narratives of the Indian Wars, 1675–1699*. New York: Charles Scribner's Sons, 1913.

Locke, John. "An Essay Concerning the True Original Extent and End of Civil Government (1690)." In *Two Treatises of Government*, edited by Peter Laslett. Cambridge, England: Cambridge University Press, 1960.

————. "Some Considerations of the Consequences of the Lowering of Interest and Raising the Value of Money in a Letter of 1691." 1692. In *Works*, 3d ed., 2:73. London: Printed for A. Bettesworth, 1727.

Lockeretz, William, ed. *Environmentally Sound Agriculture*. New York: Praeger, 1983.

Lockridge, Kenneth A. "Land, Population, and the Evolution of New England Society, 1630–1790." *Past and Present* 39 (1968): 62–80.

————. *A New England Town: The First Hundred Years*. New York: W. W. Norton, 1970.

————. "The Population of Dedham, Massachusetts, 1636–1736." *Economic History Review* 19, no. 2 (August 1966): 318–44.

Loehr, Rodney C. "Self-Sufficiency on the Farm." *Agricultural History* 26 (1952): 37–41.

Loftfield, Thomas C. "The Adaptive Role of Warfare among the Southern Algonquians." In *Papers of the Seventh Algonquian Conference, 1975*, edited by William Cowan, pp. 290–96. Ottawa: Carleton University, 1976.

Lovejoy, David. *Religious Enthusiasm in the New World: Heresy to Revolution*. Cambridge: Harvard University Press, 1985.

Lovelock, James. *Gaia: A New Look at Life on Earth*. Oxford, England: Oxford University Press, 1979.

Lovely, N. W. "Notes on New England Almanacs." *New England Quarterly* 8 (June 1935): 264–77.

Low, Nathanael. *An Astronomical Diary: or Almanack*. Boston: 1807, 1810, 1811, 1815, 1816, 1817.

————. "Cutting of Bushes." In *An Astronomical Diary: or Almanack* (end essay). Boston: John and Thomas Fleet, 1807.

Lowenthal, David. *George Perkins Marsh: Versatile Vermonter*. New York: Columbia University Press, 1958.

Machiavelli, Niccolò. *The Prince and the Discourses*. 1532 and 1531 respectively. Reprint. New York: Modern Library, 1950.

McIntyre, Ruth A. *William Pynchon: Merchant and Colonizer, 1590–1662.* Springfield, Mass.: Connecticut Valley Historical Museum, 1961.

Mackintosh, Maureen. "Reproduction and Patriarchy: A Critique of Claude Meillassoux, 'Femmes, Greniers et Capitaux.'" *Capital and Class* 2 (Summer 1977): 114–27.

McMahon, Sarah F. "A Comfortable Subsistence: The Changing Composition of Diet in Rural New England, 1620–1840." *William and Mary Quarterly,* 3d ser. 24, no. 1 (January 1985): 26–65.

_____. "A Comfortable Subsistence: A History of Diet in New England, 1630–1850." Ph.D. dissertation, Brandeis University, 1982.

Macomber, Mary M., Elizabeth Hayward, and Annie W. Wood. "Cheese Making." *New England Farmer* 2, no. 15 (July 20, 1850): 242.

Mahomet. "Petition of Mahomet . . . to the King . . . George the Second, King of Great Britain." In *Collections of the Connecticut Historical Society,* 31 vols., 4:368–72. Hartford: Connecticut Historical Society, 1892.

Maine, State of. *Laws of the State of Maine.* Hallowell: Goodale, Glazier & Co., 1822.

_____. *The Revised Statutes of the State of Maine Passed October 22, 1840.* Augusta: State of Maine, 1840.

Maloney, Francis X. *The Fur Trade in New England, 1620–1676.* Cambridge: Harvard University Press, 1931.

Malthus, Thomas. *An Essay on the Principle of Population.* 1798. Reprint. New York: Penguin, 1976.

Manwaring, Charles W., ed. *A Digest of the Early Connecticut Probate Records.* 3 vols. Hartford: R. S. Peck, 1904–6.

Marburg, Sandra L. "Man's Role, Woman's Place: Images of Women in Human Geography." Ph.D. dissertation, University of California, Berkeley, 1984.

_____. "Women and Environment: Subsistence Paradigms." *Environmental Review* (Special Issue on Women and Environmental History) 8, no. 1 (Spring 1984): 7–22.

Marini, Stephen A. *Radical Sects of Revolutionary New England.* Cambridge: Harvard University Press, 1982.

Markham, Gervase. *Cheap and Good Husbandry.* 1614. Reprint. London: B. Wilson for George-Sawbridge, 1664.

_____. *Country Contentments, Part 2: The English Housewife.* London: J. B[eale] for R. Jackson, 1615.

Marsh, George Perkins. *Man and Nature: Or Physical Geography as Modified by Human Action.* 1864. Reprint. Boston: Harvard University Press, 1965.

_____. *Report on the Artificial Propagation of Fish, Made under the Authority of the Legislature of Vermont.* Burlington, Vt.: Free press print, 1857.

Marshall, Lynn, and Mary Ryan. "The Ultimate Cause of the Civil War: Mother." Paper presented to the annual meeting of the Southern Historical Association, Atlanta, Georgia, 1973.

Martin, Benjamin. *The Philosophical Grammar.* 2d ed. London: J. Noon, 1738.

Martin, Calvin. *Keepers of the Game: Indian-Animal Relationships and the Fur*

Trade. Berkeley: University of California Press, 1978.

Marx, Karl. *Capital.* 3 vols. Edited by Frederick Engels. New York: International Publishers, 1967.

———. "Preface to *A Contribution to the Critique of Political Economy.*" In *Selected Works.* New York: International Publishers, 1968.

Marx, Leo. *The Machine in the Garden.* New York: Oxford University Press, 1964.

———. "The Two Thoreaus: Young Man Thoreau by Richard Lebeaux." *New York Review of Books* (October 26, 1978): 37–43.

Mason, John, and Samuel Mason. "Petition of John Mason [and] Samuel Mason of New London, in Your Majesty's Colony of Connecticut . . . in Behalfe of the Chief Sachem and also of the Mohegan Indians." In *Collections of the Connecticut Historical Society,* 31 vols., 5:139–59. Hartford: Connecticut Historical Society, 1896.

Massachusetts, State of. *Massachusetts General Laws Annotated.* St. Paul, Minn.: West Publishing Co., 1959.

Mather, Cotton. *The Christian Philosopher: A Collection of the Best Discoveries in Nature with Religious Improvements.* London: E. Mathews, 1721.

———. *On Witchcraft, Being the Wonders of the Invisible World, First Published at Boston in Octr. 1692 and now Reprinted.* Mount Vernon, N.Y.: Peter Pauper Press, 1950.

Mather, Increase. *Remarkable Providences Illustrative of the Earlier Days of American Colonization.* London: Reeves and Turner, 1890.

Mayow, John. "On Sal-nitrum and Nitro-aerial Spirit." In *Medico-physical Works.* 1674. Reprint. Oxford: Alembic Club, 1926.

Meadows, Donella H., Dennis L. Meadows, Jorgen Randers, and William W. Behrens III. *The Limits to Growth.* New York: Signet Books, 1972.

Mechling, W. H. *Malecite Tales.* Ottawa: Canada Department of Mines, Government Printing Bureau, 1914.

Meek, Ronald, ed. *Marx and Engels on the Population Bomb.* Berkeley, Calif.: Ramparts Press, 1971.

Meeker, Joseph. *The Comedy of Survival.* New York: Charles Scribner's Sons, 1972.

———. "A Footnote about That Awful Word." *Minding the Earth Quarterly* 6, no. 2 (June 1985): 2.

———. "Resourceful Resurrection." *Minding the Earth Quarterly* 6, no. 1 (March 1985): 1.

Meeks, Harold A. "An Isochronic Map of Vermont Settlement." *Vermont History* 38, no. 2 (Spring 1970): 95–102.

Meillassoux, Claude. *Maidens, Meal, and Money.* Cambridge, England: Cambridge University Press, 1981.

Melcher, Marguerite Fellows. *The Shaker Adventure.* Princeton: Princeton University Press, 1941.

Merchant, Carolyn. *The Death of Nature: Women, Ecology, and the Scientific Revolution.* San Francisco: Harper and Row, 1980.

———. "Earthcare: Women and the Environmental Movement." *Environment* 23, no. 5 (June 1981): 6–13, 38–40.

_____. "Ecofeminism and Feminist Theory." In *Reweaving the World: The Emergence of Ecofeminism*, edited by Irene Diamond and Gloria Orenstein. San Francisco: Sierra Club Books, 1989.

_____. "Perspective: Restoration and Reunion with Nature." *Restoration and Management Notes* 4, no. 2 (Winter 1986): 68–70.

_____. "The Theoretical Structure of Ecological Revolutions." *Environmental Review* 11, no. 4 (Winter 1987): 265–74.

_____. "Women of the Progressive Conservation Movement, 1900–1916." *Environmental Review* 8, no. 1 (Spring 1984): 57–85.

Merriam, C. Hart. "The Acorn: A Possibly Neglected Source of Food." *National Geographic* 34, no. 4 (August 1918): 129–37.

Merriam, Thomas. "The Disenchantment of the World." *Ecologist* 7, no. 1 (1977): 22–28.

Merrill, Michael. "Cash Is Good to Eat: Self-Sufficiency and Exchange in the Rural Economy of the United States." *Radical History Review* 3 (Winter 1977): 42–71.

Meyer, Balthasar. *History of Transportation in the United States before 1860*. Washington, D.C.: Carnegie Institution, 1917.

Miller, G. Tyler, Jr. *Living in the Environment*. Belmont, Calif.: Wadsworth, 1975.

Miller, Perry. "From Edwards to Emerson." In *Errand into the Wilderness*, pp. 184–203. New York: Harper and Row, 1956.

Mills, Enos A. *In Beaver World*. Boston and New York: Houghton Mifflin, 1913.

Mitchell, John. "Wither the Yankee Forest." *Audubon* 83, no. 2 (March 1981): 76–99.

Mohegan Indians. "The Humble Petition of the Major part of the Tribe of Mohegan Indians in Your Majesty's Colony of Connecticutt in New England, February, 1737/8." In *Collections of the Connecticut Historical Society*, 31 vols., 5:159–63. Hartford: Connecticut Historical Society, 1896.

Mohr, James. *Abortion in America: The Origins and Evolution of National Policy, 1800–1900*. New York: Oxford University Press, 1978.

Mollison, Bill. *Permaculture Two: Practical Design for Town and Country in Permanent Agriculture*. 1979. Reprint. Maryborough, Australia: Dominion Press-Hedges & Bell, 1984.

_____, and David Holmgren. *Permaculture One: A Perennial Agriculture for Human Settlements*. 1978. Reprint. Maryborough, Australia: Dominion Press-Hedges & Bell, 1984.

Monter, E. William. "Sodomy and Heresy in Early Modern Switzerland." *Journal of Homosexuality* 6, nos. 1–2 (1980–81): 41–55.

Mood, Fulmer. "John Winthrop, Jr. on Indian Corn." *New England Quarterly* 10, no. 1 (March 1937): 121–33.

Moore, Omar Khayyam. "Divination—A New Perspective." In *Environment and Cultural Behavior: Ecological Studies in Cultural Anthropology*, edited by Andrew P. Vayda, pp. 121–29. Austin: University of Texas Press, 1969.

Morgan, Edmund S. *Gentle Puritan*. New Haven: Yale University Press, 1962.

Morrison, Alvin Hamblen. "Wabanaki Women Extraordinaire: A Sampler from Fact and Fancy." In *Actes du Quatorzieme Congres des Algonquinistes*, edited by William Cowan. Ottawa: Carleton University, 1983.

Morrison, Kenneth. *The Embattled Northeast: The Elusive Ideal of Alliance in Abenaki-Euramerican Relations.* Berkeley: University of California Press, 1984.

_____. "The People of the Dawn: The Abnaki and Their Relations with New England and New France, 1600–1727." Ph.D. dissertation, University of Maine, 1975.

Morton, Charles. *Charles Morton's Compendium Physicae* (from manuscript copy of 1697). Colonial Society of Massachusetts Publications, vol. 33. Boston: Colonial Society of Massachusetts, 1940.

Morton, Thomas. "New English Canaan (1632)." In *Tracts and Other Papers Relating Principally to the Origin, Settlement, and Progress of the Colonies in North America, From the Discovery of the Country to the Year 1776,* 2 vols., edited by Peter Force. Washington: P. Force, 1838.

Mutch, Robert E. "Yeoman and Merchant in Pre-Industrial America: Eighteenth Century Massachusetts as a Case Study." *Societas* 7, no. 4 (Autumn 1977): 279–302.

Naess, Arne. "The Shallow and the Deep, Long-Range Ecology Movements: A Summary." *Inquiry* 16 (1973): 95–100.

Nash, Roderick. *Wilderness and the American Mind.* New Haven: Yale University Press, 1967.

Nebel, Bernard J. *Environmental Science: The Way the World Works.* Englewood Cliffs, N.J.: Prentice-Hall, 1987.

Nelson, Richard K. "The Gifts." *Antaeus* 57 (Autumn 1986): 117–31.

_____. *Make Prayers to the Raven: A Koyukon View of the Northern Forest.* Chicago: University of Chicago Press, 1983.

New Hampshire, State of. *The Compiled Statutes of the State of New Hampshire.* 2d ed. Concord: G. Parker Lyon, 1854.

_____. *The Revised Statutes of the State of New Hampshire, Passed December 23, 1842.* Concord: Carroll & Baker, 1843.

Newton, Isaac. "An Hypothesis Explaining the Properties of Light." In *The Correspondence of Isaac Newton,* edited by H. W. Turnbull, 1:364–66. Cambridge, England: The Royal Society at the University Press, 1959.

Nichols, Charles. *Notes on the Almanacs of Massachusetts.* Worcester, Mass.: American Antiquarian Society, 1912.

Nichols, George E. "The Vegetation of Connecticut: II. Virgin Forests." *Torreya* 13, no. 9 (September 1913): 199–215.

Norton, John P. "The Pursuit of Knowledge Under Difficulties." *The Cultivator,* n.s. 8 (March 1851): 103–4.

Norton, Mary Beth. "The Evolution of White Women's Experience in Early America." *American Historical Review* 89, no. 3 (June 1984): 593–619.

Novak, Barbara. *American Painting of the Nineteenth Century: Realism, Idealism, and the American Experience.* New York: Praeger, 1969.

_____. *Nature and Culture: American Landscape and Painting, 1825–1875.* New York: Oxford University Press, 1980.

Oaks, Robert. "Things Fearful to Name: Sodomy and Buggery in Seventeenth-

Century New England." *Journal of Social History* 12, no. 7 (Fall 1978): 267–81.

Odum, Eugene P. *Fundamentals of Ecology*. Toronto: W. B. Saunders, 1971.

O'Laughlin, Bridget. "Production and Reproduction: Meillassoux's 'Femmes, Greniers et Capitaux.'" *Critique of Anthropology* 2, no. 8 (Spring 1977): 3–33.

[Olbers, Heinrich]. "The Influence of the Moon Upon the Seasons." *New England Farmer* 2, no. 2 (August 9, 1823): 10–11.

Ortega y Gasset, José. *Meditations on Hunting*. New York: Scribner's, 1972.

Ortner, Sherry. "Is Female to Male as Nature Is to Culture?" In *Women, Culture, and Society*, edited by Michele Z. Rosaldo and Louise Lamphere, pp. 67–87. Palo Alto, Calif.: Stanford University Press, 1974.

Orton, Vrest. *The American Cider Book: The Story of America's Natural Beverage*. New York: Farrar, Straus and Giroux, 1973.

Osterud, Nancy, and John Fulton. "Family Limitation and Age at Marriage: Fertility Decline in Sturbridge, Massachusetts, 1730–1850." *Population Studies* 30, no. 5 (1976): 481–94.

Pagel, Walter, and Maryanne Winder. "The Eightness of Adam and Related Gnostic Ideas in the Paracelsian Corpus." *Ambix* 16 (1969): 119–39.

Pagels, Elaine. *The Gnostic Gospels*. New York: Random House, 1979.

_____. "What Became of God the Mother? Conflicting Images of God in Early Christianity." *Signs* 2, no. 2 (Winter 1976): 293–303.

Palmer, Kingsley. *The Folklore of Somerset*. London: B. T. Batsford, 1976.

Palmer, Ralph S. "Late Records of Caribou in Maine." *Journal of Mammology* 19, no. 1 (February 1938): 37–43.

Palmer, Roy. *The Folklore of Warwickshire*. London: B. T. Batsford, 1976.

Parker, Joel. "The Origin, Organization, and Influence of the Towns of New England." *Proceedings of the Massachusetts Historical Society* 9 (1866–67): 14–65.

Parsons, Howard L., ed. *Marx and Engels on Ecology*. Westport, Conn.: Greenwood Press, 1977.

Patent Office Report. "How Cities Exhaust the Fertility of Land." *New England Farmer* 2, no. 16 (August 3, 1850): 261.

Peattie, Donald Culross. *A Natural History of Trees of Eastern and Central North America*. Boston: Houghton Mifflin, 1950.

Pequot Indians. "Petition of the Pequot Indians (September 22, 1735)." In *Collections of the Connecticut Historical Society*, 31 vols., 4:319–23. Hartford: Connecticut Historical Society, 1892.

Peirce, Joseph. "MS. letter of Joseph Peirce, Esq." In Jeremy Belknap, *The History of New Hampshire*, 3 vols., 3:118–19. Dover, N.H.: J. Mann and J. K. Remick, 1812.

Perham, Sidney, Esq. "An Address Delivered Before the Oxford County Agricultural Society, October 6th, 1853." In *Transactions of the Agricultural Societies in the State of Maine for 1853*, edited by E. Holmes, pp. 181–96. Augusta, Maine: William T. Johnson, 1854.

Peterson, Abby. "The Gender-Sex Dimension in Swedish Politics." *Acta*

Sociologica 27, no. 1 (1984): 3–17.

————. *Women in Political "Movement."* Gothenburg, Sweden: University of Gothenburg, 1987.

————, and Carolyn Merchant. " 'Peace with the Earth': Women and the Environmental Movement in Sweden." *Women's Studies International Forum* 9 (1986): 465–79.

Phillips, Ronald, et al. "No-Tillage Agriculture." *Science* 208 (June 6, 1980): 1108–13.

Phillips, S. H., and H. M. Young, Jr. *No Tillage Farming.* Milwaukee, Wis.: Reiman, 1973.

Piper, Charles V., and Katherine S. Bort. "The Early Agricultural History of Timothy." *Journal of the American Society of Agronomy* 7, no. 1 (January– February 1915): 1–14.

Plato. "The Timaeus." In *The Dialogues of Plato*, 2 vols., translated by Benjamin Jowett, 2:3–68. New York: Random House, 1937.

Platt, Sir Hugh. *Jewell House of Art and Nature.* London: Peter Short, 1594.

Plattes, Gabriel. *A Discovery of Infinite Treasure.* London: Printed by I. L. & sold by G. Hutton, 1639.

Pliny. *Natural History.* 6 vols. Translated by J. Bostock and H. D. Riley. London: Bohn, 1858.

Porter, Enid. *Cambridgeshire Customs and Folklore.* London: Routledge and Kegan Paul, 1969.

Powell, Sumner Chilton. *Puritan Village: The Formation of a New England Town.* Middletown, Conn.: Wesleyan University Press, 1963.

Preston, R. A. "The Laconia Company of 1629: An English Attempt to Intercept the Fur Trade." *Canadian Historical Review* 31, no. 2 (June 1950): 125–44.

Prigogine, Ilya. *From Being to Becoming.* San Francisco: Freeman, 1980.

————, and Isabelle Stengers. *Order out of Chaos: Man's New Dialogue with Nature.* Paris, 1979. Reprint. Toronto: Bantam, 1984.

Pring, Martin. "A Voyage Set Out from the Citie of Bristol, 1603." In *Early English and French Voyages, Chiefly from Hakluyt 1534–1608*, edited by Henry S. Burrage, pp. 345–52. New York: Charles Scribner's Sons, 1906.

[Proctor, J. W.]. "Dairy Management." *New England Farmer* 2, nos. 1–3 (January 5, 19, February 2, 1850): 20–23, 36–37, 51–52.

Pruitt, Bettye Hobbs. "Agriculture and Society in the Towns of Massachusetts, 1771: A Statistical Analysis." Ph.D. dissertation, Boston University, 1981.

————. "Communication." *William and Mary Quarterly*, 3d ser. 42, no. 4 (October 1985): 557–60.

————. "Self-Sufficiency and the Agricultural Economy of Eighteenth Century Massachusetts." *William and Mary Quarterly*, 3d ser. 41, no. 3 (July 1984): 333–64.

————, ed. *The Massachusetts Tax Valuation List of 1771.* Boston: G. K. Hall, 1978.

Ptolemaeus, Claudius. *Ptolemy's Tetrabiblos.* London: Davis & Dickson, 1822. Reprint. North Hollywood, Calif.: Symbols and Signs, 1976.

Purchas, Samuel. "The Description of the Country of Mawooshen, Discovered by the English in the Yeere 1602, 3, 5, 6, 7, 8, and 9." In *Hakluytus Posthumus, or Purchas His Pilgrimes*, 19 vols., 19:400–406. Glasgow: James MacLose and Sons, 1906.

Pursell, Carroll. *Early Stationary Steam Engines in America*. Washington, D.C.: Smithsonian Institution Press, 1969.

Rasieres, Isaack de. "Letter of Isaack de Rasieres to Samuel Blommaert, 1628(?)." In *Narratives of New Netherland, 1609–1664*, edited by J. Franklin Jameson, pp. 97–115. New York: Charles Scribner's Sons, 1909.

Rasles, Father Sebastien. "Letter from Father Sebastien Rasles, Missionary of the Society of Jesus in New France, to Monsieur his Brother, October 12, 1723." In *The Jesuit Relations and Allied Documents: Travels and Explorations of the Jesuit Missionaries in New France, 1610–1791*, 73 vols., edited by Reuben Gold Thwaites, 67:133–229. Cleveland: Burrows, 1896–1901.

———. "Letter from Father Sebastien Rasles, Missionary of the Society of Jesus in New France, to Monsieur his Nephew, October 15, 1722." In *The Jesuit Relations and Allied Documents: Travels and Explorations of the Jesuit Missionaries in New France, 1610–1791*, 73 vols., edited by Reuben Gold Thwaites, 67:85–119. Cleveland: Burrows, 1896–1901.

Raup, Hugh M. "Recent Changes of Climate and Vegetation in Southern New England and Adjacent New York." *Journal of the Arnold Arboretum* 18, no. 2 (April 1937): 79–117.

———. "The View from John Sanderson's Farm: A Perspective for the Use of the Land." *Forest History* 10, no. 1 (April 1966): 2–11.

———, and Reynold E. Carlson. "The History of Land Use in the Harvard Forest." *Harvard Forest Bulletin*. Petersham, Mass.: Harvard Forest, 1941.

Reidel, Carl H., ed. *New England Prospects*. Hanover, N.H.: University Press of New England, 1982.

Reiter, Rayna R., ed. *Toward an Anthropology of Women*. New York: Monthly Review Press, 1975.

Repton, John A. "Observations on the Various Fashions of Hats, Bonnets, or Coverings for the Head, Chiefly from the Reign of King Henry VIII to the Eighteenth Century." *Archaeologia* 24 (1832): 168–89.

Rhode Island, State of. *General Laws of Rhode Island, 1956 . . . Completely Annotated*. Indianapolis: Bobbs-Merrill Co., 1956.

Ricklefs, Robert E. *The Economy of Nature: A Textbook in Basic Ecology*. New York: Chiron Press, 1976.

Risch, Stephen J. "Insect Herbivore Abundance in Tropical Monocultures and Polycultures: An Experimental Test of Two Hypotheses." *Ecology* 62, no. 5 (1981): 1325–40.

———, and Michael Hanson. "Population Dynamics of Insect Pests in Mixed Cropping Systems." *Activities at Turrialba* (Costa Rica) 5, no. 4 (1977): 5–7.

Roberts, William I. "The Fur Trade of New England in the Seventeenth Century." Ph.D. dissertation, University of Pennsylvania, 1958.

Rogers, Horatio, and Edward Field, eds. *The Early Records of the Town of Providence*. 21 vols. Providence, R.I.: Snow & Farnham, 1892–1915.

Rogin, Michael. "Nature as Politics and Nature as Romance in America." *Political Theory* 5 (February 1977): 5–30.

[Rosenberry], Lois K. Matthews. *The Expansion of New England: The Spread of New England Settlement and Institutions to the Mississippi River, 1620–1856.* Boston: Houghton Mifflin, 1909.

Rosier, James. "A True Relation of the Voyage of Captain George Waymouth, 1605." In *Early English and French Voyages, Chiefly from Hakluyt, 1534–1608,* edited by Henry S. Burrage, pp. 357–94. New York: Charles Scribner's Sons, 1906.

Rossiter, Margaret W. *The Emergence of Agricultural Science: Justus Liebig and the Americans, 1840–1880.* New Haven: Yale University Press, 1975.

_____. *Women Scientists in America: Struggles and Strategies to 1940.* Baltimore: Johns Hopkins Press, 1982.

Rostlund, Erhard. "The Evidence for the Use of Fish as Fertilizer in Aboriginal North America." *Journal of Geography* 56, no. 5 (May 1957): 222–28.

Rothenberg, Winifred B. "The Market and Massachusetts Farmers." Ph.D. dissertation, Brandeis University, 1984.

_____. "The Market and Massachusetts Farmers, 1750–1855." *Journal of Economic History* 41, no. 2 (June 1981): 283–314.

Rowlandson, Mary. "The Captivity of Mrs. Mary Rowlandson (1682)." In *Narratives of the Indian Wars, 1675–1699,* edited by Charles H. Lincoln, pp. 109–67. New York: Charles Scribner's Sons, 1913.

Rowling, Marjorie. *The Folklore of the Lake District.* London: B. T. Batsford, 1976.

Ruether, Rosemary Radford, and Rosemary Skinner Keller, eds. *Women and Religion in America.* 3 vols. Vol. 1, *The Nineteenth Century.* San Francisco: Harper and Row, 1981.

Rupp, Robert S. "Beaver-Trout Relationship in the Headwaters of Sunkaze Stream, Maine." *American Fisheries Society Transactions* 84 (1954): 75–85.

Russell, Howard. *Indian New England before the Mayflower.* Hanover, N.H.: University Press of New England, 1980.

_____. *A Long, Deep Furrow: Three Centuries of Farming in New England.* Abridged ed. 1976. Reprint. Hanover, N.H.: University Press of New England, 1982.

Rutman, Darrett B. *Husbandmen of Plymouth: Farms and Villages in the Old Colony, 1620–1692.* Boston: Beacon Press, 1967.

_____. "People in Process: The New Hampshire Towns of the Eighteenth Century." *Journal of Urban History* 1, no. 3 (May 1975): 268–92.

_____. *Winthrop's Boston: Portrait of a Puritan Town, 1630–1649.* Chapel Hill: University of North Carolina Press, 1965.

Ryan, Mary. *Womanhood in America from Colonial Times to the Present.* New York: New Viewpoints, 1975.

S., J. G. "Plain Advice to Country Girls." *New England Farmer* 1, no. 21 (September 29, 1849): 332.

Sachs, Carolyn E. *The Invisible Farmers: Women in Agricultural Production.* Totowa, N.J.: Rowman & Allanheld, 1983.

Sagendorph, Robb, ed. *The Old Farmer's Almanac Sampler*. New York: Ives Washburn, Inc., 1957.

Sahlins, Marshall. *Stone Age Economics*. New York: Aldine, 1972.

St. George, Robert Blair. " 'Set Thine House in Order': The Domestication of the Yeomanry in Seventeenth-Century New England." In *New England Begins*, 3 vols., edited by Jonathan L. Fairbanks, 2:159–351. Boston: Museum of Fine Arts, 1982.

Salisbury, Neal. "The Great Awakening and Indian Conversion in Southern New England." In *Papers of the Tenth Algonquian Conference*, edited by William Cowan, pp. 25–36. Ottawa: Carleton University, 1979.

_____. *Manitou and Providence: Indians, Europeans, and the Making of New England, 1500–1643*. New York: Oxford University Press, 1982.

_____. "Red Puritans: The 'Praying Indians' of Massachusetts Bay and John Eliot." *William and Mary Quarterly*, 3d ser. 31, no. 1 (1974): 27–54.

Salwen, Bert. "Indians of Southern New England and Long Island: Early Period." In *Handbook of North American Indians: Vol. 15, Northeast*, edited by Bruce G. Trigger, 15:160–76. Washington, D.C.: Smithsonian Institute, 1978.

Sargent, William M., ed. *York Deeds* (1642–1738). 18 vols. Portland, Maine: J. T. Hull, 1887–96.

Schreiner, Oswald. "Early Fertilizer Work in the United States." *Soil Science* 40, no. 1 (1935): 39–47.

Schuette, H. A., and Sybil C. Schuette. "Maple Sugar: A Bibliography of Early Records." In *Transactions*, 29:209–36. Madison: Wisconsin Academy of Sciences, Arts, and Letters, 1935.

Schumacher, Max George. *The Northern Farmer and His Markets during the Late Colonial Period*. 1948. Reprint. New York: Arno, 1975.

Schwartz, Hillel. "Sun and Salt, 1500–1700." *Diogenes* 117 (January–March 1982): 26–41.

Scoville, Warren C. "Did Colonial Farmers Waste Our Land?" *Southern Economic Journal* 20 (1953): 178–81.

Seebohm [Christie], Mabel Elizabeth. *The Evolution of the English Farm*. London: George Allen & Unwin, 1927.

Sellers, Charles. *The Market Revolution and the Creation of Capitalist Culture, 1815–1846*. New York: Oxford University Press, forthcoming.

Seton, Ernest Thompson. *Lives of Game Animals*. 4 vols. Garden City, N.Y.: Doubleday, Doran, 1929.

Shammas, Carol. "How Self-sufficient Was Early America?" *Journal of Interdisciplinary History* 13, no. 2 (1982): 247–72.

Sharpe, John. "John Sharpe to Francis Wilks." In *Collections of the Connecticut Historical Society*, 31 vols., 5:104–17. Hartford: Connecticut Historical Society, 1896.

Shteir, Ann B. "Linnaeus's Daughters: Women and British Botany." In *Women and the Structure of Society: Selected Research from the Fifth Berkshire Conference on the History of Women*, edited by Barbara J. Harris and JoAnn K. McNamara, pp. 67–73, 261–63. Durham, N.C.: Duke University Press, 1984.

_____. "Priscilla Wakefield's Natural History Books." In *From Linnaeus to*

Darwin: Commentaries on the History of Biology and Geology, edited by Society for the History of Natural History, pp. 29–36. London: Society for the History of Natural History, 1985.

Shurtleff, Nathaniel B., ed. *Records of the Colony of New Plymouth in New England.* 12 vols. Boston: William White, 1855–61.

———, ed. *Records of the Governor and Company of the Massachusetts Bay in New England.* Boston: William White, 1854.

Sibley, John L. *History of the Town of Union in the County of Lincoln, Maine to the Middle of the Nineteenth Century . . .* Boston: Benjamin B. Mussey, 1851.

Siebert, Frank. "The First Maine Indian War: Incident at Machias (1676)." In *Actes du Quatorzieme Congres des Algonquinistes.* Ottawa: Carleton University, 1983.

Simmons, Amelia. *The First American Cookbook: A Facsimile of "American Cookery," 1796.* New York: Dover, 1984.

Simmons, William. "Conversion from Indian to Puritan." *New England Quarterly* 52, no. 2 (1979): 197–218.

———. "The Great Awakening and Indian Conversion in Southern New England." In *Papers of the Tenth Algonquian Conference*, edited by William Cowan, pp. 25–36. Ottawa: Carleton University, 1979.

———. "Red Yankees: Narragansett Conversion in the Great Awakening." *American Ethnologist* 10, no. 2 (1983): 253–71.

———. *Spirit of the New England Tribes: Indian History and Folklore, 1620–1984.* Hanover, N.H.: University Press of New England, 1986.

———, and George Aubin. "Narragansett Kinship." *Man in the Northeast* 9 (1975): 21–31.

Slocum, Sally. "Woman the Gatherer." In *Toward an Anthropology of Women*, edited by Rayna R. Reiter, pp. 36–50. New York: Monthly Review Press, 1975.

Smart, Jesse. "Wood and Timber Lands, Planting Forest Trees, &c." *New England Farmer* 1, no. 1 (December 9, 1848): 5.

Smith, Adam. *An Inquiry into the Nature and Causes of the Wealth of Nations* (1776). Edited by James E. Thorold Rogers. 2 vols. Oxford, England: Clarendon Press, 1869.

Smith, Daniel Scott. "Family Limitation, Sexual Control, and Domestic Feminism in Victorian America." *Feminist Studies* 1, nos. 3–4 (1973): 40–57.

Smith, David C. *A History of Lumbering in Maine, 1861–1960.* Orono: University of Maine Studies, 1972.

———. "The Logging Frontier." *Forest History* 18, no. 4 (October 1974): 97–106.

Smith, James M., ed. *Seventeenth Century America: Essays in Colonial History.* Chapel Hill: University of North Carolina Press, 1959.

Smith, John. *A Description of New England.* London: Humphrey Lownes, 1616.

———. "New England's Trials (London, 1620)." In *Proceedings of the Massachusetts Historical Society, 1871–1873.* Boston: Massachusetts Historical Society, 1873.

Smith-Rosenberg, Carroll. *Disorderly Conduct: Visions of Gender in Victorian America*. New York: Alfred A. Knopf, 1985.

———. "Sex as Symbol in Victorian Purity: An Ethnohistorical Analysis of Jacksonian America." In *Turning Points: Historical and Sociological Essays on the Family*, edited by John Demos and Sarane Spence Boocook, *American Journal of Sociology*, 84 Supplement: S212–47. Chicago: University of Chicago Press, 1978.

Snow, Dean R. "Abenaki Fur Trade in the Sixteenth Century." *Western Canadian Journal of Anthropology* 6, no. 1 (1976): 3–11.

———. *The Archeology of New England*. New York: Academic Press, 1980.

———. "Keepers of the Game and the Nature of Explanation." In *Indians, Animals, and the Fur Trade*, edited by Shepard Krech III, pp. 59–71. Athens: University of Georgia Press, 1981.

———. "The Solon Petroglyphs and Eastern Abnaki Shamanism." *Papers of the Seventh Algonquian Conference, 1975*, edited by William Cowan, pp. 281–96. Ottawa: Carleton University, 1976.

———. "Wabanaki 'Family Hunting Territories.'" *American Anthropologist* 70, nos. 4–6 (August–December 1968): 1143–51.

Speck, Frank. *Penobscot Man: The Life History of a Forest Tribe in Maine*. Philadelphia: University of Pennsylvania Press, 1940.

———. "Penobscot Shamanism." *Memoirs of the American Anthropological Association* 6 (1919): 238–88.

———. "Penobscot Tales and Religious Beliefs." *Journal of American Folklore* 48, no. 187 (January–March 1935): 1–107.

Spedding, C. R. W. *The Biology of Agricultural Systems*. New York: Academic Press, 1975.

Speed, Adolphus. *Adam out of Eden*. London, 1659.

Stanford, Donald E. "The Giant Bones of Claverack, New York, 1705." *New York History* 40, no. 1 (January 1959): 47–61.

Staples, Daniel. "Instructions for Farmers." *New England Farmer* 1, no. 43 (May 24, 1823): 339.

Stilgoe, John R. *Common Landscape of America, 1580–1845*. New Haven: Yale University Press, 1982.

Stowell, Marion B. *Early American Almanacs: The Colonial Weekday Bible*. New York: Burt Franklin, 1977.

Strachey, William. "Extract from the Second Book of the First Decade of the Historie of Travaile into Virginia Britannia . . . as Also of the Northern Colonie, Seated Upon the River Sachadehoc, Transported at the Charge of Sir John Popham . . ." In *Collections of the Maine Historical Society*, 3:288. Portland: Maine Historical Society, 1853.

[Stuart, Kevin]. "My Friend, the Soil: A Conversation with Hans Jenny." *Journal of Soil and Water Conservation* 39, no. 3 (May–June 1984): 158–61.

Stubbes, Phillip. *Anatomie of Abuses*. London: Richard Jones, 1585.

Swift, Mary. *First Lessons on Natural Philosophy, Part Second*. Hartford: William J. Hamersley, 1862.

Talcott, Governor. "Governor Talcott to Francis Wilks (Hartford, Sept. 17, 1736)." In *Collections of the Connecticut Historical Society*, 31 vols., 4:376–

78. Hartford: Connecticut Historical Society, 1892.

———. "Governor Talcott to Francis Wilks (January 11, 1739/40)." In *Collections of the Connecticut Historical Society*, 31 vols., 5:195–208. Hartford: Connecticut Historical Society, 1896.

Taussig, Michael. "The Genesis of Capitalism amongst a South American Peasantry: Devil's Labor and the Baptism of Money." *Comparative Studies in Society and History* 19 (April 1977): 130–53.

Taylor, Charles. "Neutrality in Political Science." In *The Philosophy of Social Explanation*, edited by Alan Ryan, pp. 139–70. London: Oxford University Press, 1973.

Taylor, Edward. "The Description of the Great Bones Dug Up at Claverack on the Banks of Hudsons River, A.D. 1705," in Donald E. Stanford, "The Giant Bones of Claverack, New York, 1705." *New York History* 40, no. 1 (January 1959): 47–61.

Thacher, James. "Observations Upon the Natural Production of Iron Ores." In *Collections of the Massachusetts Historical Society*, 10 vols., 1st ser., 9:253–68. Boston: Monroe & Francis, 1804.

Thaer, Albrecht D. *The Principles of Agriculture.* 4 vols. 1809–12. Reprint. London: Ridgway, 1844.

Thomas, Keith. *Religion and the Decline of Magic.* New York: Charles Scribner's Sons, 1971.

Thomas, Peter Allen. "Contrastive Subsistence Strategies and Land Use as Factors for Understanding Indian-White Relations in New England." *Ethnohistory* 23, no. 1 (Winter 1976): 1–18.

———. "In the Maelstrom of Change: The Indian Trade and Cultural Process in the Middle Connecticut River Valley: 1635–1665." Ph.D. dissertation, University of Massachusetts, 1979.

Thomas, Robert B. *The Old Farmer's Almanac.* Boston: Apollo Press, 1793–1847.

Thompson, F. M. L. "The Second Agricultural Revolution, 1815–1880." *Economic History Review* 21, no. 1 (April 1968): 62–77.

Thomson, Betty Flanders. *The Changing Face of New England.* 1958. Reprint. Boston: Houghton Mifflin, 1977.

Thoreau, Henry David. "Huckleberries." In *The Natural History Essays*, pp. 211–62. Salt Lake City: Peregrine Smith Books, 1984.

———. "Journal." In *Works*. 20 vols. Walden ed. Boston: Houghton Mifflin Co., 1906.

———. *The Natural History Essays.* Salt Lake City: Peregrine Smith Books, 1980.

———. *The Portable Thoreau.* Edited by Carl Bode. New York: Penguin, 1977.

———. "The Succession of Forest Trees (1860)." In *The Natural History Essays*, pp. 72–92. Salt Lake City: Peregrine Smith Books, 1984.

———. *Walden, or Life in the Woods and On the Duty of Civil Disobedience.* 1854. Reprint. New York: Harper and Row, 1965.

———. "Wild Apples." In *The Natural History Essays*, pp. 178–210. Salt Lake City: Peregrine Smith Books, 1984.

Thresh, J. M., ed. *Pests, Pathogens and Vegetation.* London: Pitman, 1981.

Thwaites, Reuben Gold, ed. *The Jesuit Relations and Allied Documents: Travels and Explorations of the Jesuit Missionaries in New France, 1610–1791.* 73 vols. Cleveland: Burrows, 1896–1901.

Todd, Sereno E. *The Young Farmer's Manual.* 2 vols. New York: F. W. Woodward, 1867.

Tongue, R. L., and K. M. Briggs, eds. *Somerset Folklore.* London: The Folklore Society, 1965.

Topsell, Edward. *Historie of Foure-Footed Beastes.* London: W. Jaggard, 1607.

Toulmin, Stephen. "The Inwardness of Mental Life." *Critical Inquiry* 6, nos. 1–2 (Autumn 1979): 1–16.

Townsend, John E., Jr. "Looking for the Simple Life." *Whole Earth Review,* no. 56 (Fall 1987): 88–94.

True, N. T., M.D. "An Address Delivered Before the Cumberland County Agricultural Society in Portland, on the Evening of Wednesday, October 19, 1853." In *Transactions of the Agricultural Societies in the State of Maine for 1853,* edited by E. Holmes, pp. 1–32. Augusta, Maine: William T. Johnson, 1854.

Tryon, Rolla Milton. *Household Manufactures in the United States, 1640–1860.* New York: Augustus M. Kelley, 1966.

Tuan, Yi-fu. *The Hydrologic Cycle and the Wisdom of God: A Theme in Geoteleology.* Toronto: University of Toronto Department of Geography and the University of Toronto Press, 1968.

Tulley, John. *An Almanack.* Boston: n.p., 1687, 1688, 1693.

Ulrich, Laurel T. " 'A Friendly Neighbor': Social Dimensions of Daily Work in Northern Colonial New England." *Feminist Studies* 6, no. 2 (Summer 1980): 392–405.

_____. *Good Wives: Image and Reality in the Lives of Women in Northern New England, 1650–1750.* New York: Alfred A. Knopf, 1982.

U.S. Department of Agriculture. *Atlas of American Agriculture.* Washington, D.C.: U.S. Government Printing Office, 1936.

_____. *The Changing Fertility of New England Soils.* Agricultural Information Bulletin No. 133. Washington, D.C.: U.S. Government Printing Office, 1954.

_____. *Conversion Factors and Weights and Measures for Agricultural Commodities and Their Products.* Statistical Bulletin no. 362. Washington, D.C.: U.S. Government Printing Office, 1965.

[Vallemont, Pierre Le Lorrain, Abbé de]. *Curiosities of Nature and Art in Husbandry and Gardening.* London: Printed for D. Brown, A. Roper, and Fran. Coggan, 1707.

Van Wassenaer, Nicolaes. "Historisch Verhael (1624–1630)." In *Narratives of New Netherland, 1609–1664,* edited by J. Franklin Jameson, pp. 61–96. New York: Charles Scribner's Sons, 1909.

Vaughan, Alden T. "English Policy and the Massacre of 1622." *William and Mary Quarterly* 35 (January 1978): 57–84.

Vaughan, Benjamin. "An Account of the Method of Preparing Woodlands for Cultivation, used in the vicinity of Maine, From Latitude 44 to Latitude 45 North," in Gilbert Chinard, "The American Philosophical Society and the

Early History of Forestry in America." *Proceedings of the American Philo-sophical Society* 89, no. 2 (July 18, 1945): 444–88.

Vayda, Andrew P., ed. *Environment and Cultural Behavior: Ecological Studies in Cultural Anthropology.* Austin: University of Texas Press, 1969.

Vermont, State of. *Acts and Laws Passed by the Legislature.* Rutland: William Fay, 1811.

———. *The Revised Statutes of the State of Vermont, Passed November 19, 1839.* Burlington: Chauncey Goodrich, 1840.

Vickers, Daniel. "Communication." *William and Mary Quarterly*, 3d ser. 42, no. 4 (October 1985): 553–55.

Vinovskis, Maris A. *Fertility in Massachusetts from the Revolution to the Civil War.* New York: Academic Press, 1981.

Wakefield, Joanna, to John White. "Warrenty Deed." East Montpelier [Vermont] Land Records, bk. 2, p. 332. May 6, 1856.

Walcott, Robert R. "Husbandry in Colonial New England." *New England Quarterly* 9, no. 2 (June 1936): 218–52.

Walker, Mildred. *The Southwest Corner.* New York: Harcourt Brace, 1951.

Ware, Norman. *The Industrial Worker, 1840–1860: The Reaction of American Industrial Society to the Advance of the Industrial Revolution.* New York: Houghton Mifflin Company, 1924.

Warren, Karen J. "Feminism and Ecology: Making Connections." *Environmental Ethics* 9, no. 1 (Spring 1987): 3–44.

Washburn, Wilcomb E. "The Moral and Legal Justification for Dispossessing the Indian." In *Seventeenth Century America: Essays in Colonial History*, edited by James M. Smith, pp. 15–32. Chapel Hill: University of North Carolina Press, 1959.

Webster, Noah. "An Address Delivered Before the Hampshire, Franklin and Hampden Agricultural Society, at their Annual Meeting in Northampton, October 14th, 1818." *The Rural Magazine and Farmer's Monthly Museum* 1, nos. 1, 3 (March, April 1819): 50–53, 83–86.

Weiskel, Timothy. "Agents of Empire: Steps towards an Ecology of Imperialism." *Environmental Review* 11, no. 4 (Winter 1987): 275–88.

Weld, Isaac. *Travels Through the States of North America and the Provinces of Upper and Lower Canada During the Years 1795, 1796, and 1797.* 2 vols. 2d ed. London: John Stockdale, 1799.

Wells, Robert. "Revolutions in Childbearing in Nineteenth-Century America." In *Uncle Sam's Family.* Albany: State University of New York Press, 1985.

Welter, Barbara. "The Cult of True Womanhood, 1820–1860." *American Quarterly* 18 (Summer 1966): 151–74.

Westveld, Marinus, et al. "Natural Forest Vegetation Zones of New England." *Journal of Forestry* 54, no. 5 (May 1956): 332–38.

White, Anna, and Leila S. Taylor. *Shakerism: Its Meaning and Message.* Columbus, Ohio: Fred J. Herr, 1904.

White, Caroline Barrett. *Diary* (1849–50). Worcester, Mass.: American Antiquarian Society, 1849–1915.

White, Hayden. "The Forms of Wildness: Archeology of an Idea." In *The Wild Man Within*, edited by Edward Dudley and Maximillian E. Novak, pp. 3–38.

Pittsburgh: University of Pittsburgh Press, 1972.

Whitlock, Ralph. *The Folklore of Devon*. London: B. T. Batsford, 1977.

[Whittemore, Nathaniel]. *An Almanack*. Boston: B. Green, 1713.

Wilbur, C. Keith. *The New England Indians*. Chester, Conn.: Globe Pequot Press, 1978.

Wilford, John Noble. *The Mapmakers*. New York: Knopf, 1981.

Wilkinson, Ronald Sterne. "The Alchemical Library of John Winthrop, Jr. (1606–1676) and His Descendants in Colonial America." *Ambix* 11, no. 1 (1963): 33–51.

———. "New England's Last Alchemists." *Ambix* 10, no. 3 (1962): 128–38.

Wilks, Francis. "Francis Wilks to Governor Talcott (London, Aug. 19, 1736)." In *Collections of the Connecticut Historical Society*, 4:374–75. Hartford: Connecticut Historical Society, 1892.

Willard, Samuel. *A Compleat Body of Divinity*. Boston: Printed by B. Green & S. Kneeland for B. Eliot & S. Henchman, 1726.

Williams, Michael. "Products of the Forest: Mapping the Census of 1840." *Journal of Forest History* 24, no. 1 (January 1980): 4–23.

Williams, Roger. *A Key into the Language of America: Or, An Help to the Language of the Natives in that Part of America, called New England*. London, 1643. Reprint. Providence, R.I.: Publications of the Narragansett Club, 1866.

Williams, Samuel. *The Natural and Civil History of Vermont*. 2 vols. Burlington, Vt.: Samuel Mills, 1809.

Williamson, Hugh. "An Attempt to Account for the Change of Climate Which Has Been Observed in the Middle Colonies of North America, (1770)." *Transactions of the American Philosophical Society* 1 (1789): 336–45.

Willis, William. *History of Portland From 1632–1864*. Portland, Maine: Baily & Noyes, 1865.

Willoughby, Charles C. "Houses and Gardens of the New England Indians." *American Anthropologist*, n.s. 8 (1906): 115–32.

Wills, Garry. *Inventing America: Jefferson's Declaration of Independence*. Garden City, N.Y.: Doubleday, 1978.

Wilson, Harold Fisher. *The Hill Country of Northern New England: Its Social and Economic History, 1790–1930*. New York: AMS Press, 1967.

Winslow, Edward. "Letter (1621)." In *The Story of the Pilgrim Fathers: 1606–1623 A.D.*, edited by Edward Arber, pp. 488–94. Boston: Houghton Mifflin, 1897.

[Winthrop, John, Jr.]. "Description, Culture, and Use of Maize." *Philosophical Transactions of the Royal Society of London*, no. 142 (1678): 1066.

Winthrop, John, Jr. "Indian Corne," in Fulmer Mood, "John Winthrop, Jr. on Indian Corn." *New England Quarterly* 10, no. 1 (March 1937): 121–33.

Witthoft, John. *Green Corn Ceremonialism in the Eastern Woodlands*. Ann Arbor: University of Michigan Press, 1949.

Wolin, Sheldon. *Politics and Vision*. Boston: Little Brown, 1960.

Women's Work Study Group. "Loom, Broom, and Womb: Producers, Maintainers, and Reproducers." *Radical America* 10, no. 2 (March–April 1976): 29–45.

Wood, Richard G. "A History of Lumbering in Maine, 1820–1861." *Maine Bul-*

letin 37, no. 7 (January 1935): 1–267.

Wood, William. *New England's Prospect*. London: Thomas Cotes, 1634.

Woolley, Mary E. "The Development of the Love of Romantic Scenery in America." *American Historical Review* 3 (October 1897–July 1898): 56–66.

Worlidge, John. *Systema Agriculturae, Being the Mystery of Husbandry Discovered and Layd Open*. London: Printed by T. Johnson for S. Speed, 1668.

Worster, Donald. *Nature's Economy: A History of Ecological Ideas*. New York: Cambridge University Press, 1985.

Wright, John K. "Regions and Landscapes of New England." In *New England's Prospect*, edited by James T. Adams et al., pp. 14–45. 1933. Reprint. New York: AMS Press, 1970.

Wyllys, Gov. George. "Letter of Gov. George Wyllys to George Wyllys (1644)." In *Collections of the Connecticut Historical Society*, 21:67. Hartford: Connecticut Historical Society, 1924.

Yarranton, Andrew. *The Improvement Improved; by a second edition of the Great Improvement of Lands by Clover: Or, the Wonderful Advantage by, and Right Management of Clover*. London: J. C. for Francis Rea, 1663.

Young, Iris. "Socialist Feminism and the Limits of Dual Systems Theory." *Socialist Review* 10, nos. 2–3 (March–June 1980): 169–88.

Zirkle, Conway. "To Plow or not to Plow: Comment on the Planters' Problems." *Agricultural History* 43, no. 1 (January 1969): 87–89.

Zuckerman, Michael. "Pilgrims in the Wilderness: Community, Modernity, and the Maypole at Merry Mount." *New England Quarterly* 50, no. 2 (1977): 255–77.

Index

Key to abbreviations: f = figure,
m = map, t = table.

Abenaki, 44, 55; women, 38, 48; reproduction and subsistence of, 38,
52–58; worldview of, 47–49; breakdown of culture of, 50–52, 61–62;
crisis in reproduction of, 56; convert to Christianity, 59–60; caught
between French and English, 60.
See also Indians
Adam, 168
Adams, John, 200
Adams, John Quincy, 202
Agriculture: subsistence farming,
99–100, 113, 155–56, 175–85; crop
rotation, 118, 132, 163, 165, 205;
agricultural ecology, 153–56, 163–
66; girdle and burn method, 156,
159–60; methods of, 156, 163–65,
169, 211–17; "intensive system,"
156, 189–90; cut and burn method,
160–62; food preservation, 171;
poultry raising, 171; biological
control of insects, 268–69. *See also*
Dairying; "Extensive system" of
land use; Farming; Gardens; Indian horticulture; Livestock; Market agriculture
Agroecological unit, 153
Agroecology, 268
Agroecosystem, 153
Air, 121, 123, 137; as exhalations of
earth, 132–33; pollution, 232–33,
241–42
Alchemy, 9, 116, 119; Newton on,
122–23

Alcohol: lacking in Indian diet, 83
Alfisols, 30, 32m
Almagest (Ptolemy), 115
Almanac (Nathaniel Ames), 200
Almanacs, 115, 133–45, 171, 212; as
records of use value economy,
172–74; and conservation con-
sciousness, 228. *See also* individual
almanacs
Almy, William, 236
American Agriculturalist, 209
American Husbandry (anonymous),
189
American Revolution, 188
Ames, Nathaniel, 135, 140, 200–201,
212
Analytic consciousness, 21–22, 25t,
149
Anatomie of Abuses (Philip Stubbes),
42
Andrews, Joseph, 173
Animals: as consumers, 6f, 8; as
equals of Indians, 29, 68; role in
creating landscape, 36; Greek
view of, 39–40; Hebrew-Christian
view of, 40; as ancestors of native
Americans, 44–47; treatment of
remains of, 47, 48; game, 47–48,
49, 82; powers of, 49; extermina-
tions of, 61, 62, 65, 66–67; colonial
denigration of, 62–65, 100; European ecological complex of, 85, 86,
88f. *See also* individual animals
Anima mundi, 115, 131, 255
Animism, 23, 125, 137–38, 142–43,
149; of Indians, 24–25t; supplanted
by transcendence, 58, 61, 68; vege-

tative, 74, 125; purged by modernists, 127; vestiges of in transcendentalism, 254; replaced by mechanism, 260
Antinomianism, 129
Aristotle, 113, 137, 172
"Artificial Propagation of Fish, The" (George Perkins Marsh), 240
Astrology, 115–16, 133–34, 140, 305 (n. 43), 307 (n. 53); Man of the Signs, 135, 136*f*
Astronomical Diary, An (Nathanael Low), 137, 141, 212
Astronomy: Indian, 77
Avery, James, 93
Awashonks: Sakonnet squasachem, 84

Bacon, Francis, 127, 203, 260
Barrett family, 168
Bartering, 111, 150, 173, 190
Bartlett, M. B., 203
Barton, Benjamin Smith, 66
Base/superstructure theory, 3, 4
Bates, James, 247
Bateson, Gregory, 267
Batson, John, 58
Beavers: meadows created by, 36; dams of, 37, 87; pelts of made into hats, 42, 43*f*; offspring nursed by Abenaki women, 48; decimation of population, 61–62, 66; trapping of, 65–66. *See also* Fur trade
Bees: raising of, 170–71
Behaim, Martin, 51
Belknap, Jeremy, 158, 221
Benton, Thomas Hart, 202
Berkshires, 30
Bestiality, 40, 41; outlawed by Puritans, 63; as male counterpart to witchcraft, 106
Bible: effect upon Indians, 97; translated into Massachuset dialect, 97; and women, 108; used to legitimate manifest destiny, 202; evoked to subdue wilderness, 203
Biogeochemical cycles, 6*f*, 7

Biological reproduction. *See* Reproduction—biological
Bioregionalism, 266*t*
Black bears: habitat of destroyed, 66
Blackstone Canal, 193
Blackstone River, 195, 236
Blaeu, Willem Janszoon, 52, 53*f*
Blith, Walter, 118, 137
Bohm, David, 267
Boyle, Robert, 127, 137
Bradford, William, 78, 90, 101, 104, 105
Bridenthal, Renaté, 18
Brodt, Ellen, 184
Brown, Moses, 236, 240
Bruno, Giordano, 9
Buel, Jesse, 213, 218
Buffalo: disappear with colonization, 67
Bullard, John, 204
Bulkeley, Peter, 102

Caliban, 41
Calvinism, 108, 128, 129. *See also* Puritans
Cape Cod, 33
Capitalism: market expansion, 12, 188, 193; and reproduction, 17, 242–47; early industries of, 126; effects on environment, 223, 225–26, 232–33, 240, 242; and global ecological revolution, 264. *See also* Capitalist ecological revolution; Market agriculture; Mercantilism; Production
Capitalist ecological revolution, 24–25*t*, 119, 196–97, 231; period of, 2, 198; origins of, 113, 145, 185, 187, 188, 193, 196; and reproduction, 149, 175–90. *See also* Capitalism; Ecological revolution
Caribou: depletion of, 67
Cartesian grid: of industrial society, 24*t*; foreshadowed by colonial towns, 109
Cartier, Jacques, 52, 53
Catechism of Agricultural Chemistry

and Geology (James F. W. Johnston), 208

Cautantowwit, 70

Ceres, 5

Chadwick, Joseph, 62

Champlain, Samuel de, 52, 54, 56

Change theory, 6–7*f*, 13, 23, 265, 324 (n. 7)

Chaos theory, 268

Chastellux, Marquis de, 227

Cheese: making of, 169–70

Chemical paradigm, 205–11, 220

Chemical pesticides, 263

Chemistry of Vegetable and Animal Physiology (Johann Mulder), 208

Chiefs. *See* Sachems; Squasachems

Child, Lydia, 179

Childbearing: decline in, 244, 264

Children: role in Indian horticulture, 79

Christian Philosopher (Cotton Mather), 131

Christianity, 201; ethic of, 60–61; Indians convert to, 96–97; view of nature in, 100; evangelical, 129. *See also* Bible

"Civilizing" process, 41

Clark, Mr. (Wakefield, N.H., farmer), 173

Clarke, Samuel, 128

Climate, 226

Clinton, Gov. De Witt, 227

Cohoon, Hannah, 250

Cole, S. W., 246

Cole, Thomas, 251

Collins, Judith, 250

Colman, Henry, 203, 214, 219, 257

Colonial consciousness. *See* Consciousness—colonial

Colonial ecological revolution, 24–25*t*, 65–68, 69, 125, 144, 145; summary of, 2, 67–68, 230; and Indian dependence, 55–56; property relations between Indians and colonists, 57, 61–62; externally caused, 85, 109; marshes drained by colonists, 87; and reproduction, 91;

downfall of Indian subsistence, 92; origins of, 109; expansion of, 112

Colton, Calvin, 202

Commodities: in market system, 11, 172, 173; natural resources as, 24*t*, 98

Commons: supplement subsistence of farmers, 176–77, 183

Communism: of Shakers, 249

Community: social reproduction of, 16; organic, 98; cooperative, 172, 173–74

Compendium Physicae, 130, 142

Composting, 206, 212

Computer Age, 262

Concord, Mass., 162–63, 187, 189, 193, 282–85

Connecticut, 33, 178, 180, 188; Valley, 31; last wolf killed in, 67; corn festival in, 73

Connecticut River: trade networks along, 98

Connecticut Valley tribes. *See* Southern New England tribes

Consciousness, 19–23, 24–25*t*, 266*t*; forms of, 2, 22, 259; defined, 19; perceptions of time, 51; worldview defined, 70; postindustrial transformation of, 265–68. *See also* Modernity

—capitalist. *See* Modernity

—colonial, 98, 110, 134; as visual, 2, 22, 25*t*, 49, 85, 96, 112; analogical thinking, 25*t*; transcendence, 58–61, 68, 114, 144; toward animals, 62–65; origins of, 114–16; expressed in farming rituals, 116–18; ecological worldview of eighteenth century, 128; loss of efficacy of, 197. *See also* Participatory consciousness

—mimetic. *See* Mimetic consciousness

Conservation: emerging consciousness of, 227–28; and women, 252. *See also* Preservationism

Constitution, U.S., 200

Copernicus, Nicholaus, 115; heliocentric hypothesis of, 112; system of, 134, 135, 260

Corn: corn, bean, and squash complex, 69, 79, 80, 164, 165, 215; Indian's caloric intake of, 75t, 76, 80; yields of, 78, 80, 87, 180, 215. *See also* Diet

Corn Mother, 24t, 72–74; legends of, 72–73, 80; linked with crows, 73; farming system collapses, 85–92

Corporea mundi, 115

Cosmology: colonial, 23, 113–16; organic cosmos, 25t, 119, 134, 137–38, 218; of Indians, 70–74, 77; heliocentric hypothesis, 112; Copernican system, 112, 135, 260; geocentric cosmos, 112, 140; Judeo-Christian, 114; cyclical cosmos, 122–26, 303 (n. 10); hierarchical cosmos, 123, 131; mechanistic cosmos, 128. *See also* Astrology; Earth; Moon; Sun

Cotton, John, 98, 102, 107

Craig, Daniel, 215

Credit: early debtors, 99; and account books, 214

Crèvecoeur, J. Hector St. John de, 64–65, 222

Crop rotation, 118, 132, 163, 165, 205

Crows: in vegetative myths, 72–73; warding off, 79, 142

Cultivator, 209

Curiosities of Nature and Art in Husbandry and Gardening (Pierre Le Lorrain, Abbé de Vallemont), 123, 124f, 209

Cycles: biogeochemical, 6f, 7; of nature and women, 105; hydrologic, 119, 122; lunar, 122; meteorologic, 122; solar cycle, 122; cosmic, 122–26, 303 (n. 10)

Dairying, 169–70, 234, 235

Dana, Samuel L., 206, 208

Daughters: and inheritance practices, 185–86; role in dairying, 235

Davy, Sir Humphrey, 206

Dawn Land People, 44. *See also* Abenaki

Day, Mr. (of York County, Maine), 216

Deane, Samuel, 219

Declaration of Independence, 200

Dedham, Mass., 99, 100

Demeter, 5

Denham, John, 11

Depopulation: of Indians, 90, 91

Depression: of 1640s, 98

Descartes, René, 127, 199

Dialectics, 10, 13, 270; of production and reproduction, 18–19

Dialectics of Nature (Friedrich Engels), 10

"Dialectics of Production and Reproduction in History" (Renaté Bridenthal), 18

Diet: of Indians, 64, 75t, 81–82, 83; caloric intake of corn, 75t, 76, 80; of colonists, 169–72, 177, 184; subsistence requirements of farm families, 180, 183–84, 297 (n. 24), 314 (nn. 64, 65), 315 (n. 66)

Digby, Kenelm, 120–21, 257

Discourse Concerning the Vegetation of Plants (Kenelm Digby), 120

Diseases: of Indians, 56, 86, 90

Divination: of Indians, 49

Druillettes, Gabriel, 58–60

Dualism, 25t, 102

Dwight, Timothy, 189

Earth: interior of, 7, 122; *ohke*, 70; as animate, 119–20, 126, 149, 306–7 (n. 52); fertility of explained, 121; regions of, 131; as unconscious, 133; as laboratory, 210. *See also* Cycles; Mother Earth; Nature

"Earth apple," 51, 262

Earth Mother. *See* Mother Earth

Earthquakes, 140, 306–7 (n. 52)

Eaton, Amos, 252

Eaton, H. M., 202, 214

Eclipses, 135

Ecocentric ethic, 263

Ecodevelopment, 265
Ecofeminism, 269
Ecological revolution, 1–2; defined, 1, 3, 6*f*, 23; and historical approach to ecology, 1, 4, 287 (n. 2); environmental history defined, 5; and ecological approach to history, 7; causes of, 18, 19; ecological breakdown, 26. *See also* Consciousness; Ecology; Production; Reproduction
—capitalist. *See* Capitalist ecological revolution
—colonial. *See* Colonial ecological revolution
—global. *See* Global ecological revolution
Ecological succession, 8. *See also* Plants: succession of
Ecological worldview, 8–9, 263–64; view of nature, 23, 263
Ecology, 4, 8, 9, 153, 263, 268; historical approach to, 1, 4; ecological core, 5, 6*f*; ecological breakdown, 26; original New England habitat, 29–39; colonial ecological complex, 86; marshes drained, 87; tension with production, 187; farm, 193; habitats destroyed under industrialism, 264; "of mind," 267. *See also* Agriculture: agricultural ecology; Ecological revolution; Externalities
Economy: Indian, 18, 85; colonial, 99, 149–50, 172–74; coexistence of market and subsistence economies, 150; transition to capitalist, 197 (*see also* Capitalism)
Edwards, Jonathan, 129
Elements of Agricultural Chemistry (Sir Humphrey Davy), 206
Eliot, Jared, 141, 142
Eliot, John, 97
Elites: colonial, 98, 108, 112, 113, 130; shift toward mechanism of, 128, 144, 145; and almanacs, 134–35; respond to nature, 254
Emerson, George B., 228

Emerson, Ralph Waldo, 254, 255, 256
Emery, Sarah Anna, 170
Endelechia, 255
Energy: required for reproduction, 15–17
Engels, Friedrich: base/superstructure theory of, 3–4; on ecological interactions, 10; on reproduction of daily life, 17; on earth as object of huckstering, 223; on interaction between production and reproduction, 289 (n. 17)
Entisols, 32–33*m*
Environmental ethics, 263, 267, 270; and dynamic theory of change, 13, 265, 324 (n. 7); ecological thinking, 23; equality of animals, 29, 68; Indian, 47; conservation consciousness, 227–28; in transcendentalism, 253, 254–58; preservationism, 256–57, 258, 262
Environmental history, 5
Epidemics, 56, 86; epidemic of 1616, 90
Erdapfel (earth apple), 51
Erie Canal: opening of, 195
Essays Upon Field Husbandry (Jared Eliot), 141
Ethics. *See* Environmental ethics
Europeans: view of animals, 39–42; fashions of, 42, 43*f*; bring tetrad of crops to New World, 86, 164
Eve, 108, 168
Evelyn, John, 121, 137, 257, 304 (n. 16)
Evolutionary succession, 8, 29. *See also* Plants: succession of
Exchange: in production, 6*f*, 11
Exchange value: economy of, 25*t*; compared to use value, 172
Exogenous additions and withdrawals, 6*f*
Exports: from colonies, 99
"Extensive system" of land use, 24*t*, 155, 156, 185, 186, 187, 188, 193, 196
Externalities: of capitalism, 2, 223–26, 232, 262–63

Extinctions. *See* Animals: extermina-
tions of

Fallow: long-fallow system, 24*t*, 155,
156, 157, 158; fields, 74, 76, 120,
122
Familiar Lectures on Botany (Almira
Hart Lincoln Phelps), 252
Familiar Lessons in Minerology
(Jane Kilby Welsh), 252
Farmers: female, 74–81, 150, 152,
153, 167–72, 183, 216–17, 312
(n. 37); cosmology of and role in
cosmos, 113–16, 123, 130, 210, 215;
rituals of, 116–18; become chemists, 209–10, 215; entrepreneurial
values of, 213, 215–17; journals
and societies, 215; resist new technologies, 217–20. *See also* Almanacs; Farms; Indian horticulture
Farmer's Almanac (Nathaniel Whittmore), 135
Farming: subsistence, 99–100, 113,
155–56, 175–85; supplemented by
commons, 176–77; mechanism of,
211–17; decline of, 261. *See also*
Agriculture; Indian horticulture
Farms: size and division of, 18, 163–
64, 182–83, 185; of preindustrial
family, 25*t*, 57; inland, 157, 159*f*;
and problems of ecology, 193;
abandonment of, 195–96, 196*f*
Fatalism: of colonists, 25*t*, 108
Federalists, 242
Female deities, 5, 44, 46, 72–74, 120,
124*f*, 139; male-female deity of
Shakers, 248
Female farmers. *See* Farmers: role of
farm women; Indian horticulture
Feminism, 18–19, 269–70
Fences: colonial, 63
Fessenden, Thomas G., 213, 219, 228
Field ecology, 9
First American Cookbook (Amelia
Simmons), 177
*First Lessons on Natural Philosophy
for Children* (Mary Swift), 252

Fish: in beaver ponds, 37; spring
runs of, 77, 82, 224; Indians depend on, 78, 82; as fertilizer, 78,
155, 156, 296 (n. 16); in subsistence, 176–77, 183; colonial recipes for, 177; Acts, 239
Fishing: and trade, 52, 54, 62, 98; Indians' practices of, 82; affected by
milldams, 87, 224, 239–40; and
debtors, 99
Food: and reproduction of energy,
15; Indians' storage of, 78, 81;
preservation, 171. *See also* Diet;
Gathering and hunting
Forest, 224, 227, 229, 262, 283*f*; area
coverage of, 31, 225*f*; northern, 31;
types of, 31–36, 35*m*; depletion of,
61, 224; clearance of woodlands,
156, 159*f*, 162–63; primeval, 158*f*;
marketing of, 162, 191; effect on
climate, 226; oak cultivation advised, 227; succession of trees in,
229–30; agroforestry, 268; restoration of, 268. *See also* Logging; Wood
Fossil fuels, 263
Foster, John, 135, 140, 305 (n. 43),
307 (n. 53)
Foster, Oliver, 216
Foucault, Michel, 22
Foxes, red: habitats destroyed, 66
Franklin, Benjamin, 109
Frontier, American, 1
Frost, Joseph, 215
Fuller, Margaret, 253
Fur trade, 66, 87, 98; initiates breakdown of Abenaki subsistence, 52–
56; and depletion of fur-bearing
animals, 61, 65; decline of, 89

Gaia (Greek goddess of earth), 5, 206
Gaia hypothesis, 267
Gale, Hannah, 253
Gallatin, Albert, 236, 242
Game animals. *See* Animals
Garden of Eden, 123, 127, 128, 199
Gardens: herb, 169; vegetable, 169,
177, 182, 235

Gathering and hunting, 81–82; of northern tribes, 12; and human energy, 15; caloric value of to southern Indians, 82

Gaze, the: in hunting, 20, 47, 292–93 (n. 28); loss of, 48, 68; and "shining the eyes," 290 (n. 29)

Geertz, Clifford, 20

Geine, theory of, 208, 211

Gender relations, 16, 92, 264; and production, 24t, 167–68, 192; of Indians, 81–82, 84; of colonists, 167–72, 185; change under capitalism, 172, 188, 243–44, 245. *See also* Matriarchal traditions; Men; Patriarchy; Women

Geocentric cosmos, 112, 140

Georgics (Virgil), 138–39

Global ecological revolution, 1, 261–70, 266t

Glockenthon (artist who helped construct first globe), 51

Gnostics, 255

God, 252–53; manifest through nature, 48, 49, 116, 129–30; transcendent over nature, 60, 97, 115, 144; male-female Shaker deity, 248, 323 (n. 32). *See also* Female deities; Indian myths and deities

Goddess. *See* Female deities

Goldsbury, John, 204, 215

Gookin, Daniel, 78, 84, 90

Gorges, Ferdinando, 57

Graham, Sylvester, 244–45

Grains, 86, 87, 165, 176, 177, 178, 180, 314 (n. 65), 315 (n. 66). *See also* Diet

Grandmother Woodchuck (Abenaki ancestress), 44, 46, 100

Grasses: American, 165; English hay, 166, 188

Great Awakening, 129

Great Chain of Being, 130, 131, 135, 137, 199

Great Spirit, 60

Greeley, Horace, 164, 177

Green corn festival, 73

Green Mountains, 30

Green politics, 264, 266t

Greenwood, Isaac, 132–33

Habitat: ecological core of, 5; original New England, 29–39; loss of Indians', 58; destroyed under industrialism, 264

Half-human creatures, 39–40, 46

Hamiltonian politics, 25t

Haraway, Donna, 22

Havelock, Eric, 21

Heliocentric hypothesis, 112, 115

Heraclitus, 9

Hermetics, 255

History of New Hampshire (Jeremy Belknap), 221

Holmes, Ezekial, 204

"Holomovement," 267

Homocentric ethic, 263

Hooke, Robert, 137

Hooker, Thomas, 102

Horkheimer, Max, 265–66

Horse-hoeing Husbandry (Jethro Tull), 218

Horsford, Eben Norton, 208

Horticulture. *See* Indian horticulture

Housework, 245–46

Howard, J. Harrison, 218

Howell, Anna, 169, 216–17

Humus, 155, 206

Hunting: the gaze in, 20, 47–48, 290 (n. 29); practices of northern tribes, 47–49; lures used by Indians, 48; practices of southern tribes, 82; undermined by colonists, 87; relationship of hunter to animal, 292–93 (n. 28)

Hunting and gathering. *See* Gathering and hunting

Hydrologic cycle, 119, 122

"Immutable mobiles," 22

Imports: to colonies, 99

Indian consciousness. *See* Mimetic consciousness

Indian horticulture: seasonal char-

acter of, 15, 29; female farmers
dominant in, 24*t*, 69, 75, 76, 81;
methods of, 74, 76–80; shifting
cultivation, 74, 86; burning practices of, 75–76, 156, 159, 160; hoes
used in, 77; pest control, 79; weeding practices of, 79; harvesting, 80;
collapse of, 85–92; compared to
Pilgrims' horticulture, 86, 108–9,
164
Indian myths and deities, 44, 45, 46–
47, 70–74; Corn Mother, 24*t*, 72, 73,
74; Gluskabe, 44, 46; Grandmother
Woodchuck, 44, 46, 100; totemism,
46; creation myths, 46–47, 70–74;
Ketci-Ni-wes-kwe, 47; Great Spirit,
60; Kautantouwit, 70; Kiehtan, 70,
72; crows in myths, 72–73; Squauanit, 84
Indians: viewed as inferior by colonists, 2, 63–64, 295 (n. 58); gender
relations of, 24–25*t*, 81, 84; monistic thinking of, 25*t*; tribal councils
and villages of, 25*t*, 109–10; population of, 39*t*, 91, 292 (n. 15); early
accounts of, 40; locations of tribes,
45*m*; increasingly depend on mercantile capitalism, 55–56; crisis in
reproduction of, 56; and loss of
reciprocity ethic, 60; and death of
hunting economy, 62; astronomy
of, 77; production system of, 85;
wars of, 85, 90; breakdown of legal
protection of, 91; subsistence crisis
of, 92; retain ways and culture, 97–
98, 261; demise of culture, 109–10,
111; women record council proceedings, 109–10. *See also* Abenaki; Indian horticulture; Mimetic
consciousness; Southern New England tribes
Indian women. *See* Indian horticulture; Indians; Women
Industrial consciousness. *See* Capitalism; Mechanistic worldview
Integrated thinking, 267; in post-

industrial consciousness, 266*t*
*Introduction to Botany, in a Series of
Familiar Letters* (Priscilla Bell
Wakefield), 251
Iroquois: lose title to land in New
York, 187

Jantsch, Eric, 13
Jefferson, Thomas, 143, 200, 227, 242
Jeffersonian politics, 25*t*
Johnson, Edward, 65
Johnson, Samuel W., 211
Jonson, Ben, 42
Josselyn, John, 52

Kautantouwit (Narraganset god of
southwest), 70, 72
Kendall, Edward, 62, 222–23
Kennebec River, 29, 69; trading cen-
ter on, 55
Kepler, Johannes, 115
Ketci-Ni-wes-kwe (Indian Great Be-
ing), 47
Kiehtan (Narraganset god of south-
west), 70, 72
King Philip (Wampanoag sachem),
85, 89, 90, 91, 97; led southern
tribal coalition, 63, 69, 70, 84
Kircher, Athanasius, 122
Kuhn, Thomas: theory of scientific
revolutions, 3

Labor: force reproduction, 18, 25*t*,
175, 185; rise of wage, 188, 189;
farmers depend on, 216; in logging
industry, 221–23, 229. *See also*
Capitalism; Production
Land: colonial settlement of, 61–62;
viewed as "wastes" by colonists,
63, 243; requirements for food production, 87, 180–81; disputes over,
89, 91, 92–93, 94–95, 187, 295
(n. 55), 299 (n. 54); investment in,
99
Latour, Bruno, 22, 210
Lee, Mother Ann. *See* Mother Ann

Leeds, Daniel, and sons, 135
Legal-political system: reproduction of, 17, 242–44. *See also* Reproduction—social
Leibniz, Gottfried Wilhelm, 9, 128
Le Lorrain, Pierre. *See* Vallemont, Pierre Le Lorrain, Abbé de
Leopold, Aldo, 263
Letters on the Elements of Botany Addressed to a Lady (Jean-Jacques Rousseau), 251
Liebig, Justus, 207–8
"Limits to Growth" models, 265
Lincoln, Gen. Benjamin, 227
Livestock, 165–66, 192–93, 315–16 (n. 67); acreage requirements of, 87; pastures cleared for grazing of, 158, 166; nutritional requirements of, 179, 180, 181; animals per family, 181–82
Locke, John, 163; empiricism of, 230
Logging, 57, 229; laborers in, 221–22, 229; ecological repercussions of, 223–26; decline of, 262
Longhouses, 76
Lovelock, James, 267
Low, Nathaniel, 137, 141, 212
Lowell, Francis Cabot, 236
Lunar cycle and festivals. *See* Moon
Lyon, Mary, 252

McCulloch, John, 12
Madison, James, 200, 227
Magnetism: supernatural powers of, 105
Mahican. *See* Southern New England tribes
Mahomet (Mohegan sachem), 93, 94
Maine, 29, 30, 69, 178, 180, 192, 223, 229; Indian tribes of, 44; expeditions to, 54; loss of large mammals in, 67
Maine Farmer, 213, 214
Malleus Maleficarum, 106
Man and Nature (George Perkins Marsh), 1, 240–41

Manifest destiny, 199, 201–2
Manitous: defined, 49, 70; denounced by Jesuits, 59, 61
Man of the Signs, 133, 135, 136*f*, 138*f*, 212
Manual of Botany (Amos Eaton), 252
Maps: and concepts of space, 24–25*t*, 259–60; as step in colonialization, 50–52, 53*f*, 68, 109, 198
Market agriculture, 24*t*, 118, 215–17, 308 (n. 3); expansion of, 145, 156, 188, 190–96; effect of on farms, 198; industrialization of, 234–35
Marsh, George Perkins, 1, 226, 240
Marx, Karl: theory of social revolution, 3; base/superstructure theory of, 3–4; on use value, 172–73; on appropriation of nature, 223; on production relations, 287 (n. 4); on human interaction with nature, 288 (n. 9)
Mason, John (New Hampshire explorer), 57
Mason, Maj. John, and descendants, 94, 97
Massachuset. *See* Southern New England tribes
Massachuset Confederacy, 83
Massachusetts, 157, 170, 173, 179, 193, 206, 252; rivers of, 82; Puritans of, 85; settlement of Bay Colony, 98
"Massachusetts Queen," 83–84
Massachusetts Society for Promoting Agriculture, 227
Massasoit (Wampanoag sachem), 84
Mathematical Principles of Natural Philosophy (Isaac Newton), 9, 127, 199
Mather, Cotton, 106, 129, 135; view of nature, 131; fertilization theories of, 132
Mather, Increase, 105
Matriarchal traditions: maternal ancestry of Indians, 44, 46, 49, 50; matrilocal residence, 50, 294

(n. 34); *ookas*, 70; matrilineal descent, 94. *See also* Women
Mayow, John, 123, 137
Maypole tradition, 104–5, 117, 301 (n. 79)
Meat production: acreage requirements of, 87, 180–81
Mechanics, 213
Mechanistic worldview, 24–25*t*, 126–28, 220, 230–31; of nature, 7, 131, 199–205; core concepts of, 199; social expression of, 201, 262–63
Meillassoux, Claude, 16–17, 289 (n. 24); on reproduction of energy, 15, 289 (n. 20)
Men: role in Indian horticulture, 81; and tribal governance, 83; role in farming, 153; role in colonial production, 167; and inheritance of land, 185, 243; role in textile production, 237
Mercantilism: colonial trade as, 12, 55; development of, 98–100, 112, 128, 150, 188; contrasted with industrial capitalism, 197, 198
Mercator, Gerardus, 51
Merrimac River, 82, 193
Meteorologic cycle, 122
Miantonomo (Narraganset sachem), 89
Microcosm-macrocosm theory, 114, 115–16, 132–33
Middle class: women of, 251–52. *See also* Elites
Middlesex Canal, 193
Migration: westward, 187–88
Miller, Perry, 129
Mills, 239–42; saw, 25, 58, 224, 229, 237; textile production in, 236–37; build dams, 239–40
Mimetic consciousness, 20, 25*t*, 46–50, 68, 96, 97; Plato's critique of, 21; Indian worldview as, 29, 44–50, 67–68; in hunting, 47–48, 290 (n. 29), 292–93 (n. 28); disappearance of, 110, 111, 149; loss of, 259–

60. *See also* Participatory consciousness
Minerals: produced by earth, 126; animistic view of, 142–43
Mink: habitats destroyed, 66
Modernity: origins of, 127; transition to, 145, 149. *See also* Capitalism; Mechanistic worldview
Mohawk River, 188
Mohegans, 69, 73, 90; land disputes of, 93, 94–96
Monadnocks, 30
Monistic thinking, 25*t*
Monocultures, 263
Moody, Paul, 236
Moon: lunar festivals, 117; lunar cycle, 122; influences zodiac, 136*f*; influences farming practices, 141–42, 218, 305 (n. 43)
Morton, Charles, 130, 142
Morton, Thomas, 101, 104
Mother Ann, 248, 249, 250
Mother Earth, 44, 115, 125, 199, 202–5, 209, 255; goddesses, 5; interior of, 7; restorative abilities of, 11; and fertilization, 119–20; weakened by producing vegetation, 125; inseminated by rain, 126; in almanacs, 137–39. *See also* Earth; Nature
Mount Holyoke, 252
Muck Manual for Farmers (Samuel L. Dana), 206, 208
Mulder, Johann, 208
Mundus Subterraneus (Athanasius Kircher), 122
Myths, Indian. *See* Indian myths and deities

Narraganset, 70, 72, 84; cosmology of, 70–74. *See also* Southern New England tribes
Native Americans. *See* Indian horticulture; Indian myths and deities; Indians; Matriarchal traditions; Mimetic consciousness; Women

Natura, 5, 255

Nature: as active agent, 5, 23, 24t, 29, 36, 87, 266t; as female, 5, 101, 126, 139, 143, 202–3, 256, 319 (n. 18); mechanistic view of, 7, 127, 128, 199, 231; European view of, 9, 39–42, 122–23; colonial view of, 23, 100–103, 104, 105; social construction of, 23; as passive and inert matter, 24t, 127; domination of, 25t, 127, 128, 199, 201, 203, 212; spiritual resonances of, 72–74, 116, 129–30; as commodity, 99, 209, 300 (nn. 66, 67); rituals in, 104, 105, 116–18; supernatural signs in, 105; as animate, 112–26, 204, 206, 218, 255, 306–7 (n. 52); as mundane, 112, 114, 255; as clock, 128; made up of particles, 199; as teacher, 137, 205, 245–46, 306 (n. 49); modern view of under capitalism, 232; romanticized, 250–58; revolt of called for, 265–66; human partnership with, 266t. See also Cosmology; Cycles; Mother Earth; Wilderness

"Nature's Tree," 143

Nauset. See Southern New England tribes

Neoplatonism, 129

New Atlantis (Francis Bacon), 203

"New Canaan," 69

New England Almanack, 164

New England Farmer, 167, 170, 171, 213, 218, 219, 228, 234, 235; adds "Domestic Department," 246

New England Farmer, or Georgical Dictionary (Samuel Deane), 219

New England habitat, 29–39

New England's Rarities (John Josselyn), 52

New English Canaan (Thomas Morton), 101

New Hampshire, 30, 173, 179, 193; last wolf killed in, 67

Newton, Isaac, 137, 140, 253, 260;

architect of mechanism, 9; views nature as vital, 9; alchemical speculations of, 122–23; and mechanistic philosophy, 127, 199

Ninecrafts: great dance at, 73

Nipmuck–Connecticut Valley tribes. See Southern New England tribes

Niter. See Nitrous salts

Nitrous salts, 119, 120, 121, 125–26, 131, 132, 142, 143, 208, 303 (nn. 11, 12), 306–8 (n. 59); formative principle of, 115. See also Soil fertilization

Norridgewock, 44

Northern tribes, 12, 38

Norton, John Pitkin: on chemical paradigm, 208–10

Nuclear power, 264

Oak forest, 33

Of Plymouth Plantation (William Bradford), 78

Oikos (house), 29; as postindustrial space, 266t

Olbers, Heinrich, 218

Old Farmer's Almanac (Robert B. Thomas), 65, 135–36, 212

On Witchcraft, Being Wonders of the Invisible World (Cotton Mather), 106

"Oo" (Narraganset verb of motion), 70

Opticks, queries to, 127–28

Organic Chemistry in its Applications to Agriculture and Physiology (Justus Liebig), 207

Organic cosmos. See Cosmology

Origin of the Family, Private Property and the State (Friedrich Engels), 17

Ortega y Gasset, José, 293 (n. 28)

Ozone emissions, 262

Paganism: Old World, 103, 104, 301 (nn. 78, 79). See also Witchcraft

Paleo-Indians, 38

Panopticon (Jeremy Bentham), 22

Paracelsus, 119, 137

Partible system of inheritance, 18, 185, 187

Participatory consciousness: of colonial farmers, 113, 118, 144; in global ecological revolution, 266*t*. *See also* Consciousness—colonial; Mimetic consciousness

Passamaquoddy, 44

Passenger pigeons: extinction of deprives soil of phosphorus, 36

Pastoral imagery, 128

Patriarchy: subordination of women, 16, 107, 168; inheritance practices of colonists, 18, 107, 185–86; and family, 24–25*t*, 168, 266*t*; *Oosh*, 70; patrilineage in tribal rulership, 83; among Puritans, 108; conflict with ecology, 187; and global ecological revolution, 264; patrilocal residence, 294 (n. 34). *See also* Matriarchal traditions

Pearlash. *See* Potash

Penobscot, 44, 49–50; hunting observances of, 47

Pequots, 69, 90; land disputes of, 93

Perham, Sidney, 204, 213

Pest control: nonchemical means of, 79, 159, 169, 268–69

Petersham, Mass., 157–58, 158*f*, 159*f*, 162, 193, 195–97, 196*f*

Peterson, Abby, 17

Phelps, Almira Hart Lincoln, 252

Philosophical Grammar (Benjamin Martin), 143

Photosynthesis, 263

Pilgrims, 85

Pioneer trees, 36

Piscataqua River: as trade route, 57

Plants: succession of, 6, 8, 29, 33, 36, 229–30; as producers, 6*f*, 7; Indians collect medicinal, 38; as ancestors of Indians, 71; ecological indicators of planting time, 77, 117; and colonial ecological complex, 88*f*, 98, 298 (n. 35); planting cycles, 122; having souls, 125. *See also* Forest

Plato: critiques mimetic consciousness, 21, 110; Platonism, 255, 259

Pliny, 115, 119, 303 (n. 11)

Plymouth, Mass., 65, 104

Podzols, 30, 32*m*, 155

Political systems, 25*t*, 266*t*

Pollution: as market externality, 2; and ecological change, 3, 232–33, 240–42, 264

Polycultures: native American, 24*t*, 79, 80; colonial, 86, 164–65; ecological advantages of, 165, 268. *See also* Indian horticulture

"Poor, strolling," 188

Population: and demographic transition, 25*t*, 195–96, 244, 264, 316 (n. 7); equilibrium, 25*t*; and reproduction of labor force, 25*t*; of Abenaki, 56–57, 292 (n. 15); of southern tribes, 90, 292 (n. 15); of inland towns, 275, 276; effect of increase in, 316–17 (n. 71)

Postindustrial society, 264–70, 266*t*

Postmodern: science, 265, 267, 324 (n. 7); integrated thinking, 266*t*

Postpatriarchal family, 266*t*

Postrevolutionary depression, 188

Potash: production of, 191–92

Power looms, 236–37

Praying towns, 96, 97

Predestination, 108

Preindustrial consciousness. *See* Consciousness—colonial; Mimetic consciousness

Preservationism, 256–57, 258, 262

Presumscot River, 224

Prigogine, Ilya, 13, 265, 324 (n. 7)

Principles of Agriculture (Albrecht Thaer), 206

Pring, Martin, 54

Printing press: effect of, 22

Proclamation of 1763, 61

Production, 113, 230; interaction

with reproduction, 3, 16, 17–19,
52–58, 91, 185–90, 196, 233; role in
ecological revolution, 5, 149; and
extraction of resources, 6*f*, 11, 87,
89, 91, 99; theory of, 10–13; gender
relations in, 24–25*t*, 81, 84–85, 91;
Indian, 24–25*t*, 52–58, 81, 83, 84,
85; alters Indian ecology, 52–58,
85; colonial, 85, 98–100, 167–72; of
meat, 87; different cultural requirements of, 93–94; synthesis of
European and Indian methods,
144, 153; contradiction with
ecology, 186–87; of potash, 191;
machine farming under capitalism, 217; capitalist, 232–39. *See
also* Agriculture; Exchange;
Externalities; Market agriculture;
Subsistence economy; Textile production; Use value
Property relations: between Indians
and colonists, 57, 61–62
Protectionism, 91
Protoplast, 123
Ptolemy, 115, 140
Puritans: view of wilderness, 39,
100–101, 130; of Massachusetts
Bay, 85; consciousness of, 99, 100–
108, 197; popular folklore of, 103–
5; sexuality of, 107; belief in predestination, 108; patriarchal mores
of, 108
Pynchon, John, 89, 99, 273, 274
Pynchon, William, 89

Quaiapan (Narraganset sunksquaw),
84

Radical feminists, 269
Railroads, 195, 241–42, 243
Rain: inseminates Mother Earth,
126; effect of on soils, 155; acidity
of, 262
Rainforests, 261
Rasles, Father (French Jesuit), 61, 64
Reciprocity: exchange patterns

among Indians, 52; between humans and animals, 60
Recycling, 257, 265
Renaissance worldview, 9, 113, 130,
133, 137, 139
*Report on the Trees and Shrubs
Growing Naturally in the Forests of
Massachusetts* (George B. Emerson), 228
Reproduction: interaction with production, 3, 17–19, 52–58, 185–90,
196, 233, 289 (n. 20); role in ecological revolution, 5, 149, 175–85,
191; and historical change, 13–17;
defined, 14–17, 25*t*, 83, 175; of
family, 15, 113, 290 (n. 25); energy
requirements of, 15–17, 175–76,
289 (n. 20); and role of women, 17,
83–85, 106–7, 168; under capitalism, 17, 242–47; and breakdown of
Abenaki subsistence, 52, 56–57;
crisis of, 56–57, 109, 185; in colonial ecological revolution, 91; in
capitalist ecological revolution,
149, 175, 185–90; and subsistence
requirements, 175–85
—biological: defined, 14–15, 289
(n. 17); and Indians, 83; cycles of
nature and women, 105; of labor
force, 175; decline in childbearing,
244, 264; effect of increase in, 316–
17 (n. 71). *See also* Population
—social: changes in among Indians,
57; defined, 14–17; of legal-political structure, 17; of social norms,
17; role of Indian women in, 83–
85; and land disputes, 96; tensions
of reflected in witch trials, 106–7;
in Euramerican history, 175; and
contradictions arising from inheritance practices, 185–90; and wom-
en's role under capitalism, 246–47
Resources, 24*t*, 53*f*; depletion of, 2,
262; original meaning of, 11; colonial view of, 11, 29; Indian view of,
11, 29; as commodities, 24*t*, 98;

recycling of nonrenewable, 265
Restoration, 268
Rhode Island, 33, 140, 179, 195, 236, 239, 240; war in swamps of, 84
Rivers, 29, 57, 69, 82, 98, 193, 195; ecology disrupted by milling, 224, 239
Rousseau, Jean-Jacques, 251
Rowlandson, Mary, 63–64
Rush, Benjamin, 227

Sachems, 93, 97; responsibility for decision making, 16; role undercut, 56; transfer property to Europeans, 57; role in harvest, 73; patrilineal succession of, 83; Mahomet's role in land dispute, 93. *See also* Squasachems
Saco River, 29, 69
Sagamores. *See* Sachems
Saint John's River, 69
Salem, Mass.: witch trials of, 108
Salts. *See* Nitrous salts
Sawmills, 25, 58, 221, 224, 229, 239, 241
Sayword, Henry, 58
Science: theory of scientific revolutions, 3, 4; worldviews in, 4, 9, 21, 199, 210, 267–68. *See also* Mechanistic worldview
Scientia, 259
Secondary succession. *See* Plants: succession of
Senses: equality of. *See* Mimetic consciousness
Settlements, 151*m*, 152*m*
Sexes. *See* Gender relations; Men; Women
Shakers, 144, 248–50, 323 (n. 32); communism of, 249
Shakespeare, William, 41–42
Shamans: decisions by, 16; Puritans' view of, 21; role in ecosystem regulation, 49; women serving as, 49, 84; role undercut, 56, 60; convert to Christianity, 59

Shapleigh, Maj. Nicholas, 58
Sheela-na-gigs (fertility females), 105
Signatures, doctrine of, 115
Simmons, Amelia, 177, 183
Slater, Samuel, 236, 240, 241
Smith, Adam, 200
Smith, John, 52, 54
Socialist feminism, 269–70
Social norms: reproduction of, 17
Social reproduction. *See* Reproduction—social
Soil fertilization: methods of, 78–79, 116–17, 118, 142, 155, 156, 210–11, 220; theories of, 119–22, 131, 132, 144, 206–210, 303 (nn. 11, 12), 304 (n. 16); humus, 155, 206; vitalist-mechanist debate, 206–7, 208; artificial, 263. *See also* Nitrous salts; Soils
Soils, 30, 32*m*, 33, 155; biomass in, 30; top, 30; podzol, 30, 74, 155; fertilization needs of, 154–55, 206–10; under "extensive system," 166–67; decline in fertility of, 186–87; effect of potash production on, 191–92. *See also* Soil fertilization
Solar cycle and festivals. *See* Sun
Soldier's ration: as determinant of subsistence requirements, 180
Sons: and inheritance practices, 185, 188
Southern New England tribes: creation myths of, 70–74; daily lives of, 82–83; retain tribal heritage, 97. *See also* Indian horticulture
Space: concepts of, 24*t*, 266*t*; perceived differently by Indians and colonists, 50; mapped, 50–51; domains of colonial men and women, 167
Spatial metaphors, 23
Spinning: textile production, 236, 237, 238*f*
Spinsters: accused of witchcraft, 107; manage farms, 168
Spiritus mundi (world spirit), 115,

119–20, 122; rejected, 131
Spodosols, 30, 32*m*
Squasachems, 83–84. *See also* Sa-
    chems
Squauanit (Narraganset women's
    diety), 84
Star gazing, 77
Steady-state society, 266*t*
Steam power, 241–42, 243*f*
Stiles, Ezra, 73, 131, 180
Stoics, 255
Strachey, William, 101
Structure of Scientific Revolutions
    (Thomas Kuhn), 3
Subsistence economy: production of,
    10–11, 163–67; and extraction, 15;
    preindustrial, 15, 24*t*, 150; of farm-
    ers, 99–100, 155–56, 172–74; and
    reproductive requirements, 175–
    85; evidence for among inland
    colonists, 184, 308 (n. 3), 317
    (n. 73). *See also* Economy: colo-
    nial; Production: Indian
Subsistence requirements: and re-
    production, 175; determination of,
    176–85; and household consump-
    tion, 177–78
"Succession of Forest Trees, The"
    (Henry David Thoreau), 229
Sulfur dioxide emissions, 262
Sun: heliocentric hypothesis, 112;
    symbolism of, 116; solar festivals,
    117; solar cycle, 122; virility of, 139
Sunksquaws, 83, 84
Supernatural: signs in nature of, 105
Swift, Mary, 252
Sylva Sylvarum (Francis Bacon), 127
Symbolism: and exchanges, 1, 2, 11;
    alchemical, 9; pertaining to na-
    ture, 20; native American, 45–46,
    72–74; European traditions of, 113;
    of rural farmers, 113; in almanacs,
    133–37; mechanical metaphors of
    nature, 199–201
Systema Agriculturae (John Wor-
    lidge), 119

Systems theory, 12–13

Talcott, Gov. Joseph, 93, 95
Taylor, Charles, 20
Taylor, Edward, 143
Terra (John Evelyn), 139, 304 (n. 16)
Tetrabiblos (Ptolemy), 115, 140
Textile production, 236–37, 238*f*
Thacher, James, 143
Thaer, Albrecht, 206
Thermodynamics, second law of, 8
Thomas, Robert Bailey, 65, 135, 212,
    218
Thomas Aquinas, Saint, 40
Thoreau, Henry David: on plant suc-
    cession, 33, 36, 229; on fertiliza-
    tion, 121, 257; on steam power,
    241–42; and transcendentalism,
    254–55; as preservationist, 256–57,
    258; opposes market farming, 257;
    on apples, 258–59
Timaeus (Plato), 255
Time: Indian and colonial percep-
    tions of, 51
Todd, John, 244–45
Todd, S. E., 217
Tools: transform Indian economy,
    53–54; traded for fur pelts, 55
Topography: of New England, 34*m*
Totemism, 46
Townships: coastal and inland, 149–
    52, 151*m*, 152*m*
Trade: between Indians and colo-
    nists, 52–56; networks, 55, 98, 174,
    193, 196
Transcendence, 114, 144, 230; in co-
    lonial religion, 58–61; supplants
    animism, 68
Transcendentalism, 253, 254–58
Transportation: rivers, 29, 57, 69, 82,
    98, 193, 195; construction of turn-
    pikes and canals, 162, 188; access
    to, 190, 193, 242–43; canals, 193,
    194*m*, 195, 221; linking farms to
    market, 196, 211
Tree of Life, 250

Tribal councils, 25t, 109–10
Tribal villages: and social reproduction, 25t
Tricky, Sarah, 58
True, N. T., 205, 218, 247
Tull, Jethro, 218, 219
Tulley, John, 135

Uncas family: role in land dispute, 94–95, 97
Unitarianism, 108, 144
Use value: production of, 172–73

Vallemont, Pierre Le Lorrain, Abbé de, 123–26
Vaughan, Benjamin, 160, 162
Vermont, 30, 178, 193, 240
Verrazzano, Giovanni da, 52, 53
Virgil, 115, 138–39
Visual consciousness, 96; replaces oral consciousness, 2; preindustrial, 22, 25t, 112, 149; introduced by colonists, 85
Vitalism. See Soil fertilization: vitalist-mechanist debate

Waban (Wampanoag sachem), 84
Wakefield, Joanna, 186
Wakefield, Priscilla Bell, 251
Walden (Henry David Thoreau), 243f, 257
Walden Pond, 241, 243f, 257
Waltham system, 237
Wampanoag Confederacy, 84. See also Southern New England tribes
Wappinger Confederacy. See Southern New England tribes
Warfare: and Indian depopulation, 90
War of 1675–76, 85
Warren, James, 189
"Waste": doctrine of, 243–44
Water rights, 239–40, 242
Weather forecasting, 115, 116, 117, 140
Webster, Noah, 215, 227

Weld, Isaac, 161–62
Welsh, Jane Kilby, 252
Weymouth, George, 54
Wheetamoo (Pocasset sunksquaw), 84
Whigs, 242
White, Caroline Barrett, 253–54
White Mountains, 30
White pine forest, 31, 33
Whittmore, Nathaniel, 135, 141
"Whole earth" image, 262
Widows: accused of witchcraft, 107; manage farms, 168; dowers used to determine subsistence needs of, 178, 183, 186, 313 (n. 62), 317 (n. 76)
Wigwams: transportable, of Indians, 76
"Wild Apples" (Henry David Thoreau), 258
Wilderness: identification with savagery, 64–65, 201, 204; demise of, 67; Puritan view of, 100–103; Bible descriptions of, 202, 300 (n. 70)
Willard, Samuel, 107, 131, 143
Williams, Roger, 73, 78, 80, 81, 102
Williamson, Hugh, 226
Winslow, Edward, 78
Winthrop, John, 78, 79, 102
Witchcraft, 105–8, 302 (n. 84); associated with women, 40, 105; associated with wilderness, 105; witch trials, 105–8; compared to bestiality, 106; popular beliefs about, 108. See also Paganism
Withdrawals: from ecological core, 6f
Wolves: disappearance of, 67
Women: subordinance of, 16; under capitalism, 17–19, 233, 235–36, 243–47; associated with animals and sexual lust, 40, 106; dominant in Indian horticulture, 81; possible inventions by, 81; in witch trials, 106; record Indian council proceedings, 109–10; role of farm,

150, 152, 153, 167–72, 183, 216–17, 312 (n. 37); roles taken over by men, 172; and inheritance practices, 185–86; surfeit of single, 188; role in textile production, 236, 238*f*; as moral agents, 246–47; respond to nature, 250–54; middle-class, 251–52. *See also* Gender relations; Indian horticulture; Matriarchal traditions; Reproduction; Witchcraft
Wood, William, 78
Wood: subsistence requirements of, 157, 182–83, 316 (n. 69); woodlots, 157–63; woodlands served as pasture, 158; ecology of woodlands,

159; shortages of, 227. *See also* Forest; Logging; Sawmills
Working Farmer (John Mapes), 211
World soul, 119, 131, 255
Worldview. *See* Consciousness; Mechanistic worldview; Mimetic consciousness; Modernity; Postmodern
Worlidge, John, 119–20, 137

Yeats, John, 11
Young Farmer's Manual (S. E. Todd), 217

Zodiac, 133, 136*f*, 140. *See also* Astrology